Not Just The Beatles...

Not Just The Beatles...

The story of how legendary impresario Sid Bernstein brought the Beatles to America, and his association with the show business greats of our time

As told to Arthur Aaron

Jacques & Flusster Publishers, Teaneck, New Jersey

Copyright © 2000 by Sid Bernstein and Arthur Aaron

All rights reserved under international and Pan-American copyright conventions. This book may not be reproduced or copied in any form or by any means, electronic, mechanical, photocopying, recording or otherwise, without prior written permission from the publisher.

Library of Congress number 00-110109

ISBN 0-9706101-0-6

First printing November 2000

Manufactured in the United States of America

Book and cover design by Dick Lopez

Attention organizations and corporations:

This book is available at a bulk rate price for fundraising, premium or promotional purposes. For information, please contact
JACQUES & FLUSSTER PUBLISERS (201) 692-1635 or
www.NotJustTheBeatles.com

For Gerry and my kids, Adam, Denise, Dylan, Beau, Casey and Etienne

A very special thanks to veteran entertainment attorney Dick Roemer, close family friend and confidant, for his encouragement and wisdom over the years.

—*Sid Bernstein*

About the Author

Arthur Aaron resides in Teaneck, New Jersey. Since graduating from Yeshiva University in 1964, Mr. Aaron has been a music business entrepreneur. He has known Sid Bernstein for more than 30 years. This is Mr. Aaron's first book.

Author's Acknowledgements

This is my first book. Without the contributions and support of a number of people, I never would have been able to pursue and complete this project. I would like to thank the following people for their help.

Antoinette Sconamilio for her ability to decipher my scratchings. Marilyn Kaskel for her support and her overwhelming knowledge of "the biz." Vicki Beer for her insight, warm friendship, spirit, and editorial expertise. Ida S. Langsam for her quick wit and her nimble brain. Jim Kaufogiens for the pens. (Yes, I wrote this book by hand.)

Stan Satlin who knows the difference between being a warrior and a worrier and for his ability to focus. Robert Cohen for his insights and suggestions.

During this process, the following people read the book and gave me their comments: Mark and Miriam Aron, Judith Barzilay, David Fisher, Ken Jacobson, Arthur Levy, Dick Lopez and Charlotte Waldman.

To Dick Lopez for his taste and his dedication.

To my children: Ariella Ives for her perception and advice. Avrum and Eliana Aaron, whose help and support were invaluable. Ahava Leibtag for her steadfast belief that, in the end, all would be well.

And to my wife, Julia, without whose advice, encouragement, support and love, nothing would have been possible.

To all of you, thank you, thank you.

—Arthur Aaron

"Sid Bernstein is a wonderful person who was instrumental in introducing the Beatles to America."
— SIR PAUL McCARTNEY

"Sid Bernstein helped make my dreams come true. He presented me for the very first time "in concert" at Carnegie Hall, which was also my debut at this legendary landmark. It remains one of my most cherished performance memories."
— TONY BENNETT

"Sid Bernstein is the quintessential gentleman promoter. He is part P.T. Barnum, part Donald Trump and part Henry Kissinger; a negotiator, a diplomat and a brilliant builder of careers. His life is filled with the colorful, the implausible and the enormously entertaining."
— GERALDO RIVERA

"Sid Bernstein is one of those unique individuals. He's always done his best to honor God and country. He helps people at all times. He is mentally awake and morally straight. He's been able to swim in entertainment's shark-infested waters for years unscathed. He's one of the good guys. It's an honor to have him as a friend."
— DICK CLARK

Table of Contents

Foreword: *iii*
Prologue: *iv*

BOOK ONE: BUDDY BURNSIDE 1918-1941 *1*

Chapter 1: Zisselman's Farm *3*
Chapter 2: Major Bowes *8*
Chapter 3: Meeting Abe *16*

BOOK TWO: NEWSPAPERS, NIGHTCLUBS AND SHOW BUSINESS 1941-1963 *25*

Chapter 4: Defending Brooklyn *27*
Chapter 5: Newspaper Magnate and Nightclub Impresario *32*
Chapter 6: There's No Business Like Show Business *41*
Chapter 7: Geraldine *52*
Chapter 8: Tony Bennett *73*
Chapter 9: Married…Finally *89*

BOOK THREE: THE TOP OF THE MOUNTAIN 1963-1974 *97*

Chapter 10: Brian Epstein Says Yes *99*
Chapter 11: A Comet Called the Beatles *121*
Chapter 12: The Most Important Rock Concert…Ever *142*
Chapter 13: On to the Next Projects *163*
Chapter 14: Regrets *179*
Chapter 15: Big Events: One After Another *189*
Chapter 16: Sinatra and Elvis *208*

BOOK FOUR: BASHERT *225*

Chapter 17: Starting Over *227*
Chapter 18: And Then Came Laura *250*
Chapter 19: The Death of John Lennon *263*
Chapter 20: England, Hawaii and In Between *268*
Chapter 21: Oh, What Might Have Been! *295*
Chapter 22: The Attack on George Harrison *303*
Chapter 23: Bashert *305*

Author's Epilogue *310*
Glossary *311*
Index *313*

FOREWORD

I was walking away from the meter after having filled it with coins. I saw him coming towards me—Sid Bernstein—the man who brought the Beatles to America. We greeted each other with hugs, as old rockers do.

"Sid, how are you! It's good to see you," I said.

"Great, kid, I love that hat. Look at that hat! Do you have others?"

We had met over 30 years ago when I was a young fan of the Rascals, but Sid had never stopped calling me "kid." I was heading to a meeting and was wearing one of my custom-made hats.

"Yeah, Sid, I have about 11 of these in different colors. My father taught me never to go anywhere without a hat."

"And where do you get them?" he asked.

"Oh, I had them made for me, but the guy who made them passed away. Can you imagine, there are no custom hatters in New York anymore! I have to go to Buffalo or somewhere in Texas to get them."

Sid looked good with that ever-youthful smile on his face.

"You know, Sid, I think about you often. That desk you gave me—you know, the one you worked at when you were bringing the Beatles to America—that's the desk I use everyday."

"Oh, Christie's or Sotheby's would like to have that desk," he said.

"Really, why is that?" I asked.

"Well, you know, Beatles memorabilia is very hot."

"I can't sell that desk. You gave it to me as a gift. That's what makes it so special to me."

"I appreciate that, kid. There's a lot of history in that desk."

"What history?"

"Well..." he began recounting all of the famous people in the music and entertainment industry who had sat in front of his desk, hoping that he would help promote a concert or manage their career. I knew that Sid had an illustrious career. And I also understood that his presenting the Beatles at Carnegie Hall in 1964 and Shea Stadium in 1965 was instrumental in establishing them as the greatest musical and cultural phenomenon of the 20th century. But what I never realized was that Sid had the only direct line from Sinatra to Elvis to the Beatles, and the other names he listed were like a who's who of the entertainment business. "That desk, kid, is music history," he said with a nostalgic look on his face.

"And so are you, Sid. So are you."

PROLOGUE

ONE NIGHT, AS GERRY, THE KIDS AND I WERE sitting around the dinner table, the phone rang. Beau, who was then four years old, jumped to answer the phone.

"Dad, it's John Lennon," he said.

I took the phone and heard this unmistakable Liverpool accent on the other end. "Hello, Sid. This is John."

"John, how are you?"

"Sidney, I have a big favor to ask of you."

"What is it, John?"

"I cannot find three tickets for the Jimmy Cliff concert you are putting on tomorrow night at Carnegie Hall. [Jimmy Cliff is a great reggae artist.] I have a friend coming from Liverpool who is mad about Jimmy Cliff, and I promised him that I would take him to the concert. I looked everywhere, and I just can't get any tickets! Is there any possibility that you could help me with the three tickets?"

"John, the concert is sold out and I don't have an extra ticket, but let me see what I can do, and I'll call you back in a little while."

"Okay, I'd be deeply appreciative if you could help me."

When I hung up with John, I reflected on the irony of the situation. I always put aside a few extra tickets to cover just this type of last minute request. With this sold-out Jimmy Cliff concert, I had been hit so hard for tickets that even the emergency reserve was gone. As a matter of habit, I had always reserved tickets to all my concerts and shows for my wife Gerry, our three oldest kids and myself. Unlike most other promoters, producers and impresarios, I did not enjoy being backstage for my shows. I always sat out front so that I could get a feel for what the audience was experiencing and how they were reacting to the performance. My habit was that Gerry, the kids and I would sit as a family in about the tenth row and be a part of the audience.

When I hung up the phone with John, I asked Adam, Denise and Dylan, my three oldest children, "Would you mind giving up your Jimmy Cliff tickets to John Lennon?" Being pretty young themselves, they did not really know who the great Jimmy Cliff was, so they said, "Sure, Dad, but you have to tell John that we gave up our tickets for him!" They knew who John Lennon was.

I called John back.

"John, I have your tickets."

"Great, Sid! I knew you'd come through for me."

"John, I'll leave three tickets in your name. Just go to the box office and ask for them. They'll be expecting you."

"Thank you so much, Sid. I really appreciate it. See you tomorrow night."

The next night, I got to Carnegie Hall early, took care of my business backstage, and left the tickets for John with instructions that they be given only to him, and proceeded to my seat where Gerry sat waiting for me. Carnegie Hall was packed and there was a buzz of excitement in the crowd. The loyal Jimmy Cliff fans couldn't wait to see him perform.

Moments before the show was to begin, John Lennon came into Carnegie Hall with a date and his friend from Liverpool. The noisy and excited crowd grew hushed when they noticed that John Lennon had entered the concert hall. John and his party hurried to their seats. John sat down to my left, his date to his left and his friend to her left. The concert began almost immediately. As expected, Jimmy Cliff put on a great show.

At intermission, John chose to stay in his seat and what was noteworthy was that no one came to talk to him or request an autograph. Maybe the ushers kept everyone away, but John and I got a chance to talk without interruption. He told me about his current musical direction and a little about his personal life, which at that time was in turmoil. I told him about the concerts I was promoting and the acts I was managing.

Right before the end of the intermission, John gazed at me with a distant look in his eyes and said, "You know, Sid, that night in 1965 at Shea Stadium? I saw the top of the mountain on that unforgettable night."

I looked at him for a moment and thought to myself that it had been a truly unbelievable night.

"I saw the top of the mountain, too, John."

BOOK ONE

BUDDY BURNSIDE
1918-1941

CHAPTER 1: **ZISSELMAN'S FARM**

I WAS BORN ON AUGUST 12, 1918, at Mt. Sinai Hospital, between Fifth and Madison Avenues at 99th Street in New York City. I never knew my birth parents and was immediately adopted by Israel and Ida Bernstein, who had recently emigrated from Lukshivka, a small shtetl, or town, outside of Kiev. My Bubba, the Yiddish word for grandmother, Rachel and I shared one of the two bedrooms in the apartment, and I loved her with all my heart. My grandmother spoke only Yiddish, and I learned to speak Yiddish and English simultaneously. Although my name is Sid, my parents and grandmother called me Simcha, which in Hebrew and Yiddish means happiness and also is a euphemism for party or celebration. Considering that I have spent most of my life in the music and entertainment business, I would say that my Hebrew name was somewhat prophetic.

My mother lost her leg a few years before I was born. She had fallen in New York City, bruised herself and developed gangrene. Her case was mismanaged and, in order to save her life, it became necessary to amputate. This tragedy not only meant that she had to live with a cumbersome wooden leg for the rest of her life, but it also meant that she couldn't bear children. I guess that's why I was adopted. I was an only child in a family that never expected to have any children, and so I received lavish attention and boundless love.

The loss of my mother's leg did not stop her from being a terrific mother and housewife. She was a great cook and along with my grandmother, cooked some of the best food I have ever eaten. And believe me, I have eaten some good food in my life!

My father was a fine tailor who learned his trade in Russia. During the early years of my life, he worked in a factory in New York City's garment center. He labored long hours during the workweek and I never saw him much. The weekends, however, were family time. Among my earliest and most cherished memories are the walks that my father and I took in Central Park, which was around the corner from our Madison Avenue apartment. I also remember rowboat excursions with my father in Central Park on the lake. Who needed friends when I had my family?

People who know me say I am a very soft-spoken man. I guess I speak so softly because during those early years of my life, I never heard shouting at home. My grandmother was a very gentle woman and my mother was often ill. Around our home, everything was done in a quiet and calm manner.

I only remember seeing my father get angry and shout one time. He told a customer in his thick Yiddish accent, "Go a-vey! I don't vant you far a customer anymore!"

Our home was what you could call a traditional Jewish home. My parents, out of respect for my grandmother, kept a kosher kitchen. There were two sets of dishes, one for meat and one for milk. I remember seeing my Bubba Rachel lighting the Friday night candles and praying from a prayer book. Our extended family, also immigrants to America, would often come for Friday night and holiday meals.

My parents enjoyed listening to the records of Enrico Caruso, the great Italian tenor, on our hand-cranked phonograph. They also liked playing the records of a renowned Jewish cantor whose name was Yosele Rosenblatt. Rosenblatt was a sweet singer, and maybe I got my appreciation and taste for music from listening to Caruso and the Cantor.

When I was three years old, I remember going on vacation to a farm in Parksville, New York, called Zisselman's Farm, which is in the Catskill Mountains. At one time, the Catskill Mountains were one of the major resort areas in New York, populated with famous and glorious hotels like Grossinger's, The Concord and Brown's. Some of my aunts, uncles and cousins, including my favorite cousin Maxie Goldberg, came along to Zisselman's. Through the years, we would continue to go to the mountains, and as my father got more successful, we began to go to bigger and better hotels. It was at these hotels that I saw my first singers, comedians and other performers. The performers were on stage, in the spotlight and admired by the audience. What an impression this made on me. The performers were "somebody" and I wanted to be "somebody" too! I particularly remember a black performer who sang in Yiddish to the delight of his 100% Yiddish-speaking audience. His name was Napoleon Reid. He was a sensation—a black guy who spoke Yiddish as if it were his native language.

When I was five years old, my father left work at the factory in the garment center and decided to go into business for himself. He bought a tailor and dry cleaning shop on 116th Street in Harlem. The shop had an apartment attached to it, so we moved from Madison and 99th to the back of the new shop. Shortly after we moved, I started school. I was enrolled in P.S. 10, just one block from where we lived. I was pretty indifferent to school. I never did my homework. I hated the regimentation and I really didn't like being told what to do. I didn't have many friends, still preferring my parents' company to anyone else's. Throughout all of my school years, my parents never pressured me about school. It was at P.S. 10 that for a short time I began to think that my real name was Jew Boy, as that's what the black kids in school called me.

I stayed at P.S. 10 for two years. My most vivid memory of those two years is a snowball fight we seven-year-olds had, throwing snowballs across 116th Street at each other. I'm sure that I couldn't possibly have thrown a snowball from one side of that city street to the other. Yet, when a window was broken as a result of the snowball fight, Jew Boy got blamed for it. The black kids banded together to blame me. "Jew Boy did it! Jew Boy did it!" they shouted. My father had to pay to repair the window; he knew I didn't do it, but he paid anyhow.

During this time, I discovered Cushman's Bakery a block and a half from my father's shop on 116th Street. I would venture over there to eat the crullers and jelly doughnuts. Soon, I began wandering further north and found a German bakery that made the most mouth-watering napoleons for five cents. I went still farther north and discovered 125th Street, which was teeming with bustling crowds, huge stores like Woolworth's, movie theatres and the Apollo Theatre.

I went to check out the Apollo, which was across the street from Woolworth's. The huge posters at the front of the theatre with the pictures of the entertainers really impressed me. I knew instantly that the acts featured on those posters were somehow connected to the acts I had seen at Zisselman's Farm. I knew that they weren't the very same acts, of course, but I instinctively knew that these posters had something to do with being on a stage, being applauded and being "somebody."

The sign above the Apollo box office window said that anyone under 12 could be admitted for ten cents if accompanied by an adult. I would get a dime, find someone who would take me in, and enter the magic world of the Apollo Theatre. On stage, there was an orchestra, some colorfully dressed dancing girls and, of course, the featured acts. I loved the whole scene, the music, the dancing girls, the singers, and the comedians. I just loved it; it was an afternoon of complete entertainment and fun. The entertainers were attractive, they were beautifully dressed and most importantly, it was evident to me that everyone in the audience was having a good time. The shows at the Apollo would change every week or two, and I tried to get to see the new shows as soon as they debuted.

One of the most important events for me at the Apollo was when I saw the Jimmie Lunceford Band for the first time. They were just fabulous. There were 14 pieces in the band and I could tell, even at such a young age, that they were very together. Listening to the Jimmie Lunceford Band, I began to cultivate an understanding of what elements were needed to be an entertaining and successful band.

During my childhood, my family moved several more times. I was going to P.S. 165, but remained an uninspired student; I rarely did my homework but always managed to pass my classes. Eventually, my father sold his shop and bought a new store in the Bronx. My mother was away frequently in the hospital and my father was working long hours at the store, so I had to fend for myself much of the time. This nurtured my spirit of independence. When I was nine, I began delivering suits and dresses for my father, which gave me the money that enabled me to begin frequenting restaurants on my own. I loved going to restaurants. I was a big tipper and was a favorite of the waiters. I particularly liked soup. I visited the M&F restaurant located west of Tremont Avenue and Southern Boulevard in the Bronx, and I also liked going to the G&R Café, which was two blocks from Yankee Stadium and had marvelous food. You could get a complete lunch for 25 cents. I also would take the subway from the Bronx to Manhattan to go to a German restaurant, the Ruppiner Bar, on East 86th Street, which had a great big pot of beans in the window. For ten cents, you got a large roast beef sandwich and for an additional five cents, a great side dish of baked beans!

I heard talk about the Depression around the shop and even at home from my parents and relatives. Talk of it was so pervasive that I couldn't escape it. Since I had money that I was earning delivering the dry cleaning for my father, I always had the wherewithal to take myself to the movies. There, watching the old Movie-Tone newsreels, I became informed about what was going on in the wider world. I knew that the market had crashed, although I didn't really understand what that meant, and I knew that desperate people were jumping out of windows. My father's income was steady, and the crash and ensuing Depression had little direct effect on the Bernstein family.

When I was 12 years old, in addition to my job of delivering the clothes for my father, I got a job as an office boy at the Bronx Coliseum, a 7,000 seat arena which featured wrestling matches, boxing matches and a pretty decent ice hockey team made up of Canadians. I loved the wrestling matches, and for many years thereafter followed wrestling and even had thoughts of one day becoming a wrestler myself. In addition to working at the Bronx Coliseum, I got a job at the soccer stadium adjoining the Coliseum. At that job, I sold soccer programs for 15 cents each so I was good for another $1.50 per week during soccer season. I was really more interested in making money and eating in restaurants than I was in going to school.

Also when I was 12, a little man who kept smoking the same wet cigar began to come to our home to prepare me for my Bar Mitzvah. He taught me the prayers and, on the appointed day, about 20 or 30 members of my family came to the storefront synagogue that my father frequented on the High Holidays, to celebrate my Bar Mitzvah. Unlike today, when people make huge parties, I did not have a party following the service—no food, no flowers, no music. All I remember is getting one gift, a fountain pen, and that just about did it for me as far as my religious training was concerned.

After my Bar Mitzvah, I went directly from the synagogue to the illegal weekly Saturday craps game that was held in the schoolyard of P.S. 47. I was the youngest participant. For some reason, this was a protected craps game as no police ever showed up there. But, on the morning of my Bar Mitzvah, with me standing there holding my only gift, the pen, a cop came into the schoolyard and broke up the craps game. For a minute, I thought that I was going to get arrested. How would that have looked, getting arrested for shooting craps in the schoolyard on the day of my Bar Mitzvah?

My parents continued to go on their yearly summer vacations to the Catskill Mountains, and they left me in charge of the store. Phil, my father's presser, would keep an eye on me. I collected cash, took in the cleaning and gave people receipts. The store was underneath Lefty's Pool Hall, a popular hangout for my friends from the neighborhood. When they weren't upstairs in the pool hall, my friends came down to the store and we would play knock rummy, a card game that we played for money. As my rummy skills improved, I won more than I lost and that meant more money to indulge my passions, eating in restaurants and going to the movies.

Chapter 2: **MAJOR BOWES**

SHORTLY AFTER MY BAR MITZVAH, AT THE AGE OF 13 I began to go downtown to Manhattan to watch movie, stage and vaudeville shows at various theatres. The theatres began having two- for-one shows where you could watch both a movie and a stage show. Each theatre would try to outdo the next one with the extravagance of their productions. The shows were fabulous, with great performances and dazzling chorus girls. I would play hooky from school to get to the theatre early enough to get the best seat I could afford.

At this time, radio shows also became a popular form of entertainment. The *Eddie Cantor Show* was a huge favorite across America. Eddie Cantor had been a vaudevillian who made it big in the Ziegfeld Follies and was rewarded with a radio show that aired in front of a live audience every Sunday night. The show was extremely popular. I liked going downtown to see Cantor's shows. I always found a way to get in. I got to see acts who would later become big stars: Deanna Durbin, Bobby Breen, and the beautiful young Dinah Shore. After the shows were over, instead of going right home, I would hang around and watch what the producers, PR men, managers to the acts, agents and writers did. I found it all very exciting.

Another show I liked to see was the *Fred Allen Show* at NBC. The *Eddie Cantor* and *Fred Allen* shows became my university. After the audience went home, I would linger to see what was going on behind the scenes. I was absorbing and learning. Show business was evidently in my blood.

When I worked in the Bronx Coliseum selling programs, I began to notice a young man who attended the fights regularly and was very boisterous. He had flaming red hair that was so bright, it was almost orange.

One night I noticed him screaming for a fighter named Kid Tracy. I found it interesting that the redhead was going against the crowd. Everyone else was cheering for the favorite, but he was rooting for the underdog, Kid Tracy.

Soon after, I saw him in the neighborhood and recognized him immediately.

"Wait a minute," I said. "Aren't you the guy I saw cheering and screaming for Kid Tracy the other night at the Bronx Coliseum?"

"Yeah, yeah. He's my favorite lightweight fighter," he answered.

"Do you live around here?" I asked.

"Right around the corner," he replied.

He lived with his parents and he and I became friendly. He was a very funny guy. Over the years, I watched the redhead's comedic career grow. He went from burlesque to vaudeville to stand-up to Broadway theatres to television and finally to Hollywood, where he won an Academy Award for *Sayonara*, a movie that featured Marlon Brando. He stayed the same funny and engaging guy he had been in the neighborhood. The only thing that was different about him was his name. His name now was Red Buttons.

I became an avid reader of *Popular Mechanics*, a best-selling magazine. In particular, I enjoyed reading the ads about mail order offerings. One day, I saw an ad for a closeout on Eddie Cantor songbooks. The price quoted in the ad was two two cents per book. I bought 500 books and took them to the opening night of the new *Eddie Cantor Show* at the Palace Theater on 47th Street. This was a Broadway show in which Eddie performed nightly in addition to his weekly radio show. I sold the books for 10 cents each, and I sold every one. I just stood in the lobby as people showed up for the show and sold them the songbooks. I reordered the books and was on the verge of selling all of them when I was asked by the theatre management to leave. They didn't appreciate the entrepreneurship of a 13-year-old.

At the beginning of my first term at James Monroe High School, we had an assembly held in the auditorium. At the assembly, I heard a most beautiful voice singing *The Star Spangled Banner*. I turned around and didn't recognize the singer, who was a huge, swarthy fellow. I waited for the class to file out of the auditorium, and the first thing I noticed was that this young man looked much older than 14. He looked like a 17-year-old.
"Excuse me, what's your name?" I asked him.
"Sol Strausser," he replied, with the slight trace of an accent.
"You sing beautifully."
"Thank you."
"Sol, I'd like to talk to you."
"OK," he said. "But I have to go to another class."
And so we talked as we walked between classes from the auditorium period. We only had a few minutes between classes, and I couldn't find out much about him. I asked if we could talk at greater length after school.
"I can't," he said. "My mother is at home waiting for me. She's all alone."
"Well, I'll be glad to come to your home if that's okay with you."
He agreed and we walked the 12 blocks to his home on Bathgate Avenue, which was in a poor section of the Bronx. It was a street full of fruit, vegetable, fish and dry goods stands. There were a few apartment buildings on Bathgate Avenue, and Sol lived in one of them.
When we reached his home, I said, "Sol, I would like to manage you."
"What do you mean?" he asked.

"Well, you have a great voice and I think that I would like to manage you. It means that you and I will have to sign a contract and I will try to find you some work."

"I must tell this to my mother," Sol said.

Sol and his mother were newly arrived immigrants from Poland. He spoke English quite well, but his mother didn't. I learned that in Poland Sol had taken operatic voice lessons. I asked him if he knew *Vesti La Giubba*, a well-known aria from the opera *Pagliacci*, which I remembered hearing Caruso sing on my parents crank-up Victrola. Sol said he did and proceeded to sing it so beautifully that I said, "My God, I think you sing better than Caruso, and I would like to make a contract with you."

I remember I wrote up a contract that stated I would get 10% of Sol's earnings in exchange for getting him work. Sol signed the contract. I was 14 and I had my first act. Now, I had to find him some work.

There was a popular radio program on the air at that time called the *Major Bowes Amateur Hour*. Amateurs who wanted to be in show business would audition for Major Bowes, and, if accepted, would appear on his show in front of a live audience. The audience would then vote on their preference for the particular act by applauding. The performance garnering the most applause would be the winner. The weekly winners would be invited to go on the Major Bowes bus tour, which visited the 20 largest cities in the U.S. This gave the winning acts exposure to live audiences around the country. Many successful performers had their genesis on the *Major Bowes Amateur Hour* on radio and then on the bus tour.

Major Bowes had made his reputation as the managing director of the Capitol Theatre, a great vaudeville and movie house on Broadway and 50th Street, which today is the location of the Mark Hellinger Theatre. Major Bowes ran his radio show out of the Capitol Theatre building and, I found out later, had his living quarters there as well.

I said to Sol, "I would like to get you on the *Major Bowes Amateur Hour*."

Like most people at that time, Sol and his mother listened to the *Major Bowes Amateur Hour*, so they knew what I was talking about and both nodded their heads in agreement.

The following Saturday, Sol and I took the Lexington Avenue subway down to 50th Street and walked over to the theatre. There was a stage entrance at the side of the Capitol Theatre. We entered and asked the guard where Major Bowes' office was.

"Back there, two floors up," he motioned.

"Wait for me, Sol," I said, and I proceeded to go up to Major Bowes' office. I rang the bell and was admitted. When I entered, there was this rather large lady sitting behind a desk whose name was Bessy Mack, a longtime associate of Major Bowes and the sister of Ted Mack, who later hosted the very popular *Ted Mack Amateur Hour* on TV.

"May I help you?" she asked.

"My name is Sid Bernstein, and I go to James Monroe High School. Last week in our auditorium class, I heard a great singer. This young man is from Italy and he is returning next week," I concocted. "He sings only in Italian. I really would hate to see him go back to Italy before he has a chance to sing *Vesti La Giubba* for you and Major Bowes. I'm sure that once you both hear him sing, Major Bowes will want to put him on the show."

Bessy Mack broke up. "Where is this young man?" she laughed.

"He's in the Bronx, but I can get him here quickly," I responded. "He'll be here in no time flat."

"Why don't you call him? Major Bowes is here now. Do you think that your friend will sing for us?"

"Sure!" I said. "I'll ask him!"

I ran down the stairs. Sol was there, waiting.

I said, "Sol, listen. Here's what I told them—you're a young man from Italy and you're going back on a boat next week. I heard you sing at school. They want you to come upstairs now and sing *Vesti La Giubba* for them."

Sol was overjoyed. "Yeah?" he questioned with a look of awe on his face.

"Yes!" I said. "Now remember, you're supposed to be Italian and I don't want them to think I'm lying, so try not to speak. Just answer me by nodding 'yes' or 'no.' If necessary, talk to me with as few Yiddish words as possible, okay?"

"Sure, Sid!" Sol was overjoyed.

We waited several minutes and went upstairs. I introduced Sol.

"Sol, this is Miss Mack." She said hello and Sol nodded.

"What key do you sing in?" she asked. "I have a piano player here."

I had coached him not to understand a single word they said to him.

"*Sol, vus far a key zingst di?*" I repeated in English. "What key do you sing in?"

Sol answered with one letter, "C."

"C," I responded.

"All right," she said and brought out a piano player.

"He sings in the key of C," I told the piano player.

"Ok. *Sol, in das key in 'C,' zing* Vesti La Giubba *far Miss Mack*," I said. "Okay, Sol, in the key of C, sing *Vesti La Giubba* for Miss Mack."

The piano player started playing, and Sol sang even better than he did in the school auditorium. Miss Mack and the piano player were enthralled.

"When is he going back to Italy?" Miss Mack asked me.

"Let me make sure... *Sol, ven gais du zurick offen shif?* When are you going back on the ship?"

"*Ein vuch,*" he answered. "In one week."

"Will he be here for next Monday night?" Miss Mack asked me.

So I asked Sol, "*Vilst du zein du montag nacht?*"

"*Zug, yah,*" I told him to say yes, and Sol nodded, "*Yah.*"

"I want the Major to hear this," said Miss Mack.

Bessy Mack went inside and returned with a courtly elderly gentleman in a beautiful smoking jacket. Bessy introduced us to a man of great bearing and charm.

"Hello, how are you, young man?" He extended his hand with a warm smile.

I shook his hand, "Fine, Major Bowes, and permit me to introduce Sol Strausser, who is visiting here in New York, but is going back to Italy next week. I was hoping that maybe you or someone on your staff would listen to him sing. He has a beautiful voice!"

"Yes," said the Major. "Miss Mack told me that he is quite a young talent."

Turning to Sol, the Major asked, "How old are you, young man?"

I translated into Yiddish: "*Sol, zug tzu de Major vie alt du bist.* Tell the Major how old you are."

Sol said to me, "*Fuftzen.*"

"He's 15 years old," I told the Major.

"Fine, fine. Would you like to sing *Vesti La Giubba* for me?"

"*Sol, vilst singen nach a mul* Vesti La Guibba *far de Major?* Sol, do you want to sing *Vesti La Giubba* again for the Major?"

"*Yah, yah,*" nodded Sol, and I told the Major, "Yes, Major. He said yes."

"Good. Do we have his key?"

The piano player nodded in the affirmative and began to play. Sol began to sing and you could see how thrilled the Major was because Sol was in top form, and he really did have a magnificent voice.

When Sol finished, the Major inquired of me, "When did you say he was leaving?

"Next week, Major," I answered.

"Do you think he might be able to stay over so that he can be in our next show?"

"Well, Major, I could ask his mother. I talk to her often and I think it could be arranged," I replied.

"Good," said the Major.

The Major and Miss Mack spoke in hushed tones and then the Major turned to me and said, "Young man, I would like you to bring Sol to our studio early Monday morning for rehearsal. You know how our show works, don't you?"

"Of course, Major," I answered. "My parents and I have been listening to your show for years."

"Okay," said the Major, and he gave me a time to bring Sol back on Monday and said good-bye to both of us.

"Nem sein handt un zug good-bye," I instructed Sol. "Take his hand and say good-bye."

Sol shook the Major's hand and we left.

I'm sure that Bessy Mack must have fallen off her chair from laughing so hard. Of course, both she and the Major understood that Sol was not Italian, but they didn't care. All that mattered to them was Sol's sensational voice.

In the alley, Sol and I hugged and congratulated each other on our good fortune. We were ecstatic. On that subway ride home to the Bronx, we were on cloud nine!

On the following Monday, I brought Sol to the rehearsal as instructed. At the rehearsal, he was spectacular. The orchestra members, stagehands, engineers, and staff were all in awe of Sol's magnificent voice.

When Major Bowes introduced Sol that night to the live audience and to the millions of radio listeners, he said, "Ladies and gentlemen. Here's a young man that I had the privilege of hearing who's on his way back home to Italy, and I asked him to spend another few days in New York so that you could hear his magnificent voice."

Sol came out, sang *Vesti La Giubba,* and the audience went wild. The applause meter went off the charts. I later learned that Sol broke all previous records for audience reaction. Letters and cards flooded in to the *Major Bowes Amateur Hour.* Those who had phones, called. The reaction was stupendous. When Sol and I left the show that night, there were people waiting outside the stage door to see and greet him and to get his autograph. I kept telling him to just nod and shake hands, which he did. He was literally an overnight sensation.

A few days later, I got word to go see Bessie Mack at the *Major Bowes Amateur Hour* office. There I was, a 14-year-old manager in knickers, at Major Bowes' office in the Capitol Theatre renegotiating with Bessie Mack. The offer that the *Major Bowes Traveling Amateur Show* made to Sol was $200 per week for a 16-week bus tour. Sol would join with other winning acts appearing in major cities across the U.S. All expenses like hotels and food would be covered and since Sol was only 15 years old, the show would provide a tutor for him.

I accepted the offer on Sol's behalf, and he became a member of the tour. His $200 salary was sent to his mother, and I would visit her in her Bathgate Avenue apartment every week and collect my $20 commission. I was really in the chips.

One day about three months later, I got a visit from an elderly gentleman who showed me his business card. I've forgotten his name, but I remember that he had offices in the Palace Theater building and his card said he was a theatrical agent.

"Did you write this contract?" he asked me and flashed me the one paragraph contract that I had written between Sol and me. The agent must have gotten it from Sol's mother.

"Yes, I wrote it."

"Well, you know I could report you to the authorities, young man, and you'd be in a lot of trouble! You are only 14 years old and you are not permitted to write or sign contracts! You're going to be in a lot of trouble, young man!"

I wasn't frightened about getting in trouble or anything like that, but I was hurt. I went to Sol's mother later that day to plead my case, but to no avail. She just pretended she didn't understand. It was a very disappointing moment for me.

I talked to my folks and grandmother about it, but neither they nor I had the experience to deal with something like this in a professional manner. They just told me to forget about it and that I would go on to do other things in life.

The older man became Sol's manager. Sol never returned to James Monroe High School. I didn't see him again until a few years later when our family was on vacation in the Catskill Mountains and Sol was performing at the hotel where we were staying. Sol was beautifully dressed, had lost some weight, and had a polished act. The audience loved him. After he finished performing, he saw me and came over to say hello as if nothing had ever happened between us. We spoke briefly. I was still hurt.

Years later, I learned that Sol was doing a lot of work for Israel, singing and selling Israel bonds. He had changed his name to Jan Bart. I once saw him at the Young's Gap Hotel in the Catskills. He told me he had gotten married and was the father of a young son. By then, I had gotten over my hurt, and it became just another chapter in my life.

The 20 dollars a week that I received from Sol's mother enabled me to move up in class as far as the restaurants were concerned. I had read about the Brass Rail, a first-class restaurant where wealthy and influential people went to dine, so I ate there. Lindy's was another premier restaurant where I went to eat. It was located next to the *Eddie Cantor Show* and many stars and show business people dined there. I saw Milton Berle, a rapidly rising star, there one day and also John Garfield, who was a major movie star.

After my disappointment with Sol, I returned to James Monroe High School and immersed myself in the social life, the clubs and the extracurricular activities of school. I tried the drama club for a while. The girls were pretty, and I had delusions of being an actor. I liked the atmosphere, but I soon lost interest when I realized that I just didn't have the necessary talent. Although I couldn't play a musical instrument, I was attracted to the school orchestra. They had a fine teacher and were quite good, and I would often go to their rehearsals and just sit, watch and listen. I also went to their concerts. I loved the music.

When I was 16, I had a traumatic experience that affected me so much that I believe I have not recovered from it to this very day. One night as I lay sleeping in the bedroom I shared with my grandmother, I felt something strange against the back of my head as I changed positions in bed. Something was projecting from the pillow into the back of my head, and it wasn't feathers. I groped the pillow and what I felt was a folded document of some kind. I picked the pillow up and tiptoed out of the room so as not to awaken my sleeping Bubba. I went into the living room, sat down and opened the seam of the pillow. I reached through the feathers and extracted the document that was folded in three. I unfolded it and there was my name: Sidney Bernstein. It was an adoption paper, and I saw the name Rae Popkin, who I assumed was the name of the woman who gave me away. I remember shaking and the tears falling onto the paper. I realized then that I had not been born to Ida and Israel Bernstein. When I got over the shock, I buried the document back into the feathers and sewed the seam back up. Remember that I was a tailor's son, so there were always needles and thread around. I never slept on that pillow again. The name Rae Popkin didn't mean anything to me, and no man was mentioned in the document.

I never talked to anyone about what I had found out. I loved and cared for my parents and my grandmother so much that I didn't want to bring up an issue that might cause them to be hurt or aggravated in any way. Also, I was so happy that they had chosen me and were so good and loving to me that I just didn't want to mention the adoption. The truth is that I should have mentioned it, because not talking about my adoption bothers me to this day. I should have attempted to find out who my birth parents were.

Chapter 3: **MEETING ABE**

IT TOOK ME FIVE YEARS TO COMPLETE FOUR YEARS OF HIGH SCHOOL. I could never figure out algebra and geometry and that caused me to have to spend an extra year in school. In what would have been my graduating year, my popularity had grown among my schoolmates and they encouraged me to run for class president. I ran and lost. I was disappointed but I got over it.

As I approached high school graduation, I started thinking about college and my future. Like most immigrants, my parents hoped that I would become a lawyer or a doctor because those professions promised financial security, but I didn't take it too seriously. Since it took me five years to get out of high school, I wasn't about to subject myself to another four years of schooling. I just thought that something of interest would come along. I had always been entrepreneurial and had been able to generate cash, so I figured that I would always be able to earn a living and take care of myself.

Towards the end of high school, I met someone who was to become a lifelong friend and a major influence in my life. Abe Margolies was a star basketball player at James Monroe High School. He wore thick glasses because he always had trouble with his eyes, but it didn't stop him from being a fabulously accurate shooter on the basketball court. Abe hung out at Lefty's Pool Hall, which was above my father's tailor shop.

Besides shooting pool at Lefty's, you could place bets on all kinds of sporting events, and since I liked to place a wager every once in a while, I would go there. Abe and I became nodding acquaintances. Abe was charismatic, and you could see by the way people related to him that Abe was a person people respected and looked up to.

In 1936, at the age of 18 and while still in high school, I had the occasion to go to Madison Square Garden to hear Franklin D. Roosevelt make a speech in support of his re-election campaign. What I heard and saw made a lasting impression on me.

I got to the Garden early and secured a good seat near the front. I was excited because this was the first political rally I ever attended. There were several speakers and finally it was FDR's turn to speak. I was close to the stage so I saw Roosevelt as he was wheeled in and then helped up to the podium. I had never seen or heard that Roosevelt could not walk, and I learned much later in my life that the press respected FDR's request that the public not be told of his disability. Most Americans did not know that FDR had contracted polio years earlier and as a result wore heavy leg braces, and that walking was extremely challenging for him. I was touched and moved, and seeing him in the wheelchair made me think of my mother with her cumbersome and heavy wooden leg.

Seeing President Roosevelt in person and hearing his mellifluous voice was thrilling. Although the Garden was packed, it seemed that he was talking to me alone. I had seen him on the Movie-Tone newsreels that were played before the main features in the movie houses, but here he was in the flesh: President Franklin Delano Roosevelt! In his speech, Roosevelt helped crystallize the feelings and emotions that had been running through me as a result of the things I was seeing and hearing in the streets on my frequent wanderings through the city. When I left the Garden that evening, I had the fervent desire to think and believe as this great man did. FDR that night in Madison Square Garden awakened in me a political consciousness that would remain with me for the rest of my life.

For a while after graduation from high school, my father tried to persuade me to let him open another tailor and dry cleaning store which I would run, but I really wasn't interested. However, I continued my wanderings around the city. In those excursions, I would often run into people I knew from high school. I began to understand how big the school was and how many people had attended. I was lucky as well in that I had a good memory for names and faces, and people who I met were often surprised that I knew them and amazed that I remembered their names.

About a year after graduation, I got the idea that it would be nice to have a school reunion dance. I negotiated with the school and cleared a Friday night to use the gym for a rental fee of $10.00. I sent out postcards to all the graduates whose names and addresses I got from the yearbook, and hired a DJ to play records. The night of the dance turned out to have beautiful weather and I got a tremendous turnout. I charged 15 cents for the girls and 25 cents for the guys. It was a huge success and I netted $18. I was happy, since it was a goodly sum of money in those days.

A year later, I held another reunion dance. This time I added another graduating class, so I needed a larger hall. I rented the Hunts Point Palace for $25, which included two security guards. Again, it was a big success. We had a lot of people who had been there the year before, so I guess people liked what I was doing. These successes encouraged me and were my first promotions.

As much as I enjoyed setting up these dances, I needed to find steady employment. I registered with several employment agencies downtown and went on as many job interviews as I could get. When I wasn't looking for a job, I was hanging out with the kids in the neighborhood and we would sit and talk. The country was still recovering from the Depression, Europe was in turmoil, and, as young adults, politics had become a major topic among us.

Some of my friends had become young communists. They were called Y.C.L.ers (the Young Communist League) and a few had become Norman Thomas socialists. The debates we had were spirited and sometimes heated. I was basically a loner, not a joiner and I didn't get caught up with the Y.C.L. or the Y.P.S.L. (the Young People's Socialist League), but I listened carefully. It was a time of heightened social consciousness in the country. My friends and I had the same concerns as President Roosevelt about how to help the poor and oppressed recover from the Depression.

In addition to all this, I had begun listening to Father Coughlin, an Irish Catholic cleric, on the radio. Father Coughlin broadcast his Sunday radio programs from Royal Oaks, Michigan, and he was a rabid anti-Semite who simply hated Jews. His show was very popular. My father, who was not political in any way, thought that we should listen to Coughlin. He was a great orator, his message was frightening to the Jews, and I guess to my father it was "know thy enemy." Father Coughlin issued his weekly 32-page magazine called *Social Justice* in tabloid form, and it reminded me of Hitler's *Mein Kampf,* which I had bought at the age of 16 at a German book shop on Third Avenue.

One day as I was walking west on West 42nd Street from yet another registration at one of the employment agencies, I passed Stern's Department Store. In front of the entrance to the store was a burly-looking young man with a canvas magazine pouch slung over his shoulder, selling Father Coughlin's *Social Justice* magazine for 10 cents a copy. An elderly lady passed by the magazine seller and in her Yiddish accent said, "You should be ashamed of yourself, selling that awful magazine. Shame on you!"

He pushed her and said, "Get out of here, you kike!"

I reacted without thinking. The way he had pushed her and said, "Get out of here, you kike!" blinded me with rage, I rushed over to him and pushed him as hard as I could. The man fell off the narrow curb, all his magazines spilling from the canvas bag onto the street. As I was about to kick the magazines all over the street, a policeman came up behind me.

"Hey, you, come here!" he screamed at me. "Just follow me," he said, his face bright red. We walked into Stern's Department Store and he took me to a mezzanine, which was between the ground floor and the basement level. There were two other policemen hanging out there.

In his slight Irish brogue, he asked, "You were wrong, absolutely wrong! I saw the whole thing happen!"

"Yeah?" I said. "What about what he did to the old lady?"

He interrupted me immediately so that the other two cops wouldn't hear how the fascist had pushed the old woman.

"You keep still," he said, waving his finger in my face. "Don't say another word. You should be ashamed of yourself and you should also pay for those magazines that you ruined and that are out in the gutter."

I said, "Why?"

"You pushed him, you hit him, you created a disturbance and you ruined his merchandise, that's why! Now, just keep your mouth closed. Shut up!"

I was incensed and I wanted to protest, but I saw the other two menacing cops and I thought better of it. They let me go. As I left, I was seething, but there was nothing I could say. I thought to myself, this bully who had pushed the old lady was a manifestation of Hitler and his repulsive ideas; yet, the authorities protected him. It was quite sobering. My sensitivity to being a Jew was raised. I was born a Jew, and I would always be a Jew. I felt threatened.

Not long after this incident, I went to a restaurant on East 149th Street in the Bronx. Outside the restaurant, I saw a crowd of about 100 people milling about and being addressed by a man standing on a stepladder. My curiosity drew me closer to the speaker, who turned out to be Joe McWilliams, a handsome man with a beautiful head of prematurely gray hair. McWilliams was an extremely gifted and captivating orator. The crowd was mesmerized. Since I had happened upon this event by accident, I didn't quite get the context. I heard McWilliams invite the crowd to two other similar events that he would be speaking at later in the week, one in the Bronx and the other in Washington Heights in Manhattan. And then I heard him say, "And Roosevelt's real name is not Roosevelt; it's Rosenfeld."

Without thinking, I blurted out, "You're a liar!"

Had I been thinking, I would have realized that the crowd was in agreement with everything McWilliams was saying. I was physically attacked; a few women scratched me and the men screamed at me. The cops, who were there supposedly to keep order, surrounded me and several began poking me with their nightsticks. The hatred coming at me from the crowd and the policemen was palpable.

I walked away from the rally as fast as I could and delayed my return home because I noticed blood on my shirt from where the women had scratched me. I didn't want to alarm my parents. I think I walked all the way home instead of taking public transportation. When I arrived home, I waited to make sure that my parents were asleep, and as soon as I got inside, I took off the bloody shirt and threw it in the garbage.

My curiosity now led me to go to McWilliams' next two rallies. I didn't stay long at either rally, but I could see that it was basically the same thing, Jew-hating and calling Roosevelt "Rosenfeld." I had learned my lesson from the first rally and didn't say anything. What I realized was that this anti-Semitic hatred was becoming pervasive, since I had now seen it in three different neighborhoods. This was not happening on the screen in some movie house showing pictures of the persecution of the Jews in Europe. This was happening in New York City. I was so disturbed by these events that I felt I had to respond in some way.

I went up to Lefty's Pool Hall, which was above my father's tailor shop, to talk to Abe Margolies.

"Abe, could I possibly talk to you privately in a quiet spot?" I asked him.

"Sure," he said.

We went off into a corner and I told him what had happened to me and what I had discovered. I told him that I thought McWilliams was a growing menace and something needed to be done to protest his activities.

"I wonder, Abe, could you get a few of the guys to go to McWilliams' next rally, which will be at Fordham Road and Valentine Avenue? What I'd like to do is not fight them because there will be a lot of cops around, but interrupt McWilliams speech by singing *The Star Spangled Banner*."

"What day of the week is it?" asked Abe.

I told him what day it was.

"Let me talk to a few of the guys up here," he said. "And I'll get back to you."

Later, he came down to the tailor shop and told me that he had lined up Red Ryan and Don Daley and some of their Irish friends, and George Manze and a few of the Italian boys.

"Sid, we're gonna meet at one o'clock on the day of the rally and go up to Fordham and Valentine as a group, and in the middle of the speech, we're going to sing the National Anthem."

I was elated. I felt that I was going to get revenge for what had been done to me, and I felt that I had some allies. On the day of the rally, just as he had said, Abe and his group met me at Lefty's, and we proceeded to walk to Fordham Road and Valentine Avenue to the McWilliams rally. There was a big crowd. McWilliams was up on his ladder spouting his venom. We were a mixed group of guys: Jews, Italians and Irishmen. Abe had done a fine job of organizing our group. We easily infiltrated the crowd, and at a signal given by Abe, we began to sing *The Star Spangled Banner*. Abe, by the way, couldn't sing in tune if his life depended on it, but there we all were, singing the National Anthem. The police didn't know what to do. The crowd got uneasy, but there was no scuffling. McWilliams was shocked. He was speechless for a moment, but then he tried to overshout the singing.

"Ignore them, ignore them!" McWilliams shouted. "They're all kikes trying to break up this meeting, but no one is going to break up this meeting! This is what America is really about! This is what we Americans stand for!"

From nowhere came the sound of fire engines, which promptly pulled up to the rally. Out came hoses. We kept singing. The firemen turned on the water and directed the hoses at the crowd, which broke up the rally. McWilliams lost his permit to hold rallies on Fordham and Valentine Avenue. We had peacefully and, I thought, cleverly thwarted McWilliams.

The word got out about what we had accomplished and we learned that the Jewish War Veterans who had fought in World War I were interested in doing the same thing on East 86th Street in Manhattan, where McWilliams was going to hold another rally. We met the Jewish War Veterans and went to McWilliams' rally together. On 86th Street and Third Avenue, Joe McWilliams was standing on the back end of a covered wagon, holding a lantern.

"I'm looking to find one patriotic Jew," he said, as he squinted and dramatically lit the wick of the lantern.

As soon as he did that, we started singing the National Anthem. Now it was the pool room boys and the Jewish War Veterans, wearing their Army war caps.

The crowd dispersed. We went back to the Bronx and we soon learned that McWilliams had lost his permit to hold rallies on East 86th street, the heart of Manhattan's Germantown. I guess the authorities felt that he was a riot waiting to happen and they pulled his permit. We felt that we had rendered the community at large an important service.

Sometime later, I remember reading in the *Daily Mirror* in Walter Winchell's column about Joe McWilliams. Winchell, who had the most influential and widely read newspaper column in America, had exposed for the entire country the Jew-hating Joe McWilliams and had renamed him "Joe McNazi." Although I never knew whether or not our counter-demonstration had anything to do with Winchell's column, I was still pleased and felt tremendously rewarded.

But the relief was very temporary. It was 1939 and Hitler was menacing everyone now: the Jews, the Europeans, the British, and the entire world. Militarism was in its heyday and war was in the air. I was 21 years old. I was doing clerical work at Bronx Hospital and the YMHA in the Bronx on alternate days and continuing my wanderings throughout the city.

Although I had been a disinterested student, my reading and study of Tom Paine, the American patriot who published pamphlets supporting the Revolutionary War, had intrigued me. Tom Paine became my all-time hero. I knew that I wasn't ready for full-fledged pamphleteering, so I decided I would become a stickerteer.

For years, the Eveready Label Corporation had advertised on the back cover of every telephone book in New York City. The ads said that you could get 5,000 labels with any message imprinted for $2.00. I decided that instead of Tom Paine-style pamphleteering, I was going to do stickering. On the heels of my success in enlisting Abe and the pool hall boys and exposing Joe McWilliams, I would become even more of an activist and broaden my political horizons.

The first sticker I produced was directed at Henry Ford and it said, "Henry Ford Give Your Iron Cross Back to Hitler." On the bottom, it was signed "Buddy Burnside." I liked the ring of "Buddy Burnside."

Henry Ford, the great American industrialist, had been given the Iron Cross, the highest honor that Germany could bestow on anyone. Ford was a known anti-Jew who had paid for printing and distribution of a vicious anti-Semitic pamphlet known as "The Protocols of the Learned Elders of Zion." I placed thousands of these anti-Ford stickers on Wrigley Gum machines on every subway platform in New York City. I had to lick each and every sticker to activate the glue, but I did it gladly because I knew that hundreds of thousands of people who rode the New York City subways daily were probably seeing the stickers. It's a wonder that I didn't get glue poisoning with all the stickers that I licked!

After I exhausted the Henry Ford stickers, my next target was Charles Lindbergh, the renowned aviator who was the first person to fly solo across the Atlantic Ocean. Lindbergh had accepted an Iron Cross from the German government. Lindbergh was also known to be anti-Semitic. The stickers encouraged Lindbergh to give the Germans back their Iron Cross.

I was so bold in these stickering campaigns that I even pasted one on the door of Fritz Kuhn's office at the German-American Bund, which was in reality a Nazi organization whose members were all Nazis. They couldn't call themselves Nazis so they called themselves the Bund.

I became a full-time activist. I got a post office box and began to imprint in tiny letters at the bottom of my stickers, "If you would like to help spread the word, send a self-addressed stamped envelope to Buddy Burnside at P.O. Box 38 and we'll send you your own supply of stickers." I started to get stamped envelopes, and since the stickers were so cheap, I could supply all the requests. Now it was not only me licking and pasting those stickers around the city, but others were doing it, too. Now millions of New Yorkers who rode the subways were seeing the stickers. My sticker campaign was growing.

One day, two young men showed up at my parents' door and showed me their IDs. They were from the FBI. The two FBI agents looked around my room and spotted the piles of magazines, tabloids and newspapers I had collected. They interrogated me about my reading habits. I told them that I was staying abreast of what the fascists were writing and had also gotten interested in liberal publications as well. Those publications were considered by some to be communist. I wanted to be educated about the contending political forces in the world. In my bedroom, I had stacks of the various publications. The agents looked at my magazines, one of which was titled *The New Masses*, a leftist magazine. The FBI men asked me if I was a member of the Communist Party.

"No," I said.

"Then why are you reading this stuff?"

"Because I want to gather information about these people who I am opposed to and also gather as much information as I can on the people who are opposed to them as well. My reading covers a wide gamut," I said, as I pulled out several of the fascist magazines that I had been collecting. "My reading doesn't make me a communist now, does it?"

"No, it doesn't. Sorry to bother you." And with that, they left.

My sticker campaigns became so pervasive that *Life* magazine actually reprinted one of the stickers. Also, John Wilson, a young reporter at *P.M.*, a very liberal tabloid newspaper, traced me down either through the post office box or the Eveready Label Corporation and interviewed me. He wrote an article for the magazine in which he reported that "Buddy Burnside is really someone named Sid Bernstein." My secret was out!

In 1940, there was a battle within the Republican Party for who was going to be the nominee for President. Although I wholeheartedly supported President Roosevelt, the Democrat, I so abhorred the conservative Republicans who were opposing the more moderate Wendell Wilkie for the Republican nomination, I decided that I would try to do whatever I could to help get Wilkie nominated.

I had become quite adept at placing my stickers, so I placed "Win With Wilkie" stickers wherever I could. I probably placed 40 or 50 thousand "Win With Wilkie" stickers around New York City. However, I wanted to broaden my geographic reach, so I enlisted some of the guys from Lefty's Pool Hall to accompany me to Philadelphia, where the Republicans were holding their nominating convention.

Somehow, we gained admittance onto the convention floor. Surreptitiously and cleverly, we placed "Win With Wilkie" stickers on every seat and at every microphone. It's amazing that we didn't get caught, or even worse, arrested.

Wilkie won the Republican nomination. FDR won the national election. I was happy. The conservatives did not carry the day, as I had feared. Chalk up another one to Buddy Burnside!

BOOK TWO

NEWSPAPERS, NIGHT CLUBS
AND SHOW BUSINESS
1941-1963

CHAPTER 4: DEFENDING BROOKLYN

ON SUNDAY MORNING, DECEMBER 7, 1941, the Japanese attacked Pearl Harbor. I was sitting in the kitchen with my father listening to a radio broadcast by the great liberal commentator Drew Pearson. The program was interrupted by a bulletin about the attack. Although no one could be happy at the thought of war, I viewed the situation differently than most others did. The attack on Pearl Harbor signaled the end of isolationism. America would become involved and I knew that finally the Fascists and the Nazis would be stopped.

The following day, President Roosevelt addressed a joint session of the Congress of the United States to formally declare war on Japan. We all listened together in our home as a family. It was very sobering to know that our country was at war. It took Germany four full days to declare war on the United States.

I wanted to enlist, but my mother's health was still quite poor. My grandmother, who had always been such a help to my mother, was getting on in years and my father had to spend most of his time at the tailor shop. I was the only one that my family could rely on to take up the slack. I knew that eventually I would be drafted but since I didn't know when, I helped out around home and waited. In January of 1943, I received my induction notice. I was 23 years old, I was an only child and everyone at home depended on me, but it was time to serve my country. My family hated seeing me go, and I hated leaving them. Who knew when and if I would come back?

I was ordered to report to Camp Upton on Long Island and was sworn into the Army there. From there, we went to Verona, New Jersey, for basic training, which lasted eight weeks. Basic training was not too difficult as I was in reasonably good shape. From Verona, we were temporarily assigned to Prospect Park in Brooklyn. The Army had taken over Prospect Park, which is a large and beautiful park right in the middle of Brooklyn, New York's most populous borough. They put a fence around the park, built some barracks and made it a transitional stopover before assigning soldiers to advanced training elsewhere. There I was, a member of Battery A, of the 602nd AAA Gun Battalion, stationed in Prospect Park to defend the citizens of Brooklyn against air attacks. I don't know from whom and I don't know why, but there we were defending Brooklyn.

The food in the Army was so miserable that every once in a while I would have to take myself over the fence to get a decent meal. As soon as bed check was over, I would climb the fence and go to some restaurant in Brooklyn to get a meal. I went to Garfield's Cafeteria, Dubrow's and Nathan's Famous, the hot dog place in Coney Island. I was usually back in a few hours and, thank God, I never got caught. If I would have been caught, my poor parents would have had to be informed that their son was being court-marshaled for going AWOL for a piece of kishke or a corned beef sandwich!

While we were there in Prospect Park, we got to meet the girls from the neighborhood. We were young soldiers who had just come from eight weeks of basic training. We were in the best shape of our lives and the girls knew it, so they came looking for the guys. I became friendly with a very pretty blonde who was 21 years old. One night on a little hill called "Blanket Hill" for obvious reasons, she seduced me and I lost my virginity. Times were different then. I had been brought up to respect women and the sanctity of marriage. What happened, happened and I didn't complain about it afterwards.

After our assignment in Prospect Park was finished, we were sent to Fort Totten and I learned to be a member of an artillery battery. I learned how to sight the big 90-millimeter cannon and how to be a loader. Finally, to get familiar with operating the cannons, we were sent to Riverhead, Long Island, to practice firing into the ocean. The cannon made so much noise that it impaired my hearing permanently. To this day, I have trouble with certain registers, but my hearing impairment has not stopped me from enjoying music.

Late in 1943, I was shipped along with my Army buddies to Gurock, Scotland, in anticipation of the invasion of Europe. After a brief stay in Scotland, we were sent by rail to Nottingham, England, the place made famous by the *Tales of Robin Hood*. We were hanging around, waiting for the invasion of Europe.

I liked England very much, particularly the people. They were very friendly towards the American servicemen. They appreciated what we were doing for them.

We were stationed near a huge airfield. One morning, the earth shook from all the engine noise coming from the air base. It seemed as if every plane had its engine running. That turned out to be D-Day. The sound was deafening. Five days later, on D-5, our company went across the English Channel to Normandy. We landed on Omaha Beach, which we later learned had seen some of the fiercest fighting during the initial hours of the invasion. Had we been there on Day One of the invasion, most of us would have been killed. Omaha Beach had been cleared, but at night we could hear gunfire and we were told that those were Allied Field Marshal Montgomery's troops engaging the enemy. We saw many truck convoys moving men and equipment. It was there that I realized that black men were driving most of the trucks. It bothered me that we weren't integrated as an Army. I thought that it somehow made us less of a nation.

We moved farther into France and bivouacked on an abandoned farm. We knew that we were going to stay there for a while so instead of setting up our pup tent, Frank Diano, my buddy and co-machine gunner, and I got ambitious and decided to build a little hut. We found some lumber, put sides on the hut and used the pup tent as the floor. We found some straw and made our own mattresses. We made it as cozy as we could.

Since our duties allowed for some free time, we would walk into the local town to see what was going on. I remembered some of my high school French and I was able to converse with the girls in their own language.

I met a buxom French farm girl, whose name was Madeline. We got friendly and she would come out to our camp at the farm, often bringing us fresh eggs and fresh cow's milk, which was a treat for us because all we had was powdered milk and terrible Army food.

One night Diano and I were asleep in our makeshift hut. It was a pitch-black moonless night. You couldn't see your fingers in front of your face. Suddenly, I was awakened from a deep sleep by hands groping my body.

"Frank," I said. "Stop kidding around."

Drowsily he replied, "What?"

The groping continued.

"Frank," I said, this time a little louder, "*cut it out! I'm getting angry now!*"

"What the hell are you talking about, Bernie?"

"Leave me alone, Frank! Leave me the hell alone!"

"Alright, Bernie, alright, but I don't know what you're talking about."

While Diano and I were arguing the groping had stopped, but as soon as we stopped speaking, it started again.

"Frank, you'd better stop it," I growled.

"Bernie, I want to sleep! I don't have a clue what you're talking about!"

I reached down and captured the hand, which had resumed its groping, and I then realized that it was a female hand. I looked down to the foot of the bed and barely recognized Madeline's silhouette in the darkness. She moved up and lay down next to me. She started hugging and kissing me. Diano was, at this point, fast asleep and completely oblivious to what was going on.

I got very excited. Madeline was wearing a turban and I wanted to touch her hair. I reached up to remove the turban and with it, her hair came off as well! I was in shock! Madeline was bald! I immediately realized that Madeline had been disciplined in the French custom of punishing their women who had collaborated with or dated the German invaders. They would shave a girl's head and make her parade through the center of town bald. I jumped up, which woke Diano. The poor guy thought he was having a nightmare! I just told Madeline to leave. "Go away, go away," I yelled, and she left. I guess Madeline liked soldiers, and she didn't care which side they were on. Luckily, I never saw her again.

Soon after, we were transported farther inland into France. Our troops moved towards the border of France and Germany. The mission, once we had our weapons set up, was to shoot down the V-1 rockets that the Germans were directing towards Great Britain. The V-1 rockets, which we could see taking off, made the most frightful noise. I was on duty with Diano one day, manning a machine gun, when we heard and then spotted a low-flying V-1. I started firing, and Diano kept feeding the gun. One out of every 18 or 20 bullets that we fired was a tracer, so you could gauge if you were in front of or behind the target. I got lucky that day because I got the V-1 in my sight and hit it with several shots and blasted it out of the sky. Knocking down a V-1 was very uncommon. I was a big hero for a day or two and I got a promotion to private first class.

Shortly thereafter, things heated up, and we saw action as a rear guard in the Battle of the Bulge, one of the most famous battles of World War II. The Germans started their move with overwhelming forces and actually pushed our front-line troops back so far that we who were in the rear were ordered to move even farther back. We saw a lot of ambulances and wounded soldiers pass us on their way to the rear. Capt. McCarthy asked Diano and me to be the rear guard for our company as we retreated. We were positioned with our machine gun covering our guys as they fell back. McCarthy told us to hold our position until all our men had passed us on the way to the rear and that he would return for us when everyone was in the clear. Diano and I stayed there until the Captain came back and got us. We were scared, but we stayed. I remember taking the firing pin out of the machine gun we were abandoning, to render it useless as we fell back. On the way to the rear, we saw all the guns and ammo that the American forces left behind.

The tide finally turned, the American Army regrouped, and we were ordered to a town called Epinal. We stayed there for a few months, just hanging around until V-E Day (Victory in Europe), which came on May 8, 1945. We were overjoyed! The war in Europe was over!

I thought that the food at basic training camp was bad, but Army food overseas was even worse! My father, however, used to send me food packages. Katz's Deli on the lower East Side of New York had a slogan, "Send a salami to your boy in the Army," so he would send salamis, and chocolate from Nestles which came in one-pound blocks, in addition to other non-perishable foods. But the salami and the chocolate are what I remember most. My father also sent me New York newspapers, like *P.M.* and *The Daily Mirror*.

Chapter 5: NEWSPAPER MAGNATE AND NIGHTCLUB IMPRESARIO

EPINAL WAS A NICE QUIET TOWN that had not been impacted at all by the devastation of the war. We had an uneventful quiet stay there. From Epinal, we were ordered to Dijon, the town made famous by the mustard that is produced there. Dijon was the place we were sent before being shipped home. The process of being shipped back to the States was based on a point system. If you had been wounded or had a Purple Heart, you received a certain number of points. If you had fought in a battle, you earned other points, and so on. The troops with the most points got to go home first. Since we had gotten to Europe rather late in the war and had not seen that much action, our point totals were relatively low, so we stayed in Dijon longer than we would have liked. But that worked to my advantage.

Dijon was a large city of 100,000 or so, which had not been scarred by the battles in France. Most of our activity in Dijon centered on our guarding German POWs.

One day, early in our stay in Dijon, the Captain came to me and said, "Bernie, what do you want to do? Do you want to keep guarding these German prisoners or do you want to drive one of the provision trucks or do something else?" The Captain liked me, and it was nice of him to give me a choice.

"Well, to tell you the truth, Captain, I'd just like any job where I wouldn't have to carry a heavy rifle," I answered him.

"You know what, Bernie?" he said. "The battalion needs a newspaper, or at least a newsletter."

"A newsletter?" I questioned.

"Yeah, a daily one-sheet with some news that we can get out to our boys and to the other battalions. Something to let everyone know what's going on with us."

"Okay, Captain, I'll take a shot at it."

We called the newsletter the *Comeback Diary*, in honor of the fact that we now knew for sure that we would be coming back home very soon. The Captain gave me two German POWs to be my assistants. The one who spoke English fluently was my typist, and the other did the mimeographing. We quickly became friends. Even though a few months ago we had been hell-bent on killing each other, we now came to realize that we were just human beings who had been put in this position by the fortunes of war. They were just as anxious to get home to their families as I was.

I wrote an article every day for the *Comeback Diary*, and I filled it with battalion news and news that I got from the States via the New York newspapers that my father would include in the food packages he sent me.

We made sure that the *Comeback Diary* was distributed to both the soldiers and the local citizens. I included something in French in the newsletter every day. The French civilians started to read the paper. The paper had a breezy, gossipy style to it, very New York in style. The papers that my father was sending me in the food packages had articles by Walter Winchell, Max Lerner and other noted columnists of the day. These articles kept me in touch with what was going on in Hollywood, on Broadway and with the hottest music trends and current events. I was passing the news along to the troops.

The tidbits in our paper were different from the other papers, like the *Stars & Stripes* that the Army was printing. Soon, our paper became very popular. When we started the paper, we were mimeographing 100 sheets daily. The circulation built and soon we were printing 6,000 per day. Since I was including something for the French citizenry, I got into the habit of signing off my column with *"Votre garcon, Sidney"*— "Your boy, Sidney." When the armed services radio guys got wind of our newspaper, they started quoting it in their radio broadcasts and they would say, "Here's something from 'our boy, Sidney.'" This created more and more demand for the newspaper. I had become a successful newspaper publisher while waiting to get out of the Army! The work on the paper gave me notoriety, made me feel important and gave me invaluable experience and perks.

The Captain and the other officers were so happy with what I had accomplished with the paper that they procured a room for me at the Grand Hotel in Dijon where the officers stayed. The accommodations at the Grand Hotel were far superior to the Central Hotel where I had been quartered before the success of the newspaper, and the women who visited there were beautiful. I was the only non-officer living at the Grand Hotel. The food was excellent.

Through the newspaper, I campaigned against the gouging of American soldiers by the French at the bars and cafes. The French were not as appreciative of the Americans as the British had been. The French took the opportunity to overcharge our boys at almost every turn. They were rude to our soldiers and treated them poorly. This did not sit well with me. After all, we had come to France to help liberate them from the Nazis. Some of our finest young men were buried here in France, having lost their lives so the French could be free. I began to campaign for a GI nightclub. I wrote about it quite often in the newspaper.

One day, one of the captains approached me.

"Bernstein," he said, "you know this GI nightclub you keep writing about in the paper? Well, listen, you are going to organize it. There's a lot of talk about it and I want you to put it together."

I knew nothing about running a nightclub, but an order is an order. I requisitioned a vacant store on the main street in Dijon. I requisitioned tables and chairs, got the place decorated and hired the loveliest French girls to be waitresses. We made sure to keep all the windows clear so that anyone could look inside and see how well-behaved the GIs were. And we served only beer, no hard liquor. The entertainment was mostly records played by a DJ, and I insisted that everyone be on his best behavior. Anyone who had one too many and got the least bit rowdy was asked to leave.

We invited French girls to visit the club. The French felt that the club was safe, and they encouraged their girls to visit, have a beer, and dance with the Americans. The nightclub became a very popular spot.

In addition to being a newspaper mogul, I had now become a nightclub impresario. I hired the waitresses, made sure we had the latest music, arranged for the clean-up of the club and found two bright enlisted men to run the cash and keep the books. I ran that club as would any proprietor. Seeing everyone have a good time in a safe and well-ordered environment was the goal, and we accomplished it.

Because I was running the paper and the GI nightclub, I was able to requisition a car or jeep whenever I needed one. With the mobility that transportation-on-demand gave me, I got to venture out into the countryside and also to take longer trips into occupied territory. I saw tremendous devastation and ruin, and it made me realize that war was and is tragic and should be avoided at all costs. Unfortunately, this war had been unavoidable.

I made it my business to stay away from all the attractive young French girls who worked in our GI nightclub as waitresses or who came to the club as guests. I was very serious about this rule. I was determined to keep my behavior professional.

Almost every night, there was a crowd of locals standing outside the window watching the American servicemen dance with the French girls. One night, as I turned to look at the crowd that was gathered outside looking into the club, I spotted the most delicately beautiful blonde girl standing there with a very attractive woman who was obviously her mother. The older woman looked to be in her early forties. Both women were smiling at me. Since the younger woman so captivated me with her smashing looks and because they were not patrons of the club, I walked out to say hello.

My French had really become quite good. I stood talking to the two women and learned that the young beauty's name was Claudy Vilfroy. Claudy was a college student at the University of Dijon and she was 19 years old. She was quite shy.

We spoke in French for about 10 minutes or so, just chatting. Madame Vilfroy complimented me on my French. I learned that they lived just eight blocks down the road, and I asked if I could walk them home. Madame Vilfroy agreed. They lived in a little, old building, 2 Rue Liegeois. We stopped at the entrance of the building and they invited me up for tea, but I declined, saying I had to get back to the club but that I would enjoy having tea with them some other time. They said I could come any time it was convenient for me. I waited a few days, thinking about Claudy often.

When all seemed to be running smoothly in the club and at the *Come-*

back Diary, I walked the eight blocks to have tea and see Claudy. I was 27 years old and I was smitten with Claudy Vilfroy. Claudy spoke only French to me and introduced her father Georges, a traveling salesman who happened to be home on this particular occasion. I became a frequent visitor in the Vilfroy home.

One day when I visited, there were records playing and I asked Claudy if she would like to dance. We danced, and I was in heaven. I sneaked a kiss. My visits to the Vilfroy home continued. I became very friendly with Madame Vilfroy and her husband when he was home from his travels, and, of course, I found Claudy enchanting.

After many months of waiting, the point system had worked its way to my unit, and we were ordered back to the United States. Our orders were to go to Reine and from there to Marseilles to board ships for the USA.

On my last day in Dijon, I went to say good-bye to Claudy and her mother. I was quite sad saying good-bye. Claudy walked me downstairs and we kissed. I gave Claudy my address and promised to write and told her that I hoped I could get back to France soon.

The next day, we left for Reine. We went through a process of turning in our weapons and other gear. In Reine, we boarded trains that we thought would be taking us directly to the Marseilles. Late that night, the train stopped at Dijon. I never found out why the train stopped at Dijon, but I seriously considered doing an AWOL to go say good-bye to Claudy again. I felt very sad and empty, and could not get her out of my mind. I reconsidered the AWOL, knowing that the train could leave without me and, if it did, I would be in real trouble. The train moved a short time later and took us to the ships in Marseilles.

The voyage back was horrendous. The sea was rough, and I got terribly seasick. The trip took an eternity. And all of that time, I thought about Claudy constantly.

We finally arrived at one of the piers at the Hudson River. We were loaded on buses and taken to Fort Dix in New Jersey. We arrived there late in the evening and we found lots of snow on the ground. We were discharged and had the choice of waiting for the morning bus or leaving immediately. I didn't care how late it was or how bad the weather was or how much snow was on the ground, I just wanted to get out of there. So, along with a few friends, I walked through a large field to get to a train station. I will never forget how cold, wet and muddy that field was. It was a mess, but every step took us closer to home. We caught the early morning train to New York.

We arrived in New York City at the break of dawn. We were tired and looked terrible. I said to the guys who were with me, "Listen, fellas, let's not let our folks see us for the first time looking so haggard. Let's get a decent meal somewhere."

So we climbed into a cab, went down to Ratner's Restaurant on Second Avenue, and ate like there was no tomorrow.

After the meal, we all felt better, and we probably looked better, too. I got a cab with one of my friends who also lived in the neighborhood and went up to the Bronx. I dropped my buddy off and proceeded to my father's shop. I had my Army coat on and was carrying my duffel bag over my shoulder as I entered the store. My father was sitting at his sewing machine. I had tears rolling down my face. He looked up and yanked his glasses off. "Simcha!" he cried. And we hugged for a long time. He had aged. We were speaking in Yiddish and memories came rushing back at me. I had not seen my family in more than two years. I went home to see my mother and grandmother. My mother had aged as well. My Bubba looked the same. I spoke to my mother and grandmother, hung up my Army clothes, changed into civilian garb and after about two hours, went back to spend the balance of the day with my father until he closed the shop.

When we got home, I was not surprised to see that my grandmother had hastily prepared a meal that included some of my favorite dishes. As we sat down at the dinner table in that ground floor apartment in the Bronx as a family, I thanked God. I had made it through, and our small family was united again.

The next day I woke up, still in disbelief that I was actually home. I wandered around the neighborhood, checking things out and getting re-acclimated. I saw some of my old acquaintances.

I went up to see the boys at Lefty's Pool Hall, and hoped to see Abe Margolies. I was disappointed that he wasn't there. Someone told me that he had moved to Laurelton, in Queens, with his young family. I was, however, happy to learn that Abe had achieved success and had built a business of some size and depth. When the war started, Abe had tried to get into the Army but his eyesight was so poor that he was immediately classified 4F. They just would not take him for service. Abe wanted to be helpful to the war effort in any way that he could. He went to Bridgeport, Connecticut, where there was highly sensitive and important defense work being done, but, because of his eyes, Abe couldn't do this kind of work, either. So, he started a jewelry company, which he and a partner built into a large and successful enterprise.

As the weeks passed, I became reintegrated into civilian life and started to venture forth and visit some of my favorite restaurants and began to once again wander around the city. Sid, the wandering Jew.

I didn't know what I wanted to do and, as usual, there was absolutely no pressure from the family. I visited the tailor shop often and began to help my father, but the work was intermittent and I wasn't too serious about it.

When I got home from the Army there was a packet of letters from Claudy waiting for me. She had written me practically every day since I had left France. I took a long time to respond to her letters. It was cruel of me not to respond to her sooner than I did. I felt I could have been more straightforward with Claudy and should have explained to her that I could not leave my parents and that religion was an issue between us. She was Catholic and I was Jewish. Even though I was not personally religious, my parents and particularly my grandmother would have been very disappointed if I had fallen in love with and married a girl who was not Jewish. Eventually, Claudy stopped writing. I should have been more sensitive to Claudy. She was young and innocent, and I hurt her. I will always feel remorse over that episode in my life.

I came up with a business idea for my father, which turned out to be very successful, almost too successful. The Tremont trolley was still in operation in those days and the tracks ran past my father's shop. In fact, my father would sit in the large window at his sewing machine and watch the trolley go back and forth. One day, I said to him, "Pop, you know all these returning soldiers need work on their clothes. They need to have them altered. Why don't we put up a sign that says "Alterations for Returning Soldiers—Special Discount Price"? The people riding on the trolley will see it!"

My father liked the idea. I went to the local sign maker and designed a large colorful sign, which we hung in the window of the tailor shop. Sure enough, the returning soldiers came for alterations in droves. So many of them became customers that my father had to hire another tailor and I had to spend more time at the shop. We got so busy that my Pop turned to me one day and said, *"Simcha, vus hus di getoon? Ich hab tzu fil arbeit!"* What have you done? I have too much work!"

After helping my father increase his business with the discount alterations, I became itchy for involvement in causes again. Activism was in my blood.

The people who came into the shop complained bitterly about the high price of meat. The price of meat was high because the government had taken over the meat supply for use by the armed services and that meant that there was a very limited supply for civilians. It took a while for the supply of meat to catch up to the demand as more and more servicemen came home and the government loosened its grip on the meat supply. There was a great deal of complaining. I started a sticker campaign: "Don't Buy Meat" was the message on the sticker. Once again, I signed it "Buddy Burnside" and once again I had printed in tiny letters at the bottom that by sending me a self-addressed envelope, anyone could get a supply of stickers and become an ally of mine. I got plenty of those self-addressed envelopes and soon "Don't Buy Meat" stickers began to appear all over the city.

The next campaign was for affordable housing for returning veterans. Housing was a real problem. The returning servicemen were getting married and needed housing. Housing was so scarce that young married couples had to move in with their parents or in-laws. It was a very trying circumstance for all concerned.

I became so involved in the housing issue that I spoke publicly for affordable housing and even went down to Washington D.C. with a group of veterans to lobby congressmen and senators. One of the congressmen I met was a young man from a district in Boston who was very sympathetic to our cause—John F. Kennedy.

One day, I spoke at a large housing rally in Harlem. There was a young singer there who spoke before me. He was an eloquent speaker and extremely handsome. I never forgot him. He was brilliant and charismatic. Later, he became a star. His name was Harry Belafonte.

I continued to get odd jobs but none really interested me and nothing became permanent. I had enough money to get by, and I became even more involved at home as my mother's health remained poor and my grandmother continued to age. I was the family chauffeur, helped with the shopping and did various other chores. The relationships that I had with my folks and grandmother were extraordinarily special and unique. We had great love and affection for each other.

I spent a lot of time driving my family around the city. My mother, in particular, liked these outings because it helped lessen her feelings of being a shut-in. I spent hours just driving around to no place in particular and we would end up some place where we could get a piece of apple strudel, a knish, or a hot dog.

I loved having the fabulous pizza and veal Parmesan that could only be found in Little Italy in Manhattan or in the Italian neighborhoods of the Bronx. Whenever I had a craving for Italian food, I would jump in the car for a pizza or veal Parmesan. Often, my grandmother would accompany me on these food excursions. My grandmother, as I have mentioned, was a religious Jewish lady, and she would gently scold me in Yiddish, *"Ziz treif, zindele!* It's not kosher, my child!"

I would answer, *"Nein, Bubba! Zenen Italanisher Yidden!* No, Grandma! These people are Italian Jews! *Und zey kuchen nor kusher!* And they cook only kosher food!" I don't think I fooled her for one minute.

Not too long after I returned from the Army, my grandmother went to the doctor complaining of pains in her chest. Upon examination, the doctor said that he didn't like the way her heart sounded, and he admitted her to the hospital for tests and rest. I visited her every day for about 10 days, and she seemed fine to me, but that was not the case. One day, we got a call that my Bubba had passed away. The news was terribly shocking. I attended her funeral, where a rabbi said some prayers. We all went to the cemetery, except my mother who was too sick. That was it, my best pal was gone.

The burden of taking up the slack that my grandmother's death left fell on me. Till the very end of her life, my grandmother took care of my mother. With my grandmother gone, I had to do more.

With the war's end and my return to civilian life, I wanted to get involved in a politically and socially liberal organization. I thought that the Veterans of Foreign Wars (VFW) and the American Legion were too conservative for me, so I joined the American Veterans Committee (AVC). The AVC was headed by bright young returning veterans, including Michael Straight who came from a prominent family in Westbury; Franklin D. Roosevelt, Jr., the deceased President's son; and G. Mennen Williams, a scion of the shaving cream family.

The AVC had its national headquarters in Washington, D.C. I had helped organize our chapter in the South Bronx, which was known as the Harry Hopkins chapter, named after FDR's longtime friend, advisor and aide. Our chapter had secured a clubhouse loft on East Tremont Avenue and I became the first president of the chapter. We held weekly meetings of the board there, and it became a hangout where we could come to talk about the important issues of the day. We talked and debated at length about affordable housing, and equity and justice for black people.

I wrote a weekly column called The Burnside Chat for the *AVC Bulletin*, a tabloid-sized newspaper. The journal was distributed nationally to all of the AVC chapters, so Buddy Burnside became known nationally.

For months, I had an idea swimming around in my brain. I decided to promote a singles weekend for young people at the Plaza Hotel in Fallsburg, New York, in the Catskill Mountains. I traveled up to the hotel and met with the owners, Mr. Orlansky and Mr. Platt. I asked them for 50 rooms with double occupancy. I hoped that I could find 100 single people who would come to the hotel from Friday night to Sunday lunch. The hotel owners agreed to give me the 50 rooms with the proviso that should they need the rooms for their own guests, they could take them back. I gambled and took out some ads in the *New York Post* and got flooded with reservations. The weekend turned out very well and everyone had a good time, including me. I made $12.50 per room for myself, so financially it was great. Orlansky and Platt were really impressed and they offered me a job for the next summer as the social director at the hotel. I turned them down.

I was very involved in the Harry Hopkins chapter of the AVC. Since I was the chapter's first president, I knew every single person by name and interacted closely with many members on various projects in the chapter. Jay Simms was one of the founding members of the Harry Hopkins chapter. We did a lot of work together and became close friends. Jay knew Jack and Eve Lasher, a childless, middle-aged couple who had rented an old Con Ed regional office on Tremont and Monterey Avenue in the Bronx and converted it into a catering and meeting hall. The Tremont Terrace, as it was called, became a popular place for weddings, bar mitzvahs, christenings or any type of social event where food was a requirement. The Tremont Terrace also held weekly Friday night dances featuring small bands.

One day, Jay came to me and told me that he had spoken about me to the Lashers and thought that I could be helpful to them as a publicity man for the Tremont Terrace. Jay asked me to meet them, and I agreed. I met the Lashers and liked them immediately. I agreed to take the job. The salary was $25 per week.

I knew many people from my activities in the AVC. I went to meetings with other chapters around the city and made acquaintances and friends all along the way. I began establishing contacts throughout the city. For a publicity man, contacts are the lifeblood of the job. I told the people I met about the Tremont Terrace and the events we were holding there. As a result of my efforts, the Terrace became increasingly popular. Because of the popularity of the Tremont Terrace, the Lashers raised my salary from $25 per week to $125 per week within one year. That was a terrific salary for that time.

My workday was a typical show-biz workday, but of course I didn't realize then that I was rapidly gravitating towards a career in show business. I would come to work at about noon six days a week and would stay late into the evening. As time went on, I was given more responsibility, including booking the small bands and combos that were popular at the time. I would stay late into the night. The Lashers looked to me increasingly for advice and I got involved in and learned all facets of the club business. While the Lashers were the owners and bosses, I was basically in charge of the daily operations of the Tremont Terrace.

Chapter 6: THERE'S NO BUSINESS LIKE SHOW BUSINESS

IN 1949 AND 1950, LATIN MUSIC BECAME HOT. Xavier Cugat and Noro Morales were two of the most prominent Latin artists. Cugat became a sensation and was often seen on TV and in the movies in addition to his successful recording career.

With the growing prominence of Latin music, the Lashers and I decided to change the name of the Tremont Terrace to the Trocadero. The South Bronx was slowly becoming a Puerto Rican enclave, so it made sense to follow the Latin craze that was sweeping the music business. We continued to do the weddings, bar mitzvahs and other social events, but the Trocadero became known primarily as a dance club where you could have a good time in a safe, secure and fun environment. People came from all over the city to dance and meet each other.

In addition to the media that I had used when the club was called the Tremont Terrace, I also began to use radio advertising because radio helped reach a wider audience for promoting the club. At that time, there was a famous DJ on the Latin radio station WOV who called himself Pedro, but who was in reality Art Raymond, a Jewish ex-serviceman who had a beautiful announcer's voice and a gorgeous wife who would appear with him at the dances he MC'd. After the Latin craze had cooled, Art recreated himself and had a daily radio show on WEVD, the then-Jewish radio station, for 25 years.

With all the advertising and promotion I was doing, and with Art's program being heard all over New York, the Trocadero prospered and people came from everywhere. People came from New Jersey, Brooklyn, Westchester and Manhattan. The Lashers couldn't have been happier.

The club was jammed on the weekends but I wanted to fill it during the weekdays as well. I came up with the idea of having a Wednesday night lecture series. I had been reading about a high school teacher who had become a very successful humorist and wit while working in the Catskills. I contacted him and he agreed to work the Trocadero for the princely sum of $75. His name was Sam Levenson. He became a hit in the Bronx and went on to become an even bigger star when he began to appear on the national TV variety shows.

Another Wednesday night lecturer who we featured was Dr. Murray Banks, a young psychiatrist who talked about sex in a humorous and lighthearted way. Of course, Murray Banks became very popular at the Trocadero and he lectured for us often. His lectures were always sold out because people were interested in the topic. Although it was a lecture series, I also booked a young blind pianist whose name was George Shearing. George became a big draw at the Trocadero and went on to become a big star, appearing on national TV and in concert halls around the country.

The Trocadero had become a landmark in the Bronx. I was feeling really good about myself and knew that I was on a roll and it was time for something bigger. The Lashers encouraged me in anything that I wanted to do. As long as I took care of my responsibilities at the Trocadero, I was free to try anything else.

I was still active in the AVC and thought that it would be a great thing to hold a big dance for the benefit of the AVC. I rented Kingsbridge Armory, a huge Army installation in the Bronx. Putting together the dance really took a great deal of effort and a huge leap of faith. I paid the Armory $1,000 for the rental. Then I hired Sammy Kaye and his band for $2,000, which was a big price and a huge sum of money in those days. Sammy Kaye was worth it because he was in a class with the Dorsey and Glen Miller bands. I also spent money on leaflets and posters and hired Bob Maltz who worked for the New York State Boxing Commission to hang the posters everywhere that he could. He did an incredible job and the posters were plastered all over the city. At the monthly citywide meetings of the AVC, I got some of the meeting participants to take tickets and sell them at their AVC chapters and I gave them a commission on each ticket sold. They did a great job and sold lots of tickets.

Kingsbridge Armory did not have a facility or system for checking hats and coats and it was my responsibility to provide a hat and coat check for the people who were coming to the dance. I went up to Lefty's Pool Hall and enlisted some of the guys from there to help me with the hat and coat check setup. The dance was in the late fall. Most of the men who came to the dance had hats and almost all the gals came with some type of coat.

I had done a great promotion job and more than 5,000 people showed up. It was an all-time record for a dance in the Bronx. Sammy Kaye and his band were wonderful and everyone had a great time. The evening was a huge social success.

When the event ended that night, all the people who attended rushed to the hat and coat check stand. Here were these eight pool hall characters trying to return hats and coats to more than 5,000 people. It was a fiasco; no one was very organized and the situation became quite chaotic. When it was all said and done, there was a group of young women in tears looking for me.

"I lost my beaver coat," one cried.

"My fur coat is gone," sobbed another, and on and on.

What could I do? Everyone knew me as the organizer of the dance. I had run the dance for the AVC, but I couldn't use any of the considerable dance event profits to pay for the coats. It was my responsibility. I took each young lady's name and address, took their word for what they said their lost coat was worth and eventually reimbursed each and every one of them. I used my salary at the Trocadero for funds and it took me six months to pay each girl back.

After the Kingsbridge Armory fiasco, I continued to book the bands into the Trocadero. Most of them were Puerto Rican bands, groups like the Curbelos, the La Playa sextet from Central America, Tito Rodriguez and the legendary Tito Puente. After trying for a long time, I also got Noro Morales, one of the biggest Latin bands around.

Noro Morales had a younger brother, Esy Morales, who was a flutist. Esy had had a number one record of his own, a rearrangement of the classical piece, *The Flight of the Bumblebee*. I booked Esy into the Trocadero. He was a fabulous flutist and a magnificent musician.

On the night Esy played the Trocadero, between his first and second set I went backstage to talk to him because I was so taken with his performance. I found him to be a very articulate and nice young man who spoke English quite well and was very bright. He told me that he and his brother Humberto, a drummer, had started with their older brother, Noro, but had left to form a band on their own. Soon it was time for him to play again, but I found him so engaging that I asked if we could talk again after he was done with his concluding set and he agreed. At the end of the evening, I returned to his dressing room and we sat and talked.

"Esy," I said, "you had this incredible number one hit, *The Flight of the Bumblebee*, and yet your asking price for tonight was much lower than I thought it would be. Tell me, do you work a lot?"

"No, I don't. In fact, I have a very hard time keeping my band together. We don't get enough work."

"Do you have a manager?" I asked.

"No, I don't. I have a lawyer and an accountant, but no manager."

"Well, Esy, don't you think you should have one? After all, that's what would keep you working and help build your career."

It was late and he was tired and wanted to get home, so I asked him if we could continue the conversation at another time. He said okay, and asked me, "What do you want to talk about, Sid?"

"I'd like to talk to you about management," I said. "You've got such a fine band and you've already had a number one hit record. You should be working more."

I recognized the names of his lawyer and accountant, who were well-known in the music business, but I also understood that Esy was hurting himself by not having a manager. Unless Esy found a manager who understood him and how to promote and exploit his great talent, he would have a difficult time keeping his band together.

We exchanged phone numbers, and a few days later I phoned Esy. He invited me to his home to meet his wife Blanche, an attractive and friendly young woman. We talked about management, and Esy told me that he wanted me to be his manager and asked what I had in mind for a deal. I shook hands with him on 10 percent of his earnings in exchange for getting him work and guiding his career.

Esy and I decided that not only would I manage him but I would become his promoter as well. This meant that I had to give up my job at the Trocadero. I gave the Lashers six weeks' notice. They were very upset, but since I had become almost a son to them, they wished me well. I lived only ten blocks away from the Trocadero, so I told them that I would be around if they needed me.

"I'll be here," I assured them, and that made them feel a little better about my leaving. Whenever they had a problem or needed help after that, I was always there for them. I really cared about those folks. They gave me my entrée into the business and I learned a great deal while I was in their employ.

Milton Berle had worked a nightclub in the Capitol Hotel at 50th and Broadway in New York City. After he gained success and notoriety, Berle left the Capitol Hotel, which left the nightclub with a vacancy. I decided to rent the nightclub and put Esy Morales in there for several weekends. Esy was an instant success and as his reputation grew, the crowds kept getting bigger and bigger. Esy was delighted that his following was growing, his price per performance was up and his career was booming. I got Esy many club dates, and there was no more talk about not being able to keep his band together.

Mrs. Lipkin and Mrs. Bush, who owned the Morningside Hotel in the Catskills, contacted me. They had heard what I had done at the Plaza with the singles weekend and wanted me to be the social director for the coming summer at their hotel. They offered me good money, so I took the opportunity to work the summer in the mountains. Since I had a responsibility to Esy as his manager and promoter, I booked him into a neighboring Catskills hotel, the Tamarack Lodge. I could do my job at the Morningside and still manage Esy's career, as he would be nearby at the Tamarack.

I was making two salaries, one from Esy and the other from the Morningside. I had a car, and I could go back and forth between the Morningside and the Tamarack. In addition, I could afford to bring my mother to the mountains for the entire summer. My father would come up for the weekends. Everyone was happy.

Next, I met George Scheck (the father of Barry Scheck, the DNA lawyer and one of the defenders of O.J. Simpson), who managed Connie Francis. George had a show on TV that he owned called *Startime*, which featured kid entertainers. In addition to the kids performing on the TV show, George would tour them around to various clubs and hotels in a pre-packaged variety show. *The Startime Revue* came to perform at the Morningside, and George Scheck and I became friends.

I told George Scheck about Esy Morales playing at the Tamarack. George sent one of his assistants to see Esy. The assistant flipped for Esy, so Scheck came to me and asked me if I would be interested in having Esy star on a local CBS show called *Tropic Holiday*, where Esy would appear every week along with other Latin artists. The answer from both Esy and me was absolutely yes, and before long Esy Morales was on TV in New York every week.

Esy Morales was 35 years old at this time, and his horizons were unlimited. Esy had diabetes, and I remember cautioning him several times to take better care of himself. I would see how cavalier he was about his diet and how he paid almost no attention to curbing his sugar intake, which, for diabetics, is crucial.

At the tender age of 35, with a loving wife and a blossoming career, Esy Morales died from complications of diabetes. I remember getting the phone call from his wife Blanche. I was in total shock and despair. I really liked Esy. It was hard to believe that this vibrant and talented young man was gone. It took me quite a while to get over Esy's death.

Lou Walters, the father of Barbara Walters, owned the Latin Quarter nightclub. The Latin Quarter was without question one of the top nightclubs in America and known worldwide. A large nightclub, "The Quarter," as it came to be known, catered to the most varied dinner and show patrons you could imagine. The rich and famous, royalty, captains of industry, mobsters—all visited the Latin Quarter. The Quarter featured statuesque dancing showgirls, dance ensembles, acrobats, magicians and comedians.

I knew Lou casually because Cass Franklin, his associate, would book acts for me while I was at the Trocadero. Lou wanted to expand his horizons, so he, along with Cass, started an artists management company. It was a wise move for them because if they found any talent capable and worthy enough to appear at the Latin Quarter, that talent would have a leg up on the competition. Cass ran the management company.

After Esy died, Cass approached me and said, "Sid, I know what a terrible blow Esy's death is for you. You did a wonderful job for him and we know that you have management skills. Lou and I were hoping that you would come work with us in our management company."

I really didn't have anything else in mind at that time. I knew and liked Cass, so I said yes, and went to work for the Latin Quarter Management Company. It was a nice atmosphere to be around. I was treated well, the Latin Quarter was in its heyday and I met lots of famous people. Those tall, beautiful chorus girls weren't hard to take, either. I got to know some of them extremely well, including one who had caught Frank Sinatra's eye.

In the time that I spent at the Latin Quarter Management Company, we never signed an act that could break through and become a huge star. If you don't have a big star as a manager, it's tough going. Before long, Cass decided to give up the management business, and it was disbanded. I was ready for something new anyway, so the dissolution of the business did not bother me too much. No one lost a job. The principals of the management company still owned the Latin Quarter and, as I said, I was ready for a change.

The major booking agency for Latin bands at the time was the Mercury

Agency. When I was booking bands for the Trocadero, I dealt with Mercury all the time. They had all the great bands: Noro Morales, Ralph Font, the great Machito, the Cabelos, Pupi Campo and Tito Puente.

My friend Larry Meyers worked as an agent at Mercury. I would see him from time to time. When the Latin Quarter management venture failed, Larry talked to me about coming to work at Mercury. He offered to get me an interview, and I thought, Why not? I knew Lenny and Charley Green, the brothers who owned the Mercury Agency, and I liked them. They knew about my efforts on behalf of Esy. When they asked me to join them, I immediately agreed. They gave me my own office and a secretary and agreed to give me the summers off, since I had already committed myself to a job in the Catskills for the next summer.

I really didn't like being chained to a desk at the Mercury Agency. Being a manager gave you more freedom. I lost some of my independence, and working with bands that I wasn't close to did not particularly appeal to me. I took the job mainly to keep busy and because I loved Latin music. I was really looking forward to the coming summer.

The summer before Esy's death, I met Cynthia Brown, the daughter of Charlie Brown, the owner of Brown's Hotel, home of the Brown Derby nightclub, one of the most famous night spots in all of the Catskills. The action there would start at about midnight when all the staff and entertainers from the surrounding hotels would gather to unwind after their long and hectic day and evening performances. Also, famous entertainers like Eddie Cantor and Milton Berle would visit the Brown Derby while vacationing. The Brown Derby was the place to be in the Catskills and if you worked at Brown's and could go there every night, you were going to have a memorable summer—wine, women and song.

Cynthia knew about my work at the Morningside. She told me that she wanted me to meet her father. I told her that I would meet with him anytime, and one day he called me and invited me to come see him at the hotel. I met with Charlie Brown and he offered me the social director's job for the following summer, which was the summer after my first year at Mercury.

Brown's Hotel was everything it was cracked up to be. It was large, well-maintained, and had many guests. There was non-stop action, beautiful girls, a great nightclub, and even more beautiful girls. Brown's had gained great notoriety because Jerry Lewis got his start there. His parents were on the entertainment staff at Brown's. Jerry had started as a tea boy in the tearoom, and he just had a comedic gift. He could keep people entertained for hours, and eventually worked his way up to the Brown Derby. Jerry was discovered, and the rest is history. Jerry Lewis never forgot that it was Brown's Hotel that got him started. Even after he became a huge star, Jerry would go to Brown's for a month each summer to see his folks, take it easy and vacation with his wife, Patti. When the spirit moved him, Jerry would perform in the Brown Derby and have the audience howling at his antics. The first summer that I was at Brown's, Jerry and I became friendly. One day Jerry said, "Sid, listen. I like your style. I like what you do. You have a lot of class. How would you like to come to Los Angles and work with me?"

"Doing what, Jerry?"

"I need an assistant. I'd give you a good deal, Sid. You could live in the guest house on my property, which is really nice, and you'd be in L.A., which is a great place."

I was intrigued, so I agreed to go out and spend a few days in Los Angeles. Everything Jerry said was true. L.A. was beautiful, the guest house was first class, his wife Patti was very sweet, and when you spent time around Jerry, all you did was laugh all day long. It was very exciting because Jerry was hot. But in the end, I had to turn Jerry down because I simply could not leave my parents. Jerry, for his part, was very understanding.

After I told Jerry Lewis that I couldn't forsake my parents no matter how great he was and how successful I knew he would become, I went back to Brown's Hotel, finished the summer there, and returned to my desk job as an agent with Mercury Artists.

It was during this time at Brown's that I met Billy Fields, a young singer who later became a business associate of mine and a co-producer of many of my later promotions and concerts. Emil Cohen, a comic who lived and worked at Grossinger's and who I would present at the Brown's Playhouse from time to time, introduced me to Billy.

One night, Emil approached me at the Brown Derby, where he had come to unwind.

"Sid, I'd like to bring a young friend of mine over with me the next time I appear at the Playhouse for you. He's really a marvelous singer and he's just replaced Eddie Fisher as our band singer. You know, Milton (Berle) and Eddie (Cantor) have taken Eddie Fisher under their wing and he's going to be a very big star. My friend Billy Fields is taking Eddie's place as the singer with the band. I'd like it if Billy could open for me here at Brown's. It won't cost you anything because I'll pay him out of my money and I'm sure you'll love him. I'd like for the guests at Brown's to hear him."

"That's fine," I told Emil. "Bring him the next time you appear."

I remember thinking then how great it was that successful entertainers, men like Emil Cohen and superstars like Milton Berle and Eddie Cantor, would go out of their way to help struggling young talents like Eddie Fisher and Billy Fields. The magnanimity and generosity that the established stars in those days showed the up-and-coming talent was special. It's too bad that this kind of spirit no longer exists.

The next time Emil appeared at the Playhouse, he brought Billy Fields with him. Billy had a big voice and I thought he was very talented. But even more important was the kinship that developed between us. I just liked the guy.

After the summer, I returned to Mercury, and my first assignment was to take Tito Puente and his band to California on a West Coast tour. The Mexican-Americans in California were clamoring for Tito, so the agency put together a two-week quickie tour with me acting as a road manager in addition to my duties as an agent. I had never been a road manager so this became a good experience for me. As the road manager, I was responsible for making sure that the travel arrangements were made, the hotel rooms booked, the band intact and showing up to the performances on time, ready to play. I also coordinated any additional arrangements like radio and newspaper interviews for Tito, interacted with the promoters at the various venues and took care of all business and financial matters.

We flew to the San Diego area and got in a tour bus. We worked our way north, playing in a different ballroom every night. The crowds were large and enthusiastic, with the ballrooms sold out every night. The music that Tito and the band were playing was infectious, energetic and kept the people up and dancing all night. Tito was doing it about as well as it could be done.

I got very chummy with Tito's band members on the tour and they were such fantastic musicians that I just had to dance when they played. The truth is that I never learned how to dance, and to this very day I still have two left feet. The music was so exciting, however, that by the second or third performance, I just had to get up and dance, faking it every step of the way. The girls were exotic and beautiful and, if single, were always willing to dance with anyone connected to the band. For my part, I would always dance near the band so they could see me with the beautiful Latin ladies. We always had a good time with that the next day on the bus.

On one of the last nights of the tour in Oakland, I found the absolutely most gorgeous girl in the entire ballroom. She was magnificent, and I asked her to dance. We started to dance the mambo. She was a great dancer, and I was having trouble keeping up with her. I maneuvered her in front of the bandstand, and I could see that the guys in the band were bug-eyed because my partner was so beautiful.

I was playing it up for all it was worth. My dance partner did a step where she threw me out, so of course I tried to reciprocate. Somehow, our feet got tangled and I fell flat on my ass. The band started to laugh so hard that they couldn't play. Two of the guys actually put down their instruments and came down off the bandstand to help me to my feet. Every time they happened to glance at me they broke up laughing.

Tito Puente stayed hot for over 40 years. He won every award that you can possibly win in the music business and he played all over the world. He was a superstar. Whenever we would meet, he always asked me, "Hey, Sid, do you still do the mambo?" and we both crack up. I was greatly saddened when I learned that Tito passed away on June 1, 2000. He was a great and talented musician and he was a very warm and decent human being. I was privileged to count him as a friend.

I continued working at Mercury until Larry Meyers called me and told me that there was an opening for an agent at Shaw Artists, the agency where he was currently employed. The agency was in the WNEW Building on Fifth Avenue and specialized in rhythm and blues and jazz acts. The agency had among its artists Ray Charles, Fats Domino, Miles Davis, Muddy Waters, Stan Getz, Ruth Brown and others. The Shaw agency was extremely well-run by Billy and Lee Shaw, a husband-and-wife team. Jack Whittemore, a vice-president at Shaw and a great agent, was my mentor. He allowed me to spend time in his office, so I got to see him in action. Jack had a way with people, and great style. It was at Shaw that I got to meet and know many managers and promoters because we agents were the go-betweens for the artists, their managers and the promoters. I tried to let the good traits that I saw in all these show business functionaries rub off on me. When I accepted the job at Shaw, I negotiated the summers off because I had given my word to Charlie Brown of Brown's Hotel that I would continue to be his summer social director. Billy Shaw respected the fact that I was a man of my word and agreed to my taking the time off. He also knew that I would book some of Shaw's acts into Brown's.

Besides my regular duties at Shaw as an agent representing mainly nightclub acts, I was given the added responsibility of being the agent most responsible for TV. The television business was just starting to take off and it became my job to try to get Shaw artists as much TV exposure as possible.

While I was at Shaw, one act I had responsibility for was Sallie Blair from Baltimore. She was a beautiful, young, talented black singer who I thought was going to be a star. Her manager was Biddy Wood, with whom I became friendly. Together, we worked hard to help Sallie achieve success. One of the songs Sallie would sing in her act was *Old Black Magic* by Harold Arlen. Invariably, she would kick off her shoes during the song and really work the crowd. When she took off her shoes, the audience went wild. They knew that Sallie would remain barefoot for the rest of the performance. It became her signature.

I booked Sallie into the *Cotton Club Review,* which was a famous revue at the time in Los Angeles. I got good money for her and she became a co-star of the revue with Lonnie Satin. Sallie had beauty and presence and was beginning to create quite a stir. I thought that she was destined for stardom, and I started picking up a lot of bookings for her, simply on the word of mouth that her performances were generating.

After Sallie finished her engagement in L.A., I booked her into a hotel in Miami Beach. Walter Hyman, a young executive in the New York textile industry, saw Sallie's performances in Miami Beach. He went to every one of her performances, and the more he saw her, the more captivated he became. Soon, Walter and Sallie became friends.

Sallie called me one day to talk about Walter. "Sid, I met this rich businessman from New York and he wants to manage me. I told him that Biddy is my manager, but he's so persistent. I told him he has to talk to you."

"Tell him to call me," I told Sallie.

The next day, Walter Hyman called me from Florida. "When I get back to New York, I'd like to come up to see you about Sallie Blair. I want you to get to know me. I'm very sincere about getting involved in her career."

"Fine, Walter. Call me when you get back."

The following Monday, Walter Hyman called me and invited me to lunch. He suggested meeting at his office in the garment center, and then going to a nearby restaurant. When I arrived at Walter's offices, I was ushered in immediately. We shook hands and Walter motioned for me to have a seat while he finished a phone call. While I was waiting for him, I began to realize that Walter ran a large and successful business. His phones kept ringing and people kept running in and out of his office.

When Walter finally got off the phone, he said, "You know, Sid, I have to apologize to you; I'm not going to have the time to spend with you. I think that Sallie is going to be a big star. I want you to know that I'm serious about representing her. This isn't some kind of frivolous flirtation. Would you mind coming up to my home in Scarsdale this evening? You'll meet my wife and kids and we can talk at length."

Clearly, Walter was concerned that I thought he was just some guy trying to get next to a beautiful and talented girl.

"Walter, I'd be glad to visit you at your home."

That evening after work, I went to the Bronx, got my car and proceeded to Walter's house in Scarsdale. Walter had a lovely family and beautiful home. After some small talk, we began to discuss Sallie Blair.

"Sid, this is what I'd like to do. Sallie Blair is going to be a star, but right now she has no money. She isn't even signed with her manager, Biddy Wood. I'll do the right thing, but you're the man to help me get this done."

"But, Walter, what exactly do you want to do?"

"I'll do anything I have to do to buy you and the manager out."

"I'm her agent, and it's not necessary to buy me out, since we work on a ten percent commission basis. As far as Biddy is concerned, I'll talk to him and let you know what he says."

"I'd appreciate that very much. I'm determined to help Sallie become a star."

"Nothing would please me more," I answered.

I called Biddy Wood the next day and told him about the conversation I had with Walter. He asked me to have Walter call him and intimated that even though he had a financial interest in Sallie Blair, he would not stand in her way if Walter Hyman could help further her career.

I never found out the details, but Walter was able to buy Biddy out of his financial interest in Sallie Blair. Sallie never did achieve the stardom Walter and I thought she could because health problems held her back.

Because of our association with Sallie Blair, Walter and I became good friends. Years later, Walter Hyman would play an important and historic role in my life.

Chapter 7: GERALDINE

DURING THIS TIME AT SHAW, I had several bachelor friends with whom I used to pal around. We went to sporting events, spent summers at the same beach club and often ate at restaurants together as a group. One of the restaurants that we frequented was the famous Reuben's Restaurant located on 58th Street between Fifth and Madison Avenues. I became friendly with Bea, the woman who ran the coat checkroom. One day she said to me, "Sid, you know that young girl who is my assistant in the coat check? You know, the pretty one? Her name is Geraldine Gale and she's newly arrived from California. She does very nicely with me here at the restaurant, but she spends almost every penny she makes on voice and singing lessons with the hope of getting into musical comedy on Broadway. I was wondering if you could audition her and tell me if she's got a chance or is she just wasting her time?"

I explained to Bea that the place where I worked specialized in jazz and r&b acts, so I didn't know if I could help Geraldine, but that as a favor to her, I would listen to Geraldine sing. Bea asked me if I wanted to talk to Geraldine right then and there, but I declined and gave her my card and told her to have Geraldine call me at my office.

About a week later, Geraldine called.

"Hi, this is Geraldine Gale. I'm not sure if you know who I am. I'm one of the girls who works with Bea, and you're the man who never lets me help him put his coat on!" And she giggled.

"I know who you are. Tell me, Geraldine, what can I do for you."

"Bea told me that you might come and hear me sing."

"I did promise Bea that I would do that. But I don't want you to spend any money on a rehearsal studio or a pianist, and I don't have a facility here at Shaw Artists. Maybe I could come to one of your singing lessons and you can do one or two songs that you're working on with your vocal coach."

"That would be great!" she said. "Let me check, and I'll get back to you."

The following day, she called to tell me that her vocal coach had agreed, and if I could come the next day to the Osborne Building, which was across from Carnegie Hall, she would be happy to have me sit in on her lesson.

I remember that when I was walking up the steps in the Osborne Building to sit in on Gerry's lesson, I passed the famous conductor and composer Leonard Bernstein.

When I got to the rehearsal room that Gerry and her coach were using, I was surprised. For a moment, I didn't recognize Geraldine Gale. I was looking for the young girl in flat heels that I had seen a few times at Reuben's Restaurant. Instead, I saw a slender, rather tall girl in high heels with beautiful reddish brown hair, wearing a lovely dress. I thought to myself, I can't believe this is the same kid I've been seeing at the restaurant.

She's really pretty!

Gerry was very shy. She introduced me to her coach, Eva Brown, and her accompanist and thanked me for coming to the lesson. I shook hands with Miss Brown and said, "I hope I'm not intruding."

"Certainly not."

Gerry sang two songs, one of which was *I Feel Pretty* from *West Side Story* by Leonard Bernstein. I thought, how interesting it was that she had picked a song by Bernstein, who I had just seen in the stairwell. To top that off, I had been thinking that Gerry was very pretty. Someone was definitely trying to tell me something.

Gerry was a terrific singer.

"Geraldine, you're wonderful! Tell me what is it that you would hope from me?"

"I would love to audition and maybe get into some shows on Broadway," she answered.

"Have you gone on any auditions?"

"No, I haven't really learned the ropes yet. I don't know how one goes about getting auditions, or an agent. I really just got to New York a short while ago...."

"Okay, Geraldine. Give me a few days and let me see what I can come up with."

I thanked Mrs. Brown and the accompanist, said my good-byes and left.

When I got back to the office, I told some of the agents that I had just heard this wonderful singer. About a week later, Gerry called me. I explained that I had been thinking about her but that I didn't think our agency could help her because we were rhythm and blues and jazz oriented and she was a Broadway singer. I asked Gerry if she would allow me to introduce her to some agent friends of mine who worked at other agencies that did specialize in her kind of talent. She, of course, agreed.

I introduced her to an agent whose name was Biff Liff. He was a very fine agent who worked for William Morris, one of the world's leading talent agencies. After Biff heard Gerry sing, he called to thank me and said that he would try to help Gerry. Biff explained that William Morris could not sign Gerry yet because they had mostly established artists, but he would recommend her to some stage show producers and tell her where and when auditions were being held. Eventually Biff's efforts on Gerry's behalf paid off and Gerry got signed to do summer stock.

Gerry and I developed a friendship. I would call her and she would fill me in on what was going on in her life. Gerry felt comfortable with me and I with her. I kept encouraging her and became a mentor to her.

In the meantime, I was still living with my parents and hanging out with my buddies. In between her summer stock appearances, Gerry would come home to her Eighth Street apartment for a few days. On one of those occasions, I called her.

"Gerry, what are you doing for dinner? Maybe the boys and I could pick you up."

"I don't have any plans, Sid. I'd love to go to dinner."

For various reasons, one by one the boys canceled out on dinner and when I picked Gerry up, it was just her and me. I took her to Ratner's. She was unfamiliar with the Jewish-style food but she loved it nonetheless. The WASP-y girl from Southern California fell in love with whitefish salad, vegetarian chopped liver, blintzes, kreplach and kasha varnishkes.

After dinner, I walked her home. She really looked so beautiful as we walked along, and after a while it felt natural that I should take her hand as we strolled. Right before we got to her apartment I said, "Gerry, look at the fella kissing the girl over there," and I pointed into the distance.

She looked over where I was pointing and said, "Where?"

"Here," I said, and I kissed her.

We walked up the three flights to her apartment, and at every landing I kissed her again. It only took me three years after that date to ask her to marry me.

I continued working as an agent at Shaw, dealing with promoters, TV producers and managers. On the ground floor of the building where Shaw Artists made its offices was a small restaurant, sort of like a Greek diner. I preferred going out to lunch rather than eating at my desk and would often go down to the little restaurant because it was so convenient. One day, I was sitting in one of the booths enjoying my lunch when in came my old buddy from Lefty's Pool Hall, Abe Margolies.

Abe's jewelry manufacturing business was right around the corner from Shaw and we would run into each other from time to time in the street, but we were both busy and we never got a chance to talk at length. On this particular day, because I was eating alone, I invited him to sit with me. He asked about my folks. I inquired about his growing family and how he enjoyed living in Laurelton.

"Sid," he asked. "How's it going at the agency?"

I explained that the agency was a nice place to work. The people were very friendly and I had learned a great deal in my time there. I also remember saying to him, "But, Abe, I really don't enjoy being an agent anymore. I've been thinking about making a change."

"So what do you want to do?" he asked me.

"I think I'd like to be a promoter. I deal with a lot of promoters and I'd like to try my hand at that. I think I could be successful at it."

"Well, Sid, why don't you try it?"

I laughed. "Being a promoter takes a considerable amount of money."

"What do you mean?"

"Well, first of all, you have to be able to engage the services of a band.

Then you have to be able to pay for a venue, a theatre or ballroom and finally you have to have money to publicize the event. It all takes money!"

"You really don't like the job upstairs at the agency?"

"It's not that, Abe. I like the job. The people are great. I have some close friends up there. They have big and successful acts and I'm learning about television, but I really feel that I'm ready for a change."

"How much money do you think you'll need, Sid?" Abe asked me.

"Well, it depends on the act and the facility I want to rent," I replied. "Let me just say this. I've done a lot of business with the Apollo Theatre at the Shaw agency, and I once asked Bobby Schiffman, the son of Frank Schiffman (the owner of the Apollo), what it would take to rent the Apollo. The Schiffmans don't really like renting out the theatre because they do their own promotions. Bobby Schiffman told me that were they to even consider renting the Apollo, it would cost $7,000 for a week. And they would only consider it if the act being brought in conforms to the policy of the theatre, which means it has to be capable of succeeding in the heart of Harlem."

"I understand," said Abe. "And what about the act? How much would that cost?"

"Well, if you got an act that was capable of filling the hall, it would cost about $10,000 per week. And then you would need several thousand dollars for publicity, leaflets and posters."

"So, you're talking about $20,000."

"That's right. The Apollo is the place for me to do it, Abe. I know the Apollo. I go there often because the agency books acts into there all the time and I think I understand the audience. If the Schiffmans would rent it to me, the total cost is going to be around $20,000."

"Why don't you do it?" said Abe. "I'll put up the money. Do it, Sid."

"What do you mean, Abe?"

"Do it. I'll put the money up," he repeated.

"So, you want to be my partner, Abe? Right?"

"No, Sid. I just want to help you."

"I can't do that," I answered. "If we make money, you're my partner. And if we lose it, Abe, I don't make the kind of money where I could pay you back, but I would try to pay you back."

"Forget about paying me back," he said. "Okay, we're partners—do it!"

He stood up and said, "I've got to go; I have an appointment. Do what you have to do and let me know when you need the money." With that, he left.

I went back up to the agency. I was somewhat shell-shocked. I had gone to lunch and come back with a new career and a new partner. I had mixed feelings about leaving because I had spent four years at Shaw and it really was a marvelous crew and a fine place to work.

The first person I saw was Lee Shaw. I swallowed hard and I said, "Mrs.

Shaw, I want to start a new career for myself and it means I am going to have to leave the agency."

"Sid, how can you leave? You're doing so well here, and you're seeing that lovely girl! And what if that gets serious?"

In those days, if it looked like you were going to get married and you had a well-paying job, you just didn't quit to go off and chase a hit-or-miss dream. It just wasn't done.

"This is just something I want to do, Mrs. Shaw."

"Did you tell Billy yet?" she asked, referring to her husband.

"No," I replied. "You're the first person I've spoken to."

"Let me talk to Billy tonight at dinner."

When I saw Mrs. Shaw the next day, I asked her if she had talked to Billy.

"Yes," she said. "And he's really not happy about it, but I told him it's something you want to do. Billy said that he doesn't want an unhappy soldier here, but he wants to try to talk you out of it, so go see him later today."

At the end of the day, I went to see Billy Shaw in his office. He was very cordial.

"I hear you want to leave. What is it, Sid? Is it a matter of money?"

"No, Billy, it's not the money. It's just that I want to do other things. I want to be a promoter."

"You know, being a promoter is a very risky business."

"I know," I said. "But I'm a risk taker and I want to try."

"It also takes a lot of money, Sid."

"I know that, too, but I can get help. I'm okay there." I told him about Abe's involvement.

"Okay, Sid," he said resignedly.

Billy asked me how long I planned to stay. I told him that I would leave whenever it was convenient for him and the agency. He told me that he would talk to Lee about it, and I left his office.

The next morning when I came in, Lee Shaw told me that she and Billy had discussed my leaving that I should stay two more weeks, finish what I had to do, and they would pay me for six weeks.

Lee then said to me, "Billy told me what you're going to be doing, Sid, so I guess you'll be around and you'll come to say hello."

"I'll be around, Lee," I said.

I planned to be around almost immediately because I knew that I wanted to book Miles Davis as the first act that I promoted at the Apollo. Miles was a Shaw artist. Of course, I kept my plans to myself.

And that was the culmination of my four years at the Shaw Agency.

I set up my new business in our apartment in the Bronx. It was an interesting transition. For the previous six years, at two different agencies, I had worked in an office surrounded by people and now I was all by myself doing everything for myself. Of course, I spoke to Abe, who was quite generous with both his money and his encouragement. However, Abe couldn't help me with the day-to-day responsibilities; I had to do that myself.

My initial task was to persuade the Schiffmans to let me rent the Apollo for a week so that I could present the first promotion of my new career. I called and made an appointment to see Bobby Schiffman. He and I had done business while I was at Shaw. We were pretty much the same age and we got along very well.

On the day I visited the Apollo, Bobby asked me, "Sid, you want to rent the Apollo? That's fine. It'll cost $7,000 for the week and you'll have to pay up front. I've already spoken to my dad and it's okay with him, but he wants to talk to you first."

He called his father, who came down from his office into the theatre.

"Sid," he said, "you really want to do this thing? Can you afford it? You need to pay up front."

"That's okay, Mr. Schiffman, you'll have the money up front."

"Who are you bringing in?" he asked.

"I'm not sure."

"Okay, just give us enough notice. Work the details out with Bobby and make sure your check clears," he joked.

Having secured the Apollo, my next move was to go back to Shaw and book Miles Davis to be the star of my first promotion. I picked Miles because he hadn't been in the Apollo in a long time, and I felt confident that he would do well.

I went to Shaw and talked to Larry Meyers, who was close to Miles. We agreed on the $10,000 price and Larry said, "Let me talk to Miles' manager. I think I can arrange it, Sid."

Then I went to see Abe. I told him what I had accomplished. He asked me when I needed the money. I told him within 48 hours and he said that it would be there.

I went back to the Apollo and told the Schiffmans that it was going to be Miles Davis in six weeks. They said, "Hey, you're going into competition with us now, but if you can get Miles, good luck to you! We haven't had him here in quite a while!" They asked me who the supporting act was going to be and I told them that I had to clear that with Miles because it was an unwritten rule that the headliner always gave approval for the supporting act. After Miles approved it, I put Ruth Brown on the bill. She was a great blues singer and would be accompanied by the Apollo's fine house orchestra.

Everything was set. I went back to Abe the next day, and he gave me three separate checks: one for $7,000 made out to the Apollo, one for $10,000 to Shaw Artists, to be paid into the account of Miles Davis, and one for $3,000 for promotional expenses.

I placed ads in some newspapers and had some posters printed, which Bob Maltz proceeded to hang around the city. Then, I hoped and prayed that when we opened, the crowds would be there. I had to wait six weeks to find out if we would succeed. There was no Ticketron in those days, and your ticket sales came from walk-up traffic at the box office. I had to wait to find out if I was going to succeed.

When I went to the Apollo to check on the arrangements, the manager of the theatre, Honi Coles, who knew me from my years of coming to the theatre as an agent, offered his support, which meant a great deal to me.

He said, "We're going to give you a little extra help, Sid!"

I had good feelings about what was going on. It seemed like everyone was rooting for me. I did my part. Everywhere I went I handed out leaflets and handbills. I never went anywhere where I didn't have my promotional literature in my hands, ready to be thrust on whoever crossed my path.

In addition, I hired some of the guys from Lefty's Pool Hall to surround Yankee Stadium during a heavyweight championship fight and hand out thousands of leaflets as the fight fans left. While we were handing out these leaflets, Joe Glaser, one of the preeminent theatrical agents in America, exited the fight with his party, many of whom were agents who worked for him. Joe Glaser was a dynamo agent who also was the lifelong manager of the great trumpeter Louis Armstrong. Glaser never had a contract with Louis Armstrong, but the loyalty they had to each other was legendary in the business.

Glaser turned to his agents, pointed at me and said, "You see this man? He's going to be a success; he's doing it the right way."

"Sidney," he continued. "It's great to see you out here. I wish you a lot of luck. Boys, Sidney is out here with his guys working shoulder to shoulder with them. He's making sure that he's protecting his investment. I admire that!"

Joe Glaser's words gave me the confidence that my promotion would succeed.

Miles Davis was a sensation at the Apollo! Two shows a day and every seat sold. My timing had been perfect. Enough time had elapsed since the last time Miles had been at the Apollo and the public was anxious to see him again. I made a bundle.

After the sold out-week at the Apollo, I called up Abe and said, "Abe, I owe you a lot of dough."

"Okay, when do you want to come down to the office?" he said.

"How about today?" I asked excitedly.

"I can't, Sid. I have a hectic day, but how about tomorrow? We'll have lunch and talk. Come to the Diamond Club."

The following day, I met Abe at the Diamond Club at West 47th Street, the main hangout and restaurant for the jewelry industry in New York. Over the years, literally trillions of dollars of deals have been made there. Not millions, not billions, but trillions.

The first thing I did was give Abe back the $20,000 seed money. Then I took out a handwritten sheet which detailed all the costs and revenues applicable to the week at the Apollo. It showed that we had made an $8,000 profit, a bonanza in that era! Then I took out $4,000, which represented Abe's partnership share, and gave it to him. He handed it right back to me and said, "Use it, Sid. Use it for the next one."

As soon as I saw the rush for tickets to see Miles, I called the Howard Theatre in Washington, D.C. The Howard was the Apollo of D.C., and I had sold them acts while I was an agent at Shaw Artists. I told the manager what was happening with Miles at the Apollo in New York and asked if he had any open dates at the Howard when I could present Miles Davis. He did some quick checking, called me back and gave me the dates and the price. I called my buddy Larry Meyers at Shaw and said, "Larry, I want to present Miles Davis and Ruth Brown at the Howard Theatre."

"Great," laughed Larry. "You're becoming one of our better clients. The Shaws are beginning to like the fact that you left! Keep the dates coming."

Because the Howard was a smaller theatre, we agreed on a price which was somewhat less than the $10,000 per week that we had paid Miles at the Apollo.

I went down to Washington ten days in advance and plastered the town with leaflets and posters.

Miles Davis' triumph at the Howard mirrored what had happened at the Apollo. There were long lines of people waiting to see him play. I was hot and having lots of fun. It was time for me to look for my next promotion.

Shaw Artists had a young black singer who had been playing the "chitlin' circuit," the numerous night, supper and dance clubs that were to be found in the black urban areas of America. He was on the road to stardom, and, in my opinion, he was ready for a major coming-out in New York. So on the heels of Miles Davis, I booked Brook Benton into the Apollo. Luckily for me, Brook had a new record out, *It's Just a Matter of Time*, which was peaking. Everybody wanted to see him. Brook Benton sold out the Apollo for the week. We made $5,500, and again Abe would take no money. Our boy Sidney was having the time of his life. I had reclaimed my independence. I was working very hard but enjoying life.

Because Brook had recently played the Howard, I couldn't bring him to Washington to follow Miles. But the Howard management and I were anxious to do another promotion. I went to Shaw Artists, talked to Larry, and we agreed to put Fats Domino from New Orleans into the Howard.

It was one of the coldest, snowiest winters in the history of Washington. I vividly remember the bitter cold as I toured the supermarkets, meat markets and grocers, asking the proprietors' and store managers' permission to put my posters in their store windows or hang them on their walls. I also rode the trolleys through the black neighborhoods and handed out leaflets and handbills to the riders. After I had exhausted my supply, I would go to the U.S. Senate to watch the senators, the best actors in the world, perform.

When the week of Fats Domino's Howard performances arrived, I went to the street often during the day to check out the people waiting to enter. Fats Domino, with his flashy rings and clothes, would leave the warmth of his dressing room and come out into the cold and snow before each and every show at the Howard and ask, "Mr. Sidney, how are you doing out here?" Fats would talk to the fans who were waiting outside to buy a ticket to see him perform. He was the gentlest, most considerate and involved artist that I have ever met. Fats was a big hit. Again, Abe took no money, and I was building up the kitty.

Gerry and I were seeing each other all the time. She had landed a role as one of the nuns in *The Sound of Music*, a role she kept for four years. I was a "stage door Johnny," which meant I would pick her up at the stage door every night when her show ended. Our romance was blossoming.

While all this was going on, the folks at Shaw, who by now thought that I had the magic touch, approached me with an idea. The Newport Jazz Festival, held every year for the past seven years in Newport, Rhode Island, had become an international event. Promoted and produced by the highly capable George Wein, the festival was a major happening each summer, attracting jazz fans to Newport for three days during the July 4th weekend. The people at Shaw thought that with the number of jazz artists they managed and my promotional hot streak, we could recreate some of the Newport excitement in Atlantic City. They even thought that we could do it in the same July 4th time frame. I agreed.

I went to Atlantic City and secured the Warren Theatre for the July 4th weekend. I booked the Shaw Artists jazz lineup including Miles Davis, Stan Getz, Dakota Staton, and Maynard Ferguson. I also booked Duke Ellington and Count Basie. I put posters up in New York City, Atlantic City, Washington, D.C., Baltimore and Philadelphia. We handed out thousands of leaflets. I hired top security and crowd-control people for the three-day festival.

If you wanted to see or hear jazz in America on the weekend of July 4, 1960, you had to go either to Atlantic City or Newport, Rhode Island because almost every major jazz artist was in either one city or the other. We were so successful with The Jazz Festival in Atlantic City that we broke all attendance records for a live event in Atlantic City up to that time. And that included the Miss America Pageant.

On the last night of the festival, Abe, Gerry and I were in my car looking for a place to eat in Atlantic City when we heard that there had been a riot at the Newport Jazz Festival. This was the first time there had ever been trouble in the seven years that George Wein had produced the show. I felt very badly for George Wein.

By now, the Schiffmans at the Apollo were watching what I was doing very closely. I had achieved great success with my promotional efforts at their theatre. I must have recharged their batteries because it became almost impossible to clear any more dates at the Apollo. The Schiffmans decided that they were going to go back and do everything themselves and not rent out the Apollo for the foreseeable future. If I wanted to continue promoting in New York City, I was going to have to find another theatre.

In the late 50's, the number one DJ in America was Alan Freed, who broadcast his radio show from WINS in New York City. That was well before WINS became the number one all-news radio station in the U.S. A transplanted Clevelander, Freed had a huge radio following. Some journalists say that Alan Freed popularized the terms "rock and roll" and "rhythm & blues."

Alan would hold holiday rock and roll shows in both the New York and Brooklyn Paramount Theaters. During Christmas and Easter, he would assemble the top recording acts and present them at three different shows per day and the kids would line up to get in. Freed had the great advantage of being able to spin an artist's recordings on his daily radio show. As a result, the artists and their managers felt a certain obligation to Freed. After all, Alan Freed could "make you" in the most important radio market in America. If Alan Freed asked you to perform at one of his holiday Paramount show weeks, you did it.

In late 1959 and early 1960, the payola scandal hit the news. Alan Freed got caught up in the scandal. Taking money to play records over the Federal Communication Commission-controlled airwaves was against the law. Because of his association with the payola scandal, Freed was banned from the airwaves and lost his Paramount holiday shows as well.

With the successes I had recently had and the money I made, I was able to open an office on Fifth Avenue in the Jensen Building. A shaken Alan Freed came to see me in my new office shortly after his indictment. He was looking for some advice and help, but even though I liked him, I couldn't do anything for him. His troubles with the law had taken a terrible toll on him, and he died a few years later, a broken-hearted man. I wish that I had been able to help him. Alan Freed was a decent man and had given a tremendous boost to many r&b and pop artists.

Gene Pleshette (actress Suzanne Pleshette's father) was the director of the New York and Brooklyn Paramount Theaters, where Alan had presented his holiday shows. Gene had worked with Alan Freed to make the holiday rock and roll events an institution in New York. Gene called me one day and asked me if I would like to take over Alan's spot at the Paramount. Gene suggested staging a show at the Brooklyn Paramount first. This was a godsend because I needed a new venue, since I had lost the Apollo. Naturally, I went to Abe, and he, of course, said, "Do it."

So, I called Gene Pleshette and agreed to take Alan Freed's spot at the Brooklyn Paramount. The show I put on at the Brooklyn Paramount turned out to be the first big mistake in my career as a promoter.

In an effort to ensure sellouts, I mixed rock and roll with jazz acts. It was mixing oil and water. The rock and roll fans had no interest in seeing the jazz artists. And the jazz aficionados couldn't care less about rock'n'roll. The fans stayed away in droves. We lost about $18,000. In one fell swoop, I had, with just one loser production in my career as a promoter, undone the financial gains I had made with the four preceding winners.

I wasn't about to stop, even though I had just lost a bundle at the Paramount, and of course Abe wouldn't think of not going forward. I told Abe that I wanted to do a show at the Palace Theatre on Broadway in New York City. As usual, Abe supported me, but this time he thought we should try something a bit different.

Abe convinced me to let John Drew, scion of a wealthy Irish Chicago family, and his lovely wife Eleanor into our Palace promotional partnership. John and his wife were eager to get into show business, and since they had financial resources, Abe thought it was a good idea to include them. As soon as I met John, who had the map of Ireland on his face, and Eleanor, his wife, I agreed that we should make them our partners.

The Palace was the best location to put on a show in New York; it was on a par with the Palladium in London. To be a promoter who presented at the Palace had always been a dream of mine. In September 1961, in a co-production with John Drew, I presented Ray Charles and Sarah Vaughan at the Palace Theatre. Larry Storch was the comedian on the bill, and we had Johnny Conrad, a famous choreographer at the time, and his dancers. It was a great bill, but the public at large wasn't ready for Ray Charles yet, and Harlem wasn't in the habit of coming down to Broadway for entertainment. Again we failed financially. Now, Gene Pleshette of the Paramount came to me and said, "Sid, I know you've had a couple of setbacks recently, but I have faith in you, and so does the Paramount organization. Why don't you do the New York Paramount for our upcoming holiday season rock and roll show?"

I told him I had to talk to my backer first, and would get back to him. I went to see Abe.

"Abe," I said. "We've just had two losers which set us back about 27 grand. Now the New York Paramount wants us to stage another holiday show. I think I know what will be successful, but it'll be a financial risk. What do you think?"

"Let's do it," Abe said.

It was always the same response when it came to Abe.

For the New York Paramount, I came up with the idea of alternating the featured act. Instead of having one star act for all 10 days, I booked James Brown for four days, Sam Cooke for three days and Jackie Wilson for three days. As supporting acts, we had the Four Seasons, Ruby & the Romantics, Rufus Thomas, Leslie Gore, King Curtiss, Terry Stafford,

Diane Renay, Chris Crosby, The Sapphires, Dean & Jean, and Bobby Rydell. Most of them had hit records at the time or had had recent hit records. The WMCA Good Guys, the DJ lineup from the ever-popular New York rock and roll radio station WMCA, acted as the show's hosts and it was a huge success. The waiting line for tickets stretched around the block and finally the people at the end of the line extended to where it met the front of the line.

Alan Klein, who was the manager of Sam Cooke (and briefly, later in his career, the manager of the Beatles) brought me up on charges at the American Guild of Variety Artists. This was the first and only time that I ever had trouble with a union or oversight body in the industry. When I booked the three main acts to do the holiday shows, I promised each one top billing. The ads, posters and handbills that I printed showed the three top acts on an equal line, so no one had top billing or all had top billing, depending on how you chose to look at it. Allen Klein went to Jackie Bright, a friend of mine and the head of AGVA, and complained. Jackie, who was looking out for me, suggested that I try to mollify Allen with money. I offered Sam Cooke four days' pay for three days work and that seemed to satisfy Allen Klein. Neither Jackie Wilson nor James Brown, the other acts, ever complained.

While at the Paramount, I often had to go talk to James Brown before every performance. Ben Bart, his manager/agent, would come to me before James was supposed to go on and say, "Sid, he's not going on. He just doesn't want to do it." James always had a different excuse: a headache, a toothache, or his foot or stomach bothered him. It was always something.

"You have to go talk to him," Ben would implore. So I would go up to James' dressing room and talk with him and tell him how great he was and how he couldn't disappoint all the fans who had come to see him perform. James was basically a pussycat who probably needed the TLC. Of course he always went on and he always did a spectacular job. When James would finally go on stage, Ben would look over at me and wink. And then James would give his usual phenomenal performance.

The 10 days at the New York Paramount were a huge success. The shows were all sold out and we even added a show, so instead of two shows a day, we had three. We made a bundle and we were back on the plus side. But I was learning that it was hard to make money at these promotions. The margins were really small and if you charged nominal prices to accommodate the fans but did not sell out, you were probably going to lose money. Basically, it meant that you always had to be right. You could have a succession of winners, and one loser could undo it all.

About a month later, I got a call from the Mayor of Newport, Rhode Island, who said to me, "Mr. Bernstein, you know that we've had a disaster here with our Jazz Festival. The merchants are after me to continue the festival because it brings so much business to Newport. The townspeople, on the other hand, are unhappy and wish that the whole thing would go away. The town council and I would like to invite you here to make a presentation, as we hope that you would consider taking over the festival from Mr. Wein."

"Mr. Mayor, I am very flattered. Are you absolutely certain that Mr. Wein cannot continue with the Festival?"

"Yes, Mr. Bernstein, we are certain about that."

"Well, let me get back to you, Mr. Mayor. I need to confer with my associates first. I'll be in touch very soon."

I went to see Abe at his office.

"Abe, we are being offered the most important jazz festival in the world. It's going to be very expensive to produce a show of this magnitude. The acts will cost a lot and the security is going to have to be extraordinary to avoid the kinds of problems that George Wein had. Abe, we're looking at $50,000 to $75,000."

"You know what, Sid?" Abe said. "The Russians have been calling us hooligans. When they reported the riot at Newport in their newspapers, they referred to our people as the American hooligans. Let's show those bastards that they're full of it. Do it!"

I called the Mayor and accepted his invitation to present a proposal to him and the city council. I went up to Newport, made a speech to the council and a large assembly of townspeople, and went back home.

The next day, the Mayor called me and said, "Mr. Bernstein, by unanimous vote, you are hereby awarded the 1961 Newport Jazz Festival! Congratulations!"

I sent John and Eleanor Drew to be our representatives in Newport. We talked on the phone constantly, and the phone bills between New York and Newport were huge.

I used Abe's idea about leveraging the negativity that the Russians had injected into the situation to hype the Newport Jazz Festival. I went on every radio show that would have me and sat for every print journalist who wanted a story, and kept emphasizing that Americans were not hooligans and that folks should support the Newport Jazz Festival and buy tickets.

One day during our preparations for the festival, John Drew called me and said, "Sid, listen to this. I'm having a problem. Eleanor and I are being called kikes all around Newport. We walk down the street shopping or just to get an ice cream cone with the kids, and we hear people saying, 'There are those kikes.' I even stopped some ladies and asked them why they were calling us kikes when it should be obvious to everyone that I'm an Irishman, and they told me, 'We don't want you Bernsteins up here! We had enough of that last year!'"

Clearly, the residents of Newport were scared. They thought that they were going to have another riot on their hands with the coming festival.

They really didn't care about the merchants or the business that the festival generated for Newport; they were worried about safety.

I asked John if this was making him uncomfortable enough for him to get out and he said, "Absolutely not!" I told him to let me think about a solution and we would resolve everything in a day or two. My solution was to call the agent for Bob Hope, Val Irving, and ask him if I could book Bob for the Jazz Festival.

He said, "Sid, what do you want with Bob Hope at a jazz festival?"

"I need him. I'm not going to put him in the Jazz Festival. I'm going to put him on by himself on the afternoon of July 2nd."

"Okay, but it'll cost you $25,000," Val said.

"You got it."

I knew that if I presented Bob Hope, Mr. American Flag, the man most closely associated with the USO and the man who traveled literally hundreds of thousands of miles to entertain U.S. servicemen and women all over the world, that the "kike" business would stop. Anybody who brought Bob Hope to Newport would be considered a hero. Bob Hope *was* the Stars and Stripes.

I also called Judy Garland. The reason I felt that we needed Judy Garland was that, without tremendous star presence and the sellouts that star presence guarantee, we would lose every penny that we had already sunk into the Newport Jazz Festival. She told me to call her managers, David Biegelman and Freddy Fields. I asked them if Judy Garland could perform at the Newport Jazz Festival on the afternoon of July 3rd.

"$25,000," they said. "Plus, you pay her conductor, Mort Lindsey, five of her key musicians, and you supply a 22-piece orchestra."

"You got it," I said.

I had just increased our expanding budget by $60,000—$50,00 for Hope and Garland and $10,000 for Mort Lindsey and the 22-piece orchestra. The word got out fast about Bob Hope and Judy Garland, and the people in the town began to treat John and Eleanor like heroes. We had diffused the anger and animosity.

With the acts and dates set, we distributed posters and handbills in five cities: New York, Newport, Boston, Providence and New Haven. We also did some radio advertising.

A few weeks before the festival, I got a phone call from Val Irving, Bob Hope's manager. "Sid, you have to let Bob out of the July 2nd date. He owes Jimmy Durante a favor to be on his TV show, which is on the same day as your show, and he just has to do it. We'll make it up to you someday, somehow, Sid, but you have to let Bob out." Reluctantly, I let Bob Hope out. Luckily, I still had Judy Garland and I knew that I could explain the Bob Hope situation in a media blitz. I would lower my costs by $25,000 and still get some publicity, all at the same time. We held a press conference and I went on some radio stations to explain why Bob Hope wasn't showing up.

Everybody took it in stride.

Finally, we were ready for Newport. Four days of the greatest jazz acts in the world: Louis Armstrong, Count Basie, Gerry Mulligan, Maynard Ferguson, Cannonball Adderley, Dave Brubeck, Ramsey Lewis, Stan Getz, Art Blakey, Sarah Vaughan, George Shearing, Ray Charles, Oscar Peterson, Gloria Lynne, Lionel Hampton, Quincy Jones, Mel Torme, and John Coltrane, among others. If you were a jazz fan, and if you were lucky enough to be in Newport during the Independence Day weekend in 1961, you would have thought you'd died and gone to heaven.

The security was fabulous. I brought in New York detectives that my cousin Leo Kitchman helped me recruit. We hired ushers from Madison Square Garden. We had extra security men. If anything, there was too much security. But the three days went off without any problem. John Drew and I scored a big hit with the people of Newport.

On the last night, I had Mel Torme, Quincy Jones and Duke Ellington on the bill. Quincy asked me if he could have an extra 30 minutes because he was doing a live album. I agreed. Quincy did his extra 30 minutes, and Mel did several encores, and an open-air concert that was supposed to be over at 11:30 was still in progress at 1:00 a.m., with the great Duke Ellington waiting in his trailer to go on. And then it began to drizzle. I got word that the Duke wanted to talk to me. I went to his trailer. Duke Ellington was a man of great dignity and civility and we had quite a chat.

"Mr. Bernstein," he said. "It's 1:30 a.m., it's started to drizzle out there, and I should have gone on stage two hours ago. I don't believe that those folks are going to want to sit out in the rain at two in the morning listening to my band and me. I think I should go home."

"Mr. Ellington, those people want to see you and they are all still here waiting and I believe they'll stay."

I convinced him to wait around for his set to begin. I remember he got dressed in a beautiful jacket, and the tall, elegant and regal Duke Ellington went out into the drizzle and played his concert and no one left. At 2:30 a.m., the audience was all still there, and they stayed until he did his last number.

From a musical point of view, the entire four days were magical. Our costs were inflated with the expense for Judy Garland and the extra security we had arranged. Even though we broke previous attendance records, we lost money. In support of the Bob Hope and Judy Garland initiatives, I had committed unbudgeted funds for emergency advertising. Because we were functioning in a crisis situation, I just acted and didn't have time to confer with Abe or John Drew. When the bills for the advertising came due, I took the responsibility to pay them myself. Of course, I didn't have the money but I knew that somehow I would find a way to get those bills paid without involving John or Abe.

The Boston Herald did an editorial about the Newport Jazz Festival and about how we had saved it and how well it had been run. In the editorial, they quoted me as having said that I had come to Newport to perpetuate the great jazz festival that George Wein had initiated. George called me as soon as he heard about the editorial, to thank me, and we have remained friends to this very day.

During our stay in Newport, we were headquartered at the Cliffwalk Manor Hotel. On our last day there, a man came to see me with his wife and three children.

"Mr. Bernstein, I am a native of Newport, born and raised here. I was against you and this festival from the very beginning. However, after seeing how you ran these four days, the care you gave to security, the way in which you handled yourself with our children and the great show you put on, I want to tell you, Mr. Bernstein, that if you'd choose to move up to Newport and run for Mayor after Mayor Mar, we would consider it a privilege to work for your election."

I thanked him but respectfully declined.

We had accomplished a great deal at Newport. We saved the festival. We put on a wonderful four days with the best jazz acts in the world. All previous attendance records were broken. Our crowds had been well-behaved and Abe was happy that we had showed the Russians that Americans were not hooligans. I was also happy that we had put the "kike" business to rest. But the bottom line was that we lost a great deal of money. The extra security and $25,000 to Judy Garland did us in financially. I was very upset.

Billy Fields had come to Newport to help with the festival. I remember how down we both were on the drive home. To make matters worse, I had booked Connie Francis and Brook Benton into the State Theatre in Hartford as our next promotion and the preliminary indications were that we were in trouble with the event. Advance ticket sales were below expectation. I was depressed and miserable. In addition, I knew that the added costs that I had incurred for advertising the fact that Bob Hope and Judy Garland were going to appear at Newport would soon be coming due. A smart guy might have considered quitting the game and stop fighting the odds. But no, I had to be around the music. I was going to stick it out.

The State Theatre in Hartford was another loser. I never could figure out why. Both Brook Benton and Connie Francis were major recording acts and had hit records. Someone later told me that people were getting in free through a back door. Maybe that happened, but I really don't know for sure. Abe, as usual, just took it all in stride. He paid the bills for the State Theatre and never complained.

On the other hand, John and Eleanor Drew had had it with show business. Somehow, all the financial losses took the glitz and glitter out of it for them. "It's only exciting when you win." They went back to their lives in

Chicago and eventually I lost contact with them. I wish it had turned out differently, as they were fine, hard-working people and I liked them and enjoyed their company.

Despite losing John and Eleanor's involvement, Abe insisted that we go on. With his great smile, his ebullient spirit and his never-say-die attitude, Abe said, "What's next, Sid?"

I remember telling him, "Abe, you know Judy Garland is almost a sure thing if she shows up. Look at how great she was in Newport. The audience in Newport couldn't get enough of her."

"What do you mean *if* she shows up?" he asked.

"Well, you know she's had all these health problems induced by her uncontrolled drinking, and there is the possibility that we'll book her and she'll cancel out—it's always a possibility with her. And if that happens, we have to refund everybody's money. We also lose the money we put up for the venue, the advertising and the promotion. It's a crapshoot with her."

Abe's response was, "Let's do it!"

Newport and Hartford were costly in many ways. We lost a lot of time and money, but we pressed on with the next project—Judy Garland.

We had established a good working relationship with David Biegelman and Freddy Fields, Judy Garland's managers. They agreed to let us pay Judy date-by-date so we wouldn't have to put up all the money up-front for the series of concerts that we planned. As long as we paid her $25,000 per performance and paid for Mort Lindsey, her conductor, and five key men in her band, plus supplying a 22-piece orchestra, we were okay. I estimated that with all the incidental costs, it would cost us about $30,000 for each performance.

We had the amazing good fortune that Judy did not cancel on us even once. She was canceling almost as often as she was showing up for other promoters but I think she liked me and did not want me to suffer financial loss. Financially, we were quite lucky. But she sure did give us our moments.

The first concert we did with Judy in the series was at the Ice Palace in Haddonfield, New Jersey, near Philadelphia. It was the only venue in New Jersey I could get that was both large enough and available when Judy was available. Many rural roads surrounded the Ice Palace. On the morning of the concert, there was a torrential downpour that made the roads almost impassable. The police told me that cars were lined up in every direction bumper-to-bumper trying to get to the Ice Palace. Although I was a promoter who liked to be punctual with my events, I held up this first Judy Garland concert for an hour and a half. I felt that I just had to accommodate all the people who were trying to get to the show.

I was sitting in my temporary office in the Ice Palace, checking with the police and finding out how the audience was faring in their efforts to get to the show, when I got a summons from Judy Garland to come to her dressing room. I remember walking to her dressing room and thinking to myself, I wonder what I forgot? Usually, when an artist summons you to his or her dressing room moments before they are supposed to go on, it spells trouble. I went down the checklist. We had installed the red carpet that Judy insisted must always be in her dressing room. We had supplied the bottle of special liquor with the twig in the neck of the bottle. And we had installed her special lighting. Everything seemed to be in place.

I knocked on the door of the dressing room and her wardrobe mistress admitted me and whispered, "She's quite angry." The wardrobe mistress then announced me, "Miss Garland, Mr. Bernstein is here."

Judy was sitting at her dressing table, putting the finishing touches on her makeup. The bottle of liquor beside her was almost empty.

"Where are the fuckin' tissues?" she screamed at me, as she slowly began to rise.

"What's that, Judy?"

"The fuckin' tissues, Sid! Where are the tissues I asked for?" She was standing now, a bit unsteady on her feet.

She stood up, a bit unsteady on her feet, but mad as blazes.

I tried to inject some levity into the situation, "Tell me what color you'd like, Judy, and I'll send for them right away."

"I don't give a damn what color, Sid! They should be here! I'm not going on unless my fuckin' tissues are here!" she screamed.

"Don't worry. They'll be here," I said and immediately had someone run out to get her the all-important tissues.

That was Judy. You could expect anything from her.

Finally, the cops told me that the crowd had made it into the arena. I gave Mort Lindsey the signal to start the overture that always marked the beginning of Judy's concerts.

By now, Judy was really unsteady on her feet. Freddy Fields, her manager, was with her. Freddy helped her get the short distance to the stage, but she couldn't negotiate her way up the stage steps so Freddy got under her one arm and I got under the other, and we helped her get up the steps. We looked at each other, both wondering if Judy would be able to perform because we could tell that she was in pretty bad shape. When she got up on stage there was complete darkness and then a pin spotlight hit her. As soon as the pinpoint of light hit Judy Garland, she threw her shoulders back, walked to the mike and on Mort Lindsey's cue began to sing *Somewhere Over the Rainbow*. There could not have been a dry eye in the audience because all those Judy Garland fans knew that their darling was in bad shape, and they knew why. I am sure that no one who was there that night at the Ice Palace in Haddonfield, New Jersey, ever forgot Judy's performance.

After the show, we all went back to the local hotel where we were staying. After Judy changed, she came downstairs to the lounge to get something to eat and to unwind. Like most lounges, there was a musical ensemble playing dance music. Judy asked me if I wanted to dance. How could I refuse? So here I am—Sid the klutz—dancing with Judy Garland who used to dance with Fred Astaire. Judy was so drunk that I had to hold her up. I was stepping all over her feet but she was so out of it that she didn't even know it. It was really sad to see Judy Garland like this because I liked her and admired her amazing talent. She was a great artist but also a sad and lonely woman.

A few weeks later, we booked Judy at the Forum in Montreal, where the Montreal Canadiens, the most storied hockey team in history, played. The Forum was a huge arena with over 15,000 seats.

A week before the concert, Billy Fields and I drove up to Montreal to let the city know that we were coming in with the great Judy Garland fresh off her triumphant success at her comeback concert in Carnegie Hall. I had taken Gerry to see that concert after she begged me to get tickets. I probably got the last two tickets, and we sat way up at the top of Carnegie Hall. Judy had been spectacular, utterly magnificent that night. The audience stood several times during the performance, and I had vowed to myself that I would one day present this once-in-a-lifetime artist.

Billy Fields and I were in Montreal, telling everybody what Judy had done at Carnegie, at Newport and at Haddonfield. It was a marvelous week for us. We stayed at a big, beautiful hotel called the Queen Elizabeth. We had recommended it to Judy and her entourage, and they, in fact, booked their entire party into the hotel. At the same time, I found an incredible bakery on St. Catherine's Street near the hotel that made the most marvelous napoleons. Every day, as a special treat for myself, I would stop there and get a napoleon or two.

On the night of the concert, I was leaving the hotel a little early to stop at the bakery and fortify myself with a couple of napoleons. The hotel is a huge one-block-long structure. As I exited the elevator in the lobby at one end of the hotel, I heard this big voice coming from the other end.

"Hey Sid! Sid! It's Judy! I'm on my way to the Forum. I'll give you a lift!"

I really didn't want to get into her limousine and go right to the Forum. I wanted to go get the napoleons, so I yelled across the hotel lobby, "It's okay, Judy! I have a lift! I'll see you there!"

"Okay, bye!" she screamed across the lobby.

I went to the bakery, ate my two napoleons and went to the Forum ready to work.

As usual, we were supplied with an office, a phone, some writing materials and an intercom. Billy was down on the arena floor making sure that everything was set for Judy's appearance. The intercom in my office rang. It was Judy's road manager and he sounded very upset.

"Hey, Sid," he said. "You'd better come up to Judy's dressing room. We've got a problem."

"What's wrong?" I asked.

"No, Sid. You'd better come right away."

As I walked to the dressing room, I wondered what could be wrong now. I went down the mental list in my head again: the red carpet was in her dressing room; Billy had personally gotten the liquor with the twig; the tissues were there. What could it possibly be this time?

I got to her dressing room, knocked on the door and was admitted. The wardrobe mistress rolled her eyes at me and whispered, "I wonder how you're gonna handle this one."

"Sid's here," she announced to Judy.

Judy was sitting at her dressing table—hair coifed, makeup artfully applied and seemingly ready to go. I found her staring directly into the mirror with her fists at her cheeks, dejectedly looking downward.

"Judy, it's me, Sid! Judy! Is anything wrong?"

She looked up from the mirror and whispered to me in a barely audible voice, "Sid..."

"What is it, Judy?"

She whispered again, "I can't go on, Sid. I can't speak. I can't sing. It's impossible. I can't go on. My voice is gone."

I could barely hear her. But I could certainly hear the orchestra tuning up and I could visualize all the excited fans streaming into the Forum. I also remembered her shouting to me just an hour earlier across the hotel lobby.

I went into crisis mode.

"Judy, do you have a special doctor?"

She whispered to me, "Lester Coleman. But he's in New York, Sid."

"Judy, did you say Dr. Lester Coleman?"

"He's my doctor," she said in a slightly restored voice.

As soon as I heard her slightly improved voice, I knew that we had another kind of problem, which had nothing to do with her loss of voice. I stood in front of her dressing room intercom to block Judy's view of the apparatus. I picked it up and began having a one-way conversation with myself. In my hands, the intercom became a phone, and I hoped that Judy wouldn't pick up on the fact that I wasn't really talking to her doctor.

"Hello. Is this Dr. Coleman's office? It is? Good. May I please speak to the doctor? I'm here in Montreal with Judy Garland, and we have an emergency."

Now, to make Judy believe that this conversation was actually taking place, I repeated everything that the other side was supposedly saying to me.

"Doctor, this is Sid Bernstein calling from Montreal. I'm presenting Judy Garland tonight, here at the Forum, in concert. The arena is sold out, Doctor. There are more than 15,000 people waiting to see Judy, but she has a bad case of laryngitis and is having a most difficult time. Is there a possibility, doctor, that you could fly up immediately? I don't care what it costs! Charter a plane, and please come to Montreal immediately. Yes, doctor! You can? In about an hour, you say? That's wonderful, Dr. Coleman!

"What is the nearest airport?" I continued my imaginary conversation. "LaGuardia? That's good," I said into the intercom. "Whatever it costs, I'll pay, doctor. Dr. Coleman, I cannot tell you how grateful I am, along with these thousands of people who have come here from all over Canada to hear Judy! Thank you and we'll see you soon," and I hung up the intercom.

I turned around to look at Judy, and I noticed her refreshing her makup.

"Judy, what a wonderful man! He's coming right up! He'll be here in no time flat!"

"Oh, he will? That's great, Sid. You are just the best. Will we dance later?"

"You know we will, Judy."

And then Judy responded in full voice now, "Out of my dressing room, Sid. I want to put on another dress."

I got out of there as quickly as I could. I called Billy from the first intercom I could find and told him to tell Mort Lindsey to strike up the band. It was the sweetest music I ever heard. I was so relieved. This was a big event. I had met so many wonderful Canadians and had helped them get tickets to Judy's heavily sold-out concert. It had become a personal thing for me, and I just couldn't imagine myself disappointing all the fans because Judy was pulling one of her *schticks*, which in Yiddish means outlandish acts.

Of course, Judy was fabulous in the concert. She always did the job for me. I think that when Judy stepped out on a stage, she was transformed. She had been born to perform and thrill people with her ability to communicate with them heart-to-heart through her music. She had an indescribable magic as a performer. The Judy Garland concerts were all winners and I recouped some of our losses and much of my self-esteem.

Chapter 8: **TONY BENNETT**

I WAS VERY TIRED. I HAD BEEN GOING NON-STOP for almost three years. I had been busy with one promotion after the other. Some were winners, and some had been losers. The winners could never seem to make up for the losers, and accumulating any kind of money was simply out of the question under those circumstances. I was sure that Abe would choose to go forward, but I had grown weary.

Stan Scotland was an agent friend of mine who worked for the General Artists Corporation. GAC, as it was known, was one of the premier talent agencies in the world and had on its roster a who's who of show business performers. When I was promoting the rock and roll shows at the Paramount and elsewhere, I would often buy acts from GAC.

One day, soon after I had finished with the series of Judy Garland concerts, Stan and I met.

"Sid," he said, "I heard you took a beating at Newport and in Hartford. What's next for you?"

"I also just did a series of concerts with Judy Garland that was successful, but to tell you the truth, I'm tired and I'm not sure what's next. I've been up and down with this promotion stuff, Stan, and I think I need a change."

We spent a few more minutes talking, then said our good-byes, and I thought that was the end of it. But, the next day, Stan called me.

"Sid, this is Stan. I spoke to Buddy Howe about our conversation, and he would like to see you. Could you come by the office today?"

I knew that Buddy Howe was the chairman of GAC, so I asked Stan, "What does Buddy want?"

"Well, he'd just like to kick some ideas around, and he asked me to invite you up."

"Listen, Stan, I have to take my mother to the doctor today, so I can't do it, but if you pick another day, I'd be happy to talk to Buddy."

"Sid, tomorrow is Saturday. We'll be working half the day."

"I'll be there at 10 AM."

Saturday was always my day to take my mother shopping. I helped my mother into the car and told her I was going to a meeting, but that she could sit in the car and rest. I promised to make the meeting short and be back to her as quickly as I could, and we could go shopping then. My mother was only too happy to get out of the apartment and watch the passersby on Fifth Avenue. I parked my car across from Rockefeller Center. In those days, you could still park a car on Fifth Avenue. I went up to the GAC offices.

I had known Buddy Howe casually through the years. He had been a dancer in his younger days and his wife Jean Carroll was a famous and successful comedienne. Buddy had been a great agent with a lot of heart and had worked his way up to the chairmanship of GAC. Stan took me in to see Buddy, and he got right down to business.

"Sid," he said, "Stan tells me that you're contemplating leaving promotions for a while. If that's true, we would love to have you join GAC."

I was surprised at Buddy's offer; it was a bolt out of the blue. My mind immediately went to all those advertising bills from Newport I still had to pay.

"That's interesting, Buddy. I'm flattered that you want me at GAC. What do you have in mind?"

"Well, Sid, we'd like you to head the one-night department. Rosalind Ross has been running our one night department, which books all of our rock and roll acts. But Roz just went over to William Morris, and I know she's going to try to take all our rock acts with her. It's a natural fit for you and us, Sid. You know the talent, and there's a lot of respect for you in the industry, and we have to make sure that Roz doesn't steal our acts. I'll pay you $200 a week to start and we'll naturally give you your own office and secretary."

I knew Roz Ross to be a very formidable, bright and capable agent. I knew that she would be tough competition. On reflection, however, I knew that I could compete with her and that if I took the job, I could deliver for Buddy and GAC. But I had other concerns.

"Buddy, I've just come through a very tiring and taxing time, and I don't know if I'm up to handling the responsibility of running a department just right now."

Buddy sensed my hesitancy.

"Sid, I'll tell you what. Why don't you come up on Monday and work whatever hours you want. We'll give you an office away from the rest of the staff and leave you alone. You'll get all the company memos; you'll read the trade papers; you'll slowly work your way into it. There will be no pressure, and we'll pay you as if you were working full-time. It'll be good for you and good for us."

"Buddy, your offer is very generous and your sensitivity to my feelings is really heartwarming. My friend Abe Margolies, who I think you have met, backed me at Newport and my other promotions. He really has been a great and loyal friend to me. I incurred some bills outside the budget at Newport, and I don't want to show those bills to Abe because he'll insist on paying them and he's lost enough money with me already. I want to pay those bills myself."

"Oh, come on, Sid. Abe can pay those bills easily! It's nothing for him. Why should you have the burden?"

"I know that, Buddy, but I still want to pay those bills myself."

"Okay, Sid, here's what we'll do. Prepare a list of the creditors and give it to my secretary. We'll call each creditor and tell them you're joining GAC and that we are going to deduct a certain amount from your weekly paycheck and remit the money to them. That way, you'll pay them all back. They'll go for the plan because GAC will stand behind the pledge to pay them. We'll make sure that they even send the bills here to the agency. How much do you want us to deduct, Sid?"

I felt a weight being lifted from my shoulders.

"Buddy, I want to pay them back rather quickly, so if you can deduct half my salary, that will start the ball rolling."

"Good. We'll deduct half and soon you'll get some salary increases and before you know it, those guys will be repaid and Abe won't know a thing about it."

We shook hands, and I was a new employee of GAC.

By this time, Abe Margolies had opened Les Champs, a fancy restaurant located on 39th Street between Madison and Park Avenues in New York City. Opening a restaurant for Abe seemed like a good idea on paper. After all, he knew so many people and his dedication to quality in all things was well-known. The problem was that Abe's generosity made it impossible for Les Champs to ever make a profit because Abe was forever picking up tabs. There was no way the restaurant could ever make any money.

I remember meeting one of Abe's meat suppliers. He said to me, "You know your buddy Abe? He'll never make any money at that restaurant. He insists on the absolute best that we have to offer and then charges prices that are too low! Abe insists on the best of everything. The best meat, the finest produce, home-baked goods—everything! The best at low prices and then to top it off, he picks up everybody's check."

I went to Les Champs to tell Abe that I had accepted the GAC job. As usual, his only concern was for me. "Are you sure that you want to go back to a desk job?" he asked. "You know, I'm here for you if you want to keep promoting. I think you should stay with promoting."

"Abe, I'm tired. You know how much pressure I've been under. Let me try this for a while and get my head clear, and we'll see. It'll be just for a while."

"Okay," said Abe. "As long as you're happy. If it's good for you, it's good for me. Let's eat."

On the next Monday, I reported to work at GAC. Buddy had been true to his word, and they put me in an office so far away from everybody that I thought of it as the "isolation ward." He also gave instructions to everyone to "leave Sid alone" and to let me integrate myself at my own pace.

I circulated and said hello to everyone. There were several agents who I knew there. I returned to my office to be met by the agency PR man.

"Sid," he said, "I'm here to do a press release which Buddy wants to get into *Variety* as soon as possible. With your reputation, Buddy figures we can keep Roz from raiding our roster of rock acts, but we need to get the word out immediately."

I filled in the blanks for him and he wrote the press release. A week later, there was an article in *Variety* and some of the other trade papers. The word was out that Sid Bernstein, who had produced shows at the Paramount, the Palace, the Apollo, the Newport Jazz Festival, and the recent highly successful Judy Garland tour, had joined GAC as head of the one-night department. For the time being, the rock acts took a wait-and-see attitude and Buddy Howe's strategy had worked. No act left GAC. It was damage control at its best.

I worked my way in slowly. Working from the "isolation ward," I read the memos, sat in on meetings that I was invited to and began the all-important task of meeting the artists that were on GAC's roster. At that time, GAC had Patti Page, Dion & the Belmonts, Brenda Lee, Bobby Darin and Tony Bennett, to name just a few. Everyone left me alone, but Buddy Howe was a frequent visitor to the "isolation ward," stopping in to inquire about how I was getting along and asking if I needed anything. That man really had a lot of heart.

A few weeks after getting to GAC, I decided at the end of a workday to catch the Second Avenue bus down to Auster's Egg Cream Stand in lower Manhattan. Egg creams, a drink made with chocolate syrup on the bottom of a glass, topped with an equal amount of milk, then topped with approximately three times the amount of seltzer and mixed together, had become another one of my food and drink passions. I would think nothing of getting in my car very late at night and driving all the way from the Bronx to Auster's for an egg cream.

As I was walking east from GAC to catch the bus to Auster's, I heard a voice call my name. "Hey, Sid! Sid Bernstein!"

I looked around and there was this young comedian who had recently been signed by GAC. He was standing in front of the Living Room, which was a popular nightspot on the East Side.

"I'm so glad you're coming, Sid!" he said. "No one from GAC has been here to see me perform yet, and I've been here three days already! It's so good of you to come!"

I recognized him as one of the acts that I had been introduced to during my first few weeks at the agency. Recovering very quickly, I asked, "When are you going on?"

"The first show is in 45 minutes, but we can go to my dressing room and talk until the show starts, if you'd like."

I decided to put my egg cream on hold.

We went to his dressing room and he lamented the fact that no one from GAC had been there to see his new act, which he said was "very different." He was very bright and engaging and the time passed quickly. Before show time, he took me out and gave me a choice of seats. I opted to sit at the bar instead of at a table.

The performance was great; he had everyone wrapped around his finger after the first five minutes. I was glad that I had stumbled onto him. After his first show, we went for a walk around the block. He was pleased that I was so genuinely impressed with his act. "I wish Buddy Howe could see my act," he said. "I know that he's not the agent responsible for me, but he is the chairman of GAC, and he could be very helpful to my career."

"Don't worry, I'll tell the guys at the agency about you," I said. I agree you are different, and they should all get to see you. You have something very special to offer."

We said goodnight. He thanked me again for coming to see him, and I went to get my-egg cream fix.

The next morning, when I got to GAC, I wrote a memo in which I related my previous evening's experience. "...I must say that the guy is unbelievably clever, different, and a very charming young fellow." I concluded that "...although I had been on my way to get an egg-cream fix, I had the good fortune of having a double fix, because the guy had me and everyone else in the audience howling. I think everyone at GAC should make every effort to see this incredibly gifted young comic, George Carlin."

The following week, the phone rang in my office.

"Hi, Sid. This is Tony Bennett. How are you?"

Right, I thought. One of these jokester agents here at GAC is putting me on because they know that Tony Bennett is my absolutely favorite singer of all time.

"Who is this?" I asked in an annoyed tone of voice.

"It's Tony Bennett, Sid," said the voice.

Something about the voice this time tipped me that this was indeed Tony Bennett.

"Wow," I thought, "Tony Bennett!"

"Sorry," I said apologetically. "For a minute there I thought someone was putting me on. How can I help you?"

"Sid, I read that article about you joining GAC in *Variety* and I thought it would be a good idea for us to talk in person."

"Sure," I responded. "When would you like to come up?"

"You know, I'd rather not come to the office. Why don't we meet at Schrafft's for lunch?"

"Fine. How about tomorrow?"

"That's great. I'll meet you at Schrafft's tomorrow, at one," he said.

The next day at 1 p.m., right on the dot, we met at Schrafft's restaurant, which was next door to GAC.

The waitresses and patrons were all excited to see Tony Bennett and most recognized him from his frequent TV appearances.

"Sid," he began, "As I mentioned on the phone, I read the article about you in *Variety*. I think you're going to be a great asset for GAC. Your background as a promoter with acts in the music business is quite extensive and impressive. You've worked with a lot of stars. You know, the guys up there at GAC all take me for granted, and I'm thinking of leaving the agency."

"Why?" I asked him.

"Well, I haven't had a hit record for a couple of years, and I haven't done *The Ed Sullivan Show* in who knows how long. Maybe they think I'm finished. Mainly, they give me saloons to work in. Take the Copa, for instance (referring to the world-famous Copacabana), two shows a night, seven days a week. We know they have great Chinese food, but you would think that if they have a headliner performing on stage, they would stop the food service. Instead all you can hear when I'm up there are dishes and silverware clanging and dropping to the floor! It's terrible!"

I could see that Tony was really wound-up now.

"I don't have a manager at the moment, and I don't really feel like I have an agency either," he continued. "And after reading about you and what you've done, I wanted to talk to you and see if you have some thoughts about me and GAC."

To me, the Tony Bennett sitting at that table that day at Schrafft's was a sad and dejected man. I really felt bad for him. I didn't know how to respond.

We had been in the restaurant for a while so I said, "You know, Tony. I have to get back upstairs. Let me give our conversation some thought."

"Okay, I'm meeting my conductor Ralph Sharon at Columbia. We're working on some new material. Would you like to walk down there with me? It'll only take a few minutes."

"Sure," I said, "I'll walk you down."

We took the short, leisurely walk. When we got to Columbia, Tony introduced me to Ralph Sharon, who was a very fine, dignified British gentleman. I looked at my watch and said apologetically, "I have to get back to my office, Tony."

"Shall we talk later?" he asked.

I realized that he was reaching out to me and I quickly responded, "Sure, if that's what you'd like. How late are you rehearsing?"

"Oh, I don't know. Five thirty or six...around that time. How late do you work?" he asked me.

"Six o'clock. Where do you want to meet?"

"I'll come up to the office at six, if that's okay with you."

"Sure, that'll be just fine. I'll see you at six."

As I walked back to the office I was troubled. Tony Bennett was a great artist. He was a man of civility, which I had witnessed at lunch. He had a feel for people and treated everyone in a friendly and respectful way. He had given so much of himself to others and brought such enjoyment to countless numbers of people. He was my favorite singer and I wanted very much to help him.

My wheels were spinning and I felt challenged. As soon as I got to the office, I placed a call to Felix Gerstman, who along with Sol Hurok, were the most prominent promoters of shows at Carnegie Hall. Felix Gerstman was the dean of pop attractions at Carnegie. I had met him, and I admired what he was doing in bringing great acts to Carnegie Hall.

"Mr. Gerstman, how are you? This is Sidney Bernstein," I said.

"How may I help you, Mr. Bernstein?"

"Well, Mr. Gerstman, I have a client here at GAC that I think would do a magnificent job at Carnegie Hall. He's worked the Copacabana and been on television and has had hit records, but, as yet, no one has engaged him to do a concert. I have a feeling that, in concert, he would be sensational. I would love to see you be the first one to promote Tony Bennett in a concert."

"Sidney," he said, "let me think about it, and why don't you call me back in a few hours?"

At four o'clock, I called Felix Gerstman back.

"Sidney, I've done some checking and I have to report to you that it is my belief that Tony Bennett will not sell out Carnegie Hall. I appreciate your enthusiasm, but I will not make money with Tony Bennett. He has not had a hit record in a while, and he will not sell out. I'm sorry to disappoint you."

"Thank you for your time, Mr. Gerstman." I hung up, disappointed.

Felix Gertsman was a pro and a gentleman. He had done his homework, and my respect for him remained undiminished even though he had turned me down.

Next, I called Bill Grummond, who was a promoter who in the past years had produced shows at the Forest Hills Tennis Stadium in Queens, New York.

"Bill, this is Sid Bernstein."

"Hi, Sid. How ya' doin'?"

"Bill, I don't know if you're aware of it, but I've recently joined GAC."

"No, I wasn't aware of it. How's it goin'?"

"Fine, Bill. It's very interesting."

"What's up?" he asked.

"Well, you know we have Tony Bennett here at GAC as a client, and I'd like to talk to you about booking him into the stadium. He's never done a concert before, and I have a feeling that he would do very well for you."

"Wait a minute, Sid. You do realize that we have a 14,000 seating capacity? Tony hasn't had a hit in a while, and I don't think he can fill the place."

"I know how big the stadium is, Bill, but he has a following and there are legions of his fans who can't afford to go to the Copa, who are dying to see him perform live."

"I don't think so, but let me think about it. I'll get back to you."

When I hung up with Bill Grummond, I knew that he would not call me back and that he had no interest in promoting Tony Bennett at the Forest Hills Tennis Stadium.

It was now about six o'clock. I waited for about 10 minutes and told myself that Tony was not going to show up. Probably tied up at the rehearsal, I thought. As I reached for my jacket, in strolled Tony Bennett.

"Sorry I'm late. We went a little over at the rehearsal. I'm not keeping you, am I?"

I liked his gentility. I had seen at lunch how he treated the waitresses and handled the fans who came over for his autograph. He is a considerate man.

"No, you're not keeping me."

"Well, Sid, did you think about our conversation?"

"Yes, I did. I've thought about it a lot."

"Tony," I launched into it. "You know, I recently came off a tour with Judy Garland. We did about a dozen concerts that were all sold out except one, and all to great critical acclaim. I'd like to see you do a concert at Carnegie Hall. Judy Garland did her comeback concert there, and it was unbelievable. She had Mort Lindsey conducting and her five key musicians and a large orchestra, and it was just terrific. It also reignited her career! You know that GAC and I as agents are not permitted to act as promoters. I'd love to promote you in concert and that's really my background, but industry rules forbid me from doing that. I've thought this out carefully, and if you rented out the hall, placed the ads, printed the posters and flyers and hired the musicians, I think you could sell out Carnegie Hall. Tony, I am trying to persuade and press you to do this because I believe that it truly can work for you, and it won't cost you any money."

"What?" he asked, with a look of disbelief on his face. "It won't cost me any money? How is that possible, Sid?"

"I have a line of credit at the advertising agency and the printer."

I was, of course, referring to the Newport debts that I was paying off with the help of my salary at GAC.

I continued, "The only money you're going to have to put up is a deposit for Carnegie Hall, and that's $500. The musicians can be paid after the concert and Ralph Sharon, your conductor, is already on your payroll. What I'd like to see are big posters that say 'Tony at Carnegie Hall,' the date and the price. But in really large letters, just 'Tony at Carnegie Hall'."

"Oh, I like that. I really like that," he said. And I knew then that I had him.

"That's all you need. Just $500 and everything else will be taken care of. I'll do all the pre-concert work."

"You think I'll do good?"

"Believe me, you'll do good," I said. "We'll do a job in this town that hasn't been done in a long time. We'll print 1,000 posters and put them up all over New York City."

He was really into it now. "Wait a minute, Sid. I have an artist's caricature of myself. I'd love to see the caricature on the poster instead of a picture."

"Yeah, Tony! Great idea!"

"When do you think we should do it?"

"I called Carnegie Hall before you got here, and June 2 is available," I said. I neglected to tell him that earlier in the day, both Gerstman and Grummond had passed on the opportunity to present him in concert.

"Sid," he said. "I know that I only have to put up $500 to start with, but we both know that if we don't sell any tickets, I'm going to have to pay all the bills, so what are we really talking about?"

"We both know that there is no way that you're not going to sell tickets, but the worst-case scenario is that you would lose $10,000, give or take a few bucks."

We continued talking, getting excited at the idea of actually putting on a show at Carnegie Hall.

"Sid, you think the show should be just me for the entire evening?"

"Yes, just you," I said. "You'll do a short first half, then we'll have an intermission. The audience will have a chance to get some refreshments and socialize, which is always a big thing at Carnegie, and after the intermission, you'll go on for as long as you like, until 11 o' clock. But, remember, Tony, we can't go past eleven, because then the overtime costs for the house, the ushers and the rest of the staff gets to be very expensive."

"Could we use a comic?"

"Not a bad idea," I responded. "Who did you have in mind?"

"Well, if we use a comic, I'd love to get Henny Youngman," he said. "That guy really breaks me up!"

"I know Henny, and he's a funny guy. I'll call him and see if he's available."

I felt great. Tony was upbeat now when a few short hours ago he had been dejected. I was going to present the great Tony Bennett, my favorite singer at Carnegie Hall. I knew that my name couldn't be on the posters and handbills, and GAC would have to maintain some semblance of distance from the event, but I didn't care. I was doing all of this for Tony Bennett. We said good night, and I went home with my head bursting with plans for the concert.

The next morning, I got to work early and went directly to see Buddy Howe. I told him about the meeting I had had the day before with Tony and that Tony's continuing relationship with GAC was in jeopardy because of the lukewarm treatment he felt that he was getting from the agency. I also told him about the plan I had worked out for Carnegie Hall.

"Sid," Buddy said, "I appreciate your taking the initiative on this, but do you really think that Tony can fill Carnegie Hall?"

"Absolutely, Buddy, I plan to work on it after-hours, weekends and whenever I have a free moment. I promise that it won't interfere with my duties here. I want this to succeed."

"Okay, don't even tell the other guys here what you're doing."

I knew from this request that Buddy Howe was concerned about the industry rules prohibiting agents and agencies from being promoters.

"Who's going to present the concert?" Buddy asked.

"Tony. Tony is going to present himself."

"That's good. That's good. And you're sure he'll be all right? I don't want him to come up here and give us aggravation when something doesn't go right. He'll be coming up here asking me, 'What did Sid get me into?'"

"Rest assured, Buddy. Everything will work out fine."

Generally, I'm not this cocky, but I had a gut feeling about Tony's appearing at Carnegie Hall. I called Tony. "Everything is set. I reserved Carnegie Hall and Henny is available to do the date. I think that you should ask Henny to do just 20 minutes. He'll warm up the audience and then you'll do your show. All I need from you now is a check for $500."

"Fine, Sid," he said. "I'll be rehearsing with Ralph again tomorrow at Columbia, so we can have lunch and I'll give you the check or, if you like, you can come over there and get it."

"Let's skip lunch. I'll just come to the rehearsal to pick up the check."

The next day, as planned, I picked up the check. When Tony excused himself for a moment, I told Ralph Sharon, who was rehearsing with Tony, how excited I was about the concert at Carnegie Hall. Ralph confided to me that Tony was excited but also a little nervous about it.

"It's gonna be good," I said to Ralph.

I returned to my office and called Julius Bloom, the head of Carnegie Hall at that time. I explained that I had the $500 deposit and asked him if he wanted me to messenger it over or bring it myself the next day.

"Tomorrow will be fine. I'm looking forward to meeting you," he said.

I called Phil Scheff, the head of my ad agency, and we devised a schedule of ads for the concert. I called Bob Maltz to alert him that we were going to do an extensive poster campaign and asked him to set aside the time necessary to hang the posters. I went to the printer with Tony's caricature in hand, laid out the copy and contracted for the posters. I called Columbia Records and spoke to Bill Gallagher, president of the label. I explained to Bill about the concert and he committed Columbia Records to purchasing 12 tickets to the concert for members of the press. Imagine, only 12 tickets for an artist who had made tons of money for Columbia.

Bill was less than enthusiastic and he said to me, "Sid, can you please get Tony Bennett off my back! He's constantly coming up here urging us to do a better job with his records."

I really didn't appreciate Bill's comment. I respected Tony for his work ethic and his doggedness. He had explained to me how hard and long and diligently he had worked on his current record release, *I Left My Heart in San Francisco*, and how disappointed he was with the results and how unhappy he was with the label's commitment to the record. I knew that Tony was a pro and that his frequent visits to the record company was nothing more than his attempt to invigorate Columbia Records on behalf of *I Left*

My Heart in San Francisco. I felt that, if nothing else, the concert was going to help Tony at Columbia Records.

We were ready to go, and I was as excited as I've ever been about any of my previous projects. I told Buddy Howe that everything was in place and we were just about ready to start promoting the concert.

"Sid, I told Herb Seigel, the owner of GAC, about what you're doing and he wants to talk you," said Buddy.

A little while later, Herb Siegel came back to the isolation ward. "I want you to know, Sid, I've been telling everyone around here that I don't want us to lose Tony Bennett. Do you think this will enable us to keep him?" he asked.

"It'll be no problem, Herb," I assured him.

"Thanks, Sid. I'm counting on you."

After the posters were printed, Bob Maltz began plastering New York City with them. Bob could distribute posters better than anyone else. In addition to Bob's efforts, I took several hundred posters to hang myself. Gerry would drive my convertible, and we visited every Italian neighborhood in Brooklyn, the Bronx and Long Island. Gerry would drive and keep lookout, ready to honk the horn if she spied cops. There was a law against hanging posters without a permit and we didn't have the time to wait for the city bureaucracy to issue a permit. We were like Bonnie and Clyde. I would find a wooden lamppost or another kind of facing that could take a poster, jump out of the convertible, whack in four staples and leave. Hit and run. Remember that I had lots of experience from my previous sticker campaigns.

Gerry and I did this every free minute that we had, either in the late afternoons before Gerry had to report to the theatre where she was one of the singing nuns in the long running *Sound of Music*, or on weekends.

The posters looked great; the caricature of Tony was really distinctive and the copy was sparse. Every once in a while, in the Italian neighborhoods, I would hear people exclaim after seeing the poster, 'Wow, Tony in Carnegie Hall!" He was, after all, one of their very own.

Four weeks before the concert, our first ads appeared. Since I was being very careful with the limited budget, I scheduled three small ads for that first weekend. One each on Friday in the *New York Post* and the *Daily News* and one in the Sunday Arts & Leisure section of the prestigious *New York Times*.

On the following Monday at about noon, I visited the Carnegie Hall box office to check on our progress. Nat Posnick was one of the top box office professionals in the industry and I was interested in hearing what he had to say. Also, I was anxious for any advice he might offer. When I got to the box office, I really didn't know what to expect, but I was hopeful. Mr. Posnick buzzed me into the box office and invited me to sit down.

"How are we doing on the Tony Bennett concert, Mr. Posnick?" I asked him.

"There's been no big rush yet. We have three people working these windows and I know some tickets have been sold."

We agreed that I would check with him again in a few days, but I really didn't know what to think.

Two days later, I called him. "Mr. Posnick, it's Sid Bernstein. I called to check on the concert."

"Just a minute. Let me check." He came back on the phone in a minute. "About 100 seats," Nat said to me.

"Is that good, Mr. Posnick?" I asked quite doubtfully.

"Yes, it is. You've sold 86 tickets since you were here on Monday, and that's very good. It's really good. Tell me, Sid, when are your next ads running?"

"Not this week, Mr. Posnick. I thought we'd wait a week because of how costly the ads are and run them again the week following."

"Well, that'll be fine," he said. "I think it's going to be all right. Call me again after the next ads.

After the ads ran again, I called Nat Posnick. He told me that he thought we were going to sell out. When I asked him how many seats had been sold, he told me two hundred.

"Two hundred tickets?" I said. "Nat, there are 2,830 seats in Carnegie Hall. We've sold a grand total of two hundred tickets. There are two and a half weeks to go til the concert, and you think we're going to have a sellout? How can that be?"

"Sid," he reassured me, "the sales are picking up momentum. Your next ads are scheduled for this weekend. Don't worry. It'll happen."

After the next weekend of ads, I checked again and we had sold a total of three hundred tickets. It was now two weeks before the concert.

On the next Monday when I called Nat again, he told me that the Hall had been half sold out. Nat then said quite convincingly, "Sid, it's a sellout."

"Can I tell Tony?"

"Absolutely."

I called Tony to deliver the great news. "Really, Sid?" he asked. "Sold out? Sold out!?" He couldn't believe it. We were both overjoyed.

During that last week before the concert, I visited the offices of Columbia Records. I was giving away tickets to everyone from the mailroom personnel all the way up to the president's office. If a ticket recipient was married, I gave him or her two tickets. Everyone who got the tickets was appreciative and I told Tony that I thought it was an investment that I believed would pay off.

Tony asked that I secure a rehearsal room for the Friday of the concert. Every time I went outside during those rehearsal hours, I would see people lined up at the box office trying to buy tickets to Tony Bennett's concert that evening. They were all turned away, and I could see the frustration on their faces.

That evening I arrived early for the concert, and I could see that there was a large crowd of people milling about in front of the closed doors of Carnegie Hall. Many had come to get in early, but many others came to see if they could buy tickets from scalpers. Tony's show that night was the hottest ticket in town. When the doors finally opened, there was a rush to get into the Hall. I knew that this was going to be a very special night.

Everyone in the great concert hall was excited, counting the minutes to show time: the ticket takers, the ushers, the milling audience and the musicians who were assembling. It was the kind of excitement that could only come from a sold-out concert.

I went up to see Tony in his dressing room. Henny Youngman was already there loosening Tony up with his wonderful humor. We reminded Henny that he should do only 20 or 25 minutes and he said, "No problem."

I sought out Bill Gallagher, who had again asked me to get Tony off his back when I delivered the 12 tickets that the label had bought for the press.

"How are we doing, Bill?" I asked.

Viewing the sold-out audience representing potential record sales, he gave me a big smile and a thumb's up. Everybody loves a winner!

The show began with Henny. As promised, he did 20 minutes. After Henny came off stage, we had a short intermission. The anticipation in the Hall was at a fever pitch. The people just couldn't wait. These were the diehard Tony Bennett fans.

After intermission, Henny came out to introduce Tony. Tony walked out impeccably dressed as always, with a beautifully-cut suit and a gorgeous tie. The applause was deafening. Tony was looking down at the people in the orchestra seats who began to rise as the applause picked up in volume. The crowd screamed and whistled. "Tony, Tony," they called. "Hey, Tony!" in that inimitable Italian way. I knew now that all the time Gerry and I had spent in the Italian neighborhoods had paid off.

Tony began to look up through the various levels of Carnegie Hall. They were all standing now. He began to blow kisses to the audience and to hold his head in disbelief. He was incredulous and overwhelmed. And I knew that the audience was in for the show of their lives. The fabulous welcome turned Tony on, and he gave his fans a show they would always remember. I also knew that from that moment on, Tony Bennett's career was going to take a new and exciting path.

Tony did encore after encore, and he could have remained on stage all night, but he was aware of the time and cut it off just moments before eleven o'clock. When I finally worked my way to his dressing room after the concert, family and friends surrounded Tony. It was truly a festive atmosphere. We hugged each other, and he whispered in my ear, "Thank you, Sid. Thank you, thank you." I felt a friendship that was deeply genuine and very special. Gerry and I then left Tony and his family so we could celebrate on our own. I was floating on air.

When I got to work on Monday morning, I was greeted like a conquering hero. Tony Bennett had sold out Carnegie Hall and the reviews of his concert were unanimously glowing; GAC had secured one of their biggest and most important artists. Buddy Howe came to the isolation ward to congratulate me; he gave me a raise in pay and suggested that I move from the "ward" to an office more in the mainstream of the company.

In the late morning, Tony called me.

"Sid, I called to thank you again. I really don't know what to say. I haven't talked to him in more than two years, but Ed Sullivan called me and he wants me on his show! Can you believe that? Sid, I don't know how to thank you, and I don't know what to say!"

"Sure, I believe it! Why not? You're great and Sullivan read the reviews! Good for you, Tony!"

"Sid, I'd like you to come up to the house in Englewood Cliffs on Sunday for brunch. Can you make it?"

"That's nice. I'd love to come, but I usually reserve the weekends for my folks."

"No problem, bring your folks with you."

On Sunday, I loaded my folks into the car, and we took the short ride from the Bronx over the George Washington Bridge to Tony Bennett's house in Englewood Cliffs, New Jersey. We spent about an hour meeting his wife Sandy and his two boys, Danny and Dagal, just chatting and reliving the concert. My mother, who was a Tony Bennett fan, having seen him on TV, was sitting next to Tony. She leaned over and gently took hold of his Adam's apple and said to him in her Yiddish accent, "Tony, you know vy you sing so gut? Because you have such a beautiful *gurgal*!"

"What's a *gurgal*?" he asked.

"An Adam's apple," I replied, as we all roared with laughter.

The Monday following Tony's triumph at Carnegie Hall, Columbia Records executives met and decided that Tony Bennett's record *I Left My Heart in San Francisco* was to become what in the record business was called a "push" record. Everyone up and down the line was instructed that *I Left My Heart in San Francisco* was to be worked, worked, and then worked some more. With all the extra effort, *I Left My Heart in San Francisco* speedily made it up the charts. It has become a standard and Tony Bennett's signature song. Those 300 tickets that we gave away at Columbia Records paid off a million times over.

One day during the following work week, I got a call from the head talent booker at the famous Red Rock Amphitheater located outside of Denver, Colorado.

"Mr. Bernstein," she said. "I've been directed to speak to you about booking Tony Bennett for Red Rock. Can you please tell me what you get for him in concert?"

"Ten thousand dollars," I answered. I just picked that amount because it felt right to me.

"That's fine. Would he be available for any of the following dates?" She proceeded to list them for me.

I checked the date book we kept on all of our artists and told her which dates Tony would available. She picked a date, and the deal was done. I immediately called Buddy Howe and related to him the phone conversation with Red Rock.

"Wow!" he said. "Ten thousand dollars? That's fabulous, Sid! Have you told Tony yet?"

"Not yet, Buddy, but I will after I hang up with you."

"Good, Sid. And by the way, I'm sending a memo to all the GAC offices around the world that if anyone wants to book Tony Bennett in the future, the price from now on is $10,000 per performance, and they have to clear it with you first."

In one fell swoop, I had gotten Tony out of the seven day/two shows a night/$5,000 per week salary to $10,000 for one night's work. I had also gotten him out of the 400- and 500-seat "saloons" and into concert halls with thousands of seats, filled with fans hanging onto his every note. I called Tony and he was ecstatic. No more clattering dishes. No more unruly, drunken dinner patrons who were getting a show with their supper. No more necessity for two shows a night and no more working seven days a week. Tony had arrived! He couldn't have been more thankful, and I couldn't have been happier for him.

A few weeks later, Tony came up to the office and stopped in to see me. We chatted for a while, and then he said, "Hey, Sid, I'd like you to give some thought to coming on the road and working with me. I'll pay you more than what you're getting here. Give it some thought."

I promised him that I would think the offer over. He was starting to make really big money. He was my favorite singer and if I took the job, I could hear him sing every time he worked. Tony's offer was most tempting.

The following day, I called Tony and explained how much I would have liked to accept his proposal, but I had to stay near my folks and help them out. I proceeded to assure him that I would continue to do all things necessary at the office as far as he was concerned, but I couldn't leave New York City. Tony accepted what I said with complete graciousness.

Years later, after I was no longer his agent, Tony was booked into the prestigious Empire Room at the Waldorf-Astoria. Lena Horne, Victor Borge, Maurice Chevalier and other international superstars appeared at the Empire Room. Tony invited Gerry and me to come as his guests. The room was packed. Dinner was served and then it was time for the show. Times had sure changed for Tony. Before he came on stage, all dishes, flatware and glasses were removed from the tables. Even the waiters and busboys moved to the back of the room so that there would be no distractions during his performance. Tony was magical as usual. In the middle of his performance, he made the following statement:

"Ladies and gentlemen. I want to talk about a gentleman sitting in the audience here with his wife. I want to tell you that this gentleman has been such a dear friend and I respect him so much. I'm so glad that he's here in the room, and I want to acknowledge him and thank him again for the wonderful friend he's been to me."

I thought that he was talking about a songwriter who had written a hit song for him and who might be in the audience. Tony often did this while performing. I looked around to see who he was acknowledging.

"Sid, he's talking about you," Gerry whispered.

"You're kidding!"

"Sid, could you please step up here?" he said. "Ladies and gentlemen, my friend, Sid Bernstein."

I was too overcome to say anything so I just stepped up on stage, shook his hand, and thanked him.

Buddy Howe and Herb Siegel were so pleased that I had "saved" Tony Bennett for GAC that when I told them I wanted to do the same kind of promotion with two other GAC artists, they said, "Go right ahead."

Nina Simone was an up-and-coming and extremely gifted but temperamental artist. She had issues with some of the agents at GAC, but I liked her, and we got along well. I thought that she should "graduate" from performing in clubs to doing concerts. I persuaded her record label to present her at Carnegie Hall. Nina played to a good-sized audience and did a great job. The net result was that GAC was able to raise her per-engagement price, which pleased Buddy Howe no end.

Jerry Vale was an Italian singer with a beautiful voice who had some recording success and was a big draw on the nightclub circuit. He had a wonderful mane of graying hair, was attractive and very likeable. Playing Carnegie Hall was a dream come true for him. I used the "Tony strategy" of postering the Italian neighborhoods. It worked like a charm, and Jerry's concert sold out. Because of Jerry's success at Carnegie, GAC could command more money for Jerry Vale. Jerry presented himself at Carnegie, so we had no problem with the agent/promoter rules.

My bosses at GAC loved my concert strategy. I enjoyed working on these concerts because it kept me in promotions even though my name was not directly associated with the productions. The concerts kept the fire in my belly alive and made the day-to-day "agenting" at GAC less onerous.

Chapter 9: **MARRIED…FINALLY**

ONE OF THE THINGS I DID ENJOY ABOUT BEING AN AGENT was accompanying my clients on occasional short trips—it was exciting to travel and discover new restaurants and local delicacies. A memorable adventure was when I went with Billy Fields to Europe to try and promote a record he had out on the MGM label. The last stop on the seven-city tour was Paris. We arrived in Paris on a Friday, took care of our business on Saturday and were prepared to take an early morning flight home on Sunday.

I decided that I wanted to bring my family éclairs from Le Coqelin, a famous pastry shop on the Rue Passy. Early on Sunday morning, Billy and I took our suitcases, got in a cab and went to Le Coqelin. The cab arrived and the doors to the pastry shop were shuttered. The sign said Ferme [Closed] and the window shade was down.

"OK, Sid. It's closed," Billy said. "Let's go to the airport, so we don't miss our flight."

"Wait a minute. I'm sure there must be someone here; they're probably in the back, baking. Let me knock on the door; someone's got to be here."

I proceeded to knock on the door for several minutes and got no answer. The streets were deserted and there was no one to ask about when the shop was scheduled to open its doors. I continued rapping on the front door.

By now, Billy was getting pretty agitated. He kept looking at his watch.

"Sid, we're going to miss our flight. Let's go already," he pleaded.

"I'm not leaving until I get some éclairs."

Billy just sighed and probably thought, That's crazy, Sid.

After about 15 minutes of knocking on the door and peering in the window, looking for anyone who could help me, someone lifted the shade and opened the door.

In French, I explained to the annoyed proprietor that I was on my way to the airport, but I wanted to purchase some éclairs to take home to my family in the States. By the expression on the man's face, I could see Billy now had an ally and that they both thought I was nuts.

The man quickly boxed up some éclairs. Billy and I made a mad dash to the airport.

We missed our plane, but I got my éclairs. Of course, Billy and I ate most of them waiting for the next flight to New York, which was not for several hours. I really wanted to go back and get more éclairs, but I was afraid that Billy would kill me!

Gerry and I had been dating now for almost four years. She had been through my roller coaster career as a promoter, and I had watched her blossom into a beautiful young woman with a promising career on Broadway.

We frequented the best restaurants, went to shows and movies and enjoyed each other's company immensely.

One of the things we did not do was introduce each other to our parents. I was sure that my Jewish parents would be less than overjoyed to see us together. And Gerry felt that her parents, particularly her career Army father, did not have much use for Jews.

One night, we were sitting in my car in front of Gerry's apartment building on upper Broadway in New York, having a pretty serious conversation, when Gerry said, "Sid, let's get married."

After recovering from the shock, I said, "Gerry, do you know how old I am? I'm 41 years old, and you're 22. I'm really much too old for you."

Gerry started to cry; she wasn't upset at our age difference but the fact that I had an objection to marriage.

"I don't care," she said. "What does it matter?"

"Gerry, we're of different faiths and you know your parents will be livid. My parents are from the old country, with the old beliefs and traditions. Forget the age difference for a minute, we have other obstacles to overcome. Think about it, Gerry. We have a lot of problems."

"I don't care!" she said again.

"You know what, Gerry, let's think about this. It's late. I'll take you upstairs and then I'll go home and we'll talk about it tomorrow."

On the drive home and for the rest of the night, I pondered this dilemma, weighing all the pros and cons and trying to figure out what to do. I concluded that it was unfair of me to waste any more of Gerry's time, but that I just could not spring my marriage to a non-Jewish girl on my parents. I also thought about the wrath of Gerry's parents, and by no means did I want to face their abuse.

The next day, I took Gerry to the Brasserie, our favorite after-theatre hangout. I told her that I just did not know what to do. I loved her and cared about her, but I just could not marry her now. She started to cry, and I started to cry, and the waitresses and the manager who knew us well came over to inquire if everything was all right. Even after talking some more, we had no resolution to our problem.

The next day, Gerry called me at GAC.

"Sid, I don't want to give you any more pressure. I know you're concerned about your mother. Let's just be good friends."

"Gerry, we're more than good friends."

"Well, then let's just be whatever we are, Sid. But, we'll leave the subject of marriage alone."

"Okay," I said, somewhat relieved.

"Sid, Sunday is supposed to be a beautiful day. Let's spend the day in the park."

"That's a nice idea, but I promised my folks I'd take them up to Manero's." Manero's was a terrific restaurant in Greenwich, Connecticut that I liked. After thinking for a minute, I said, "Maybe the four of us should go together."

"Are you sure you want to do that, Sid?"

"I'm sure, Gerry. I'll just tell them I'm bringing along a good friend."

"Okay, if you think it won't be a problem."

On the fateful day, I picked Gerry up at her apartment in Manhattan. We proceeded to get my folks in the Bronx and then all drove to Manero's in Connecticut.

Manero's is a nice suburban restaurant with fabulous food. We had a lovely dinner, but it was very subdued. No one spoke much; it was uncommonly quiet. Gerry tried hard, but my folks knew from the way Gerry and I looked at and talked to each other that this beautiful young woman was not just Simcha's good friend. They knew that there was serious business going on here.

After dinner, I dropped my folks off and took Gerry home. It was quite late when I returned home to the Bronx. The lights were still on and my parents were not asleep, which at this late hour was uncharacteristic of them.

"Simcha," my mother said, "*zeyer a shaine maidel*. Sid, a very beautiful girl. *Sie is frum California*? She is from California?"

"*Ya frum California*," I answered.

"An actress?" she continued.

"*Nicht an actress, a zinger*. Not an actress, a singer," I said.

"*Sie zingt zeyer shain?* She sings beautifully?"

"Yeah, she sings very beautifully," I said.

"*Bist far leibt in ir?* You're in love with her," my mother continued with her interrogation.

"*Ich glach ir asach*. I like her a lot. *Zie is zeyer a fina maidel, uber zeyer ying*. She is a very fine girl, but very young," I told them. "*Erger sig nicht. Es is nicht zeyer serious*. Don't worry too much. It's not very serious."

I really chickened out. I just didn't want to face the music. A music guy who didn't want to face the music.

My parents went to sleep, and I felt that I had weathered the initial storm. I went to Abe for some advice.

"You're nuts," he told me. "This is a beautiful, charming girl and you've been wasting her time for four years. Where are you going to find another girl like this? You're crazy and you're going to lose this girl. You want to have a family. You're always talking about having children. How long are you going to wait?"

I didn't have an answer.

Then Abe said, "Maybe you don't want her. You're coming up with all these excuses: your age, your parents, her parents, the religion—who knows what else? Maybe you don't want to marry her!" Abe was very upset with me.

Abe wasn't the only one who was upset. All of my friends advised me to stop procrastinating and "do the right thing and marry Gerry before you lose her!"

Now that the subject of marriage had been brought up, it began to crop up in every conversation that Gerry and I would have. I would try to shun it, but the subject of marriage would always rear its insistent head.

One day Gerry told me that she was going on vacation to California. She asked me if I would like to come to meet her grandparents. Not her parents, mind you, but her grandparents whom she adored and who, when I finally met them some years later, turned out to be just the nicest people. I declined because I knew if I went to California with her, I would have had to meet her parents as well, and I was not ready for that. I declined the invitation to California and Gerry opted to stay in New York.

"We'll spend more time together," she said.

During her vacation, she came to the office more often and got to know my business associates, and we had a nice time. But behind this curtain of seeming tranquility and acceptance, the tension was building.

A few weeks later, out of the blue, Gerry said to me, "Look, Sid, I have another vacation coming up and if we're not going to get married, I'm going to go home, and I'm not coming back. I'm going to stay in California. I don't want to come back to New York."

It was an ultimatum. I knew that Gerry meant every word that she said.

"Gerry, are you just going to walk away from *The Sound of Music* and your career, just like that?"

"Yes, I don't really want to come back."

I let her go. I can't really say why. I didn't fight it and I didn't protest. I just let her go. Maybe I thought she was bluffing, and she would never walk away from a career that she had built so painstakingly. I really don't know what I thought, but I just let her go.

What I do know is how miserable I was during that first week that Gerry was gone. Perhaps depressed would be a better way to describe it. I didn't want to write her because I knew that if her parents saw the letter from Sid Bernstein, they would probably make some nasty remark about my Jewishness. I also didn't want to phone, because they would know from my name unquestionably that she was involved with a Jewish guy. It definitely was a major issue for them, particularly for her father.

Finally, after a week, I couldn't take the pressure and the depression anymore. I was in love with Gerry, and I didn't care who picked up the phone or what they thought about my being Jewish. I placed the phone call and her sister picked up the phone.

"Hi, Kathleen, this is Sid Bernstein. Is Geraldine at home? I'd like to say hello."

"Yes, Sid. She's at home," she answered very pleasantly. "Hold on."

Gerry came to the phone. "How are you, Sid?" she inquired.

"I'm miserable, Gerry."

"So am I."

"Are you going to come back, Gerry?"

"Do you want me to come back, Sid?"

"Yes, Gerry. Yes, I want you to come back. I miss you."

"I miss you, too. I'll be home."

"When, Gerry? When will you come back?"

"Well, I have to come back to start in the show again next week."

Obviously, she hadn't given the show notice that she was leaving.

"What flight are you coming back on? I want to pick you up."

She gave me the flight number and I told her I would be there. I met Gerry's plane when it arrived from California. She was very tired from the trip so we didn't talk much on the drive home. I didn't bring up the subject of marriage and neither did she. But I was glad she was back.

During the next few weeks, Gerry went back into *The Sound of Music*. We saw each other often and we talked about our marriage plans.

Gerry was very sensitive to the fact that my parents were elderly and that my mother was in need of almost constant care. She suggested that we find a two-family house where my parents could live on the ground floor so my mother could get in and out relatively easily, and we would live on the floor above. I appreciated her sensitivity.

My father had given up the tailor shop on East Tremont Avenue in the Bronx. We tried to sell it but when no buyer emerged, he just closed it up. Pop was too active to retire completely, so he took a job at the Sutton Cleaners and Tailoring Shop located on First Avenue between 58th and 59th Streets in Manhattan. My father would take the subway down to the shop three days a week. He didn't need the money; he just did it to keep busy. Sutton Cleaners was a short walk from GAC and I could surprise Pop with visits to take him to lunch.

On Monday, April 15, 1963, I had made a lunch date with Pop. I remember looking at my watch, thinking that I had to get ready to leave GAC for lunch, when the phone rang. It was someone from Sutton Cleaners.

"Sid, your dad had a heart attack in the shop, and they've rushed him to New York Hospital."

I was on the run and out the door immediately. I caught a cab and shouted at the driver to step on it. Fortunately, the hospital was not far way from GAC and I got there quickly. At the inquiry desk I was instructed to go immediately to the emergency room. A doctor met me there and told me, "Your father has had a severe heart attack, and we are trying to save his life. He is conscious and you may see him for a brief moment."

When I got into the room, I saw my father surrounded by a team of doctors. He looked ashen. I held his hand and kissed him several times and said, "Pop, you'll be fine. You'll be okay. I'll be right next door."

The doctors asked me to leave the room. About a half-hour later, with Gerry and Abe by my side, one of the doctors came out.

"Mr. Bernstein, I am sorry to tell you that we couldn't save your father. We tried everything, but the heart attack was just too severe. I'm sorry."

Thank God that Gerry and Abe were with me because I was in shock and a basket case. One minute my father was a reasonably healthy and functioning human being, and the next minute he was gone. Gerry and Abe drove me home, and Gerry stayed with me. My mother had been spending most of her time in bed, going through still another rough health crisis. I dreaded having to tell my mother. Later on, Gerry had to leave to make her show, and I went in to see my mother. I told my mother that Papa had a heart attack and that we would not be seeing him that night.

"When will we see him?" she asked.

"Not tonight, or tomorrow or again, Mama. He's gone!" I sobbed.

She began to sob uncontrollably and we both cried until we couldn't cry anymore. I spent the night keeping an eye on her, and no one slept much in our home that night.

We had the funeral the next day, as is the Jewish custom, and my dad was buried in the Elmont, New York, cemetery. It all went by in a blur. My mother and I sat shiva, which is the Jewish mourning period, and were visited by family and friends. Immediately after the shiva period ended, I arranged for my mother to have full-time help and companionship. A very nice lady came to take care of her. I felt that she would give my mother the care she needed, and I returned to work at GAC.

One of the great and beautiful lights in my life had gone out.

I was basically useless when I returned to my job those first weeks after my father died. I just went through the motions and moped around. Everyone at GAC understood and, once again, the policy was "leave Sid alone." As soon as work was over for the day, I would rush home to be with my mother. After she went to bed, I would hurry back down to the city to be at the Lunt-Fontanne Theatre around eleven o'clock when Gerry finished working in *The Sound of Music*. My life was harried and hectic.

On July 16, 1963, two months after my father died, Gerry and I eloped. We drove to Cape Cod and checked into the Moor's Motel in Provincetown. The Moors was on the tip of Cape Cod, a venerable hotel with a terrific Portuguese restaurant that served the best meatballs.

The next morning, Gerry and I went looking for a justice of the peace who would marry us, but we just couldn't find one. So we took the next ferry to Nantucket. When we got there, we inquired about a justice of the peace and were referred to a man named Coffin who came from an old New England family. The justice married us, with his secretary serving as the other witness. Sid, the confirmed bachelor, had finally run out of excuses and was now a married man. We then took the ferry back to Provincetown.

Gerry and I had a lovely honeymoon week on Cape Cod.

For a wedding gift, my old buddy Walter Hyman loaned us his beautiful apartment on Fifth Avenue for six weeks. He was off on vacation in Cannes, France, with his family. The apartment was quite large and had a wrap-around terrace with a great view of Central Park and the New York skyline. We took my mother with us to Walter's apartment, and she enjoyed sitting on the terrace and looking out at the park in the daytime and the lights of New York City at night. The fact that Gerry wasn't Jewish never came up with my mother. I guess she was so wrapped up in her infirmities that she just ignored any feelings that she may have had about it.

Gerry and I found an apartment on West 12th Street, so by the time Walter came home from Cannes six weeks later, we were ensconced on West 12th Street and Mom was back home in the Bronx. I went back to work at GAC. Gerry got pregnant. Her show business career was over, and mine was about to go for the ride of the century.

BOOK THREE

THE TOP OF THE MOUNTAIN
1963-1974

The first time I spoke to Brian Epstein on the phone I was immediately struck by his most dignified tone and manner. I remember that my tongue actually stuck to the roof of my mouth. I froze. Somehow, I knew that this was the most important phone call of my professional life. I was literally tongue-tied"

– Sid Bernstein, on his legendary call that brought the Beatles to America, from Not Just The Beatles

Your First FREE Phone Call with Net2Phone Direct® might also be the most important phone call of your life...

Get up to 20 Minutes of FREE Phone Calls

with the 3.9¢ Net2Phone Calling Card!

Detach your complimentary calling card now!

Use your FREE minutes & then easily recharge your card by calling

1-888-429-7599

net2phone℠
RECHARGEABLE CALLING CARD

UP TO 20 MIN FREE

START MAKING FREE CALLS TODAY!

net2phone℠

Your complimentary 20-minute 3.9¢ Net2Phone Direct Prepaid Calling Card is ready to use...

Just refer to the preprinted Account Number and PIN to talk up to 20 MINUTES for FREE!

U.S. calls are as low as 3.9¢ a minute! International rates as low as 3.9¢ a minute!

- Call any phone anytime — all day, all night — and save!
- No connection charges, no sign-up fees, no activation charges!
- No minimum call length!
- Use it from your cell phone, too!
- Keep your current phone company!
- Auto-recharge feature never lets you run out of talk time!

When your FREE time is up, just call us to re-activate this card and keep making calls for as low as 3.9¢ a minute!

CALL 1-888-429-7599

How to use your Net2Phone Direct® prepaid calling card:

1. Dial **(800) 840-7438** or the appropriate local access number, wait for the chime and greeting.
2. Enter the card number and PIN when prompted.
3. At prompt, for calls in the U.S. and from the U.S. to Canada, dial 1 + area code + number. For international calls from the U.S., dial 011 + country code + number.
4. For additional calls, don't hang up. Just press the (#) key 3 times and wait for prompt, then dial as described in step 3.

Your card number is: 5238525076
Your PIN number is: 3768

Customer service 1-877-N2PHONE (627-4663).

Services provided by Net2Phone. Non-refundable. Not responsible for loss, theft, or unauthorized use of card or card number. An additional fee may apply when using a payphone or a cellular phone. Calls must be made from a touch-tone phone. © Net2Phone 2000, Inc.

*Free minutes based on domestic local access 3.9¢ rate. 3.9¢ domestic rate and international rates available in select metro areas with local access numbers. For a complete list of local access numbers visit net2phonedirect.com. Rates subject to change without notice. A payphone surcharge may apply.

Chapter 10: BRIAN EPSTEIN SAYS YES

WHEN I WENT BACK TO GAC AFTER THE HONEYMOON, I went to see Buddy Howe. I told him that what I really wanted to do was be a promoter and that I was planning to leave GAC.

"Listen, Sid," he said to me, "I know you love promoting, but it's such an iffy business. You're doing well here, and you have a future with us. You just got married and your wife is pregnant. Don't you think that you should give this very careful thought and consideration before you leave? Your future is secure at GAC. I really don't think you should leave. Let's table this idea for a while and we'll revisit it after you've had some time to think about it."

Buddy didn't want to have to deal with replacing me. I let myself be put off. Buddy was such a nice guy, and his allowing me to work myself into GAC slowly after I had been bruised and battered by Newport engendered great feelings of loyalty to him.

One of the good things about working as an agent at GAC was that I had more free time than I did being a promoter or a manager. I decided that to keep my mind active and my spirits up, I would enroll in some courses at the New School for Social Research in Greenwich Village. The most outstanding teacher and lecturer that I had the privilege of listening to was Dr. Max Lerner, who was also a prominent columnist, first with *P.M.* and then with the *New York Post*. He was a brilliant lecturer and he would always fill up the 700-seat auditorium in which he lectured.

I enrolled in Max Lerner's course on democracy. One of the first things he explained was that if we wanted to learn about democracy, it was incumbent upon us to read about other great democracies in the world. He suggested a reading list comprising books about the evolution of democracy in England. Since I had little time to read the books, I decided that I would read an airmail edition of English newspapers instead. I took myself to the international newsstand, Hotelings, which is located on West 42nd Street now, but used to be in the basement of the old New York Times building. I started reading the *Daily Express* from London and later graduated to the *London Times*, the *Manchester Guardian* and others. I enjoyed reading the English newspapers; they reminded me of my time as a soldier in Great Britain and helped me to remember the wonderful British people I had encountered while there. For the first time in my life, I was enjoying school.

Each Wednesday, I would buy my British newspaper at Hotelings. On one Wednesday in late 1962, I picked up a copy of an airmail edition of the *Daily Express*, a breezy, gossipy tabloid newspaper that was the largest circulating paper in England at that time. I took the paper back to my office and browsed through the news section. When I got to the entertainment page, I paid more diligent attention. The entertainment page was filled with noteworthy items about theaters, concerts, movies and other entertainment highlights. On this particular Wednesday, I happened to notice a small one-column item of about five lines with a Liverpool dateline talking about a group called the Beatles. The group, made up of four Liverpool boys, was creating lots of local excitement with big crowds and some hysteria. The use of the word "hysteria" in the newspaper caught my eye.

The next Wednesday, I went to Hotelings to get my British newspaper. I browsed through the *Daily Express* and proceeded to the entertainment section. I was not particularly looking for any mention of the Beatles because the item that I had seen the previous week had been almost inconsequential. But there was another item on the Beatles.

The two-column-wide article reported that the Beatles had done it again. The article also noted that the crowds filling the clubs outside of Liverpool were young and exubérant. I noticed the word "hysteria" again. My attention was piqued. The only time I could remember the word "hysteria" being used with regard to entertainment was in reference to Frank Sinatra and Elvis Presley.

The following week, I decided to pick up several newspapers in addition to the *Daily Express*. In all the newspapers, I saw articles about the excitement that the Beatles were generating. This time, the newspapers reported that people were being turned away; Beatles shows were selling out. I had been through the experience of turning people away from a show, and I knew that it was very uncommon. The cash register was ringing for these four boys and they were attracting crowds and the crowds were not just in Liverpool.

I picked up my papers the following Wednesday with great anticipation. This time, I purchased some more conservative daily newspapers, including the *London Times*. Because I was also interested in what the music trade papers might be writing, I purchased *Melody Maker* and *The New Musical Express*. All had articles about the Beatles. Maurice Kinn, the publisher of *The New Musical Express*, wrote an article under a pen name. In his article, he said that this group, the Beatles, was going to "explode all over England and the British Isles."

I was reading more and more about how the Beatles were picking up momentum in England. I found a kiosk at 57th Street and Eighth Avenue that sold *Melody Maker* and *The New Musical Express* and I realized that any day now Americans might soon be reading about the Beatles.

I was still running the one-night department at GAC. I was a devoted employee, dedicated to doing the best job that I could for the company. I thought that the audiences I had put on shows for at the Palace and Paramount theatres were probably just like the British kids who were getting excited by the Beatles. Maybe there would be an American audience for this new British group. The Beatles' momentum was feeding on itself and the stories documenting their success were proliferating geometrically. And even I, who could never pass geometry, knew that this meant more and more press and greater notoriety. I was sure that this phenomenon, as I had come to think of it, would eventually spill out over the borders of England.

I started to read the ultra-conservative British newspapers: *The People, The Observer, Reynolds News* and the *Manchester Guardian*. I wondered how the elite daily newspapers were reacting to this burgeoning musical development. Interestingly enough, almost all the newspaper reports that I read had reported on the group's long hair and the hysteria they created in the clubs. No one wrote about the actual music—the quality of the music or the musicianship. The articles were only about sellouts, hair and hysteria.

One day, the conservative *Manchester Guardian* ran an article on the third or fourth page with a headline: "Beatlemania Is About To Sweep Great Britain." I decided then that I had to find Brian Epstein. Many articles had named Epstein as the entrepreneur guiding the careers of the Beatles. His family owned a large retail furniture establishment in Liverpool and he had established a record shop in the furniture store. One day, a customer requested a record by the Beatles and Brian Epstein became curious about this new local group. He had found the Beatles working in a tiny Liverpool nightclub and was so impressed with them that he had stepped in and succeeded Alan Williams, a local theatrical agent and manager, as the guiding force in the young career of the Beatles.

Vic Lewis was in charge of the GAC London office. I sent him a memo: "Vic, I have been reading about a group, the Beatles, out of Liverpool, that's creating a furor in England. I'd like to contact their manager, Brian Epstein. Do you know anything about the group and can you get me Brian Epstein's phone number?"

In a few days, Vic responded with a memo of his own: "Of course, I know about the Beatles, but, Sid, no one in America cares or will ever care about them. It's a local phenomenon. There's currently no airplay in the U.S. Epstein books the band himself so they don't need agents. There is nothing here for GAC to pursue. Forget about it."

As the newspaper articles that I continued to read proliferated and grew more enthusiastic about the Beatles, I sent Vic a series of memos, becoming more insistent with each one. After a while, he stopped responding to my memos entirely. He probably thought that I was crazy. In Vic's defense, I have to say that bands like the Beatles were, until that time, not appearing in the U.S., nor were they getting any radio airplay. The Beatles were becoming a sensation in England with almost no airplay there, too. I really don't blame Vic for thinking I was nuts. I still wanted to pursue the idea of bringing the Beatles to the U.S., so I went to my boss, Buddy Howe.

"Buddy," I said, "I've been writing memos to Vic in London about a band in England that's got the kids going wild. They've had no airplay in the U.S., and not that much in England, so Vic thinks that they're just a local club fad. Their manager, Brian Epstein, books them himself, so Vic thinks there's nothing there for GAC, but I think that something is going on, and we should try to sign this group."

Buddy looked at me doubtfully. "What do you want me to do about it, Sid?"

I thought to myself, "Here's another guy who thinks I'm nuts."

"Well, I'd like you to talk to Vic about getting involved in this," I said. "I think we should try to get involved and sign the group. Something is definitely going on."

"Okay, Sid. I'll call Vic," Buddy said in a dismissive manner.

The next day, Buddy came to my office and told me that Vic thought it would be a "waste of time to chase this Beatles thing." Vic said that he wanted me off his back. Buddy was concerned with the day-to-day operations of GAC. Furthermore, he had to look out for the bottom line. A group with no airplay in the U.S. and a manager who booked the group himself represented zero dollar potential to GAC. Buddy's message to me was: Stop bothering Vic, and leave it alone. Forget about the Beatles.

By around March of 1963, I was really frustrated. I was getting *spielkes* (Yiddish for agitated or impatient) again. My time at GAC had been pretty good. I had had the terrific experience with Tony Bennett. I had orchestrated the Carnegie Hall debuts for both Jerry Vale and Nina Simone. I had repaid most of the advertising debts I had incurred at the Newport Jazz Festival. The truth, however, was that my first love was being a promoter. I thought now would be my chance to escape and still have the moral high ground. I had tried every which way I could to get GAC interested in the Beatles but had been rebuffed. It was time for me to take the initiative. I wanted to promote the Beatles in the United States.

I called information in Liverpool looking for Brian Epstein's number, but could not find a listing. I called information in London thinking that now that the Beatles were in fact exploding all over the British Isles, Epstein would have an office there. "No Brian Epstein in London, sir," the operator politely said. I couldn't get his number! I was wracking my brain trying to figure out a way to contact Brian Epstein without attracting too much attention to myself at GAC.

A few days later, I went to lunch at Stouffer's. As I was sitting there thinking about how I could find Brian Epstein's phone number, I noticed Bud Halliwell, an independent record promotion man, come in. While record companies maintain record promotions men on their staffs, they often hire independent (indies) promo men to augment their permanent staff. These indies have contacts or relationships at radio stations that enable them to get airplay, the lifeblood of the record industry. Bud was a successful indie promo man.

I was eating alone so I invited Bud to sit with me. We exchanged chitchat. Bud remarked about my success with the Tony Bennett concert and the giveaway of the three hundred tickets to the Columbia Records staff, which had become well-known in the record industry.

"That was a stroke of genius," he complimented me.

"Thanks, Bud. You know, I've been reading about this group in England called the Beatles."

"I know them, Sid," he interrupted me. "I'm promoting their records."

I could almost hear my jaw hit the floor. "You are?" I asked incredulously. "How's it going?"

"Not too good. No one in America wants to play their records. No one wants to hear about the Beatles. No one cares."

"That's too bad, but that'll change. Eventually, you'll be able to get their records on the air. Tell me, would you happen to know their manager, Brian Epstein?"

"Sure, Sid. I'm working for him. He hired me."

What an unbelievable stroke of luck!

"Do you happen to have his phone number?"

"It's Childwall 6518. It's in Liverpool."

I repeated the number and wrote it down on a napkin. It was as easy as that. When God wants it and it's destined, it happens. In Yiddish, the word for that is *bashert*.

I rushed back to my office and asked my secretary to place a call to Childwall 6518 in Great Britain. In a minute, my secretary buzzed and said, "Sid, I have your call on the line. It's a woman on the phone."

A very pleasant voice said, "Hello."

"Hello," I said. "This is Sid Bernstein in New York, and I would like to speak to Brian Epstein."

"Oh, my son is home," Queenie Epstein said. "Mr. Bernstein, may I ask a question of you before I call him?"

"Certainly, Mrs. Epstein. What would you like to know?"

"Does *The New York Times* still print its weekly book review section?" she asked me. "I have not seen it in the longest time."

"Yes, Mrs. Epstein, it appears every week."

"My gosh! I used to read it all the time because I am an avid reader, but I can't find it now."

"Mrs. Epstein, may I have your address? I get the *Times* every Sunday, and I'll mail the book section to you."

"Oh, that's too much to ask."

"Not at all. It would be my pleasure to send it to you."

She gave me her address and proceeded to ask me a series of questions about New York, as she hadn't visited the States in a while. And, yes, I did send her the book review section every week.

"Oh, Mr. Bernstein, I must be costing you an awful lot of money. This call must be so expensive for you. Let me call my son."

I heard her call out in a loud voice, "Brian, there's a gentleman from New York wanting to speak to you. I've kept him on the phone far too long."

A voice answered, "I'll be right there, Mother." In a moment, a male voice came on the phone. "Hello, this is Brian Epstein."

I was immediately struck with his most dignified tone and manner. I was finally on the phone with Brian Epstein.

I remember that my tongue actually stuck to the roof of my mouth. I froze. Somehow, I knew that this was the most important phone call of my professional life. I was literally tongue-tied.

"Mr. *Epsteen*. This is Mr. *Bernsteen*," I said, finally recovering my composure.

"Excuse me, Mr. *Bernsteen*; my name is pronounced *Epstyne*."

"Oh, I see" I said. "My name is pronounced *BernSTEEN* and yours is *EpSTYNE*. Mr. *Epstyne*, this is confusing. Perhaps we could call each other Sid and Brian?"

"That will be fine," he said. "How may I help you?"

"Brian, I have been reading about your group, the Beatles, for some time now, and I would like to present them here in America. I'm sorry to call you at home, but it's the only phone number I could get for you."

"I understand," he said. "Tell me, Sid, why would you want to present my boys?" Brian always called them "my boys" or "the boys" when he referred to the Beatles. "They've had no radio airplay in America. I'm having great difficulty breaking through or getting any response from the American market, and I will not permit my boys to play to a house that is not 100 percent full."

"But you will, Brian! You'll get your airplay. I'm sure you will."

I was feeling it. I wasn't just trying to sell him. From what I had read in the newspapers, I could tell the Beatles' success would not be limited to the British market. I just had a feeling that the Beatles would be a phenomenon in America, too.

"Tell me, Brian, has anyone other than me called you from the States?"

"They have not. You are the first. Where would you present them?" Brian asked.

I was not prepared for this question at all. I had planned to talk to

Brian and win him over. I had thought that we were just going to have a get-acquainted conversation, not an in-depth, detail-oriented discussion. I had no idea that he would move along this quickly.

"Carnegie Hall," I said.

"What? You want to present my boys in Carnegie Hall?"

"Yes, Carnegie Hall is one of our most cherished, most prestigious and most famous concert halls in America."

"I know Carnegie Hall," he said with a tone of reverence. "Not three or four days ago, I saw a movie on British telly. The film was called *Carnegie Hall*."

I remembered having seen the movie. I said, "That's the place, Carnegie Hall."

"Wait till I tell the boys at Isow's!" Brian sounded somewhat excited now.

[I later found out that Isow's was the popular hangout at lunchtime for the managers, agents, and publishers of British pop music in London. When I went there some years later, I saw the directors chairs with the names of famous people I had been reading about stenciled on the backs of the chairs, just like on movie sets in Hollywood.]

I said, "Oh yeah! Good!" I didn't know anything about Isow's, but I think Brian might have thought that I was really plugged in to the British music scene.

Brian continued, with a tone of pride, "Have you any idea how much my boys are earning in England right now?"

I thought for a second, Oh, no, here it comes... and replied, "No, I don't know, Brian."

"We are earning top dollar. The equivalent of $2,000 U.S. per show. This is what we earn in the music halls of Great Britain."

I breathed a sign of relief. I had paid Judy Garland $25,000 per night. I had been prepared to pay Bob Hope $25,000 for one afternoon. I had gotten $10,000 per show for Tony Bennett. Two thousand dollars for the Beatles was definitely something that I could handle.

"What are the capacities of those music halls, Brian?"

"Oh, easily upwards of 1,500 seats, and at some venues, even better," he said proudly.

"Carnegie Hall has 2,830 seats, but I believe the Beatles will fill it. Not to worry."

"We are now getting so many requests for the boys that it is getting impossible to fill them all. We are getting superstar money," Brian said quite excitedly.

Four months earlier, I had started reading about the Beatles, and my instincts had now been confirmed. The Beatles phenomenon had grown out of small, local clubs and into the big music halls, and the price was climbing in England. My judgment had been validated.

"When would you present them?" he continued with his questions.

"Three months from now."

I was so eager to get the Beatles to New York that I arbitrarily picked three months.

"Brian, I will offer you $6,500 for two shows in one day at Carnegie Hall."

He was really excited. "Wait till I tell the boys at Isow's that an American is offering me $6,500 for two shows in one day! I can't wait to tell them!"

"Yes, that's what I'm offering, Brian," I said. "$6,500 for two shows in one day."

"Three months is too soon, Sid, because we don't currently have any U.S. airplay."

"Well, then, let's make it four months, Brian."

"No, Sid. I do not want my boys to play to an empty house."

"Okay, Brian. When would you want to come over?"

He thought for a moment. "Not till early next year," he said.

"Next year?" I said incredulously. I almost fell over. I had been dreaming about this for several months now. It was paramount in my mind to get the Beatles, and especially to be first. I just *had* to be first. It would be a long wait, but if I agreed, I would have them. I had a very strong feeling that this man would keep his word.

"All right," I said. I began looking at my calendar. I turned to February 1964. It was after the Christmas holidays and New Year's festivities. The first holiday in the new year was Lincoln's Birthday. It was also a Wednesday, and I thought that Carnegie Hall would probably be available on a weekday.

"How about February 12, 1964, Brian? It's a legal holiday here in the U.S. The kids will be out of school and we can do the two shows."

"Okay. The idea of playing Carnegie Hall is intriguing and the money is sufficient. I will agree to everything, with one proviso. If there is no airplay in America by this coming October, October of nineteen hundred and sixty three, I have the right to cancel."

"That's fine," I said. At that point, I was prepared to agree to almost anything. "That's okay with me, Brian."

"If we have to cancel, Sid, how much will that cost you?"

"If you have to cancel, so be it. I'll absorb the loss. But I'm confident that the airplay will materialize. Don't worry about it. I can handle it."

I was struck by the man's decency. He was concerned that I not lose money. Brian Epstein was a businessman to be sure, but he also had great sensitivity, which would remain consistent through all the dealings that I would have with him. He was a gentleman.

"Fine," he said. "We're going to be busy for a while now. Why don't we talk again in about six or eight weeks."

"Okay, I will call you again in the first week of May. In the meantime, can I go ahead with my plans?"

"Yes, go right ahead, Sid. However, I just want to reiterate that if there's no airplay in your country by October, I have the right to cancel. That's the only proviso."

"Agreed," I said.

We said good-bye and hung up.

I was elated! I did a jig around my small office. I had to contain my desire to blurt out to the world that I would be the first to bring the Beatles to America!

As soon as I hung up with Brian, I called Julius Bloom at Carnegie Hall, who informed me that Iona Satescu had become the head booker. I was transferred to her office and made an appointment to meet with her during my lunch hour the following day.

At 12:30 p.m. the next day, I went to Mrs. Satescu's office on the 10th floor at Carnegie Hall. Gilda Weissberg, her secretary, ushered me in and introduced us, and I proceeded to take a seat opposite Mrs. Satescu.

"Mrs. Satescu," I began. "I have an act from England that I would like to present next year, and I was wondering if you have February 12, 1964, available?"

"Let me look at the calendar." After leafing through her book, she responded, "Yes, Mr. Bernstein. It's available."

"Would it be possible to do two shows that day?" I asked.

"What time would you like to do the two shows?"

"Well, one would be at 7 PM, the other would be at 9:30. Would that be okay?"

"Yes, the whole day is free," and turning to Gilda, Mrs. Satescu inquired if there were any rehearsals or special events in the building on that day. Gilda responded that all of Carnegie Hall was free that day.

"What would the costs be, Mrs. Satescu?" I asked.

"For the afternoon and evening, with staff and liability insurance, the two shows would run about $5,000."

"That's fine."

She turned to Gilda. "Gilda, would you please issue a contract to Mr. Bernstein?"

Turning to me, she continued, "You do not have to give me the $5,000 now, Mr. Bernstein. All that is required is a $500 deposit. By the way, who are these people that you want to bring?"

"They are four young men who are a phenomenon in Great Britain. Just four."

"And what are their names?" she inquired.

"They're called the Beatles. B-E-A-T-L-E-S," I spelled it out. She didn't question the name at all.

Gilda led me out into her office so that she could type up the contract. After filling in the requisite information, she asked me for a check for $500. I was not prepared to hand over a check right then. I didn't have $500. I needed to stall for time so I said, "May I come back tomorrow? I completely forgot that I would need a check."

Gilda said, "That's okay, Mr. Bernstein. The contract will be here tomorrow and if I'm not here, see Mrs. Satescu. Make the check out to Carnegie Hall."

I thanked both the ladies, told them that I would be back the next day and hurried to GAC to call Abe Margolies.

Once inside my office, I closed the door and phoned Abe immediately. "Abe, I need $500."

"Why don't you come over to the office?" he said. "I can't do it right now, but let's have lunch tomorrow."

"Okay, Abe. I have something really important going on."

"Come to the office for lunch, Sid, and I'll take care of it."

No questions asked. I had the $500 for Carnegie Hall. All I had to do was pick it up. The next day, I took an early lunch and went to Abe's office. We had a sandwich and he took out his checkbook.

"Who's this for, Sid?" he asked, his pen poised.

"The check is for Carnegie Hall, Abe. I have a show that I must do."

"Who are you presenting, Sid?"

"It's an act from England. You've never heard about them. You'll probably never hear about them, so what's the difference?"

He laughed, "Sid, tell me who it is so that I can at least tell my kids. Tell me."

"Okay, Abe. It's like this. The name of the group is the Beatles." I spelled it out for him. "B-E-A-T-L-E-S. Beatles, with an 'A', Abe, not with a double 'E.' Beatles that make music, not insects that sting you. The Beatles are from Liverpool, England."

"The Beatles, Sid? The Beatles?" he asked, and the look on his face said it all. Leaning forward, he put his pen down. "What kind of a name is that, Sid?"

"Abe, that's their name. That's their name!" I explained with my palms turned heavenward.

Abe looked at me as if I was nuts. "Sid, listen, do you think for one moment that I'm going to tell my kids or anybody that I backed you or loaned you $500 for a music group with a name like that? In the last days of my life, I will never let anybody know that I backed you to put a group called the Beatles in Carnegie Hall. Never."

"Okay, Abe, but I'm telling you. I've got a feeling about this; don't worry about it."

He wrote out the check, looked up at me and said, "Sid, I don't want to be your partner on this one. Do it. Good luck. For your sake I hope you're right, but I don't want to be involved. I don't want anybody to know that I gave you this money. And you have to promise me, Sid. Promise that you will never, ever let anyone know that I had anything to do with a thing called the Beatles."

He gave me the check, and I left. I thought to myself, Abe really thinks I've gone off the deep end this time. He thinks I've flipped my lid, and I'm really gone now. Gee, I hope he's not right.

Of course, Abe told some of his closest friends and associates about my new venture. For a few months after that, our mutual friends would kid me and say, "Hey, Sid! What's with that group you sold Abe? You know, that insect group? Where's that group? What's happening? We don't hear a word!" Everybody was having a good laugh at crazy Sid.

I took the check for $500, went directly to Carnegie Hall and gave it to Mrs. Satescu. "Mr. Bernstein, we're not aware of this group. Who are they?" I figured she had looked in some classical magazines and had not found their name anywhere.

"Believe me when I say they're a phenomenon in Britain." I hurriedly signed the contract, turned over Abe's $500 and got out of there as fast as I could.

I then went down to see my friend Nat Posnick at the box office. Aida, his assistant, buzzed me in. Nat said, "How've you been, Sid? We haven't seen you for a while! That Tony Bennett concert was great, Sid! It was terrific! You did a fabulous job! What's up?"

"I just came from Mrs. Satescu's office, Nat. I signed a contract for a group from England that I'm bringing in next February on Lincoln's Birthday. No one has heard of them yet."

"Good, good, Sid. You want to give me the details so we can print the tickets?"

I started to give him the copy for the tickets and realized that I had a serious problem. Since I was an agent, I was precluded by industry rules from being a promoter. Either you were an agent or you were a promoter. You couldn't be both. I could not have my name on the tickets, the posters or any of the ads. Nothing could say Sid Bernstein Presents. And Abe had forbidden me from breathing a word to anybody about his involvement, so I couldn't use his name. I had a big problem.

"Nat, I just thought of something. Can I call you back later or tomorrow with the copy?"

"Sure, Sid. Let me know what you want to do."

As I walked back to GAC, I weighed my options and tried to come up with a plan that would enable me to forge ahead. I decided to call my old friend Walter Hyman.

"Walter, hi, it's Sid."

"Sid, you son of a gun! How the hell are ya?"

"Great, Walter. Listen, I just booked an act you've never heard about. They're doing very well in England and I'm bringing them to Carnegie Hall next year. I'm going to be the first one to bring them to America. Their manager told me I was the first American to call him."

"Well, what's the deal?" Walter asked me.

"I have a problem, Walter. I'm going to promote this concert, but I'm still here at GAC as an agent, and you know I can't be an agent and a promoter at the same time. Abe Margolies, who has always been my backer, can't get involved in this for unspecified reasons. He can't front for me and I can't use his name. Would you do it? Can I use your name?"

"Sure, Sid! My buddy Hank Barron has been telling me for the longest time that he'd like to get involved in show business and he's been saying to me, Let's do something with Sid! You can put his name and my name on the tickets and posters."

"Walter, that's great. I'll do it any way you guys like."

"Okay. Let me call Hank and discuss it with him and by tomorrow we'll have it figured out. Call me tomorrow, Sid."

The next day I called Walter and he said, "Hank's in but he wants to use the name Theatre Three Productions. It's a name that Hank likes."

"Great, Walter! It's a good name. We'll use that."

Once again, my friends had come through for me. Abe put up the deposit and Walter had helped me solve the agent/promoter problem.

I went back to Nat Posnick at Carnegie Hall. "The name I want to use, Nat, is Theatre Three Productions," I said. "Two shows on Wednesday, February 12. One at 7 PM and one at 9:30."

"Fine, Sid. And what do you want to charge?"

"Well, what do you think Nat? What is the going price these days?"

"If you really feel that the act is that good, Sid, and you think they're going to make it, then charge top dollar."

"What's top dollar, Nat?"

"Three fifty, four fifty and five fifty." $3.50 for the balcony, $4.50 for the golden circle, which were the boxes, and $5.50 for the orchestra.

"Okay, Nat. If that's what you think is best, let's do it."

"The tickets will be ready in ten or twelve days, Sid. I'll call you when they come in."

I thanked Nat for his advice, said good-bye to Aida and left. I can never say enough about how wonderful and helpful the people who ran Carnegie Hall always were to me. Ten days later, Nat called me and I went over to pull some tickets for the press. I pulled twelve of the best seats and told Nat to put the rest of them away until I had a need for them.

I continued doing my work every day at GAC. Since the Beatles concerts were still 11 months away, I had no pressure about raising the additional money that I would need for the ads, posters and handbills. I continued picking up the British newspapers and music trade papers and reading with delight that fuel was being added to the fire and the Beatles' flame was growing bigger and wilder. Beatlemania in England was raging.

In early May, as agreed, I called Brian to confirm our verbal contract. He was effusive about the progress of his boys, but he continued to lament the lack of airplay in America.

"Don't worry, Brian. It'll happen. You'll get your airplay. It'll come."

"I hope so, Sid, I hope so."

No one hoped so more than I.

The waiting game was now on.

Anything I wanted to do with Tony Bennett had the support of my bosses at GAC. I had an idea and called Bill Grummond, who had previously turned down the opportunity to have Tony appear at Forest Hills.

"Bill," I said, "Tony filled up Carnegie Hall."

"I'm well aware of that, Sid."

"Well, let's put him in Forest Hills."

"No, Sid. I still don't feel it. This venue is too big; Tony won't fill it."

"Okay, how about if Tony buys the venue and pays for everything himself? Would you give him a date then?"

"That's fine," Bill said. "It'll cost you $9,000 for everything. It's your house. I'll have nothing to do with it. It will be your show."

"Good. But can we at least say it's a Forest Hills production? You know that, as an agent at GAC, I can't have my name associated with the show."

"Okay, Sid. I understand. You can use the Forest Hills name. It's okay with me."

I called Tony and told him about my idea and my conversation with Bill Grummond. I explained to Tony that it would cost about $9,000 for the house, and with advertising, the band and other expenses, he would be on the line for about $18,000.

"Once we get past the $18,000, Tony, the rest will be yours. I don't want any of the money because I'm working at GAC."

"Sure, Sid. I'd like to try it."

Tony had a renewed confidence since his success at Carnegie Hall. He had appeared on Ed Sullivan's TV show, he was in demand to make appearances both nationally and internationally and he had a new image of himself. I was so pleased for him and his success. I knew that Tony trusted me and my advice.

"Do you think we'll be alright, Sid?"

"Yes, Tony. I'm sure we'll be alright."

Gerry and I went to work. We were once again the poster-posting pair. Gerry would drive the car through the Italian neighborhoods and I would hang the posters on every available surface. Four staples with the gun and go. Hit and run, and then off to the next target.

I had handbills printed and did an ad campaign. We sold 10,500 seats. Forest Hills looked full; it wasn't a capacity audience, but it was close. The concert was held on a beautiful summer evening. Tony gave another spectacular performance. After recouping the $18,000, he made about $8,000. The concert was a big success if for no other reason than to solidify Tony's reputation as a live performer. He would go on to perform in concert venues all over the world.

After the concert, Tony once again asked me to join his organization and tour with him. Once again, my answer was the same: "Can't leave my mother, Tony. Sorry."

When I went to pay Bill Grummond, he took the money and said, "Sid, I guess I don't understand this Tony Bennett thing like you do."

"Guess not, Bill," I said.

Ed Sullivan's weekly TV show on Sunday nights was the highest rated show in the country. Everybody in the entertainment business considered *The Ed Sullivan Show* to be the most important vehicle for achieving stardom. If you appeared on *The Ed Sullivan Show*, you had made it.

Ed and his wife Sylvia were returning to New York from a European holiday when they were delayed at Heathrow Airport. The Beatles were returning from an engagement on the Continent that same day. While waiting for their plane, the Sullivans saw hundreds of teenage kids milling about the airport carrying placards and posters which said Welcome Home Beatles!, We Love You Beatles! and the like. The kids were all very excited. Sullivan asked an airport attendant what the Beatles were, thinking that they might be some kind of animal or circus act. The attendant told him imperiously, "The Beatles? Sir, they are England's foremost singing quartet."

When Sullivan arrived in New York, he called Brian Epstein in England to discuss putting the Beatles on his show. Sullivan later told me that he simply wanted Americans to see this latest British fad. Brian told him that a New York promoter by the name of Sid Bernstein had booked the Beatles into Carnegie Hall for February of 1964. Sullivan said to Brian, "I know Sid, and I'll talk to him."

Sullivan called me. "Sid, this is Ed Sullivan. Let me ask you a question."

Ed always got right down to business.

"Go right ahead, Ed."

"I was in Heathrow Airport last week, and I saw this rather large crowd waiting for a singing group, the Beatles. I called Brian Epstein, their manager in Liverpool, and he informs me that you are bringing them to America to perform in Carnegie Hall on February 12th and that you are the first promoter to bring them. Is that true?"

"Yes, Ed. That's all true."

"What do you think of them?"

"Ed, they're a phenomenon. An absolute phenomenon."

"That's all I want to know, Sid. Thanks."

"You're welcome, Ed," I said. "It's always a pleasure talking to you."

Ed Sullivan reached out again to Brian Epstein and booked the Beatles on his TV show for Sunday, February 9, and for the following week, Sunday, February 16. He had no idea at that time that he would be making television history.

When I found out that Sullivan had made a deal with Brian Epstein, I was exhilarated. Having the Beatles appear on *Ed Sullivan* three days before Carnegie Hall would almost guarantee a sellout. I wouldn't have to borrow any money to pay the bills. I wouldn't have to sweat it out. It would almost assuredly be a sellout. This was the break I was waiting for. I was home free.

I knew then I could double or triple the ticket price for the Beatles, but I opted not to. My plan originally had been to do the shows on Lincoln's Birthday so that the kids who would be out of school that day could see the concert. I was not about to price the tickets beyond their means. No, I thought to myself, I'm going to do just fine financially on these two Beatles concerts. We'll leave the ticket prices just where they are.

By October, I was becoming more excited, and more nervous. The Beatles were so popular in England that the four of them had to disguise themselves whenever they went out in public. They were indescribably hot. Brian had campaigned vigorously and strenuously for EMI, the British parent company of Capitol Records, to release and promote Beatles records in the U.S. None of his appeals to the record company seemed to work. EMI would not consent to Capitol releasing Beatles records in the U.S. Consequently, I worried that Brian would exercise his right to cancel because there was no American airplay.

In early October, Carroll James, an American DJ for a Washington, D.C. radio station, went to England on holiday. While there, he experienced the hysteria that circulated around the Beatles and their music. When he returned to the U.S., James brought with him a copy of the single *Love Me Do*. When he played the single, the audience reaction was instantaneous and unprecedented. The station received a flood of phone calls, burning out the switchboard. From Washington, D.C., the wildfire spread to New York City, where Jack Spector of the WMCA "Good Guys" played the record. The reaction in New York, the number one radio market in America, was the same as in Washington, D.C. Almost overnight, all the pop music radio stations in New York were playing Beatles music. Beatlemania had finally made its way across the ocean to America.

Capitol Records was completely unprepared for the enormity of the American reaction to the Beatles' music. Less than one month prior, they had staunchly refused Brian Epstein's requests that they release Beatles records in the U.S. Now every Capitol Records plant was pressing Beatles records in order to try to keep up with the demand.

As I drove around in my Plymouth, switching radio stations and finding nothing on the airwaves but Beatles music, I was thrilled. Brian Epstein would not cancel now. I was counting the days until February 12th.

The Beatles' breakthrough had opened up the music scene for everybody in Britain. In the fall of 1963, the British music trade papers and popular daily newspapers that I was reading began reporting on a group called the Rolling Stones. The press said that the Rolling Stones was another long-haired group like the Beatles, but with a rougher and more hard-driving image. They reported that the Rolling Stones' music had a harder edge to it. The papers also said that the Rolling Stones had even more of a working class following than the Beatles. The Rolling Stones' popularity was building. They were playing to sold-out venues and were creating a hysteria of their own.

I decided that I wanted to introduce the Rolling Stones to America, too. I called information in London and got the phone number of their manager, Andrew Loog Oldham, whose name I had seen in the trade papers.

I called the number and a secretary answered.

"This is Sid Bernstein calling from New York City. I'd like to speak to

Andrew Oldham."

A moment later, a charming, soft-spoken voice came on. "Sid, this is Andrew. I was hoping that you were going to call me."

"Really, why is that?" I asked, caught completely off guard.

"Well, I've heard through the grapevine that you are the man who's bringing the Beatles to the States to play in Carnegie Hall."

"Who told you that?" I really wanted to know.

"I don't recall exactly, but I know it was someone at Isow's."

"Yes, Andrew, it's true. But let's keep it a secret between us. I have special reasons for not wanting everyone to know about that just yet."

Everyone knew that the Beatles were coming to Carnegie Hall, but no one knew that Theatre Three Productions was really Sid Bernstein.

"No problem, Sid. It's just between us."

"Now, Andrew," I continued. "I would like to bring the Rolling Stones to play in Carnegie Hall."

"How marvelous!" he exclaimed. "And when would you like to do that?"

"How does this coming March sound to you?"

"We are committed for the Spring of 1964. But, the Rolling Stones would be available after that."

"Okay. How about sometime in June?"

"That would be just fine with us, Sid. Since we're so far away from the date, why don't we firm it up in December? We won't pick an exact date until December but will leave the first two weeks in June free."

"Great, Andrew. I'll look forward to talking to you in December, then."

I hung up feeling very good about our conversation. The Rolling Stones did not have the popularity of the Beatles, but I knew that something really huge was happening on the British music scene, and I was on top of it.

But I was still working at GAC. I would be calling Carnegie Hall to book the Rolling Stones and I would have to put someone else's name on the tickets. I didn't want to ask Walter Hyman and Hank Barron to do a repeat Theatre Three deal because I knew that the Stones were definitely not their kind of music. They had helped me with the Beatles, and I wanted to leave it at that. So, I called Billy Fields.

"Billy, I just booked a group called the Rolling Stones to play Carnegie Hall sometime in June of next year. They're not the Beatles, but they're making a lot of noise in England, and they're gaining momentum. I'm still here at GAC, and I'm not sure when I'm going to leave so I'd like to book the Rolling Stones concert under your name. Is that okay with you?"

"No problem," replied Billy. "Go right ahead."

Next, I called Abe. "Abe, I need $500 for a deposit for another group from England."

By now, Abe had heard and read all about the Beatles. He knew that I was onto something, so he just said, "Come to the office anytime, Sid. The check will be here waiting for you."

"Thanks, Abe. I'll pick it up tomorrow."

"By the way, Sid, what's this group's name?" he asked warily.

"The Rolling Stones."

That name didn't seem to bother Abe as much as the Beatles had. The next day, I picked up the check and went to see Mrs. Satescu. She looked in her book and we agreed on a date in June 1964.

The British Invasion was starting to take shape.

On Friday, November 22, 1963, I was working in my office at GAC when the terrible news came that President John F. Kennedy had been shot. We all huddled around the TV set in Buddy Howe's office, listening and hoping that the President would survive. At one o'clock in the afternoon, we, along with millions of other Americans, heard Walter Cronkite announce that the President was dead. It was shocking. I had liked Kennedy immensely. I was attracted to his youth, his enthusiasm, his style, and his beautiful family. Kennedy's compassion and his efforts on behalf of civil rights for all struck a chord with me.

It was a very sad time for America.

The tragedy of JFK's assassination came as my anticipation and euphoria for the Beatles' coming grew. I moved my mother and her companion from the Bronx into an apartment in the building where Gerry and I were living. Gerry was great about it. She often looked in to see how my mother was faring. Having my mother in close proximity afforded me great relief. I could now keep an eye on her without having to travel back and forth from Manhattan to the Bronx. This new living arrangement really saved me time and wear and tear. I wondered why I hadn't thought of it sooner!

The press in America and, in fact, all over the world had finally caught up to the Beatles story. Wherever you went, in whatever newspaper or magazine you looked at, there were stories about the Beatles. *Time, Life, Newsweek* all ran a picture of the boys on their front cover and all reported on the unprecedented musical phenomenon that was creating hysteria all over England. My participation was still a secret, and I was literally tingling with excitement.

Brian called me sometime in December.

"Hello, Sid. This is Brian."

"Brian, how are you!"

"Well, you can imagine, Sid! All hell has broken loose! I'm being sieged from everywhere. The press wants to interview the boys constantly and the demand for them to appear is nothing short of incredible!" He continued, "Of course, we can't be everywhere. It is all very hectic!"

"I can well imagine. Tell me, Brian, how can I help you?"

"Well, I'm concerned about the boys coming to America and particularly stepping off the plane practically into Carnegie Hall. I was wondering if some kind of warm-up date someplace out of New York might not be in order. I want them to get the feel for an American audience before they play Carnegie Hall."

"That's not a bad idea, Brian."

"Could you set up something not too far from New York for us? Someplace that we can get back and forth to in the same day?"

"It's a great idea and you should do it, but I can't leave New York right now because my ailing mother is not doing too well. If I agreed to do this, I'd have to go to whatever city we choose, and spend time there making sure that it was handled properly. I really can't commit myself to that now. I'm sorry. I really am."

"That's okay, Sid," he said. "I understand fully. I'm sorry you can't do it. But, I'm happy that you concur about it's needing to be done, and we will set it up. Sid, we will be staying at the Plaza Hotel when we come to New York and will be arriving on Friday, February 7th. Capitol Records is hosting a reception for the boys in the hotel at around three o'clock. Why don't you come by our suite prior to that and meet the boys, and then come to the reception?"

"Thank you, Brian. I will look forward to that."

"Thank you for everything, Sid," he said, and hung up. Brian was a gentleman as always, but I could tell from his tone that his responsibilities and concerns were all-consuming and that he had entered the fast lane.

The holiday season came and went. First Chanukah and then Christmas. It was a bittersweet time, as the country was still mourning the fallen President, and the holiday spirit was somewhat diminished for everybody. But the joyous, effervescent, hopeful music coming from those four boys from Liverpool helped to salve the terrible wound Americans had experienced after the tragedy of November 22, 1963. The build-up for the Beatles was in full force. Every radio station that played pop music played the Beatles all day long: *Love Me Do*, *I Wanna Hold Your Hand*, and *She Loves You*.

One of the hottest acts at GAC was Trini Lopez. His record of *If I Had a Hammer* had gone to number one on all the charts, and he was in big demand for personal appearances. In January 1964, Trini was booked into the

Olympia Theatre in Paris, France. The Olympia was a prestigious venue, and Norman Weiss, a GAC agent and a vice president of the company, was dispatched to Paris to cover and service Trini Lopez. It was common practice for agencies to have their agents in attendance when their acts performed, and the more successful the act, the more comprehensive the attention and service.

The Beatles were being presented on the same bill as Trini Lopez. It didn't take long for Norman Weiss to recognize that these four boys from Liverpool were indeed the real deal. By now, the hysteria that had happened in England had crossed the ocean, and the magazine covers and radio play were adding fuel to the fire

Norman had a chance to meet Brian Epstein. He told Brian that GAC was the second largest theatrical agency in the world, with many acts and great power and prestige in the entertainment world. He asked Brian to consider allowing GAC to be the Beatles' agent in America. When Norman told Brian that GAC would get ten percent for all bookings, Brian said, "Yes, we would consider GAC as agents but I will not pay ten percent." Norman told Brian that he would report back to GAC that the Beatles would not pay the standard ten-percent fee and then get back to him with the agency response.

When Norman Weiss came back to New York and reported to Buddy Howe about Brian Epstein's reluctance to pay ten percent, Buddy made an executive decision that GAC would make an exception to get the Beatles for the GAC roster. GAC would agree to take a five-percent commission.

After the Beatles were signed, a memo was circulated throughout GAC's worldwide offices and in it, Buddy said, "GAC has scored a coup."

I went directly to Buddy Howe.

"Buddy," I said.,"why wasn't I sent to Paris? I found the group! Neither you nor Vic had any interest. I'm the guy who alerted everybody to the Beatles."

"Sid, listen. I sent Norman over there to cover Trini. He met Brian Epstein by coincidence and one thing led to another. Norman is a vice president. He saw the opportunity and he seized it."

I was really hurt, and I realized what having stripes and a title meant. I called Walter Hyman and told him what had happened.

"Sid, here's what's really happening. First of all, no one knows who Theatre Three Productions is, including your boss, Buddy Howe. Everyone is running around trying to get a piece of the Beatles' deal. Tell me, how much are you going to make from the two Beatles performances at Carnegie?"

"Easily $10,000 after expenses," I answered.

"That's a little less than you make for a full year's work at GAC," Walter said. "You don't need GAC anymore. This is *your* concert. You're Theatre Three. Neither Hank nor I want any of the $10,000. It's all yours. You found the group. You did all the work. All we did was come up with a name. It's your deal. If I were you, I would go see my pal Buddy Howe and tell him you're leaving GAC unless you get a vice presidency and a $100 raise. They're going to give you that $100, and the vice presidency. You deserve it."

I took his advice and went to Buddy Howe. I told him I wanted $100 more per week and the title of vice president.

"Listen, Sid, it took me four years to become a vice president at GAC. You've been here less than two years. I can't give you a vice presidency yet, but you've got the $100 raise. I know you can use it. You just got married, your wife is pregnant, and you're taking care of your mother."

I called Walter and related the conversation with Buddy to him, and he said, "Quit, just quit. The knowledge in the business of you and the Beatles is nil because you've managed to keep it a secret. You quit, announce it to the world, and you take all the bows. You're the first one to bring the Beatles here. You deserve the credit." Walter was really angry.

Walter's encouragement really charged me up. I went back to Buddy.

"Buddy, I'm leaving," I said. "I hate to leave. I owe you a lot for bringing me in, but I'm going to leave, and I'm going to present the Beatles at Carnegie Hall."

The cat was out of the bag.

Buddy sat up straight in his seat. "*You're* Theatre Three? Are you doing the right thing here, Sid?"

"I know I'm doing the right thing, Buddy. I started on this thing months and months ago when I was sending memos to Vic Lewis in London. I tried to get you to intervene. I did the right thing and you guys dropped the ball. I think I'm entitled to have my name attached to all the activity surrounding the Beatles. That's why I think I have to go. Forget that I've even been asking about a vice presidency. This is my chance to get back to being myself—to being Sid—to being what I've always wanted."

"Okay, Sid. If you've made your decision and that's what you want, I wish you good luck."

Buddy knew that there was no way he was going to talk me out of leaving.

"We'll still be friends, Buddy. You and Jean (Buddy's wife) and me and Gerry. But I have to do my own thing."

I gave him three weeks' notice and when the time came, I moved "my stuff" (as George Carlin refers to it) and started working from my West 12th Street apartment.

Events were moving at tremendous speed.

Mrs. Satescu from Carnegie Hall called and informed me that a February 15th show had been canceled and would I be interested in taking the date. I took the date. I had been in Los Angeles months before, covering an act for GAC at the Whiskey A Go Go. Someone told me about Shirley Bassey, a young black female entertainer from Wales, who was appearing at Charlie Morrison's Macombo. Everyone I spoke to raved about her and insisted that I go see her. When I had some free time, I went over to see Shirley and she was fantastic. She reminded me of a young Judy Garland.

When I accepted Mrs. Satescu's offer of the February 15th date, I had Shirley Bassey in mind. I called Charlie Morrison to inquire about Shirley. He told me that her husband, a Yugoslavian count, was her manager. When I called the count and explained to him that I wanted to present his wife in Carnegie Hall, he couldn't accept fast enough.

"Oh yes, absolutely, Mr. Bernstein," he said.

This would be another first. I would take Shirley out of the nightclub circuit and put her in a concert venue for the first time. I felt that she was ready. Walter Hyman put up the money. But this time, he would be my partner in every sense of the word.

Mrs. Satescu called again. "Mr. Bernstein, we have another opening for February 21st. I know that you've taken the 12th and the 15th, but could you use the 21st as well?"

I called Tony Bennett and asked him if he's like to "do" Carnegie Hall again on February 21st, which was the eve of the Washington's Birthday holiday. Tony said yes, and all that he would require was a good band to work with. I got him Count Basie, a pretty good band, I would say.

When I called Mrs. Satescu to accept the 21st date, she said, "My, but you're a busy man, Mr. Bernstein."

I was hot. Everybody wanted to extend me credit and I was prepared to keep rolling the dice. This was what I was born to do. I started to think about the ads that I would run to publicize these three events, and I came up with an ad that said, Bernstein Presents: The Beatles, Bassey, Bennett & Basie. I liked the ring of that. When that ad broke, all hell broke loose with it. Ticket requests came from everywhere. I had 300 requests for press passes for the Beatles at Carnegie.

Chapter 11: A COMET CALLED THE BEATLES

ON JANUARY 27, 1964, THE BEATLES TICKETS were put on sale at Carnegie Hall. When I went to see Nat Posnick at noon to gauge sales, I noticed a trail of cigarette butts, cigarette packages, gum wrappers and other assorted garbage, from Sixth Avenue and 56th Street, all the way up to Carnegie Hall at Seventh Avenue and 57th Street, which was almost 1/5 of a mile. Aida buzzed me into the box office. Nat was there and they both looked stunned.

"Nat, don't they ever clean up around Carnegie Hall anymore?" I asked.

Nat looked at me, shaking his head and laughing, "Sid, what just happened here has never happened in the 74-year history of Carnegie Hall. It is simply unbelievable. We were totally unprepared. Some of the kids camped out all night waiting to buy Beatles tickets the minute we opened the window at nine o'clock. When we finally opened, the line was all the way around the block, down Seventh Avenue and almost to Sixth Avenue! You should have seen it, Sid! It's never happened before! We sold the Beatles concert out in 40 minutes, and they are still coming! Just look outside! We could have sold tickets for three or four times the price you're asking, and I know they'd buy them up. The mess outside will be cleaned up soon. We just never expected this!"

"It's okay, Nat. I know we could have raised the prices, but I wanted the kids to be able to afford the tickets." I was elated, but not surprised.

"Sid," Nat said with a look of wonderment on his face. "This is big!"

"Yes, sir," I laughed. "It's big, Nat, and it's getting bigger!"

Nat probably thought to himself, How much bigger can it get?

I was in trouble with Beatle tickets. I didn't have enough for press and friends. My best friend and backer, Abe Margolies, who had sworn me to secrecy, Mr. "Promise me, Sid, you will never ever tell anyone that I had anything to do with something called the Beatles," needed 300 tickets. Every day he would call me adding to the number of tickets he needed.

"Abe," I would tell him, "we're sold out! I'm getting requests from all over the world! I'm getting requests from the press! The phone doesn't stop ringing! Where do you expect me to get 300 more tickets?"

"Don't worry, Sid," he would say. "You'll figure it out." And the next day, he'd call me to add a few more tickets to his request list. Abe just didn't know what the word no meant.

Thank God, Hank Barron and Walter Hyman did not need that many tickets or I probably would have had to change my name and leave town. I had a real dilemma; I simply didn't have access to extra tickets.

Then one day, about 10 days before the concert, Doc, the Carnegie Hall stagehand that I knew best, came to me when I was visiting Carnegie Hall and said, "Listen, Sid, I don't need any tickets because my son is grown up, but some of the guys have kids and they want them to see this concert. It would really be nice if you could accommodate them."

"So what do I do, Doc? I can't even accommodate my oldest and best friend! Doc, I don't sleep nights. People are calling me from all over the world at all hours of the day and night. I don't know what to do, because I definitely don't have even one extra ticket."

"I'll tell you what, Sidney, you're allowed a limited number of seats on stage. Tell the stagehands it's okay to bring their kids. Limit them to two tickets per family and ask them to put as many folding chairs as they can on stage. We know the fire department, and we'll talk to them. We'll take care of them. Ask Nat in the box office to punch out some special tickets for our people and for your best friend. We'll put the seats in the wings. We'll put them behind the band. After all, it's only the four boys up on the stage. I think we can get you 300 extra seats without creating a stir. You've got enough security here. We'll use folding chairs and we'll have everyone seated."

And with that, I had just found 600 extra seats. Three hundred for the early evening and another three hundred for the later show. I was saved from a very frightening fate indeed.

When I told Abe he had his 300 tickets, he blithely said, "I knew you would work it, Sid!"

Those 600 tickets were gone immediately. Now, I was getting calls from people I attended high school with and who I hadn't seen in over 20 years!

The Beatles arrived at Idlewild Airport on Friday, February 7, 1964. (The airport had not yet been renamed for the assassinated President.) When they landed in the U.S., the Beatles had six records in the Top 100, including numbers one, two, three, four and five in New York. Hundreds of members of the press and thousands of kids showed up at the airport to greet the group. Murray the K, a top New York DJ, and the WMCA "Good Guys" had broadcast lots of Beatles information on their radio shows, including the arrival time of their Pan Am flight.

I had decided that I would not go to the airport but instead would go to the Plaza, as Brian Epstein had suggested to me. When I arrived at the Plaza, I was astonished to discover that there were barricades all around the hotel, with policemen and mounted police everywhere. In front of the Plaza there were between 1,500 and 2,000 kids with signs and placards. I was really interested in what the kids were saying, so I went to stand among them for a while, since the Beatles had not yet arrived at the hotel. In addition to all the kids and security, I noticed some adults and members of the press with television cameras and microphones. The kids were singing Beatles songs, looking up at the windows of the Plaza, screaming and having a good time. I thought to myself, here I am in the middle of this amazing crowd, having some responsibility for what is happening, and nobody even knows who I am. I felt good to see the kids having a great time. I felt proud to be a part of what was happening, even though no one in the crowd knew who I was.

Standing there in front of the Plaza, I realized that what I had been reading about in the papers for months was real and that I had been right. These kids standing out in the cold were an army. A peaceful army to be sure, but an army. I was beginning to see great social and cultural change because of the four mop-heads from England. Hairstyles, clothing, language and social mores had begun to change and would continue to change because of the music that the Beatles were making. I also began to feel that not only social and cultural changes would happen, but also political change might come to the world because of all the singing about love and peace. It was a very powerful thing to experience.

Suddenly, the limos drove up to the front of the hotel. I remembered Brian had told me that for security reasons the boys would not travel in the same car. I am not sure whether that was done, because it seemed to me that when the cars in the entourage drove up, all the Beatles were there. The four boys ran up the stairs and through the revolving doors of the Plaza. Brian was with them. They all waved perfunctorily, but Paul McCartney turned to the crowd, waved, and blew a kiss to the kids standing across the street.

I spent another 15 or 20 minutes with the kids outside, watching and listening to them being interviewed by the radio, television and newspaper press before I worked my way to the front and passed thought the barricades. I must have looked like I belonged, because no one stopped me or even questioned me. I made my way across the street, and walked up the steps and into the lobby of the Plaza.

Immediately upon entry, I was stopped by a security man and asked, "Excuse me, sir. Are you a guest of the hotel?"

"No, I am not," I said.

"Then would you please state your business here, sir?"

"Yes, I am here to see Mr. Brian Epstein."

"And may we have your name, sir?"

"Sid Bernstein."

The security guard glanced through a notebook and said, "Okay, yes, sir. Here is your name. You may proceed, sir. Just tell the elevator operator who you are here to see, and he will take you right up. And, thank you sir, for your patience."

Nodding to the security guard, I got on the elevator and told the operator I wanted Mr. Epstein's floor and was promptly delivered to the 12th floor. As soon the elevator doors opened, another security man directed me down the hall, where another man was standing in front of the suite. I told him my name, and he opened the door for me.

As I walked into the suite, I recognized several Capitol Records executives. Brian Epstein was just finishing a phone call. I remember seeing a photographer hanging around with many cameras around his neck. Brian finished his phone call and turned to me. I walked the few steps toward him, my hand extended.

"Brian, I'm Sid Bernstein."

"Sid!" He took my hand and gave me a warm smile. "It's good to finally meet you! I'm so glad you came. The reception is going to start in a little while."

Brian was a very pleasant-looking young man in his early thirties. He was in shirtsleeves and his tie was loosened around his neck. He seemed both exhausted and exhilarated.

"Sid, I'd like to introduce you to the boys," he said, taking me over to a closed door, which looked like it opened into another suite. He knocked on the door, which was opened by another security man, and we entered. All four of the Beatles were standing at the window, looking down at the large crowd assembled there.

Ringo was the first to come forward.

"Ringo, this is Mr. Sid Bernstein, our promoter," Brian said.

Ringo stuck out his hand, I clasped it and said, "Welcome to New York."

The other three also came forward and Brian introduced me to them. Ringo struck me as being a very funny guy. I thought that Paul was very handsome, and George and John struck me as excited kids who were just having a good time with all the popularity and special treatment. We chatted for a few minutes. Brian told me that they were all overwhelmed by the fans' reception, both at the airport and at the hotel.

John said, "This is one crazy place, this New York."

George kept looking out the window at the kids below, gathered at the front of the Plaza. "Can you believe this?" he kept saying. "Can you believe this?"

Their long hair struck me as somewhat odd, but after talking to them for a few minutes, I completely forgot about it. They were well-groomed and neatly dressed. I was struck with the similarity between these boys and other kids that I knew. They were just nice kids who were very excited and awed by what was happening to them.

I asked them, "What do you think of New York?"

Ringo said, "Well, we just got here, but it's a happening place!"

"New York is fantastic," Paul piped in.

"You haven't seen anything yet," I said.

John said, "This is unbelievable! Just unbelievable!"

"Listen, guys," I said. "If you get a chance, and you can manage to get out of here, you should go to Paolucci's. Paolucci's is the best Italian restaurant in New York. I'm sure you'd all love it."

Brian just smiled. And I knew he was thinking that with the crowds and the press, it would be difficult to go anywhere.

The boys went back to look out the windows. Brian and I talked about security. I told him that I had contacted the precinct responsible for Carnegie Hall and spoken to the police chief, and had been assured that the police were prepared for any situation that might arise. Brian told me that he and his people had also been in touch with the New York police, and he was satisfied with the reassurances he had received. He thanked me for my concern.

"Brian," I said, "the demand for tickets is non-stop. The phone rings 24 hours a day. I'm getting requests for press credentials from all over the world. There is even a contingent of press coming from Japan."

"That's great!" He was ecstatic.

"How about Washington? Are you all set there?" I asked, referring to the warm-up concert that had been scheduled for D.C. that I couldn't promote because of my mother's precarious health.

"Yes, Sid. We were going to fly, but the snow made us change our plans. We're going to take an early train on Tuesday, do the show that night and come back early on Wednesday for your two shows at Carnegie Hall."

I remember thinking that I hoped there wouldn't be a major snowstorm stranding them in Washington. If I had been able to arrange the warm-up show as Brian had requested, I never would have let them go to Washington to perform on the night before the two shows in New York. Washington, D.C. was a little too far away for comfort.

Brian must have been reading my mind because he said, "Tomorrow we start rehearsals for the *Sullivan* show, and then Sunday is the actual broadcast. I left Monday open for a rest day, and on Tuesday we go to Washington."

I understood then that the Beatles had a very tight schedule.

We went to look out the window together. After a moment, Brian said, "You know, Sid, the fever in the States for the Beatles even exceeds England.

It's just unbelievable."

It was just as I had predicted.

"America loves the Beatles, Brian, and you haven't seen anything yet."

I looked at my watch and saw that the reception was less than a half-hour away. "I'm really happy to have met you all and proud that I am going to present you in Carnegie Hall," I said to Brian and the boys.

"We're happy to be here, and thanks for presenting us," John said, in his inimitable way.

We all shook hands and I said, "See you later." I waved to them as I left.

Brian walked me out of their suite and back into his own. The Capitol Records people were still there. I knew the executives from the business. We chatted for a few more minutes and shook hands all around. Brian escorted me to the door and said, "I'll see you downstairs in a little while. Thanks for coming by, Sid."

I went downstairs to the reception. There were hundreds of press people and record executives. I knew many of them, but many were from out of town and overseas. I circulated and greeted many old friends. The Plaza served hors d'oeuvres and more food, and I busied myself with the delicious offerings. Once the Beatles and Brian came down to the reception, everything became quite hectic and I made my exit.

As I made my way home from the Plaza, I was overwhelmed with a feeling of great elation. I was finally doing what I liked to do best. I had married the girl I loved and soon she was going to have our first baby. My mother lived nearby and I could look out for her well-being. And I was a part of the biggest music and entertainment story in the history of the world. I had just met Brian Epstein, who had become a friend, and with whom I knew I could and would do further business. And, I had met the four boys and they turned out to be quality kids. This Beatles thing was going to get better and bigger and I was an integral part of it.

When I got home, I asked Gerry if she would like to be in the audience when the Beatles did the Sullivan show. She said, "No, I'll watch it on TV, Sid."

I called Bob Precht, Sullivan's son-in-law and executive producer of the show, and asked him for just one ticket. Bob and I knew each other because I often covered GAC acts that were on the Sullivan show.

"Sid, of course, you can have a ticket," he said. "I'm glad that you're only asking for one, though, because the requests for tickets are unbelievable."

"Tell me about it, Bob," I laughed.

I had been at the CBS Studio where *The Ed Sullivan Show* was broadcast many times before, but the excitement in the room on that Sunday in February was amazing. Adding to the excitement were the many celebrities that Sullivan had invited, as he often did so he could introduce them to the national TV audience during the show. There were about 750 people in the audience and there was a lot of screaming. The Beatles were great, but it was in a TV studio, not a concert venue. I was really looking forward to experiencing that energy at Carnegie Hall. Elvis Presley and Colonel Tom Parker sent a congratulatory telegram, which Sullivan read during the show. It was a classy thing for Elvis and the Colonel to do. As I sat there in the electric environment, I realized that there were people all over America seeing and hearing the magic that I had only imagined more than a year ago. At that moment, I was truly grateful for the medium of television. When I left the show, one of the TV executives present told me that the preliminary estimate was that over 70 million people had seen the broadcast. I couldn't believe it and said to him that this was mind-boggling.

When I arrived at my West 12th Street apartment building, dozens of people were hanging around, waiting to ask me for tickets to the forthcoming Carnegie Hall concert. They milled about on the sidewalk and sat along the cement balustrade that framed the walkway to the entrance of the building. I stopped to talk to them, but I had to disappoint everybody.

"Sorry, folks, there are no tickets left."

I hated having to disappoint those hopeful kids who had the ingenuity to find me.

When I went upstairs to our apartment, Gerry told me that the neighbors had been complaining about all the commotion at the front of the building. I didn't know exactly how to respond to that. She also told me that she had watched the Sullivan show and it seemed like pandemonium. I told her that the audience had been absolutely electrified, totally wired and in a frenzy.

"Yes, Gerry, this is something that one rarely sees in a lifetime. It really is unimaginable!"

Early the next morning, I read that the Sullivan viewer audience had been estimated at 73 million people. I was overwhelmed with requests for tickets again. The phones just would not stop ringing. We had taken them off the hook to get some sleep, but as soon as we replaced the receiver on the cradle, it started ringing all over again.

The germ of another idea was beginning to percolate in my brain. Early on Monday morning, I called John Goldner, the head booker at the old Madison Square Garden on 52nd Street between 8th and 9th Avenues.

"John, this is Sid Bernstein. I was wondering if the Garden is free a week from this Wednesday or Thursday, February 18th or 19th?"

"It's free on the 19th, Sid. Why?"

"John, I don't have the approval yet, but I'd like to put the Beatles in the Garden on Thursday, the 19th. I've had so many calls requesting tickets for the shows at Carnegie that I think we could sell the Garden out."

"Sid, from what I saw last night on the Sullivan show, and from what I've been reading in the newspapers, you probably can."

"Tell me, if I can get clearance from the group to do another show, how long would it take for you to print tickets?"

"That's no problem. We can get tickets printed in 24 hours if necessary."

"Okay, John. Give me a couple of hours. I'm going to call Brian Epstein, the Beatles' manager, and discuss this with him. If there's any possibility at all of this happening, I'll bring him down to see the Garden. I'll call you and let you know what's happening."

"Fine, Sid. Let us know, and we'll help you in any way we can."

I called Brian at the Plaza and was put through immediately.

"Brian, it's Sid."

"Yes, Sid, how are you?"

"Great, Brian. That show last night was spectacular, wasn't it?"

"Quite fantastic, Sid. And the audience! Sullivan's people and the papers are saying 73 million! That's absolutely astonishing!"

"What's even more astonishing, Brian, is that all 73 million want tickets to the Carnegie Hall shows!"

He laughed.

"Brian," I continued. "I have an idea, and I would like you to hear it. Actually, it would be better to show you in person. Could you possibly spare an hour? It will be well worth your while."

"When, Sid?"

"It's around ten o'clock now, so how about noon? Could you spare an hour then?"

"How about 12:30? I think I could make it then."

"Great! I'll pick you up at the Plaza at 12:30 sharp."

"See you then."

I called John Goldner at the Garden and told him to expect me at 12:45. My cousin Leo Kitchman came along because he wanted to meet Brian Epstein. Leo and I got to the Plaza at 12:15; I didn't want to be late.

"I'll be down at 12:30," Brian said when I called his suite.

At exactly 12:30, Brian exited the elevator, we shook hands, and I showed him to the cab. I introduced Leo and started to explain my idea.

"Brian, we're going down to Madison Square Garden." (Brian was familiar with the Garden from all the political rallies and championship fights that he had read about over the years.) "The Garden has an open date a week from this Thursday. It means that you would have to come back from your holiday in Florida a few days early. The Garden has 17,000 seats, but I can guarantee a sellout and you and the boys can keep all the money. I'm not interested in making a dime, I just want to accommodate the thousands and thousands of people who are desperate to see the Beatles in person and have been calling me non-stop for tickets."

"You're sure we can sell it out, Sid? You know that I will not let the Beatles appear in a venue with empty seats, and 17,000 seats is far more than we've ever filled!"

"Positive, Brian. Right now, I think we could sell out a venue five times the size. It's not going to be a problem.

We had reached the Garden. We waited in the reception area for a moment and then John Goldner came out to greet us. After I introduced Brian to John, he brought us right into the middle of the floor of the Garden. Brian stood there and turned around slowly. I could hear him musing to himself. "Hmmm, hmmm," he kept saying. He looked way up into the uppermost reaches of the cavernous old Garden. I could see him thinking and visualizing "his boys" playing in front of the biggest crowd yet.

"What do you think, Brian?"

He took another look, turning a complete 360 degrees.

"The public and the fans will eat this up, Brian. I think you should do it. I figure you can take home $100,000 clear," I said.

"Let's keep them wanting, Sid. We'll do it another time."

And that was it.

I thanked Goldner; we were both disappointed.

"We'll do other stuff," I told him.

Leo and I took Brian back to the Plaza in a cab. Brian told me that the boys were in awe of New York City and had even managed to sneak out and go to a nightclub with Murray the K, the top DJ in New York City, and by now the self-proclaimed fifth Beatle.

Brian got out at the Plaza. "See you on Wednesday," he said.

Although I was disappointed, I felt great that Brian said he'd consider the Garden at a later date. My mind was already working on it.

On the morning of February 12th, Gerry told me that she was concerned about the crowd at the concert and thought it would be better for the baby if she didn't attend. She was six months pregnant with our first child, and she didn't want to overexert herself. I tried to persuade her otherwise, but she was adamant about keeping herself and the baby in good health.

In the days and weeks leading up to the Beatles' appearance at Carnegie

Hall, I was working so hard supervising every aspect of the concert, from security to publicity. It always seemed that I was doing several things at once, and I was always on the phone checking on various arrangements. I must have been in the middle of one of those frenzied moments when we had to approve both the posters that were going to be hung right outside Carnegie Hall and the program for the performance. It wasn't until just hours before the concert that I discovered two glaring errors: the printer had misspelled Carnegie Hall as "Carngie" Hall and had listed the members of the Beatles as Ringo Starr, George Harrison, John Lennon and *John McCartney*! I understood that these kinds of mistakes happen in the middle of the unprecedented insanity that accompanied these concerts. There wasn't anything I could do, and I hoped that Brian Epstein would not be terribly upset.

I decided to get to Carnegie Hall early to check on the house and talk to Aida and Nat in the box office about the other concerts that would follow the Beatles, particularly Shirley Bassey, whose ticket sales were not doing that well. I got to Carnegie Hall about four o'clock. The Beatles' road crew was already there setting up for the boys.

The first thing Nat said to me was "Sid, we've got to be careful about how we bring the Beatles into the building. The kids are all over the place. They're lined up backstage; they're trying to figure out any way to get in here and break through. We gotta be careful. We've never seen anything like this!"

"I've talked to the police chief, Nat, and he told me that they're prepared. They told me not to worry. I think they have it covered," I said hopefully.

"Well, they sure have plenty of cops around here," Aida said.

"That's good. That's the way it's supposed to be," I said.

The last thing I needed was a crowd that was completely out of control.

I went back into the hall. The folding chairs were set up onstage and I could just picture how wonderful a jammed Carnegie Hall would look and sound. The excitement was building.

I went outside and saw people coming to the box office in search of tickets, only to be turned away. Scalpers were waiting nearby, selling tickets. If ever the word "scalper" had a meaning, this was it. Tickets that had been bought for a top price of $5.50 were being sold for $150.00—almost 30 times their face value. When I saw that happening right outside Carnegie Hall, I realized that there were probably tickets that had been sold for even more.

One of the stagehands informed me that the Beatles had arrived at Carnegie Hall at around 6 PM.

"Mr. Bernstein, your act is in the building and in their dressing room," he said.

I was relieved that they had made it back from Washington, D.C. without any problems, even though there was indeed snow on the tracks from a previous snowfall.

I walked around Carnegie Hall greeting people and stopping to chat with friends. Al Aronowitz, the dean of rock and roll reporters and a friend of mine, walked over to me, put his arm around my shoulder and said, "Sid, history is being made here today, and I'm going to say so in the *New York Post* tomorrow."

As I stood in front of the stage in Carnegie Hall, I noticed an usher standing in the back near the entrance doors with a man dressed in a state trooper uniform, complete with the pinched three-cornered hat and the high black boots. The usher was pointing at me. The state trooper started walking towards me and I wondered, Uh-oh, what have I done now? Standing ramrod straight, the tall, impeccably uniformed trooper introduced himself.

"Mr. Bernstein," he said, "I am here with the Governor's wife, Mrs. Rockefeller. She is in the lobby and she is short a ticket for one of her daughters. Is there a possibility, Mr. Bernstein, that you might have an extra ticket?" I remembered that I still had Gerry's ticket in my pocket. It was for the seat right next to mine.

"Yes, I do, sir. I happen to have a ticket for my wife, but she was unable to use it."

"Is it possible that you would give that ticket to the Governor's daughter?"

"Certainly," I said, and handed him the ticket.

The trooper walked to the back of the hall, out the doors and into the lobby. In a moment, he walked back in with Mrs. Rockefeller and several young girls. They came forward and he introduced them to me. Mrs. Rockefeller was very thankful and left her daughter with me, since she was going to sit beside me in the seat I had reserved for Gerry. I believe the beautiful young girl's name was Winnie and she looked to be 10 or 12 years old. The bell rang and people began to take their seats. The opening act I had booked was the Briarwood Singers, a folk act. I had booked them because they had very little equipment, so it would be easy to re-set the stage for the Beatles. The Briarwood Singers were a good group, but unfortunately no one cared. After they did their 20 minutes, there was a short intermission.

In the row in front of us was a young girl of about 13 who had a cast on her leg. As I was settling into my seat for the opening act, I had asked her what her name was and she told me it was Kelly. At intermission, I leaned over and whispered to Kelly, "Would you like to meet the Beatles?" When she recovered from the shock, she said, "Yes!" so I took her and Winnie and we proceeded to the dressing room.

Mal Evans, who was the Beatles' security man (and the nicest guy), knocked on the door and we were admitted. I saw Brian first.

"Brian, how are you?" I asked, as we shook hands.

"I'm tired, Sid."

"I can imagine," I replied. Turning to the girls, who were quite poised for their age, considering how excited they must have been, I made some preliminary introductions. "Brian, this is Winnie Rockefeller, the Governor's daughter, and this is Kelly."

"How do you do, young ladies?" he said and shook their hands.

"Brian, would it be possible for Kelly and Winnie to meet the boys and perhaps get their autographs?"

"Certainly, Sid, go right ahead."

We went farther into the room where the Beatles were sitting in their shirtsleeves, tuning their instruments, drinking sodas and eating some of the fruit I had provided.

John came over and joked around with the kids, and signed Kelly's cast and Winnie's program.

"Ringo, I'd like you to meet Winnie and Kelly. Girls, this is Ringo Starr."

He made a funny face at them and had them giggling. He also signed Kelly's cast and Winnie's program.

I could almost hear the pounding of those two young girls' hearts.

Paul was next. "How are you?" he greeted them, and signed his name.

George signed his name and wished Kelly well with her recovery.

I was so pleased to have been able to give these two girls an experience that they would never forget and could perhaps one day relate to their grandchildren.

"Thanks, guys, I appreciate this. I'll see you later! Have a great show!" The girls and I left and returned to our seats. I walked, but I think those two girls floated all the way back to their seats.

The intermission bell rang and everybody rushed back to settle into their seats. As I sat down, I could feel the walls of Carnegie Hall palpitating with excitement. I thought to myself, This is it. The moment of truth. I had first read about this group more than a year ago. I had followed their emergence from the club scene to the music halls and finally to the largest venues in Great Britain. I had seen them fight their way into the music pop charts in England and then, like a tidal wave, flood the charts. I had agonized with Brian over the lack of airplay in the U.S. and rejoiced with him when the Beatles had finally replicated the overwhelming acceptance in the States as they had done in Britain. I had heard the music on the radio and on records and I knew that these boys were great songwriters, destined to have their songs live forever.

The only thing left for me was to experience the Beatles performing live in a concert venue. The live performance is the decisive factor in determining an act's ultimate value for a promoter. I had been in the music business now for more than 20 years. I knew that clever producers and audio engineers using state-of-the-art equipment in a recording studio could make a marginal act sound decent, and then take a decent act and make them sound good. The only way that you knew if a singing act really had it was to hear a live performance. An act standing in front of a live audience has nowhere to hide and no studio tricks to fall back on. They either have it or they don't. It's that simple.

Carnegie Hall was packed. You could not have squeezed in another person. The people in the folding chairs were so close to the Beatles' setup that Carnegie Hall had the intimate feel of a small club. That intimacy just fed the excitement. The proximity of the audience to the group was such that I knew the boys would get immediate feedback and be able to connect with the audience.

The MC said, "Ladies and gentlemen...The Beatles!" The four boys ran onto the stage dressed in their mod suits. The welcome from the audience was something that I had never experienced before. The screaming was ear-splitting. It took them about a minute to get ready, and they began.

For the next 34 minutes, the Beatles created sheer magic. They were so tight as a group, their musicianship honed by thousands of hours of playing together. Their anticipation of each other and the space they gave each other as members of a precisely tuned team was awesome. Their singing was spectacular. The blend of their voices was as if they were brothers born of the same mother. The combination of the songwriting, the musicianship and the singing was something I had never experienced before.

The audience seemed to feel the same way that I did. I felt that the screaming and the deafening applause could be heard all over Manhattan and the rest of the boroughs.

As soon as they ended their last song, the Beatles were spirited out to waiting cars and driven back to the Plaza. There were no encores or curtain calls. They just played their songs, bowed once and left. It was enough.

After the first concert, Abe came over to me and said, "Sid, are you kidding me? This is music? Everybody is crazy!"

Abe just didn't get it. He had been brought up on the music of Benny Goodman, Glen Miller and Frank Sinatra. Although he was very pleased that I was able to produce his requisite 300 tickets, Abe simply did not understand the impact of the Beatles' music or the concert.

I just smiled at Abe, motioned to the crowd, and said, "Those four boys have changed the music business forever, Abe."

For the next hour, the Carnegie Hall staff cleared the house and prepared for the next show. Since the Beatles had left the building, the assembled press, of which I think there were at least 350 present, besieged me with questions:

"How did you learn about the group, Sid?"

"When did you contact them, Sid?"

"What's your impression of the Beatles, Mr. Bernstein?"

"Mr. Bernstein, tell us— what was the deal you made with them?"

I did my best to answer each question, but I couldn't spend too much time with them because it was time to seat the crowd waiting for the next show.

The Carnegie Hall staff and the police did a fantastic job. They cleared the house, got it cleaned up and got the second show's audience into their seats. By now, we were running two hours late. We brought the Beatles back into the building at 10:30 p.m., spiriting them in through a cordon of police and heavy security. I had real concerns about the lateness of the hour. The next day was a school day and I didn't want to be responsible for kids sleeping in and missing school. At the pace we were going, I knew that the late-show audience would not leave Carnegie Hall until midnight.

When I visited the boys and Brian in the dressing room before the second show, I found them relaxed, drinking sodas, kidding around, but understandably tired. I complimented them on the incredible show they had put on and commented on how their American fans had raved afterwards. I told them that people outside were still trying to find tickets!

"You guys own New York," I said to them. "You know, I met Al Aronowitz, who's an important New York rock critic, in the lobby and he told me, 'Sid, you're making history here today.'"

The boys, by that time, were familiar with Al Aronowitz and they had become friendly with him as well. They just couldn't believe that Al had said that to me. They were very modest, even after witnessing the fervor of their fans.

I thanked the boys and told them to have a great show and wished them well on their trip to Florida, where they were going the next day. They were excited to be going.

"I'll see you soon," I said, shaking hands with each of them.

Brian walked me out of the dressing room. Clasping my hand, he said, "Sid, thanks for everything."

"No, Brian, thank *you*!" I said. I knew that our friendship was cemented and felt we would do other historic things together. Brian was a very likeable gentleman, enduring the stress of his responsibilities with great grace.

"I'll talk to you soon, Brian."

"Yes, Sid, I'll look forward to that."

I went back into Carnegie Hall. The Briarwood Singers had warmed up the late crowd, which was already at fever pitch. The bell rang and everyone was seated. At 11:15 PM, one hour and forty-five minutes later than scheduled, the Beatles came out and proceeded to whip that late-night audience into a frenzy. The screaming was so loud, I thought I was going to be rendered permanently deaf.

I was so impressed with the Beatles' professionalism. They were young men full of energy and enthusiasm, but they had a backbreaking, whirlwind schedule of constant travel, and many pressures and obligations. Their first day in New York had been spent meeting record executives and answering questions from the press. Then for the next two days at Ed Sullivan's CBS studio, they rehearsed and prepared to appear in front of the largest American TV audience in history. On Monday, after having appeared on the *Sullivan* show, the boys finally had a chance to rest. On Tuesday morning, they were off on a train to do a warm-up concert in Washington, D.C. Then they dashed back to New York and were now doing the two shows for me.

They had an exhausting week and yet their second show was as good as their first. The Beatles played the same music and connected with this audience just as they had with the first. I think the additional 300 people sitting on the stage really gave them energy. Exactly 34 minutes after they started, they made their quick bows to the audience, were out the stage door and whisked away to the Plaza, accompanied as always by Brian Epstein.

When I got home from Carnegie Hall, it was well past midnight. I was astonished to find dozens of kids sitting on those cement balustrades waiting for me. What now? I thought. The concert's over! They can't be waiting to get tickets!

"Do you have any ticket stubs, Mr. Bernstein?" the kids implored.

"No, I don't," I answered.

"Did you shake hands with the Beatles, Mr. Bernstein?"

"Yes, I did."

"Have you washed your hands yet?"

"Well, not since I shook hands with the Beatles."

"Can we please shake your hand?"

I shook the hand of each and every kid who was there waiting for me and I hoped that, in some small way, it made up for their not being able to attend either of the concerts.

I went upstairs and related the entire evening's events to Gerry. "This is a once in a lifetime thing," I told her. "It's amazing." I went to sleep with the now-familiar and wonderful music of the Beatles resonating in my head.

The next morning, I picked up the newspapers. They all extolled the Beatles concerts. History had indeed been made in New York during the past week, and I was hailed as the man who had brought the Beatles to the U.S. And, I knew that it was just going to get better.

For days after the Carnegie Hall concerts, kids kept coming to my West 12th Street apartment building wanting to talk to the man who had brought the Beatles to America, wanting to shake the hand of the man who had shaken the hands of the Beatles. I marveled at the power of those four boys from Liverpool. They had made me into an overnight celebrity.

I didn't have time to relax and enjoy my triumph; I had two more concerts at Carnegie Hall coming up in the next eight days.

The Shirley Bassey concert was just three days away and it was not going to sell out. Shirley's limited fan following in New York and lack of a hit record were the main factors in the low ticket sales. I had been a little too hasty in making the Shirley Bassey date. I decided to accept that we would lose some money, but it wouldn't be terrible.

On the other hand, the Tony Bennett/Count Basie concert was doing well. Nat Posnick assured me that we were going to have a sellout and that I needn't worry about it.

Shirley Bassey's concert was an artistic triumph even though Carnegie Hall was only half full. Shirley was simply thrilling in concert. She reminded everyone of a young, dynamic Judy Garland. Shirley had a great voice, beauty and a fabulous stage presence. When she finished, the half-filled house created applause that was almost as loud as if the hall had been filled. The audience loved her, and the stage was filled with flowers. People just kept bringing flowers to her as she took her bows. I was proud that I had brought her to Carnegie Hall. Later in her career, Shirley sang the theme song to the James Bond *Goldfinger* movie. It was a huge hit, and she enjoyed a long and profitable, if not superstar, career.

Six days later, Tony Bennett and Count Basie performed to a soldout Carnegie Hall. The Count did a 15- or 20-minute warm-up and then he said, "Ladies and gentlemen, please welcome my friend, Tony Bennett." Tony then came out to tumultuous applause. His recording of *I Left My Heart in San Francisco* had been a top 10 record. His albums were selling, and he was playing concerts all over the world to packed houses. His career was in full bloom.

He and Count Basie put on a wonderful show. During the performance, Tony told the audience how honored he was to work with Count Basie and his great band. The Count acknowledged Tony, and everyone in the audience got to see the teaming of two great artists. There were several encores, but we finished before 11 o'clock when the overtime charges kicked in.

After the show, I went to Count Basie's dressing room and expressed my appreciation.

"Sid, anytime and anywhere, I'd do this again in a heartbeat," the Count said.

"Thanks, Count. I'll keep that in mind," I said. I paid him and left.

By the time I got to Tony's dressing room, the crowd of well-wishers was beginning to disperse. When I approached Tony, he hugged me and said, "Thanks, Sid. Thanks. You did it again."

"No, Tony, *you* did it. It was really a great evening. It was very special."

For some reason, when I had booked this concert with Tony, we had neglected to talk about money. I leaned over to him and whispered, "Tony, what do I owe you? I want to pay you."

It was customary to pay the artist right after the engagement. I expected that he would charge me between $5,000 and $6,500, even though his customary fee was $10,000 a night, because he knew that I would be paying Count Basie as well. He looked at me and said, "All I asked was that you get me a great band. We're even."

"What?" I said, not fully understanding.

"Sid, all I asked you for was to get me a great band," he repeated.

"But, Tony, we did very well! We sold out! I have to pay you. We just never got to discuss it before now. I want to pay you."

"Sid," he said indignantly. "I had told you that I just wanted a great band, and you gave me that. That's it! Thanks!" With that, Tony turned to talk to some of his guests.

I was amazed. It was really unheard of for a performer not to get paid for a concert appearance, unless it was a charity benefit. As a promoter, I had never experienced anything like this before. What Tony did reminded me of the old Italian adage which says, If someone offers you something, take it with two hands. I took it with gratitude.

Tony Bennett is a great man.

On May 3, 1964, Adam Bernstein, our first child, was born. I was almost 46 years old and I was happy and thrilled to finally be a father. I now had an outlet for all the loving feelings I had for children. I could not thank Gerry enough. I didn't want to miss any time with Adam, so I now included a carriage during my wanderings around the neighborhood. I spent lots of time walking through Washington Square Park and the neighborhood around the New York University campus with the two most beautiful people I knew: my wife and my newborn son. Washington Square is a city park, not overly large, but it has many benches and attracts a varied and interesting mix of people of all ages, ethnicities, races and cultures. It wasn't long before I became reasonably well-known in Washington Square Park. The college kids began to trail me like I was the Pied Piper. They would ask me about my next project or about the Beatles or the Stones, and who was the next new group from England that I was going to import.

The Rolling Stones concert sold out immediately. The frenzy was not as intense as with the Beatles, but by then the Rolling Stones weren't a secret to American teenagers and they were in demand. As we got closer to the sold-out concert, the phones began to ring incessantly and the kids were back to waiting for me at the front of the building, just like when the Beatles played. The kids wanting to go see the Rolling Stones were rougher and tougher-looking than the Beatles fans were, and there were more boys than girls in the crowd.

When the Stones arrived at the airport, a lot of kids and a small gathering of press were there to meet them. But the reception was nothing like the frenzy that surrounded the Beatles' arrival in New York.

The Stones stayed at the Park Sheraton, right across the street from Carnegie Hall, and I met them on the day of their two performances. This time I booked one show for 2 PM and the other for 7 PM so that we would not run behind like we did when the Beatles played.

I got to Carnegie Hall early, and the Rolling Stones were already there doing a sound check. I introduced myself to Andrew Loog Oldham and the group. They were all very nice boys and not nearly as wild as the British press had portrayed them. Charlie Watts and Brian Jones were particularly friendly and they bombarded me with questions about where to have a good time in New York. They had probably heard from the Beatles that I knew the best places to eat.

The Stones did a great show. I noticed that the Stones' fans were a blue jean/motorcycle jacket crowd. They were much more physical in their enthusiasm; when the Stones played, they jumped up and down and stood on the seats. It was definitely a rougher, tougher crowd. After the first show, I went backstage to tell the Stones that I was impressed with their energy and showmanship. They appreciated that and seemed anxious to please. I offered to take them next door where there was a German-style beer and sandwich pub, but only Brian Jones seemed interested.

Brian and I exited Carnegie Hall through a backstage door, which was only a few feet from the pub. We sat in the most out-of-the way booth we could find. Brian had his back to the front door and window. After just a few minutes, I could see several young faces pressed up against the front window panes of the pub. In no time at all, the number of faces multiplied, as if someone had made an announcement on a loudspeaker that one of the Rolling Stones was in the pub. The crowd of onlookers swelled even more and some came into the restaurant. When Brian and I had first come in, there had been only a handful of patrons, and now, in no time flat, the restaurant was mobbed. The manager, a big burly guy, told his staff to lock the door and allow no one else inside. The crowd pressing on the windows continued to grow, and I feared the glass would shatter. The restaurant manager came over to Brian and me and suggested in not too gentle terms that we leave and do so immediately. They unlocked the door to let us out and I realized that the only way we could get into Carnegie Hall was to go around to the front. We were going to have to negotiate our way through some of the remainder of the crowd that had left the first concert and some of the new crowd that was assembling for the next show. I motioned for Brian to follow me, and we made a mad dash across Seventh Avenue to the Park Sheraton. I figured if we could get into the lobby of the hotel, we would be safe. A mob of kids ran after us. They were all grabbing at Brian's beautiful strawberry-blond hair. Had we not made it into the hotel when we did, the crowd would have rendered Brian Jones bald. However, we did make it safely through the doors of the hotel, and security prevented the kids from getting inside. I stayed in the hotel for a while, and then went back to Carnegie Hall. Later, police and security escorted Brian back into Carnegie. The crowds at the evening show were even more unruly and raucous than they had been for the afternoon show. After the show ended at 9 PM, some members of the press were interviewing me when Mrs. Satescu came over and asked me, "Mr. Bernstein, can I speak to you in private, please?"

"Yes, Mrs. Satescu, what can I do for you?"

"Mr. Bernstein, the pictures on the walls were shaking. The kids were jumping on our plush seats and the armrests. They were rude and disobedient to the ushers, and you are lucky, Mr. Bernstein, that no one was hurt here today. Please do not bring any of your presentations here again!"

She was livid and practically shaking. I tried to say something that might placate her, but nothing I said calmed her. She just kept saying, "Mr. Bernstein, please do not come back to Carnegie Hall." She didn't want me there anymore, period. I was very unhappy because she and the people at Carnegie Hall had been very good to me, and together we had had a string of successful and highly acclaimed concerts.

"Mrs. Satescu, I promise you this will never happen again. I just did not expect this kind of enthusiasm from the crowd. It will not happen again, I assure you."

"I know, Mr. Bernstein, because you will not be here." She was very angry and adamant.

I loved Carnegie Hall and the people who worked there. The tiff I had with Mrs. Satescu disturbed me. Fortunately, I had begun negotiating with other venues. The word was out to the managers and agents in Great Britain that American audiences filled concert halls to hear British groups. The British Invasion was now in full swing, and I was the lead "General." If you want your act to play the United States, Sid Bernstein is the man to arrange it.

When the Dave Clark Five became available to me, I was anxious to bring them to the States, but I needed a new venue since I was persona non grata for the time being at Carnegie Hall. I was also in preliminary negotiations with the Animals, the Kinks, Herman's Hermits, the Moody Blues, Manfred Mann, and Gerry and the Pacemakers. Eventually, I signed them all and had the privilege to be the first person to present 11 of the top 13 British rock acts in the United States. It was imperative for me to find a new venue to present all these shows. The aftermath of the Rolling Stones concert had taught me that the kids could get you thrown out of almost anywhere, so I also needed to secure back-up venues.

The Paramount Theatre, one of my old stomping grounds, had ceased to function as an everyday venue. Instead, it was being rented for special events and concerts. I went back to my old friend Gene Pleshette.

"Sid!" he greeted me warmly. "You're really doing it with these bands from England! I'm happy for you!"

"Thanks, Gene, but I need help."

"What's up?

"To make a long story short, they don't want me in Carnegie Hall anymore, and I need a new venue."

"Why is that?"

"I'm not really sure, Gene. Maybe they don't like rock and roll. You know Carnegie's a venerable old hall, and rock and roll is not what you call venerable."

He laughed. "I understand, Sid. We're here and we're available. My daughter Suzanne loves rock and roll. Let's go."

We made the deal, and I had the Paramount for the Dave Clark Five. Even though the Paramount was a bigger venue than Carnegie Hall, we sold out. In fact, we had to turn a few thousand away. The Dave Clark Five was a nice, clean-cut group more on the style of the Beatles, and the event ran smoothly. Gene Pleshette was not a guy to be disobeyed. In Yiddish, we call it being a no *chochmas* guy. No fooling around. What you saw was what you got. When Gene told his ushers and staff to control the kids, that's just what they did. There was no jumping on the seats at the New York Paramount.

Next to invade the States from Britain was Eric Burdon and the Animals. Their record *The House of the Rising Sun* was a gigantic hit. Practically every time I changed the station in my car, if I didn't hear a Beatles record, I heard Eric Burdon and the Animals singing *The House of the Rising Sun*. I got carried away with the enthusiasm for the Animals and made a bad business decision. Instead of booking them into the Paramount for one or two days, I rented the venue for a week, thinking that the hit record would generate sellouts or near-sellouts every day.

The Animals sold out for the first two dates, but by then they had reached their audience. They were neither the Beatles nor the Rolling Stones and attendance diminished daily from then on. The Paramount had given me a good deal, but not good enough to make up for five days of a half-filled venue.

I decided to move to the Academy of Music on 14th Street. The theatre there had 200 fewer seats than the Paramount. The Skouras Organization, the owner of the theatre, gave me a very good price. We presented the other British Invaders at the Academy of Music: The Kinks, Herman's Hermits, the Moody Blues and Gerry and the Pacemakers. The Academy of Music was a few blocks from my apartment.

When Denise Bernstein, our first daughter, was born on November 26, 1965, I could get home in no time flat to be with my growing family. I enjoyed strolling with my kids through the neighborhood and particularly around Washington Square Park. Many young people frequent the park and music played by aspiring musicians emanates throughout, competing for the ears of the visitors. The kids loved Adam and Denise and my beautiful wife, and of course I was known as the man who had brought the Beatles, the Rolling Stones and all the others to America. The kids would always ask me during my walks in the park, "What's next, Mr. Bernstein? Who are you presenting next?"

Chapter 12: THE MOST IMPORTANT ROCK CONCERT...EVER

I HAD AN IDEA IN MY HEAD AND BEGAN TO MAKE IT A REALITY in late October of 1964. I called Jim Thompson, the head of Shea Stadium, the baseball home of the New York Mets, built as part of the World's Fairgrounds and owned by the City of New York.

"Jim, this is Sid Bernstein. I'm the guy who brought the Beatles to New York last February."

"Yes, Sid, I know who you are. How can I help you?"

"Well, Jim, I'm going to bring the Beatles back as soon as I can, and I was considering presenting them in Shea Stadium."

"Sid, we have never had a concert here before, and we have 55,000 seats. Are you aware of that? Fifty-five thousand seats!"

"Yes, I know that you have that many seats, but I think the Beatles can fill them."

"Okay, here's what's involved," Jim said. "First of all, you will need a stage because we do not have a stage that can accommodate your needs. Secondly, you'll need insurance. You'll have to secure that yourself because ours won't cover you. Also, Sid, you have to pick a date when the Mets are on the road and your date must allow for several days after the concert just in case there is any damage to our grass. Our first concern is that the field be in good playing shape because that's a League rule. So we need to be ready to make major repairs to the field just in case it gets damaged."

"I hear you, Jim. Could you look at your schedule and tell me what date would work for you?"

"That'll only take a moment. Hold on and let me take a look," Jim said, as he leafed through some papers. "Sid, the Mets will be on the road the second week in August for an extended road trip. We could do it in the middle of August."

"Nothing sooner, Jim?"

"Well, there is another extended road trip in mid-June. It's not as long as the one in August, but we could do it. You might want to take a date in that time frame."

"No," I answered immediately. "The kids are all still in school and they've got finals and graduation. No, I think August is better."

Then, looking at my calendar, I asked him, "Jim, how about Sunday, August 15 at 8 o'clock in the evening?"

"Yes, Sid, that would be fine with us, as long as you supply the stage, the insurance and the extra security. I forgot that, Sid, this thing is going to need extra security."

"I know, Jim. I'm always concerned about security and we'll have more than enough. Be assured."

"Good."

"Now, Jim, what is this going to cost me?"

He thought for a moment and said, "Well, we've never done this before, but how does a guarantee of $50,000 plus a percentage sound to you?"

"Jim, first of all, I can't give you a percentage because I've got to give that to the group. Second of all, I know that the stage is going to cost me a bundle, so is the insurance and then we have to get into the security issues. On top of all that, I need a reserve for your grass repairs should they be required. If I give you $50,000, I won't make anything for myself. I can't pay $50,000. If that's your price, I need to look elsewhere, maybe Yankee Stadium."

"Okay, Sid, I get your drift. What is your budget for the venue?"

"I was thinking more in the neighborhood of $25,000. At that number for the venue, I think I could do it."

He thought for a moment and said, "Okay, $25,000 guaranteed gets you the venue, ushers, lights, dressing rooms and scoreboard. You take care of the insurance, stage and extra security, and we have a deal."

"Great, Jim. Put a hold on August 15th, and I'll get back to you in a few days."

"Okay, Sid. You have the date. Good luck."

The next call I made was to Brian Epstein in London. He had established a large office to handle what had become a major enterprise. A secretary spoke to me while Brian finished another call.

"Sid, how are you? It's Brian."

"I'm fine, Brian, and how are you?"

"My life is so hectic, Sid. I am getting calls from all over the world for the boys and requests for endorsements and the like. And by the way, Sid, thank you so much for sending those book review sections to my mother! She does so enjoy them!"

"It's my pleasure, Brian. Send her my regards and assure her that I will continue sending them. And how are the boys?"

"Working hard. Recording in the studio, working locally and doing a lot of TV. The studio work is just wonderful. George Martin (the Beatles' record producer) tells me that the musical growth of the boys never fails to astonish him. And, the song writing is resulting in hit music! It's a good but very hectic time. I've also begun to sign some new acts, Sid, so we'll have to talk about bringing them to America. Actually I was thinking of calling you. To what do I owe the pleasure of this call?"

I got right to it. "Brian, when would you consider bringing the boys back to the States?"

"Not until next summer. That is the earliest we could come."

I breathed a sign of relief. My timing was perfect.

"We made history ten months ago, Brian. Let's do it again. We have a baseball stadium in New York called Shea Stadium, and it's on the grounds of the most recent World's Fair in Queens. It has 55,000 seats and I would like to present the Beatles there. It would be a history-making event."

"Fifty-five thousand seats, Sid? Do you really think that the boys can fill 55,000 seats?"

"Absolutely, Brian. If I didn't think so, I would never present this to you."

"Tell me, Sid, what would you sell the tickets for?"

"I was thinking of $4.50, $5.00 and $5.65."

"And you really think we can fill a 55,000-seat stadium at those prices? Amazing!"

"Yes, I am so sure that we can fill it that I will pay you $10.00 for every unsold seat."

He laughed and said, "Even though the top ticket price is $5.65, you would be willing to give us $10.00 for every unsold ticket? Why would you do that?"

"Because I know there will be no unsold tickets. We will have a sellout and the boys will gross $300,000 and be able to clear $150,000 for one night's work. It's never been done before. It'll make history. What I am saying is that I will guarantee the Beatles $100,000 against fifty percent of the gross to play Shea Stadium in New York on August 15, 1965."

"That sounds fabulous! Quite astonishing, really! Let me talk to the boys, and I'll get back to you tomorrow."

"I'll look forward to that, Brian, and remember me to Queenie."

"I shall do that. Good-bye."

The next day, as promised, Brian called.

"I talked to the boys and they are keen on coming back to New York. We require only two things. One, the $100,000 guarantee is fine, but we would like sixty percent of the gross instead of fifty percent and, two, we will need a $50,000 deposit up front."

"Agreed," I said immediately.

I expected this from Brian. A good manager would want half the guarantee up front and would always push for a little more. Brian was a great manager and had the hottest act in the world, so I was prepared to give him whatever he asked.

"When would I be required to give you the $50,000?"

"Well, as soon as possible."

"My money is tied up at the moment. What would be the latest date I could give you the money?"

"Investments and the like, Sid?"

"Yes, investments. But I will be liquid in the not-too-distant future."

He thought for a moment. "Sid, I will be at the Waldorf-Astoria on January 10th. Why don't we meet then, and you can give me the deposit."

"Okay, that's perfect. I'll have no trouble giving you the $50,000 in January."

"Okay, Sid. We'll firm it up in New York come January."

"Brian, can I advertise the Shea concert?"

"No. We'll need the $50,000 in hand before you advertise."

"Okay, how about PR, publicity and mentioning it in interviews that I seem to be sitting for with increasing frequency these days?"

"No. Please no publicity, no ads, no interviews until we firm up in January."

"Okay, Brian, but can I talk about it?"

"Of course! How can I stop you from talking about it? That wouldn't be fair now, would it?" I could see the smile on his face.

That was my saving grace. I wasn't sure exactly how yet, but I knew that the okay to talk about the concert would somehow get me the $50,000 I needed to give Brian.

"Great, Brian, that's all I need to know. You have my pledge. No ads, PR or interviews. I'll see you at the Waldorf in January, and I'll give you the $50,000 then. Tell the boys I'm really excited and looking forward to seeing them soon."

"I shall, Sid, and I can tell you they are just as excited as you are. They love New York, and playing before 55,000 is a heady prospect. We have a deal. I'll see you in New York this January."

"Bye, Brian. God bless."

When I hung up with Brian that day, I knew that we would once again make history.

I called Jim Thompson at Shea Stadium and told him, "Jim, we're good for the August 15th date. It's absolutely a secret. We can't do any PR or publicity yet, but that'll only be for about two months, so bear with me. Just hold the date for me and mum's the word."

"You got it, Sid. Call me when you want to move forward."

"It'll be sometime in January. Is that okay?"

"No problem, January is fine. And happy holidays to you!"

"And, to you, too, Jim."

The first two elements, the Beatles and the date at Shea, were set. Next, I had to see to the insurance, the stage and, most importantly, the $50,000 deposit, which I of course, did not have. I called Chip Munk, the top lighting and sound consultant of the day. Over the years, Chip has created stages, lights and sets for most of the major rock acts.

I told Chip that I was going to put on an all-star show at Shea Stadium sometime in mid-summer. I explained to him that Shea Stadium did not have a stage sufficient to my needs. I told him that I envisioned the stage somewhere around second base on the diamond so that everyone in the ballpark would be able to see. I also explained that I thought we could use the stadium lights, so additional lighting would not be necessary. When he asked me who was going to appear, I was purposely vague and said that the acts had not been firmed up yet, which was the truth. Finally, I asked him for a ballpark number (no pun intended!) of what he thought the stage would cost so I could plug the number into my budget. His almost immediate response was $10,000 to design and erect the stage. I told him that as soon as the acts were firmed up, I would get back to him. He said we had plenty of time and that I should call him when I was ready.

I then called some insurance friends that I had and explained the situation. I sensed immediately that insurance for this event was not going to be easy. It took five weeks before my friend Jerry Rosen made contact with Lloyd's of London, which finally agreed to issue the insurance. The cost was $10,000, and I was happy to get it.

Immediately after starting the process that would result in Lloyd's insuring the concert, I turned my attention to the $50,000 deposit money. I always knew that if push came to shove, I could go to either Abe Margolies or Walter Hyman for the money. For some reason, I vetoed that in my mind. I wanted to do this on my own and not go to my friends. It was just a feeling that I had.

A day or two after my conversation with Brian, I was pushing baby Adam's carriage in Washington Square Park when a group of kids converged on me. "Mr. Bernstein," they began. "What's next? Who are you going to present next?"

"The Beatles at Shea Stadium...August 15th," I whispered.

The word spread like wildfire and in a moment I was surrounded. Pandemonium erupted in the park.

"Mr. Bernstein, can I give you the money now?"

"Mr. Bernstein, how many tickets can I buy?"

"Mr. Bernstein, I don't have any money with me right now! Where can I send it, Mr. Bernstein? Can I please sit up front?"

The requests were coming from everywhere.

"Listen, kids. I don't even have tickets printed yet. We'll let you know in a few days. I promise I'll let you know when and where you can get tickets."

I took Adam home and took myself to the Old Chelsea Post Office on 18th Street between Seventh and Eighth Avenues. I filled out some papers, paid $4.00 and was given the key for Post Office Box 21.

I strolled back home and said to Gerry, "It's so beautiful outside, I think I'll take Adam back out and you can rest." That was just fine with her.

I went back into the park. The minute I entered, a mob of kids surrounded me. All they wanted to know was how they could get tickets for the Beatles at Shea. The grapevine was in full operation.

"Okay, kids, what you have to do is send a check or money order to Box 21 at the Old Chelsea Post Office on 18th Street in New York. Please don't send me cash. Make out the check to Sid Bernstein. The prices are $4.50, $5.00 and $5.65, and make sure you let us know how many tickets you want."

They were all passing around pens and small pieces of paper and zealously taking down the information. The next day, I went into the park again, and again I was besieged. I repeated the information and the kids wrote it down. I could see that this was a different group of kids than the day before, so I knew that the grapevine was working overtime.

During the next few weeks, as Gerry, Adam and I walked in the park and around the neighborhood, kids would ask me for the P.O. box number. The number of kids approaching me wasn't large, but it was steady.

"Can I have that address for the Beatles tickets again, Mr. Bernstein?" they would ask and I would oblige.

Three weeks exactly to the day that I had gotten the okay from Brian Epstein on the August 15th date, I went to the post office to see what was in the P.O. box. As I walked over from the 12th Street apartment, I thought to myself, if I have 50 pieces of mail, I'll do a jig right there in the post office, and I won't care who is there to see it. If I have 100 pieces, I will celebrate by getting drunk, which for me was a big deal since I never drank at all. The amount of mail in the P.O. box would be an indication to me that even without ads or publicity, word of mouth could generate a demand for tickets to see the Beatles.

As I walked up the steps of the post office, I realized that I had forgotten the key to Box 21. When I looked through the frosted glass that was the door to the P.O. box, I could see that it was jammed and I got ready to do my jig and look silly. To the right of the P.O. box was the inquiry office of the Post Office station. There was a fellow manning the inquiry office.

"Sir," I said, getting his attention, "I seem to have forgotten the key to my post office box. I know you're closing soon, and I don't think I have enough time to run home and get back with the key. It seems that my post office box is full of mail. I do have my driver's license, and I could show that to you."

"What's your post office box number?" he asked.

"Number 21. And my name is Sid Bernstein."

"You're Sid Bernstein!" he exclaimed.

"Yes," I said.

He called across the post office to a giant of a man who was stuffing boxes. "Hey, Eddie, Box 21 is here!"

I wondered what he was doing.

Eddie yelled, "Did you say Box 21, Mack?" and he started to saunter across the post office floor toward me.

"Yeah," said Mack from the inquiry office. "Box 21, Sid Bernstein," and he motioned toward me.

I pulled out my license and showed it to Mack.

By now Eddie had come across the floor and was looking down at me.

"Hey, buddy, what's your racket?" he inquired.

"What do you mean?"

"Well, you gotta lot of mail!" said Eddie. "What do you do?"

"I'm in the mail order business."

Mack said, "You got a hot item, buddy! What are you selling? You got some hot item!"

"What do you mean?"

Mack looked at Eddie and said, "Eddie, I'm going to need some help. Come on in here and give me a hand, will ya?"

Eddie went into the inquiry room and he and Mack emerged with three huge duffel bags. Bigger than the one I had in the Army.

"What are these guys doing?" I thought. They must be making a mistake.

"Wait a minute guys. That's a mistake. I'm Box 21." For a minute I thought they had gotten me confused with the phone company or the electric company because I had always in the past paid my utility and phone bills to a post office box at this same post office.

"It's a mistake, guys," I repeated.

Eddie opened one bag, and Mack another, and both took out a handful of letters.

"Look here," Eddie said, "these letters are all addressed to Sid Bernstein, P.O. Box 21. This is all your mail."

"That's right," said Mack, holding up his handful of envelopes.

I was flabbergasted. In my wildest dreams and imagination, I had never expected this.

"Look, guys, I have a bad back. Do I have time to go home and get my car? I'm only six blocks from here."

"Sure," said Mack, "but be quick. We're closing soon."

I flew back to the garage in the apartment building. Fortunately, since it was a Saturday, the garage was empty, so the attendant was able to get my car quickly. I sped back to the post office. I backed the car up to the loading dock and Eddie and Mack helped me load the three bags into the trunk. I was elated. I kept saying to myself, I don't believe this! I don't believe this!

When I got to the apartment house, the doorman helped me unload the bags, which I left in the lobby while I parked the car. The doorman helped me lug the bags into the elevator and I took them upstairs. I dragged them off the elevator and into the apartment.

As I pulled the three extremely heavy bags into the apartment, Gerry gave me a strange look and asked, "What's this, Sid?"

"Gerry, I don't believe it. This is mail that we got at the P.O. box I rented at the post office."

"Oh, come on, Sid. It must be some mistake."

"No, Gerry, look," I said, as I started to remove some envelopes from one of the bags. "It's all addressed to me and look—checks and money orders." There were even coins jiggling in some of the envelopes, and I realized that many of the kids I had given the post office box number to did not have checking accounts and had probably never bought a money order in their young lives. We were going to find a lot of cash, too.

I threw the mailbags behind our living room couch and sat down to catch my breath.

"Gerry, this is unbelievable! How are we going to process all this mail?"

She thought a moment and said, "Let's call Kathleen and see if she and some of her friends can help us."

"Great idea, Gerry," I said and I called Kathleen immediately.

Kathleen was a student nurse who sometimes baby-sat Adam for us. She lived across the street in the residence of St. Vincents nursing school. The young student nurses all vied for the opportunity to baby-sit for the Bernsteins, because they thought that one night while they were baby-sitting, a phone call would come and it could be Mick Jagger, Paul McCartney or another rock star. We never had trouble getting a baby-sitter.

When Kathleen finally came to the communal telephone on her floor, I said, "Kathleen, it's Mr. Bernstein. I have some work that would require you and eight or ten of your fellow students."

"What kind of work, Mr. Bernstein?" she asked me.

"Well, for one thing, it requires opening a lot of mail. It won't be very hard work and we'll all sit around a table and do it together. I'll pay everybody baby-sitting wages."

"Sure, Mr. Bernstein. Let me talk to the girls. I'm sure we can help you."

"Thanks, Kathleen, I could sure use the help."

The following Monday evening, Kathleen showed up at our apartment with seven of her friends. We set up a system whereby everyone sat around a table in the living room. Two of the girls would slit open the envelopes. One person handled checks; another money orders; a third handled five- and ten-dollar bills; another handled singles and still another took care of the coins. We filled out index cards for each order. If the envelope had a clear return address we just wrote the number of tickets on the envelope. It was tedious and time-consuming. We did it every night, five days a week, and it took us almost three months to go through all the envelopes. Most of the orders were for the better seats. When we had filled all those seats, we downgraded the order to the next best seat available. The orders were filled randomly. I didn't have a system in place because I did not expect such a tremendous response for a concert that had no publicity other than word of mouth.

When we reached the sold-out point, we took more than 3,000 orders with money in the envelopes and wrote Return to Sender and mailed them back. We took in $304,000. I never ran an ad, printed a poster, sat for an interview or did any PR. All I did was tell a couple of hundred kids where they could send money if they wanted to see the Beatles at Shea Stadium on a summer night in August. I kept my word to Brian. The mail came from all over the world: Japan, England, Europe, and even behind the Iron Curtain. The grapevine stretched literally around the globe. The power of those four boys was beyond description.

On January 10th, I went to the Waldorf to see Brian. As always, he was very cordial and looked very dapper. He was in a suite, and it seemed to me that he was there alone.

"Sid, how nice to see you," he said.

"Likewise, Brian! How are you?"

"I'm working very hard. When I first started with the Beatles, I never anticipated that it would turn into this! It's rather overwhelming."

I looked at him. I could clearly see that he was under tremendous pressure.

"How is your mother?" I asked.

"Oh, she's quite well, but complains that she never sees me and worries that I am working myself to the bone. And, by the way, you can stop sending her those book review sections. I am able to get them for her, now that I spend so much time in London. It was very nice of you and we both appreciate it. My mother has very fond feelings for you, Sid."

"My pleasure, Brian. Queenie is a lovely lady. Tell me, how are the boys?"

"In the studio presently, which is why I took the time to come over and attend meetings. The music is quite extraordinary, really. They are very excited about coming back to the States this summer."

With that, I handed him a check that I had drawn that morning, written on my account at Citibank.

"Here, Brian."

He took the check and looked at it.

"Sid, there seems to be an error. You were to give me $50,000, and this check is for $100,000."

"Yes, Brian. I've done well, and I thought it best to take care of the guarantee now. It's not a mistake."

"Sid, your investments must have done really well for you!"

"Yes, I'm quite liquid now."

"The boys will certainly be happy to hear of this. How does the Shea concert look?"

"Not to worry, Brian. I don't believe you'll be getting that ten dollars for every unsold seat!"

"You're not going back on your word?" he asked, laughing.

"No, I'm just feeling very good about it."

"Great. As soon as things get less hectic, I want to talk to you about some of these other acts I've signed recently."

"Good, Brian! Anytime you're ready, we can get into that."

I knew how busy he was, so I stood up and we shook hands.

"Send my regards to Queenie and the boys. Tell them I'm looking forward to seeing them in August."

"I shall do that, Sid, and much thanks for the $100,000! The boys will really appreciate that!"

As I left, I pondered the price this man was paying for the ride on the comet he was on. There is a price for everything.

While we were still in the process of counting the money and filling the orders for Shea, Andrew Loog Oldham called from London.

"I want to bring the Stones back on an American tour in the spring, Sid," Andrew said. "Can you promote a New York concert for us in that time frame?"

I looked at my schedule. The Beatles concert was not until August. I knew that the Academy of Music was available and that the Rolling Stones would be a guaranteed sellout.

"Andrew, I think I can do it, but we can't do it in Carnegie Hall because you guys got me thrown out of there!" We both laughed. "I've been using the Academy of Music. It's larger than Carnegie by 400 seats and it's a wonderful theatre."

"Okay, Sid. If you say it's a good place, let's do it. When do you have in mind?"

"May 1st, Andrew. Ten thousand dollars for two shows; how's that?"

"Great, Sid. You got a deal. We'll see you on May 1st, and I'll talk to you or Billy Fields before that."

When I hung up, I thought, Not bad, Sid. Not bad. The Stones in May and the Beatles in August!

During the next few months, I prepared for both the Stones and the Beatles. We did some ads and billboards for the Stones and, as projected, they sold out both shows.

On the day of the concerts, I got to the theatre early and visited with the Rolling Stones. It was amazing to me that the calm and gentlemanly men in the dressing room turned into something completely different for their stage personas. When I left them and Andrew a few minutes before show time, I said, "Listen, guys, take it easy out there. We don't want to get thrown out of this place, too!" They all just waved at me and laughed.

Of course, they didn't take it easy. They did their Rolling Stones thing, which meant Mick Jagger strutting, jumping and dancing around with boundless energy. And, of course, the audience got into it.

The Academy of Music was an old vaudeville theatre which had an orchestra pit separating the audience from the stage. Theatres like that are still found on Broadway and are utilized for musicals like *Les Miserables* and *Phantom of the Opera*. At any rate, the kids at this Stones concert got so excited that they began to rush the stage, trying to leap over the chasm created by the pit. There were so many of them that they overwhelmed the security men, and Billy and I found ourselves flat on our fannies. There were bodies flying all over the place, and a number of the kids fell on top of each other in the pit. Tiny, our 6'6" lead security man, jumped into the pit and started throwing the kids back out. There were bodies flying everywhere. Through some miracle, no one got hurt, but it was scary. Fortunately for the Stones, they had their own security men, who blocked the kids who attacked the stage from the sides. It was really something to behold that day in May of 1965 when the Rolling Stones played the Academy of Music.

We were building up to the Beatles. The workload was fantastic. The hype and demand for tickets was beyond belief, and right in the middle of this extremely hectic time, I got a call from Walter Hyman.

"Sid, I'm out here in the Hamptons vacationing with my family. Some guys took an old French barge and turned it into a discotheque. You have to walk across a gangplank to get onto the barge and into the disco. They have a band playing there called The Rascals and they're fabulous and drawing big crowds. I want you to come up here and see them."

"Walter, are you kidding me? I'm getting ready to do the biggest concert in the history of rock and roll! My wife is pregnant; my mother is sick! I don't know where to go first and you want me to drop everything and come out to the Hamptons (a two-hour drive from Manhattan without summer traffic)? Walter, give me a break!"

"Sid, I'm telling you…these kids are great! And all the rich and beautiful people out here are standing on line to see them play. I saw Senator [Jacob] Javits here last night. Bette Davis is a frequent attendee and Ahmet Ertegun from Atlantic Records comes here all the time and wants to sign them."

"Great, Walter, but I don't have the time. Maybe after the Beatles, but not now. Sorry. Call me after Shea."

The next day, Walter called again.

"Sid, you *have* to come up here. I'll send Mike and my car and you'll be here in no time at all. I told the kids that you're a friend of mine and that I'm going to bring you to see them, and they're all excited. You *have* to come, Sid! Please don't make a liar out of me!"

I begged off again.

The next day, a Monday, as I exited my office, two very strong arms wrapped themselves around me in a vise-like grip and a voice said, "You're coming with me." I was startled for a moment, but as I was maneuvered towards a car, I saw that it was Walter Hyman's Checker limousine. Walter was in the back seat, laughing hysterically. Walter's chauffeur, Mike, shoved me gently into the car.

"You're coming with me to the Hamptons. Don't worry, I cleared it with Gerry, and I promised that I'd get you home at a reasonable hour."

We drove right to The Barge, as the disco was called, and Mike stopped the limo immediately in front of the gangplank. When we got inside, the four members of The Rascals were waiting. There were perhaps six or seven other people in the place. It was the band's night off; the band members, Felix Cavaliere, Eddie Brigati, Dino Danelli and Gene Cornish, were dressed in knickers, shirts with Lord Fauntleroy collars and pilgrim shoes. I thought they looked ridiculous and I thought that Walter was nuts. But then they started to play and sing and I knew immediately why they had become the darlings of the Hamptons summer scene. They were great! They covered songs that other artists had written and previously recorded. But they played and sang in their own style with high energy and great showmanship. I knew that if they could get some original material with hit potential, they could become a major band. They had the intangible "it."

When they finished playing, I talked to the boys for a while, and then Walter drove me back to New York.

Once we were in the car, he began to sell me. "I want to be your partner on this deal. I am crazy about this group. The reaction of the people who come to see them, not just the kids, but the adults, is fantastic!"

He took out his checkbook.

"Here, I'm going to write out a check for $10,000 right now, and if you need more, let me know. I want you to take them into the studio immediately and record them. Make a record."

"Wait a minute, Walter," I said. "Yes, we can be partners. After all, you found the group. But we can get a record company to pay for their recordings, so put away your checkbook. What we really need is a lawyer. I'll tell you what. Get a lawyer and on August 16, the day after the Beatles appear at Shea, we'll meet The Rascals at your apartment with the lawyers, and we'll sign them right then and there. In the meantime, we'll invite them to the Beatles concert."

"Okay, Sid. Consider it done. August the 16th it is. And I have the lawyer. His name is Steve Weiss."

About a month after my meeting with Brian, I got a call from Barry Gotterer of New York City Mayor John Lindsay's office.

"Sid, are you aware the Mayor has stuck his chin out for you on this Beatles concert?"

"Why is that, Barry?"

"Well, Shea Stadium is owned by the city. We had to approve the stadium use for the concert. The Mayor and all of us here on his staff are concerned about security. A group of 55,000 wild-eyed screaming kids represents some challenges in crowd control, and the Mayor wants to make sure it comes off without any hitches and in complete safety."

"I appreciate that, Barry, and I'm grateful to the Mayor for letting the concert go forward. I've built a reputation as someone who is ultra-concerned about security, and the Mayor should have no cause for concern."

"Sid, it would make us more comfortable if during the numerous meetings that you are going to have over the next few months with police, traffic and security people, we could have a representative or two from the Mayor's office along."

"Believe me, it's not necessary, but if you want to tag along, it's fine with me."

I had many meetings about security over the next several months and the Mayor's office always sent a representative. Dick Aurelio was the deputy mayor who attended the most meetings. Dick is a brilliant guy and gave valuable input. He later became a vice president at Time Warner Cable operations.

Our first concern was how were we going to get the Beatles in and out of Shea Stadium quickly and safely. I had numerous conversations with Brian and his staff about that, and slowly a plan began to emerge.

Initially, we thought that we would take the Beatles in limousines under police escort from the Warwick Hotel, where they would be staying, to a Wall Street heliport and fly them directly into Shea Stadium. When we presented that plan to the police, the Mayor's office nixed it immediately. They thought that taking the helicopter into Shea would be too dangerous, particularly if there was a rush of kids to get to the Beatles.

The plan we finally agreed on was that we would use the helicopter with the only difference being that we would land the helicopter in the old World's Fairgrounds, across the way from Shea Stadium. The Beatles and Brian would exit the helicopter and get into a waiting Wells Fargo armored car that would then proceed through the Shea Stadium outfield gates. Once under the stands, the Beatles would run to the umpires' dressing room and prepare for their appearance. The exit plan was that the armored car would wait outside the stadium until the Beatles had completed their last song. As they were taking their bows, the outfield gates would be opened and the armored car would speed right to the stage. The boys would then hop in and the armored car would speed out of the stadium to the waiting helicopter for the short flight back to Manhattan. The security people, the Mayor's office and I felt that once we got them through those outfield gates, we would be home free.

It took several months but finally the plan to get the Beatles in and out of Shea Stadium had everyone's approval, including the most important approval of all: Brian Epstein's. When he gave me his final okay, he asked me again, "Sid, are you absolutely sure the boys will be safe under this plan?"

"Absolutely, Brian. The security plans for this concert are as extensive and well-thought-out as if we were protecting the President of the United States."

"Okay, I trust you. We will be arriving at the Warwick on the 13th. Why don't you come by then and we can say hello?"

"That's fine. I'll see you then."

My overriding concern through all those months leading up to the August 15th date was for security.

Chip Munk kept coming back to me and telling me that the $10,000 estimate that he had given me for the stage was off and it was going to cost at least twice that. And the initial insurance estimate that I had received for $10,000 was also off by more than half. However, these issues paled when it came to security concerns.

Until this time, no one had ever attempted a rock concert of this size and magnitude. Another complicating factor was that the Beatles were the number one group in the world, with a fan base of enthusiastic teenagers. The potential for a disaster was there, and it was on everyone's mind. I was determined that this concert would take place without incident. It was a promise I had made to Brian, to the Mayor and to myself.

The first thing we decided to do was have an initial obstacle of triple barricades between the seats and the field. Then, in addition to the stadium ushers and security men who would be patrolling the aisles and the corridors, I asked my cousin, Leo Kitchman, to provide some moonlighting cops who would act as a buffer between the barricades and the stadium security personnel, just like we had done at Newport. Finally, I hired 40 black belts in karate to give an exhibition before the concert. In reality, I hired them to act as the final deterrent to anyone trying to rush the stage. Anybody rushing the stage would have to get by the ushers and extra security we had hired, leap over the stadium field gates, over the three barricades, past the uniformed security people, past Leo's moonlighting cops and then make it through the black belts. If they got past all those people, they would still have to run 200 feet to the stage to be greeted by Neil Aspinall and Mal Evans, the Beatles' road manager and assistant, who were prepared to give their lives for the Beatles.

I figured anyone who could negotiate all that probably deserved the right to shake the Beatles' hands. No one got even close.

Finally, just in case the concert ever got out of control, a full coterie of New York City cops and mounted police were poised outside the stadium, prepared to enter on a moment's notice.

How could I not be confident in the security?

I hired Murray the K to be the MC. He had developed a close personal relationship with the Beatles and Brian Epstein. Murray was a very engaging guy who had a winning way with kids, and he and I were very good friends. His wife and Gerry were also good friends and we often socialized together. Murray was a natural to be the MC for the concert, and he was elated when I told him I had chosen him as MC.

I booked King Curtiss and his band, Brenda Holloway, Cannibal and the Headhunters, Sounds Incorporated and some dancers to be the warm-up acts. King Curtis and I had known each other since the Shaw Artists days, and Murray suggested the dancers.

About ten days before the concert, I got a call from Ed Sullivan. I had previously asked him to introduce the Beatles and he had accepted, so when my secretary told me he was on the line, I hoped he wasn't calling to cancel.

"Ed, how are you? Are you ready to get up in front of those 55,000 screaming kids?"

"Looking forward to it, Sidney! What I'm calling you about is that I'd like to film the concert. Would that be okay?"

"Sure, Ed, go right ahead. Have your people talk to Billy Fields, and we'll issue the necessary passes."

"Thanks, Sid, I'll see you on August 15th. It should really be something."

"You bet, Ed," I replied, relieved that he was still agreeable to introducing the Beatles.

The demand for tickets was once again insane. No matter how many seats I had for the concert, I always needed more. I got requests for and issued 1,100 press passes, a completely unheard of amount of press passes to any event. People started calling my home and accosting me at the front entrance to my apartment building. I just dealt with all the madness as best I could. I did not, however, have the Carnegie Hall stagehands to save me by adding seats, and I had to say no more often than I liked. I tried to get Shea to let us put seats on the field but Jim Thompson nixed that idea, saying that if they allowed that, they would never be able to get the grass into playing condition in time.

Late in the day on Friday, August 13th, two days before Shea, I went to the Warwick to welcome Brian and the boys back to New York. The scene was reminiscent of the one in front of the Plaza the previous winter. Police and barricades were surrounding the hotel and kids were screaming and waving placards.

As soon as I stepped into the hotel, a uniformed security person asked me if I was staying at the hotel. When I answered in the negative, he asked my name and who I was there to see. My name was on the list.

Brian was in an adjoining suite to the boys. He was very warm and pleasant. By now, he, of course, knew that there was a sellout.

"Well, we're not going to get that $10 a ticket!" he joked.

"You never had a chance."

Brian told me that after New York, they were going on a whirlwind tour to large venues all around the U.S. and Canada—seven cities in 15 days, I believe it was.

"I hope they're as good at security as you are, Sid."

"I'm sure you'll be fine, Brian."

Security was his main concern. Not the music, not the performance, just the safety of his boys.

"Come in. I'm sure you'll want to say hello to the boys. They're just next door."

He took me into the adjoining suite and the Beatles were there, just hanging out, joking and having a good time.

"Sid!" they all greeted me effusively.

Paul shook my hand and said, "It's nice to be with you, again."

John said, "Good to be back again, Sid! I love New York! It's still a crazy place!"

Ringo joked and remarked about how there were girls trying to get at them in the hotel and that he had heard that some had even secured rooms weeks in advance as guests of the hotel in the hope that they could get to see the Beatles.

I remember telling them that New York loved the Beatles and that there was great anticipation for Shea.

"It's never been done before, gentlemen," I said. "A soldout stadium the size of Shea! It's going to be spectacular!" They all grinned at that.

"We'll be making history again," I continued. "I'll see you on Sunday. I'm really looking forward to it."

John laughed and, with a gleeful look on his face, replied, "So are we, Sid!"

On Saturday, August 14th, Chip Munk began to erect the stage at Shea. By then, the cost had escalated to $25,000. I was in no mood to complain about the $15,000 overrun; I just wanted to see it done.

On Sunday, the day of the concert, I got to Shea Stadium very early. Chip was putting the finishing touches on the stage, and I must say it was a first-rate stage.

The Shea grounds-keepers and the security people were erecting the barricades. Billy and I circulated around the huge ballpark, checking and rechecking arrangements.

The Mayor's office assigned a young intern to spend the day with me. He observed everything very carefully, and he was a super bright kid, not only well-mannered but extremely well-dressed. That young man was Jeffrey Katzenberg, who today is partners with David Geffen and Steven Spielberg at Dreamworks.

In mid-afternoon, we assembled all the security people for final instructions. I explained ardently that no matter how provoked they might get, no matter what the young fans might do, the concertgoers were to be handled with kid gloves.

"If anyone tries to rush the stage, just lift them off their feet, let them dangle and put them back over the gates as gently as possible. If they don't go, carry them out of the ballpark. Under no circumstance are you to use clubs, hit them or use any force at all."

Billy then told them where they would each be stationed.

Naturally, the crowd came early. I think we opened the gates to Shea at about six o'clock and there were many people waiting to get in. The anticipation was electric and I knew we were in for something extraordinary.

The Rascals, invited by me, came to the Shea concert early. I had issued them passes and they had no trouble getting in. I put them in the third-base dugout so they could be as close to the action as possible. The kids on the other side of the stadium, the first-base side, saw them and thought they were the Beatles. It was very early yet, around 6:30 or so, and kids began to filter down from across the stadium for autographs from people they thought were the Beatles. When they realized that this was another group, they were undaunted and clamored for autographs. Since it still was early enough and the kids were well-behaved, I allowed them in small groups to come into the third-base dugout and get The Rascals' autographs. In addition, Billy Smith, a friend of The Rascals, had made up buttons that said, I'm a Rascals Fan, and he gave them out to the congregating kids. Before long, there were 2,000 kids roaming the stands wearing Rascals buttons.

While I was in the dugout with what later became "my four boys," Bill Tooley from the Shea Stadium staff came to me and said, "Sid, the stadium is yours for the night and that includes the message board. What's your next event, and we'll advertise it on the board."

"Thanks, Bill," I said. "With this and the recent Rolling Stones concert, I haven't really had time to plan another event, so I have nothing to promote at this time."

"But, Sid, you paid for it! You might as well use it."

"Okay, if that's the case, here is what I'd like said: Please, for your safety and your neighbor's safety, stay in your seats throughout the concert. Failure to do so could result in the cancellation of this event.

"Sid, you can get another message up there."

I thought for a second and then said, "Okay. Tell them to flash The Rascals are coming...The Rascals are coming!

"You got it, Sid," he said, and left to make the arrangements. The flashing, The Rascals are coming...The Rascals are coming! turned out to be a fortuitous and important message indeed.

As planned, the Beatles were taken by police escort in limos to the heliport in Manhattan and flown to the Fairgrounds in Queens. The helicopter did a turn around the stadium to let the boys see the crowd, which was almost filled to capacity by 7:30. When the helicopter flew over Shea, I knew who the occupants were, but I'm not sure if the crowd did. The copter landed in the Fairgrounds and the Wells Fargo armored car brought the Beatles and Brian into the stadium. They quickly got out of the armored car and ran under the stands to the umpires' dressing room. No one except a very few of us knew that the Beatles were in the ballpark.

The screaming in the ballpark was unbelievable. I have never heard noise like that in my life. The place was in a frenzy.

I went to see the Beatles in the umpires' dressing room. They were absolutely in awe. They could not believe what was happening. They were in Shea Stadium in New York, fifty-five thousand seats, and the place was packed. No rock'n'roll act had ever played to an audience anywhere close to that size. We could hear the screaming in the dressing room.

The boys were tuning their instruments, getting dressed and preparing for the momentous performance. They were nervous. I had never seen them nervous before, but this event was so unique and so different that you would have to have had nerves of pure steel not to be nervous.

Five minutes before show time, we proceeded from the dressing room along a walkway to the visitors' dugout. When we got to the entrance of the dugout, I said to the boys, "Okay, guys. I'm going to get up on stage and introduce Ed Sullivan. He will come up and introduce you. When he does, and I hope you can hear him, just run up these dugout steps onto the field and up to the stage. It's only a short run. There are a few steps at the left rear of the stage. You'll be surrounded by security, so don't worry about safety. (Years later, George Harrison commented on how impressed he was with the security that night. And it's not easy to impress George Harrison!) We have everything under control, but be prepared—there are 55,000 people out there. If you think it's loud now, wait till you step out of the dugout! It will be absolutely deafening!"

They all nodded. I wished them good luck and left them to their Shea Stadium debut.

I walked across the infield. When I got to the stage, Murray the K introduced me as the man who had brought the Beatles to America and I stepped forward to introduce Ed Sullivan.

What can I say? It was somewhat humbling to stand up in front of those 55,000 people moments before the Beatles were to come on stage. The little boy from Zisselman's Farm was about to introduce Ed Sullivan, perhaps the greatest name ever in American television, and Ed was going to introduce the number one act in the world, in what I knew was a history-making event. It was unbelievable!

I introduced Ed and said that he was a great American, which he was. He then walked out and, with little fanfare, thanked me for the introduction and said just five words: "Ladies and gentlemen—the Beatles!"

The boys ran out of the dugout waving and turning and surveying the crowd as they ran to the stage. Thousands of flashbulbs went off. I wondered if the Beatles were in as much wonderment about the scene in front of them as I was. They got up on stage, checked their tuning, looked at each other and began to play *Twist & Shout*. Brian and I stood stage right, right next to each other.

"This is quite amazing," he practically shouted in my ear. "I hope we can get them out of here."

One would think that Brian would take a moment to bathe in the glory of his and the Beatles' success. He, truly, *was* the fifth Beatle. He had discovered the group. He had guided them and nurtured them. He had worked tirelessly to make this a reality, and this, to be sure, was the apex of both his and the Beatles' career. Yet all he could think about was getting them out safely.

Brian said something like, "I hope we can get them out of here," or "I hope we get out of here alive," at least five times during the time that the Beatles were on stage.

Each time he voiced his concerns, I reassured him, "Not to worry, Brian, we have it covered. We'll get you all out." I knew that we had so many lines of defense that, in the end, we could and would control the crowd and no one would get near his four beloved boys.

Some kids tried to jump out of the stands onto the field, but no one ever came close to being a threat. We were too well-organized and prepared. I may have lost money at Newport, but what I had learned there about security stood me in good stead here. We were covered.

I can't really say much about the music that night. The screaming crowd was so overpowering that I doubt anyone heard the music. I know I didn't—and I was standing right at the foot of the stage.

Ringo's fans had a custom of tossing jelly beans onto the stage for him. One of the security men told me that throughout the duration of the concert, jelly beans rained down from the upper deck, hitting everyone sitting in the lower deck and on the field. The security guys were concerned, until someone remembered about Ringo's fans and the jellybeans. As it was, everyone complained because, as I was told, "those damn jelly beans hurt!"

As soon as the Beatles finished playing, the armored car sped across the field to the stage. I shook hands with the four boys and Brian. I could see that Brian was relieved. "Great, Sid," he said. "Just marvelous. Thanks again. I'll talk to you soon."

The five of them got into the waiting armored car and I slammed the door shut. They and Brian were in that armored car and on the move no more than 20 seconds after they stepped off the stage. The back gate of Shea opened, the armored car sped through, and they were gone. The Beatles were on their way to Canada.

The screaming continued, but the audience soon realized that there would be no encore. The crowd began to empty out of the stadium very slowly, as when one departs from a loved one or object of admiration. I waited until everyone was out of Shea Stadium; I wanted to make sure that no one was injured or harmed in any way.

We had set up an emergency First Aid station, staffed with doctors, nurses and ambulances. I wanted to ensure that we would be prepared for any possible medical situation. I made my way to the emergency station to thank the doctors and nurses for their services. I was also interested to see if anyone had required medical attention during the concert. When I arrived, there were about 10 to 15 kids in the emergency area lying on stretchers. They were all young girls who had been overcome with excitement and hysteria. As I walked into the First Aid area, one of the young doctors recognized me and said, "Hi, Mr. Bernstein. It was quite a night."

All of a sudden, the kids jumped off their stretchers and besieged me. Once again, the kids wanted to know if I had shaken the Beatles' hands.

"Yes I did," I replied.

"And did you wash your hands yet?" they asked, almost in unison.

"Not since I shook John, Paul, George and Ringo's hands, no."

"Wow! Can we please shake your hand?" they implored.

"Sure," I said. And they all lined up and one after another shook my hand.

"Look how I cured these kids with just a handshake," I joked to the young doctors. "I should have become a doctor myself!" The doctors and nurses just grinned.

The kids all left, vowing never to wash their hands again. After thanking and saying good night to the doctors, nurses and remaining stadium personnel, I got into my car and drove home.

In the car, I tried to remember if I had ever had an experience with any of the hundreds of other artists I had been involved with, like the one I just had at the First Aid station. I could not remember another performance when fans rushed up to me to shake my hand because I had shaken the hand of the evening's performer. It further solidified my view that the Beatles phenomenon had never happened before in entertainment history. And it probably never would happen again.

It was beyond amazing.

The GI nightclub we opened in Dijon, France was a big success.
It was here that I met Claudy.

The beautiful and vivacious Geraldine Bernstein, mother of my six children.

Preceding page: Here I am in front of the *Lennon* marquee in New York.
The show ended with three shots. Every night when those three shots rang, out I cried.

The great Charles Aznavour (whom I presented five times), me and Billy Fields.

Due to the pre-concert frenzy, there was a mistake in the poster.
Check out the two different spellings of the Hall!

THEATRE THREE PRODUCTIONS

PRESENT
THE FIRST NEW YORK APPEARANCE OF THE

BEATLES

CARNEGIE HALL
WED. FEB. 12

2 SHOWS 7PM & 8·30PM

PRICES $4·00 $4·50 $5·00 **TICKETS GO ON SALE AT CARNGIE HALL FROM JAN 27**

When I first saw the Beatles, they were in their suite at the Plaza Hotel, looking out their window, surveying the crowd that had gathered.

For the first time in the renowned history of Carnegie Hall, 300 extra seats were placed on the stage so that I could accommodate my longtime friend and backer Abe Margolies.

CARNEGIE HALL / *72nd Season*

Wednesday Evening, February 12, 1964, at 7:00 and 9:30 o'clock

THEATRE THREE PRODUCTIONS

presents

The Briarwood Singers

New York disc jockeys' salute to The Beatles

THE BEATLES

John Lennon

Ringo Starr

John McCartney

George Harrison

If you look closely at this official program for the Beatles' first appearance at Carnegie Hall, you can see Paul McCartney is incorrectly listed as John McCartney. No one picked up on the oversight in the pre-concert frenzy.

The first time I saw these four guys, they looked ridiculous in their knickers and ruffled shirts. History proved me wrong. The Rascals eventually became the number one group in the U.S. and wrote some of the most popular songs of their time.

The Bay City Rollers in their tartans.

SID BERNSTEIN
PRESENTS THE
BEATLES
IN PERSON

★ John
★ Paul
★ George
★ Ringo

THE NO. 1
GROUP IN THE WORLD

SHEA STADIUM
SUNDAY 8.00 P.M. AUG. 15

ALL SEATS RESERVED $4.50, 5.00, 5.65 phone 265-2280 FOR INFORMATION

This poster never appeared anywhere because the concert sold out before there was any advertising.

The Beatles tuning up in the umpires' dressing room before their first historic concert at Shea.

Overleaf: I am in the lower far right-hand corner, near the guy in the white shirt.
John Lennon is telling me how amazed he is by the scene at Shea.

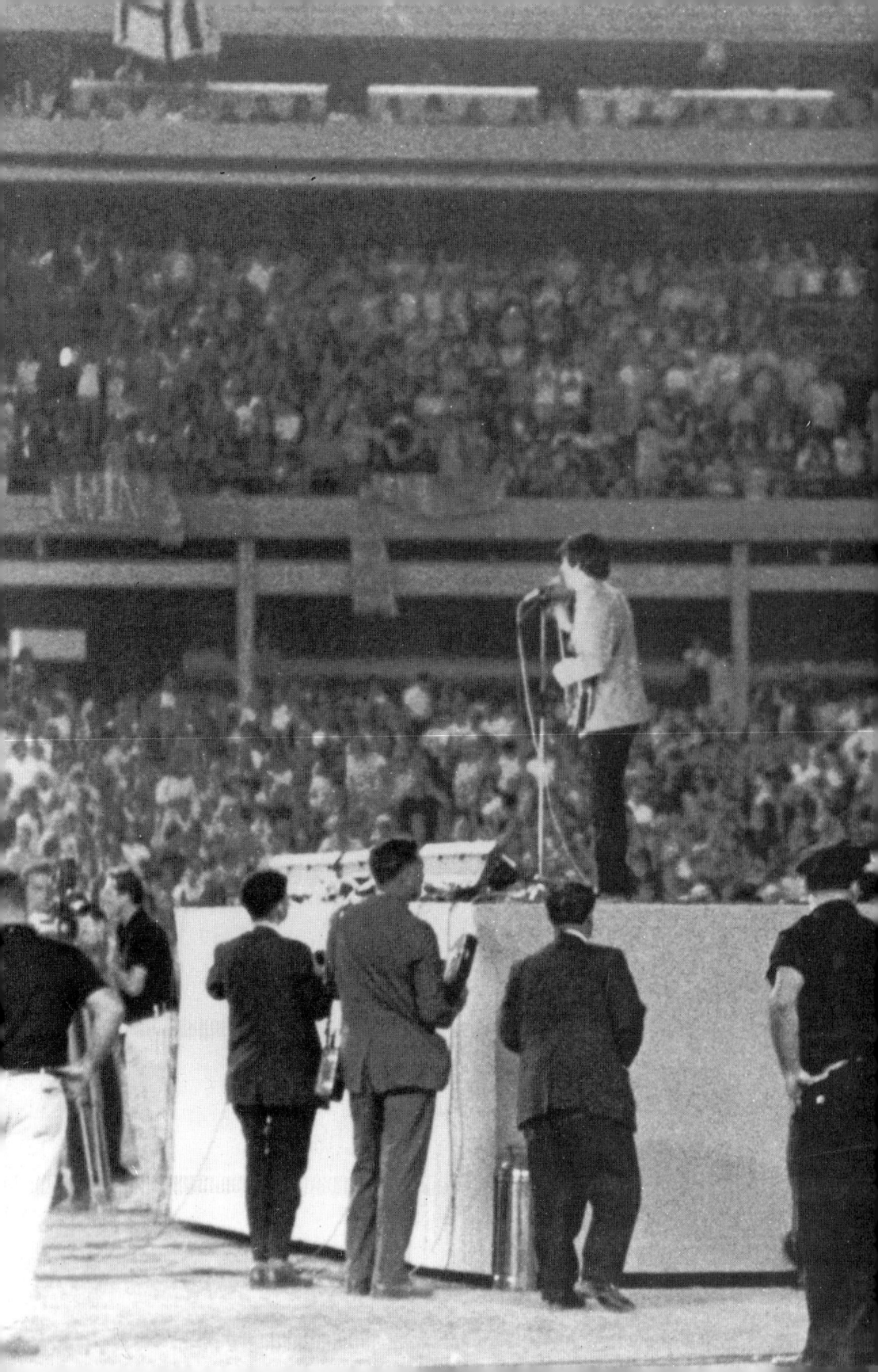

New York's Mayor Ed Koch, songwriters Sammy Cahn and Charles Strouse and me at the off-Broadway production of Mr. Koch's book *Mayor* at the Village Gate.

Madison Square Garden
MUSICAL SPECTACULAR
7:30 P.M. FRIDAY, OCTOBER 27
★ APPEARING IN CONCERT ★

DIONNE WARWICKE ★ TINA TURNER & THE IKETTES ★ MARY TRAVERS JUDY COLLINS ★ CASS ELLIOT MARLO THOMAS ★ MELINA MERCOURI GWEN VERDON ★ CHITA RIVERA SHIRLEY MacLAINE ★ BETTE DAVIS and other SURPRISE PERFORMERS

MRS. ROSE KENNEDY

Star Spangled Women for McGovern Shriver

MRS. ELEANOR McGOVERN

Produced by: SHIRLEY MacLAINE & SID BERNSTEIN

CELEBRITY USHERS ★★★★★★	CELEBRITY USHERS ★★★★★★	CELEBRITY USHERS
ROBERT ABRAMS	DANTE FERRARI	KEVIN McCARTHY	DENNIS SMITH
BELLA ABZUG	WILLIAM FRIEDKIN	MRS. EDWARD R. MURROW	GLORIA STEINEM
WARREN BEATTY	BEN GAZZARA	JACK NICHOLSON	PERCY SUTTON
JIMMY BRESLIN	DAN GREENBURG	ELEANOR PERRY	FAT THOMAS
PAT CUNNINGHAM	GOLDIE HAWN	ALICE PLAYTEN	JOSE TORRES
COLEEN DEWHURST	MARY HEMMINGWAY	GEORGE PLIMPTON	MATT TROY
HELEN GAHAGAN DOUGLAS	JAMES EARL JONES	REX REED	ELI WALLACH
NORA EPHRON	ALAN KING	FRANK ROSETTI	and many more
MEADE ESPISITO	SAM LEONE	ROBERT RYAN	564
JULES FEIFFER	SIDNEY LUMET	TINA SINATRA	

TICKETS: $25, $15, $10, $5. AT THE BOX OFFICE, 2 PENN PLAZA (564-4400) AND ALL TICKETRON OUTLETS (644-4400)

Check out the names on the program for the concert Shirley MacLaine and I produced for George McGovern's 1972 presidential campaign.

Benji Greenberg with his valid New York State
license plate and You-Know-Who!

To commemorate and celebrate the 30th anniversary of
the first Beatles concert at Shea, I was invited to throw out the first ball
at that night's Mets game.

Sunday
September 19, 1976

Dear George, John, Paul and Ringo,

You have made the world a happier place to live in. Your music has found its way into the hearts of millions of people in every corner of the world. For almost ten years now, your dedicated old friends, and countless new friends—have hoped, have waited, and patiently watched for a signal from you—that you might play from one stage, just one more time, individually, or together.

In a world that seems so hopelessly divided, engaged in civil war, scarred by earthquakes, and too often living in fear of tomorrow's encore of tragic headlines—more than ever, we need a symbol of hope for the future. Simply by showing the world that people can get it together.

Let the world smile for one day. Let us change the headlines from gloom and hopelessness to music and life and a worldwide message of peace. You four are among the very few who are in a position to make the dream of a better world come together in the hearts of millions in just one day.

The burden of the world is not on your shoulders—we all share that responsibility. This proposal is made for your consideration—only if you can find the time—and the strength to put it together.

We out there would welcome your return.

THE PLAN: Your appearance on one stage; whether you play individually or collectively, or both, would be seen by an audience of millions Moderately priced tickets would be sold in advance, at every theatre, auditorium, concert hall, and arena—where closed circuit television cables could be placed.

On the day of the event, ticket holders would be required to bring, in addition to their ticket of admission—a can of food, or an article of new or useful clothing, to be deposited in boxes at each facility. These gifts could feed and clothe an impoverished nation for years.

A 'volunteer' foundation or worldwide organization such as CARE or UNICEF could lend their resources to pick up these life-giving gifts, the day after your concert, and distribute them five days later to an area, changed over-night into a nation of hope and life.

*THE POSSIBLE REVENUES: $100 million from the sale of an album recorded 'live' of this event...$40 million from the sale of seats at a moderate ticket price to every closed-circuit venue around the world...$15 million for TV rights around the world; to be shown the next day, or the next week, free, to all who couldn't buy tickets; the night of the concert...$60 million from a movie of the event itself, and an equal amount of footage devoted to each of you—to talk, play, or share in your own way, your lives as individuals—with your friends who want to see you...$15 million from the sale of program books and souvenirs.

THE TIME: New Year's Day or Easter 1977.

THE PLACE: Bethlehem! Liverpool! Or wherever it is right.

Respectfully,

Sid Bernstein

Sid Bernstein

Preceding page: Here is the ad I placed in *The New York Times* on Sunday, September 19, 1976, urging the Beatles to "come together" to lift the spirits of the world.

PHOTO BY STEVE SHERMAN

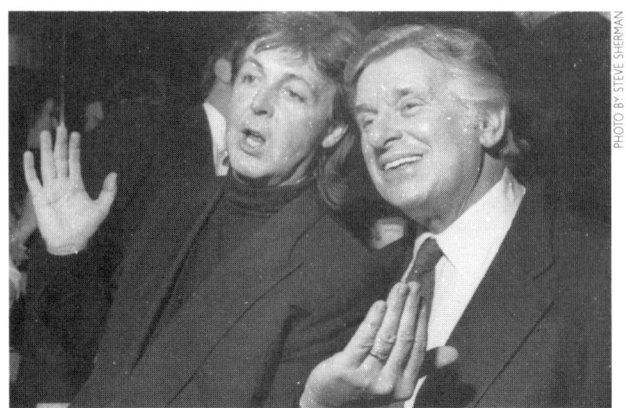

Long live Sir Paul!

Clockwise from top left: Etienne, Casey, Beau, Adam, Denise, Dylan, Gerry and me.

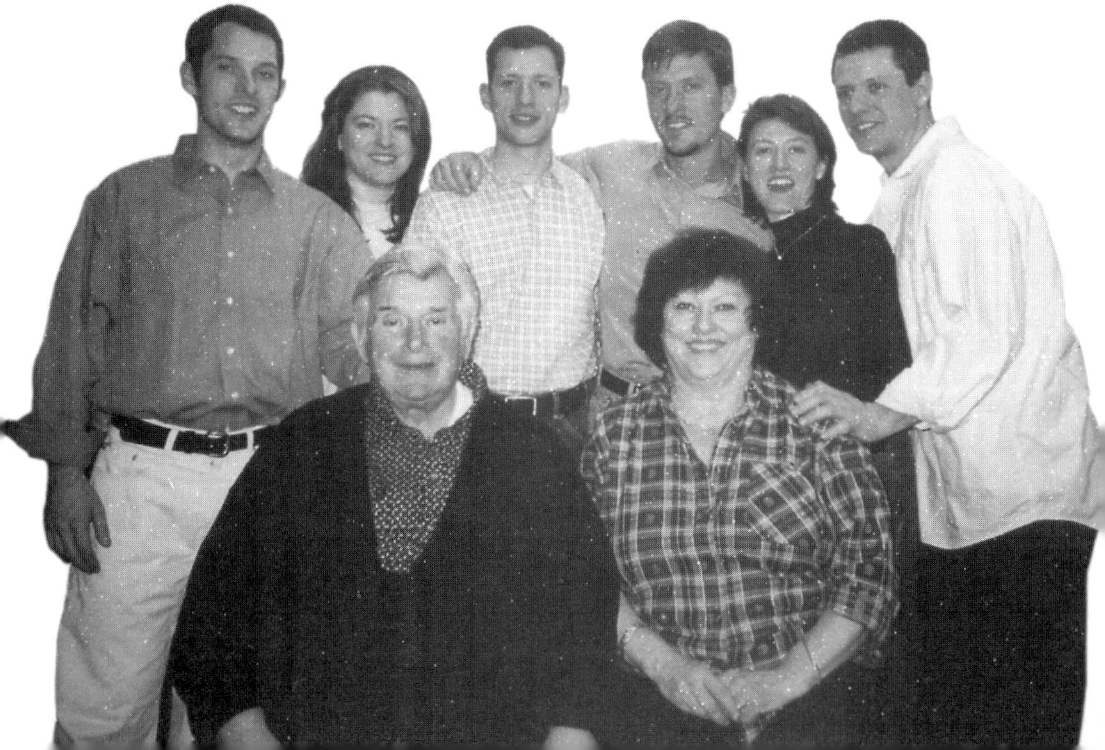

Chapter 13: ON TO THE NEXT PROJECTS

I WAS COMPLETELY DRAINED. I HAD BEEN ON MY FEET for over 18 hours. The excitement and the noise were exhausting. At that point, all I wanted was to get home as quickly as possible. I had no time to reflect on what we had accomplished. There was no time to celebrate. I had Walter Hyman propelling me towards the management of The Rascals now. It was on to the next project.

The next afternoon, August 16, 1965, at Walter Hyman's apartment on Fifth Avenue, Walter, Steve Weiss (an attorney), the four Rascals and I held a meeting. Steve Weiss presided over the meeting, and he actually represented both sides, which, on second thought, was not a good idea. We hammered out a deal whereby Walter, as a silent partner, and I, as the active partner, would manage The Rascals. We agreed on a twenty-percent commission. I was excited because I just knew that with a break or two, The Rascals could be a major act.

We also made a gentleman's agreement that they would do 10 charity events every year. They readily agreed because they desperately wanted me to be their manager. I knew that one day soon, The Rascals would command tremendous amounts of money for their appearances. I thought that we should try to do some good and give something back.

I got to work right away. I called the owners of The Barge in the Hamptons and secured The Rascals an immediate $800-per-week raise. That doubled their salary. I contacted all the record companies that had shown interest in them and told them that I was managing the Rascals and from now on they should deal with me. Many of the leading record companies were keen on signing The Rascals.

Ahmet Ertegun, along with his brother, Nesuhi, and Jerry Wexler had built a formidable record company called Atlantic Records. Specializing in jazz and r&b, Atlantic had well-known artists like Ray Charles, Aretha Franklin, Sam & Dave, Otis Redding, and King Curtiss, but did not have any major white pop music acts at the time. They were desperate to sign a white act so that Atlantic could compete with top record companies like Columbia, RCA and Decca. Ahmet and Jerry Wexler owned homes in the Hamptons and had witnessed the rise of The Rascals and wanted very much to sign them.

During that time when we were searching for a record label, Phil Spector, the legendary record producer, called me from Los Angeles.

"Sid, did you sign The Rascals to anyone yet?"

"No, Phil, I haven't. But I'm close."

"Sit tight," he said. "I'm flying in tomorrow just to see them."

"Okay, Phil," I laughed. "We're not going to do anything before tomorrow."

The next day, Phil picked me up in his limo, complete with his bodyguard, and took me with him to see The Rascals at The Barge. Naturally, Phil was taken with them, and The Rascals were awed that the great Phil Spector had come all the way from Los Angeles to see them and wanted to sign them!

During one of their breaks, I explained to the group that Phil was not going to leave Los Angeles. He would be based on the West Coast, and they would be on the East Coast.

"You need a producer with close proximity to you, especially at the early stages of your recording career," I said. "With Phil, you can never know where he's going to be. Let's find someone who's based closer to home."

The fact that Phil worked out of L.A. and the fact that The Rascals really wanted to produce their own records caused us to turn down the great Phil Spector. He got angry, stormed out and kicked either a stone or a fire hydrant and broke his foot. An ambulance came to The Barge and carted him off to the hospital.

I continued to negotiate with the top record executives, who were all interested in signing The Rascals. The world of record people had been to Shea and that flashing sign, The Rascals are coming...The Rascals are coming! got into their psyches and they all wanted to sign them.

While in the middle of the record negotiations, the summer ended and I booked The Rascals into a small New York City club called Harlow's. For the three weeks the group was there, Harlow's was sold-out every night. Limos were lined up outside of the club waiting for their owners to exit after having seen the Next Big Thing in American music.' Every night was like July 4th or New Year's Eve.

From Harlow's, I booked The Rascals into an even smaller club, the Phone Booth. As the name suggests, the Phone Booth was tiny. I was determined that my group would play only in the smallest, most intimate clubs until they had a hit record. Every night The Rascals played, the crowds at the Phone Booth, like Harlow's, were lined up to see them. Night after night the place was jammed, and quite a few stars, such as Bob Dylan and Bill Wyman of the Rolling Stones, came frequently to see the group. Brian Epstein also came a few times, always looking like he had stepped out of the pages of *Gentleman's Quarterly*.

One night, I went to check out the scene at the Phone Booth and spotted Burt Bacharach and Angie Dickenson, two friends of mine, standing on line, waiting to get in. I knew how modest and unpretentious Burt was and that he would not use his fame to gain access into the club, so I just walked over and took them both by the hand and took them in to see The Rascals. After The Rascals had finished their set, Angie and Bert came over and told me that they thought The Rascals were going to be a "huge" group.

On another night, I was sitting in the packed Phone Booth and Tom Jones, the great Welsh singer and showman, came into the club. He had not called ahead to tell anyone that he was coming. When the people at the front door saw him, they brought him to my table. I had never met Tom Jones before. Tom introduced himself and explained that he was in New York for business and had inquired about what he should do with his free evening. Several people had suggested to him that he go check out a new group that was playing at the Phone Booth. The group was The Rascals.

We sat and watched the boys perform. The club was packed and, as usual, there was high energy and excitement in the air. When The Rascals finished their set, Tom Jones told me that he thought they were "awesome" and he was delighted that he had stopped in to see them. We wished each other good luck and he left. The Rascals were thrilled to hear that a star of the magnitude of Tom Jones thought that they were awesome, but they were starting to get used to that kind of response to their act.

Finally, we made a decision about a record label. The deciding factor for me was when Ahmet Ertegun said, "Look, Sid. We don't have any white acts. We need this group. If you sign them to Atlantic, you'll get every possible promotion and production advantage you can get. We will stay with this group and see them through until they make it. No matter how long it takes. I know some of the major record labels are offering you more money, but they don't need you like we do, and I think that's an advantage you should not give up."

I agreed, and I told the boys that I was recommending that they sign with Atlantic. They knew Ahmet and Jerry from the Hamptons so they agreed, and The Rascals became Atlantic recording artists. When we finally announced the decision, there were many unhappy record executives at the companies we had rejected. Atlantic assigned Arif Mardin and Tom Dowd to assist The Rascals in the studio and agreed to allow them to produce their own records. They also granted us free studio time, which was unheard of then. Arif was then, and is now, a magnificent arranger and producer and has produced some of the great recording acts of all time. Tom Dowd was one of the finest recording engineers in the business.

The Rascals were getting press even before their record came out. There was a buzz about them that had started in the Hamptons at The Barge and carried over to Harlow's and then the Phone Booth in New York City. I got a phone call from the manager of the Harmonica Rascals, who were a famous group that had been in movies and on television. Basically he said that the Harmonica Rascals owned the name "Rascals" and that we should stop using it. I took this information to Atlantic and they did legal research and learned that if we put another word in front of "Rascals," we could continue to employ the name. The executives at Atlantic thought that the "Young Rascals" sounded pretty good, so they changed the group's name to the "Young Rascals" and that stopped the harassment over the name.

The boys had not really started to write their own songs yet, and the most pressing order of business during late 1965 was to find a piece of material that everybody thought was a hit. The search was on. Arif Mardin, Tom Dowd, and Atlantic were looking. The boys were contacting friends and anybody they knew who could write, and I put the word out to music publishers that I knew that we were looking for a hit song. We got hundreds of submissions and listened to them all.

Pam Sawyer and Laurie Burton, two songwriters, submitted a tune called *I Ain't Gonna Eat Out My Heart Anymore*. The consensus was that the song would be a hit. There was great enthusiasm and expectation for the record once it was recorded, and we did everything we could to make it a hit.

The most important market for record play and sales has always been New York, with its large, diverse population and its reputation as the media capital of the world. New York is most definitely the place to have your record heard. However, New York is also the most difficult city in which to get a new record played. Invariably, a record has to be on the Top 100 charts and have demonstrated its ability to get airplay and sales in other markets before it will even be considered for play in the New York market.

However, I had some advantages in the New York market. My association with the Beatles, the Rolling Stones, Tony Bennett and many other acts had afforded me the opportunity to get to know the music programmers and disc jockeys at most of the local New York radio stations. Often, when I ran concerts or shows, I would call on local DJs to be the MC. Over the years, I had developed many friendships.

One of the DJs with whom I had developed a close friendship was Bruce Morrow, who was more widely known as Cousin Brucie. For years, Bruce was the top jock at the leading station in New York, WABC. With its 50,000-watt clear-channel signal, WABC could be heard all the way to Florida and even reached parts of the Midwest. Additionally, WABC was the flagship radio station of the ABC Network. The station had a huge audience. Also, the station's music program director, Rick Sklar, was highly respected and copied. If Rick chose to air a record, soon other program directors around the country would start playing that record, too.

It was important to me that Brucie see and hear the Rascals. I thought Brucie could be the first one who played the boys' record.

The boys and I had developed a plan. I arranged for the Rascals to meet Cousin Brucie at the WABC offices. It was winter and they were all wearing muskrat overcoats. When I contacted Brucie about the meeting between him and the Rascals, I asked him to play along with them. I gave the Rascals an extra muskrat coat to take with them to WABC. They threw the extra coat over Brucie, spirited him out of the station and took him to the Phone Booth, where they were appearing. It was reminiscent of Walter Hyman's "kidnapping" of me to hear the Rascals for the first time.

This was the first time that Bruce saw the Rascals perform live. He had heard about them through the buzz they had created in the clubs around New York. Brucie had been onstage at the Beatles' concert at Shea and had seen the message board flashing The Rascals Are Coming... The Rascals Are Coming! As Brucie always says, "It was love at first bite." He thought that the Rascals were terrific.

Rick and Brucie agreed to air *I Ain't Gonna Eat Out My Heart Anymore* as a favor to me. They wanted to help me, so they played the record. They even encouraged the other ABC radio stations around the country to play *I Ain't Gonna Eat Out My Heart Anymore*.

Through Bruce Morrow and Rick Sklar and WABC, we had been successful in getting airplay for *I Ain't Gonna Eat My Heart Out Anymore*. However, I knew that in order to get on Bill Gavin's all-important tip sheet, which music program directors depended on to learn about hot new records. I had to get at least one more credible radio station to play it. We really needed the record to be mentioned in Gavin's sheet.

For years I had been reading in the industry trade papers about a great young DJ who worked for the largest radio station in the Buffalo area. His name was Joey Reynolds and he was so outstanding that he became well-known in national DJ and radio circles. I had met people who had promoted records in the Buffalo area and they had only positive things to say about Joey. Joey Reynolds had a great reputation.

I called the station where Joey worked and I asked the secretary who answered the phone if I could come and visit. I explained that I had a hot new group in New York called the Young Rascals and that they had a record out on Atlantic Records and I wanted to talk to Joey about playing it for the Buffalo radio audience. She told me that if I came during Joey's radio show, he would see me. I flew to Buffalo the very next day and went to the station. While I was waiting to see Joey Reynolds, I watched him work through the studio glass and heard his work over the speakers in the waiting room. I could tell right away that he knew what he was doing and was creating a lot of energy and excitement in Buffalo. At the news break, Joey stood up and waved me into the studio. He greeted me with a big smile and was warm and hospitable.

"Sid, it's a pleasure to meet you," he said. "As you can see, I'm on the air, but I should be finished in about 30 minutes. Would you mind waiting? I can spend some time with you when I'm done with the program."

I had time to wait, since my plane home was not leaving for a few more hours. I spent the time watching and listening to Joey work, and I was really impressed with the heart he put into his broadcast. He was a terrific radio personality.

When he finished doing his show, Joey and I sat and talked for about a half-hour. I told him about the Young Rascals and a little about myself. I did not tell him that I was the promoter responsible for bringing the Beatles to America. I only spoke about the Rascals. Joey listened intently, but made no commitment to air *I Ain't Gonna Eat My Heart Out Anymore*.

On the plane home, I thought about my meeting with Joey and felt that I had made a good impression and that there was a 50-50 chance that he would play the record. I later found out that Joey put the record on the very next day and continued playing it until it peaked in the 30s on the radio station record chart. He had bought the record on the merits.

The fact that Joey was playing the record enabled us to get listed in the Gavin Report and helped us gain momentum for the record. It went as high as 52 on the national charts, but that's as far as it got. It was a good beginning, but the Rascals still needed a top 10 record.

Even though we didn't have a hit record, I was able to keep escalating the live performance price for the Rascals. They were such dynamic performers that before long, we were getting $2,000 for one show, which was a high price for a group without a hit record. We played high school and college gyms, social halls and auditoriums. The word was getting out that these four boys could put on some "hell of a show."

Walter Hyman, my partner on the Rascals, came to see me one day.

"Sid, I have become very friendly with Dore Schary. He's no longer head of MGM and he's moved back to New York. As you know, he's constantly getting projects that people want him to do and he's asked me to come in on one of them, and I want to do it."

"What's the project, Walter?"

"He has a play called *The Impossible Years* that he wants to produce on Broadway and he's thinking we can take it to Hollywood after that and make it into a movie."

"That's good, Walter," I said. "What's the problem? Do it!"

"Yes, Sid," he said, "but I'm involved with you and this Rascals thing. Look, Sid, it's not my kind of music. I'm not crazy about the scene. I'd like you to buy me out."

"What would you like, Walter?"

"Well, give me $25,000, and I'm a happy man."

"Okay, let me see what I can do."

I went to Jerry Wexler at Atlantic and told him that Walter Hyman wanted me to buy out his interest in the Rascals. I told Jerry that I was inclined to do it, but I didn't have the $25,000.

Jerry immediately said, "Sid, we'll lend it to you."

The owners of Atlantic couldn't wait to get Walter out of there. They figured it would be easier to deal with me than with a tough-minded, rich businessman like Walter. They were right. They were delighted to see Walter go.

I gave Walter the $25,000. He got involved with Dore Schary's project, and it became a hit on Broadway. It was later produced as a Hollywood film starring Alan King. Everyone was happy.

The pressure was on to find another song for the Rascals to record and release. Songs were coming from everywhere. One day, Felix Cavaliere of the Rascals came to me and said, "Sid, I have very strong feelings about *Good Lovin'*. People are always telling me that we should release it as a single, and I agree. I think it's a hit."

Good Lovin', a song written by Rudy Clark and Artie Resnick and recorded by the Olympics, had been a hit several years previously. The Rascals did it in their act, and it was always a favorite of the audience.

"Felix, if you believe in it so much, let's take it up with Arif, Ahmet and Jerry Wexler."

Felix did a good sales job because the big *machers* (a Yiddish word meaning big shots) at Atlantic decided to release *Good Lovin'* as a single.

Good Lovin' was an overnight sensation that began to fly up the charts, getting into the Top 10 in just five weeks. I raised the Rascals' price to $5,000 per engagement. We could not accommodate all the promoters that were more than willing to pay the $5,000 price.

I had read an item in one of the trade papers about an interview with Brian Epstein in which he had said that he was planning to bring the Beatles to America during the coming summer. I immediately called Brian in London. I got right down to business.

"Brian, I read that you are going to take the boys on a tour of many of the major cities and stadiums in the U.S. this coming summer. I hope you were including New York. I'd love to bring them back to Shea Stadium."

"Sid, as long as these boys are together and I am their manager, New York will always be your city."

I appreciated his loyalty.

"How about if we do the same deal, Brian? We'll do everything the same. We had such a great experience the last time. We really should try to duplicate it."

"I agree. Let's do it."

"What about a date? When would the Beatles be available to play in New York?"

He thought for a moment and then said, "We are going to be in St. Louis on Saturday, August 20, and I promised the promoter in Seattle Thursday, August 25. Could we do Shea between those two dates?"

"That sounds okay to me, but I need to check on the stadium's availability. In the meantime, I'll wire the $50,000 to you."

"That's fine, just have the check made out to NEMS [the name of Brian's holding company]."

It was as easy as that. No talk about ten dollars a ticket for unsold seats. No talk about a gag on PR, advertising or publicity.

"Oh, by the way, Sid, I really have been meaning to talk to you about some of these new acts I've signed, but I just can't find the time. We'll really have to do it soon. I want them to come to America."

"Brian, I know what you mean. I'm so busy now with the Rascals. They're starting to happen and I've still got some concerts to promote. Let's wait till after Shea and we'll get into it then."

"Good. Let's definitely do it then."

"Okay, Brian, we'll do it after Shea. I promise. And as soon as I have Shea confirmed, I'll call you."

When I hung up with Brian, I got to work. I called Jim Thompson at Shea and asked him if the stadium was available for August 23. Luckily for me, the Mets were on a road trip.

"Jim, do we still have that stage that Chip built for us?"

"Yes, Sid, it's stored here at the stadium. I kind of figured we would be needing it again."

"Great. Can your crew erect it for me?"

"Yes, sir. We took it apart; we can put it back together again."

I was licking my chops. I had just saved $25,000.

"Can we have the stadium for the same price as last year?"

He thought for a second and said, "Ah, what the hell, you got it Sid. Just get the insurance."

"Okay, Jim, we're on. I'll talk to you as we get closer to the date. But, it should be much easier this time because we're going to do the exact same thing."

"Good, Sid, we're ready."

The sound for the first Shea concert had been inadequate. The screaming kids had overwhelmed the stadium's sound system so that no one could really hear the music. I called Bill Hanley, a sound genius who worked out of Boston, and he agreed to supply me with a system for the show. The price was $7,500 and the sound system Bill set up proved to be a vast improvement over the first Shea concert.

Jerry Rosen, who I called next, assured me that we could get Lloyd's again to do the insurance. "Why not, Sid, they made $25,000 the last time and it turned out to be no risk at all for them. They'll definitely do it. Don't worry, I'll take care of it for you."

Two days later, I wired the $50,000 to NEMS. I called and left a message for Brian that the 23rd of August was confirmed, and he could put it on the tour schedule. I was excited about the Beatles coming back to Shea. But something kept gnawing at me. I knew that Brian was going to book the Beatles into stadiums in Boston, Philadelphia and Washington, D.C. I had a feeling that somehow this might be too much exposure in a relatively small geographic area. I still thought that the concert would sell out, but I didn't want to try for another P.O. Box 21 miracle. We would promote this concert in the traditional way: posters, handbills, ads and PR.

About one week after I made the deal with Brian, my old friend Norman Weiss from GAC called me. Norman was now the agent responsible for the Beatles.

"Sid, I know that you made a deal with Brian Epstein to pay the Beatles $100,000 against 60 percent of the gross, just like the last time, but we'd like 65 percent this time."

I knew that I had picked up an extra $25,000 because we wouldn't need to build a new stage, so I agreed, but not before letting Norman know how I felt.

"You know, I made this deal with Brian, and I could discuss this extra five percent with him, and he would probably rescind it. But, I'll agree, Norman, for old times' sake. You can go back to Brian, and tell him you got the extra five percent. I don't care."

And, I really didn't care. All I wanted to do was get the Beatles back into Shea. A tougher businessman like Abe Margolies or Walter Hyman might have objected, but I just let it go.

I projected that we would start selling tickets for the Beatles in early July. To that end, I began to design posters and handbills for the event. The official concert poster that I designed has become a very valuable piece of

Beatles memorabilia.

I went to some police and security meetings, but it was all old hat. We all knew that we could get it done with little trouble. We were so sure we had enough security that I decided we would dispense with the karate black belts this time. Everybody concerned with security agreed, including the Mayor's office. I never got one call from Brian's office about security either. He was confident in our ability to protect "his boys."

During the planning of the second Beatles concert at Shea, I got a call from Andrew Loog Oldham about the Rolling Stones.

"Sid, this is Andrew."

"Uh, oh," I said, and we laughed. "Which venue do you want to get me thrown out of this time, Andrew?"

"Don't worry, Sid, I'll tell the boys to really behave this time."

"Right, Andrew. That'll be the day."

"Seriously, Sid, I want to bring them back to New York. How about it?"

He was such a sincere and nice guy and I knew the Stones were a sure sellout, so I accepted immediately.

"Same deal, Andrew. Ten thousand dollars, two shows, the Academy of Music, early May. And this time, I'll double the security!"

"Thank you, Sid. We're on!"

I really was on. I had the Rascals, the Rolling Stones were coming back, and that could only mean the Beatles were not far behind.

In May, the Rolling Stones came to the Academy of Music. They did their usual, high-energy performance and the kids went wild, but this time I was prepared. We had twice as much security as before and the carnage was mitigated. My most vivid memory of the Stones concerts, after their first appearance at Carnegie Hall that got me banned, was the constant parade of girls coming to my Academy of Music office asking, "Could you please introduce me to the Rolling Stones?" or "Mr. Bernstein, can you get me a date with one of the Rolling Stones?" I just laughed and declined to fulfill these requests. Although I felt sorry for these moonstruck teenagers, the last thing the Rolling Stones needed was for me to introduce them to girls.

During the time before the Beatles' return to Shea, I got a phone call from Al Diccio, a vice president at the Singer Sewing Machine Company. I had met Al through Tony Bennett. Tony and Al were old and dear friends.

"Sid," Al said, "Singer Sewing Machine is putting a new store at Rockefeller Center overlooking the skating rink. You could really do me a big favor by making the new store an outlet for Beatles tickets. The traffic and the publicity that would ensue would do wonders for the store! And to make it worth your while, Sid, we'll take 25% of all the tickets and guarantee their sale. If we don't sell them, we'll buy them."

I did a quick calculation. I had set up a ticket window at Shea and tickets were available at my office. Now I could have a sales outlet in mid-town Manhattan, which would certainly be helpful. It was before the days of Ticketron and Ticketmaster.

"You've got a deal, Al."

"Thanks, Sid. I really appreciate it."

Today a deal like that is called cross-promotion or cross-marketing. I just did it because it made good business sense and I liked Al.

I could tell pretty early on by the way the tickets were moving that the Beatles were not going to sell out Shea this time. I worked hard at publicizing and promoting the concert. We did the posters and hung them diligently. I gave interviews, and we printed and handed out a lot of handbills, but it was humanly impossible for any act to stay at that frenzied peak. The ticket sales diminished every week. I thought that perhaps my instinct was correct and that all those concerts so close to New York were a drain and had cost us a sellout.

A few days before the Beatles were to come to New York, Rick Sklar from WABC called and asked if I could get Bruce Morrow an interview with the Beatles. "Five to ten minutes is all we ask, Sid. Can you set it up?" I promised to try.

I called Rick on the day the Beatles were to arrive at the Warwick.

"Listen, Rick, I am going to see Brian and the Beatles at 5 PM at their hotel. Be down in the lobby with your equipment, and, Bruce, I think I can arrange the interview. But you have to be ready to roll!"

"We'll be there," he said.

I went to visit the Beatles on Monday at 5 o'clock at the Warwick. Brian and the boys were exhausted from having been on the road and performed nine concerts in 10 days. I marveled at their ability to withstand such a grueling pace. They were still very warm and friendly, but now everything seemed to be rather matter-of-fact. I had become a familiar fixture to them.

For his part, Brian looked extremely tired. Personally, I thought, he even looked unwell, but he was still very cheerful. The fact that the concert wasn't going to sell out never came up. I was sure that Brian had gotten the information from GAC that many of the venues on this current Beatles tour had failed to sell out, and that took some of the pressure off me. We sold a little more than 52,000 of the 55,000 seats, so the situation wasn't too bad. I was pleased that we had not made the "ten dollars a ticket for unsold seats" deal. That would have spelled financial disaster for me.

I asked Brian if it would be possible to get a few minutes for Bruce

Morrow to interview the boys.

"He's one of New York's top DJ's, Brian. Right up there with Murray the K. He's really a nice guy, and his program director, Rick Sklar, is the number one program director in America."

"We know all about Cousin Brucie and WABC. Let me ask the boys."

I stepped out of the suite, and Brian came back to me almost immediately. "The boys say okay. How soon can you have the WABC people here?"

"Well, WABC is right across the street from the hotel. They could be here in a few minutes. I can go and get them."

"Go get them, Sid."

I took the elevator down. Rick and Bruce were on the move as soon as they saw the smile on my face. We waited a few minutes, and then I took Bruce and Rick up to the suite. I introduced them to everyone. They proceeded to set up their equipment and taped the interview in ten minutes. I thanked Brian and the boys and left with Rick and Bruce. That night, Bruce Morrow went on air with an exclusive interview with the Beatles that was heard coast-to-coast on all the ABC stations. I had repaid my debt to Rick and Bruce for helping me with the Rascals.

I also realized once again that Brian Epstein and the Beatles were extremely decent people. After all, Murray the K was the DJ closest to them, and yet, because I had asked them to see Bruce and Rick as a personal favor to me, they had agreed to do it. In Yiddish, they call that being a *mensch*—a real person. They were real people.

On Tuesday, August 23, 1966, the Beatles played Shea Stadium for the second and last time. A group called the Cyrcle, who had a hit record, *Red Rubber Ball* opened the show. Jeffrey Katzenberg, the same sharp, smartly dressed kid, was with me again in the dugout, representing the mayor's office. We had used the same game plan as the previous year, except for the new improved sound system. However, the extraordinary excitement and frenzy of the fans didn't seem to be there. There was still plenty of screaming and some kids tried to rush the stage, but what had happened the previous August was a once-in-a-lifetime experience. It could not be duplicated.

I think Brian and the Beatles understood this, too. As we were standing in the walkway at the entrance to the dugout, Ringo said to me, "Sid, we hear that your wife Gerry is pregnant again. We haven't met her and we hear that she's a very beautiful young lady. This is the third time we're here in New York with you, Sid, and we still haven't met her!"

"The screaming and the frenzy are a bit too much for her," I said.

With that, John piped up, "Ah, Sid is trying to raise a baseball team, Ringo! He's going to go for nine!"

Everybody had a good laugh, and it signaled to me that the empty seats were not an issue.

As usual, Brian and I stood together on the field during the concert. We made small talk, but I remember him saying that he was glad that the tour was almost over.

"Two more dates on the West Coast, and we can go home," he said. "The boys have played almost every day since we got to Chicago 11 days ago. We even had to play two cities in one day on Sunday because of a rain postponement! Everybody is running out of energy, but New York seems to turn the boys on. I'm glad it's almost over."

I could see how tired he was, and I could detect in his voice that all the pressure was getting to him. Brian really never got any peace. People were always tugging at him from all directions. The boys sang and played while Brian did everything else. He had carried enormous responsibilities. It was really too much for one man, in my opinion.

"I don't see how you do it all, Brian."

He just smiled at me.

When the concert ended and just before the Beatles took off, I shook Brian's hand and said good-bye to him. I think we both knew that the Beatles' touring days were coming to an end.

Rock historians say that there were about 10,000 empty seats that night. However, I know that there were only 2,500 unsold tickets. It's like the mistake that has become part of the Beatles myth that I paid the Beatles $6,000 for the two performances at Carnegie Hall, when the reality was that Brian and I agreed on a price of $6,500, and that's what I paid. It's important to me that the record be set straight.

Good Lovin' reached number one. The Rascals were awarded their first gold record and, as their manager, I was entitled to receive a gold record, too. In all the years that I had been in the music business, I had never achieved a gold record.

We had a small ceremony at Atlantic Records. The Atlantic executives handed the Rascals and me our gold records. Pictures were taken that appeared about a week later in *Cashbox, Record World* and *Billboard*, the leading record industry publications. I took my gold record and hung it in a prominent spot in my office. I was very proud of this milestone we'd achieved. *Good Lovin'* was the first of ten Rascals gold records I have received.

I took the Rascals to Hawaii. Tom Moffat, the top promoter and top DJ in Hawaii, called me and offered us a super deal. The Rascals were booked into a mid-size arena for five nights. They were underpaid from a cash point of view but compensated in many other ways. We took everyone with us on this trip. My entire family and all of the Rascals' families enjoyed a fully paid working vacation. Tom paid all of our expenses, from airfare to sightseeing. When we got to Hawaii, two Rascals' records were in the top 10, so we were treated like royalty. Tom Moffat and I became good friends and we are still good friends to this day.

During these years, the Bitter End on Bleecker Street in Greenwich Village became a favorite hangout of mine. My friend Freddie Weintraub owned it and Billy Fields managed it. Billy had traded in his career as a vocalist and sometime promoter with me for something a little more predictable and secure. The Bitter End specialized in showcasing young comedians, and a number of very big stars like Woody Allen, Richard Pryor and Dick Cavett got their start there and in other clubs in the Village.

The Bitter End was also a hangout for show business professionals and managers. Albert Grossman, who managed Bob Dylan, Peter Paul & Mary and later Janis Joplin and The Band, would come to the Bitter End to relax and see what was new and upcoming.

Albert and I had become friendly, and I considered him to be the best personal manager when it came to dealing with several acts simultaneously. Albert could maintain his equilibrium and his relationship with his acts, even though they were megastars and subject to jealousies and needs that they thought only he could fill. I marveled at his ability to juggle it all.

Across the street from the Bitter End was the Café Au Go Go, where all the underground music groups performed. Alice Cooper, Richie Havens and the Blues Project eventually emerged from the Au Go Go. What the Bitter End was to comedy, the Café Au Go Go was to music on Bleecker Street.

The Blues Project, five guys from the Village, became a "big buzz" act out of the Café and I got to know them quite well. Al Kooper, Steve Katz, Danny Kalb, Roy Blumenfeld and Andy Kulberg were extremely bright and highly educated young men. They were liberal, left-thinking young guys with a lot of ideas and passion. I responded to that and we became friends. I made it a point to follow their careers and monitor their progress.

I was amazed to learn that the Blues Project, who I considered to be somewhat of an underground group, had managed to secure a booking at the Phone Booth, which was a more mainstream club. I went to check them out, and after their set, they came to sit with me. I congratulated them because I thought that they were great musicians. We talked for a while and then one of them, I think it was Danny Kalb, said "Sid, we need a manager. Would you consider taking us on?"

It was a request out of the blue (no pun intended). I understood that, at that particular moment in time, I was a pretty hot commodity. I was promoting groups like the Beatles, the Rolling Stones, and the rest of the British Invasion. I still had my hand in some of the pop music promotions at Carnegie Hall, and my band, the Rascals, had a number one record.

Although the Rascals' future looked very bright on the surface, I had my doubts. It is a strange axiom of life that sometimes success is intolerable for the successful. As soon as the Rascals achieved a number one hit, they began to fight with each other. Nothing major, mind you, just petty annoyances which had them cursing and berating each other. I was very disturbed by this. As a person who disdains the use of foul language and who avoids confrontation and arguments like the plague, the Rascals' bickering caused me great consternation and had me wondering if, in fact, they would self-destruct.

When Danny Kalb asked me to consider managing the Blues Project, I told him that I would think about it. That night at home I called my friend Albert Grossman. He had proven that you could manage several hit acts at the same time. I also thought about Brian Epstein, who was managing several acts besides the Beatles. I figured that it was just a matter of building an organization. I thought that I might be able to do it.

The Blues Project, I thought, were bright guys and fine musicians. They had paid their dues by playing in small clubs, and I knew that with the right kind of management and a record contract, they could be commercially successful.

A few days later, I called Danny and set up a meeting with the Blues Project members. We sat down, had a heart-to-heart talk and made a deal.

Walter Hyman and Jackie Green, a VP at Associated Booking Company (ABC), headed by Joe Glaser, socialized often. When Walter was still actively involved with the Rascals, he strongly suggested that I give the booking responsibilities for the Rascals to ABC. Sol Saffian became the responsible agent and reported to Jackie. I had wanted to give the Rascals to Frank Barsalona ,who had worked with me at GAC and had recently opened his own agency, Premier Talent. William Morris and, of course, GAC expressed some interest, too. But in deference to Walter and his relationship with Jackie, we went with ABC.

So many people knew me from my past activities within the music business that they called me to book the Rascals more often than they called Sol Saffian or Jackie Green. I fielded most of the calls, so I was able to convince the promoters who wanted to book the frequently unavailable Rascals to take the Blues Project instead. I wondered why promoters who had sought to book a number one record act, the Rascals, would agree to take a relatively unknown act instead. Maybe because after all those years as a manager, agent and promoter, they knew and trusted me. The Blues Project did not let them down.

The boys in the Blues Project had become accustomed to getting $150 a night. I immediately got their price to $500, and, in short order, I worked them up to $750 and then to $1,250. They stayed at that price for a short time, and then I got them a record deal on Verve Records, and their price went to $2,000 a night. They were relishing every moment as they watched their careers advance. The Blues Project was on the verge, and a hit record would put them over the top, when Danny Kalb took an overdose of LSD and got arrested in San Francisco. It took a plea from Tom Moffat in Hawaii to Tom Rounds, the top DJ in San Francisco, to get Danny out of jail, but that incident destroyed the Blues Project. They broke up and went their separate ways. Later, Al Kooper and Steve Katz would go on to be founding members of the supergroup Blood, Sweat & Tears.

Chapter 14: REGRETS

ONE DAY, I GOT A CALL FROM NAT WEISS, a very successful show business attorney and a close personal friend of Brian Epstein's. Nat was also the manager of the group that opened for the Beatles at the second Shea Stadium concert, the Cyrcle.

"Sid," said Nat, "as you are well aware, you have a very special relationship with Brian Epstein. Robert Stigwood, who you no doubt have heard about, manages the Bee Gees, Eric Clapton and Cream. I think that you, Brian and Robert should meet to discuss a partnership arrangement. The three of you together would make a formidable combination. You have the Rascals and the Blues Project (no one knew yet that the Blues Project had self-destructed). Brian has the Beatles and some other acts that he's wanted to talk to you about. I think the three of you should sit down and talk."

It sounded like an interesting idea.

"Nat, when is Brian going to be in New York again?

"He's going to be at the Waldorf Towers in a couple of weeks," he said. "I'll arrange a meeting and let you know the date."

Several weeks later, I went to the Waldorf Towers. Brian told me that his boys were off on holiday: John was making a movie, George had gone to India and Paul and Ringo were hanging out back home. Robert Stigwood, an Australian, was at the meeting, too. Nat Weiss introduced Stigwood to me. I found him to be a very nice young man, modest and bright. Nat repeated what he had said to me on the phone. Stigwood had the Bee Gees, Clapton and Cream and was working on some other exciting projects. I had the Rascals and, at that point, the Blues Project. Nat didn't have to repeat who Brian was managing. If we pooled our acts and started a new management company, Stigwood would cover Australia. Australia was considered to be a spawning ground for new talent. I would cover America, specifically New York, the home of most of the record companies and Brian would contribute his great reputation and stature in Great Britain and the rest of the world.

"You three together would be unbeatable," Nat continued. "If you pool your acts and resources, there's no telling what you could accomplish!"

Brian spoke first. "I'm all for this, and I think it could be very exciting, but I cannot put the Beatles into the partnership. Any other acts I manage will certainly be pooled and put into the new management company, but I cannot include the Beatles."

There wasn't much argument. Everybody understood that, for personal and business reasons, Brian couldn't include the Beatles in our partnership.

We spent about two hours discussing who would do what and where we would maintain offices. It was very exciting.

I told Stigwood, Brian and Nat Weiss that I wanted to discuss the plan with my wife and some of my advisors and that I would get back to them in a few days.

"In principle, gentlemen, this sounds very good to me," I said.

Stigwood was all for it and Brian had only the one caveat. No Beatles in the deal.

When I got home, I told Gerry about the meeting. "I think it's a great idea, Sid, and I think you should give it a try."

"I do too, Gerry. I'm going to pursue it."

The very next day, I went to discuss the proposal with my accountants. They listened very carefully and then one of them said, "Wait a minute, Sid. What are you doing? You're going to put the Rascals in the deal and they are as hot as a pistol! Blues Project is starting to make a name for itself and you've really gotten their price up. (They didn't know about the Blues Project's imminent breakup.) You're making money with them. Also, if you do this deal, the major part of the workload is going to fall on you. You're in America, by far the largest market, and almost all of the record companies are here in New York. You are going to be doing most of the work. The only way we see this working is for Brian Epstein to include the Beatles; otherwise we think it's not a fair deal."

"Listen," I said, "I'm really not too concerned about the work part of it. I like the action, so I'm happy to do the work. But if you're telling me that this is going to cost me money and it's not financially sound, I'll back out. I can assure you that Brian will not put the Beatles into the partnership. I can also tell you that Robert Stigwood is very bright and ambitious and the Bee Gees are going to be a gigantic act."

"All well and good, but right now it's not a good deal for you."

I thought about what the accountants said and decided to take their advice. I had been so cavalier about money in the past, and had had so many ups and downs, that I just thought it would be best to listen to them and not take a chance.

I called Brian in London. "Brian, I would really like to do this. I like Robert and nothing would please me more than to be partners with you. You know how much I respect and admire you, but my accountants think that without the Beatles, this is a bad deal for me. And Brian, I know you can't include the Beatles."

"Sid, it's okay. I understand that you don't want to argue with your accountants. I certainly don't want to precipitate anything between you and them. Let's leave it for another time. Maybe things will change."

"Thank you for understanding, Brian. And please tell Nat about my decision. And thank him for trying. It's a great idea."

"Yes, I'll tell him and he'll tell Stigwood."

"I'll talk to you soon, Sid."

"Be well, Brian, and don't work too hard."

He laughed and hung up.

As the years have passed, I have often wondered what might have been if Brian Epstein, Robert Stigwood and Sid Bernstein had become partners. The idea certainly was pregnant with possibilities. Nat Weiss was right on the money. We would have been a powerful and formidable troika, one of the most potent forces in the history of the music business. I am certain of that.

My accountants rejected the deal because they felt there was a chance that they would be replaced. I wasn't sophisticated enough to understand the ramifications. It's one of the few regrets I have in my life.

After *Good Lovin'* became a number one hit in the U.S., Atlantic Records decided to release the record worldwide, which is a common practice in the record industry. You get a hit in the biggest market, the U.S. and then try to get it to be a hit worldwide. To support Atlantic's release of *Good Lovin'* in Great Britain, I decided to book the Rascals into several small clubs in London and across England. Jackie Green set it up for us through some friends of his in London. At our first engagement, Blazers, in London, I sat at a table in the middle of the room. My boys took to the stage and began to play. At a table to the right of the stage were Paul McCartney, Brian Jones and Bill Wyman of the Rolling Stones and Keith Moon, the drummer of The Who. A few minutes after the Rascals began playing, Brian Epstein came in and sat down next to me. I had extended an invitation to everyone weeks earlier when I knew that the Rascals and I would be in London. I had completely forgotten about the invitation, but was pleased and appreciative that Brian, Paul and the others had come to show their support. Everyone in the club was excited. Paul and Brian stayed till the set ended and then accepted my invitation to visit with the Rascals. Brian and Paul spent about a half-hour with the Rascals. They both were very complimentary and encouraging. Gene Cornish, the Rascals' guitarist, was always in awe of Brian and could never get over what a sharp dresser he was.

Brian came to another Rascals performance with John Lennon. Whenever big rock stars came to a performance, there was always additional excitement in the club. The Rascals were doing more than holding their own in the presence of so many great musicians and performers. Someone told me that the Rascals were Bill Wyman's favorite group.

During one of the dates on the Rascals' first trip to Britain, Dino's tom-tom drum was sliding off the stage, so Keith Moon propped himself against the drum to make sure it would remain on stage. Someone told me that in exchange for that great courtesy, Dino taught Keith how to twirl drumsticks while playing. No one in the entire world of drummers could twirl his sticks like Dino! It was a show unto itself!

Throughout our stay in England, members of groups who were becoming famous in the U.S visited us. It was a very new and exciting time for all of us. We were all trying to navigate through the uncharted waters of fame and fortune together. We were like an extended family of explorers and pioneers.

I wanted to help Atlantic with their continued efforts on behalf of *Good Lovin'* worldwide. Our trip to London had gotten the record started in England and there was the beginnings of airplay in Germany, too. I thought it would be a good idea to make a quick trip to Paris and play the Olympic Theatre, the same venue the Beatles had played at immediately before coming to Carnegie Hall. I also wanted to meet Eddie Barclay, Mr. Music in Europe. Barclay's Records was the label that released the British and European version of *Good Lovin'*. Sol Saffian, who was the responsible agent for the Rascals at ABC, arranged the date at the Olympia, which would feature the Rascals and a great Spanish band, Los Bravos, who had the hit *Black Is Black*.

Felix Cavaliere of the Rascals shipped his Hammond B-3 organ to Paris. The sound of the Hammond organ differentiated the Rascals from almost all other groups playing at that time. The Hammond is a very large and unwieldy instrument that comes in two parts, a very heavy keyboard and an equally heavy speaker cabinet. When Felix plugged the B-3 into the available power source at the Olympia, it blew up. A mini mushroom cloud, like something after a nuclear explosion, appeared. American and European electric currents are incompatible and that caused the circuit to blow. Everyone searched frantically for a substitute organ, but we could not locate a suitable replacement in Paris. The substitute organ that we eventually found was beat-up and broken-down. It was like a toy; it was not a B-3. Felix was beside himself. He thought the substitute organ was a joke.

As I was sitting in the front row in the Olympia Theatre trying to figure out what to do and seeing Felix so disconsolate, I felt a hand tap me on the shoulder. I turned around to see Brian Epstein, as elegant as ever, with a friend.

"How nice to see you," I said incredulously. "What brings you here?"

"I heard you were here, Sid, and just came over to say hello."

I was really touched. Brian had flown over to Paris just to say hello and wish us good luck. I told him about our B-3 problem and asked if he had any ideas.

"If we had a little more time, we could bring one across the Channel, but we'll never get it here in time for tonight's performance. Have you checked with any other groups?"

"Everybody is out looking for us, Brian. Eddie Barclay's people, the theatre staff, but no luck yet."

By then, the Rascals had congregated and said hello to Brian, with whom they felt a kinship.

Brian turned to Felix and said, "Felix, I have been listening to the rehearsal with the substitute organ and I can assure you that no one here tonight will know the difference. Don't even give it a second thought."

Brian's comments seemed to calm Felix. Brian wished the Rascals good luck on the evening performance and listened to the rest of the rehearsal, clearly enjoying the music.

After a while, he leaned over to me and said, "Sid, I have to catch a flight back to London." I escorted him out of the theatre and thanked him again for making the trip.

"Think nothing of it," he said.

When I took my boys to dinner before their performance that night, all they talked about was how Brian Epstein had flown in for an hour just to show his support and lend encouragement.

When I returned to the States, I had the opportunity to promote a Ray Charles concert in Central Park. I jumped at the chance because I loved Ray Charles. He is one of the most important and beloved artists in the music business. Dino Danelli, the Rascals' drummer, had always been a big fan of Ray Charles. Right before the concert, I introduced Dino to Ray. Ray Charles had a 40-foot trailer with absolutely no furniture other than a chair that was placed in the middle of the trailer. There was no furniture in the trailer to make sure that Ray, who is blind, would not bump into anything and hurt himself. After making the introduction, I left the two artists alone so that they could talk.

Dino spent about a half-hour with Ray Charles. When he emerged from the trailer, his face was glowing. I was happy to have made a dream come true for Dino.

Pearl Bailey had always been a favorite performer of mine. I had met her during my Lou Walters days when we were managing Diahann Carroll and Diahann appeared in the Broadway show *House of Flowers* starring

Pearl Bailey. Pearl's singing, acting and comedic talents were outstanding. I had always wanted to present Pearl in concert. I approached Pearl to see if she would like to do a concert at Carnegie Hall. Her husband, Louis Bellson, who was a widely known jazz drummer, was also her chief advisor. When I outlined the proposal to him and Pearl, they nodded to each other and said in unison, "Let's do it."

I couldn't clear a date at Carnegie Hall, so we took the Pearl Bailey concert to Lincoln Center's Avery Fisher Hall, where the New York Philharmonic played. Seats were in such demand that I could have done three shows with her. It was particularly thrilling because she put on a great performance, and many record industry and Hollywood executives and artists from Broadway were in attendance. It was a gala evening in a magnificent hall, and Pearl couldn't have been better. It was a big event in New York. The best thing about Pearl Bailey's concert was that, for me, it was less a quest for money and more an issue of presenting someone who I thought was a very special artist.

I was making money from many sources. The Rascals were hot, and I was making a percentage from their personal appearances, their record royalties and their publishing. The promotions that I did were successful, so the money was flowing from there as well.

I decided to do a big show. The old Madison Square Garden had never had a rock and roll concert. I wanted to be the first to promote music in the Garden. I had tried to put the Beatles in the Garden, but Brian had nixed the idea.

I thought that James Brown was capable of filling the Garden. I believed that he had become a very major artist. I called Ned Irish, the owner of the Garden and the New York Knicks. Irish had made his reputation and fortune by putting college basketball doubleheaders in the Garden and from his ownership of the Knicks, New York's pro basketball team. (The Rangers, New York's hockey team, also played their home games at the Garden.)

"Mr. Irish, this is Sid Bernstein."

"Oh yes, Mr. Bernstein! How can I help you?"

"Well, Mr. Irish, I would like to present an attraction at the Garden."

"Who would you like to present here?"

"There is an artist that I think is perfect for the Garden. I would love to present him, Mr. Irish. Are there any dates available for me to present him?"

"Wait a minute, Mr. Bernstein. Who do you want to put into the Garden?" he asked emphatically.

"James Brown. I want to present James Brown."

"What does Mr. Brown do?"

"He's an artist who sings and performs and has a great following nationwide," I answered.

"I've never heard of him."

I didn't know what to say to that so I quickly said, "Well, he does sell a lot of records and is extremely popular."

"Mr. Bernstein, I am very busy right now and I'm going to be out of town for the next few days. I should be back by the end of the week. I'll call you and if you don't hear from me, give me a call and we'll continue this conversation."

"Fine, Mr. Irish," I said "If you don't call me by Friday, I'll call you."

The very next day, Ned Irish called me at my office.

"Mr. Bernstein, please listen to me carefully."

"I'm listening, Mr. Irish."

"I want you to make me a hero with my grandchildren."

"What do you mean, Mr. Irish?" I was very curious now.

"Well, I mentioned the conversation that you and I had about James Brown to my grandchildren and they were very excited. 'Grandpa,' they said, 'he's the man!' They want to see James Brown in the Garden, Mr. Bernstein."

"So, let's make a deal," I said.

"Okay, Sid. I'll give you the Garden at a bargain price of $25,000, and that's only because of my grandkids. You get everything for that: tickets, ushers, lights, stagehands. It's all yours."

"Great, Ned. You've got a deal."

I called Ben Bart, James Brown's agent and manager. The same Ben Bart that I used to collude with several times a day at the Paramount when James Brown headlined for me and would refuse to go on for every conceivable reason.

"Ben, I want to present James Brown in the Garden."

"What? Did you say the Garden, Sid?"

"Yeah, you heard me right, Ben. James Brown in Madison Square Garden. I'm guaranteeing the Garden, Ben."

"Sid, you're kidding! James would love to play the Garden."

"Well, you've got it. The deal with the Garden is set. Is James available?"

"Don't worry. He'll make himself available. How many shows?"

"Only one. There are 17,000 seats in the Garden. I'll offer you guys $20,000 for the one show. How does that sound?"

"No problem! I have to check with James, of course, but $20,000 sounds just fine."

I was really happy after I hung up with Ben, because it was going to be another first. The first rock music concert at the Garden.

A day later, Ben called and confirmed our deal.

"Sid, James is really excited."

"Good, Ben, he should be."

Every seat for James Brown at the Garden was filled. James was stupendous and rocked the Garden. The crowd loved him. My fondest memory of the concert was when James got the entire audience to hold hands and sway to the music. It was a sight to behold. Black and white people holding hands, the chain extending all around the Garden. It was a real show of solidarity, but such is the power of music.

The success of James Brown at the Garden confirmed to me its viability as a venue for concerts.

I decided to promote my own group there. The Rascals were by now becoming a fixture on the charts, first with *I Ain't Gonna Eat Out My Heart Anymore*, then *Good Lovin'* followed by *You Better Run*. I thought they were ready.

I called Ned Irish.

"Ned, I'm going to make you a hero again."

"Really, Sid? How's that?" he asked. I could picture the grin on his face.

"Tell your grandchildren that Sid Bernstein is going to bring the Rascals to the Garden."

"Who?"

"The Rascals."

"Listen, Sid, you were right on the last one. I'll take your word for it."

"Same deal, Ned?"

"Same deal, Sid."

When I hung up, I realized that Ned Irish was very happy because the James Brown concert had opened a new revenue stream for him. I had probably become one of his favorite people.

The crowd in the Garden really turned on to the Rascals. There is nothing like 17,000 people screaming, whistling and applauding to get the adrenaline going. It was sheer energy.

After the Rascals concert in the Garden, I knew that I had a major act on my hands, and I escalated their price from, $5,000 to $7,500 per show. I couldn't fill even a fraction of the requests for their appearances that were being offered.

After playing the Garden, the Rascals played at the Singer Bowl in New York's old World's Fairgrounds. They performed to an audience of 12,000, and again all the seats were gone and many were turned away. The Rascals owned New York.

It was my habit to call Brian Epstein in London from time to time to chat and find out how he was doing. The Beatles had stopped touring and he had more time and was less harried. He was always very cordial, and we had a running gag. He would ask me about Gerry and the kids and he would always ask, Any new ones? And there always was!

On one such call in the summer of 1967, Brian told me that he was coming to New York in two weeks.

"Sid, I'm going to be at the Waldorf. Why don't you come by and we can talk about some of my new acts and spend some time together?"

"Great, I'll look forward to that."

I called Brian at the Waldorf.

"Do you have any free time today?" he asked me.

"Sure. I have my wife with me. Your boys always kidded me about never seeing or meeting her. Now you can tell them you actually met her."

He laughed, "I'd love to meet her. Come on over."

Gerry and I went over to the Waldorf. Brian looked absolutely worn out to me, but he went out of his way to be courteous and solicitous of Gerry, who was very pregnant at the time with our second son Dylan, who was born on April 8, 1967. We drank tea and he asked her about our children, Denise and Adam, and we made small talk. I inquired about his mother and the Beatles as well, and we spent about an hour talking about plans he had for some of his new acts and ways I could be involved in presenting them in New York. After a while, Brian told us that he had to leave for a meeting with Murray the K and offered to drop us at home.

I accepted the offer, and we all got into his limo. Brian just didn't have the same energy that I had always seen him exhibit.

"Hey, Brian, is anything wrong? You don't look too well to me."

"There's just so much pressure, it has not been an easy time."

"You have to take care of yourself, Brian. I'm concerned about you."

"Thanks, Sid."

He got out of the limo and told the chauffeur to take Gerry and me home and then to come back and wait for him until he was finished with his meeting.

We shook hands. He told Gerry how nice it was to finally meet her, and said he would send my regards to his mother and the boys and call me from London. And then he left. It was the last time I saw Brian Epstein.

On August 27, 1967, as I was sitting at home doing some paperwork, someone called to inform me that Brian Epstein had been found dead in his London townhouse. I had to catch my breath. True, he had not looked well the last time I had seen him, but he was a 32-year-old man in the prime of his life, extraordinarily successful, with no known health problems. We had spoken about future plans and I thought that even though he seemed extremely exhausted, he had everything to live for.

I was completely shocked. Brian was a man who I respected and admired, and it hurt deeply to think that he was gone! He had played such an important role in my life. He was a man, who by saying yes to me, had allowed me to participate in the making of music history. Brian had said yes and changed my life forever. I was shattered.

I called each of the Rascals. They had known and admired Brian. They were shocked, too. Brian had exhibited great support for them by coming to see them at the Phone Booth in New York, by stopping in with Paul McCartney and John Lennon when they had performed in England, and by flying to Paris just to wish them good luck when they played the Olympia.

During that sad day, I thought about my relationship with Brian. I thought of his gentility, his grace, his sartorial splendor and his love for "his boys." I wondered what would happen to them now that he was gone, and I knew that, as far as they were concerned, they would never be able to replace him. Brian's loss to all of us was devastating. The loss for me was both personal and professional.

Later that week, I made a call that I dreaded making. I called Queenie Epstein, Brian's lovely mother. It was a very difficult conversation. Her pain was immeasurable, but as always she was so gracious and expressed to me how "Brian was so fond of you, Sid." She was trying to console me. It really was so terrible. We had all lost something dear and precious, and she had lost the most of all.

For a while after Brian died, I heard rumors that I was going to be asked to become the Beatles' manager. I did not give much credence to the rumors and was never contacted by anyone in the Beatles' organization to discuss the possibility. I remember thinking back to the meeting with Nat Weiss when Robert Stigwood, Brian and I had met about a possible merger of our companies. I wondered what would have happened if we had gone ahead with our plans. Would that have lessened some of the pressure on Brian and possibly prolonged his life? It's the great What If game at its ultimate.

Chapter 15: BIG EVENTS: ONE AFTER ANOTHER

FROM A BUSINESS PERSPECTIVE, I WAS HOT. My friend Manheim Fox called me. He was a folk music expert.

"Sid," he stroked me, "you've promoted everything! Jazz, r&b, Latin, pop, the Beatles, the Rolling Stones."

"Stop, Manny. Flattery will get you everywhere. What do you want me to do?"

"Sid, you've never done a folk concert. Folk is hotter than hell, and I think you should do a folk festival."

I liked the idea. I had been exposed to many folk acts in the Village. Some of my friends, like Albert Grossman and Mort Lewis, were successful managers of folk acts. What Manny Fox said was true. Folk was hot.

"Manny, I like the idea, but I really don't know the folk music scene very well."

"Don't worry," he assured me. "I'll help you."

I agreed to do it. Manny helped, and Billy Fields was great at booking the acts. We booked Carnegie Hall for a four-day folk festival. Mrs. Satescu knew that the folk audience would behave. We booked Dave Van Ronk, Mississippi John Hurt, the Greenbriar Boys, Buffy Ste. Marie, Phil Ochs and Jesse Colin Young. To spice it up and for no logical reasons we added Chuck Berry, the Staple Singers, Mose Allison, the Statler Brothers, June Carter and Johnny Cash. Looking at it now, it was more an amalgam of country, jazz, r&b and folk rather than pure folk, which I think was what Manny had originally envisioned.

Manny brought in his friend John Stevens as a co-promoter, but I put up the money. The festival ran for four days in mid-June, 1968. It got great critical reviews and we had fun, but I lost about $18,000. It was okay; I had the money and I considered it to be a learning experience.

One of the highlights of the folk festival was visiting Johnny Cash in his dressing room and having him ask me, with a big question mark written all over his face, "Sid, can you please tell me what the hell I'm doing here?" He couldn't figure out what a country star like him was doing at a festival with folk and r&b acts. I wish you could have seen the expression on Johnny Cash's face when he asked me that question. I laughed so hard that tears came to my eyes.

In early May, my mother was admitted to the hospital for still another attempt to relieve her from the pain that she had been suffering with her whole life. She made it through the operation, but fell into a coma shortly thereafter. I visited her three or four times a day. On May 15, 1968, she passed away. It was unexpected, and I was devastated and lost, but what could I do? My mother had been in pain almost all the days that I knew her. We buried her, sat *shiva*, and were visited by family and friends.

A short while after my mother passed away, Soshana Damari, an Israeli singing star, convinced me to do an Israeli all-star show in the Garden. It was the last event I promoted in the old Madison Square Garden on 52nd Street and Eighth Avenue. I did this show in my mother's memory.

Peter Nero had been the piano player at Jilly's restaurant. Frank Sinatra had made Jilly's his hangout so the restaurant became quite famous and very successful. I would go to Jilly's from time to time, and Peter and I became friendly. He was making records and they were selling. I thought he was ready for a concert career, so I approached him about performing in Carnegie Hall. He agreed and we scheduled the concert. We did the posters and the handbills, but what assured the concert's success was the fact that Peter's wife was a member of the Jewish women's charitable organization Hadassah. Peter's wife galvanized the Hadassah ladies to get behind the concert, and they sold a lot of tickets. The Hadassah ladies assured me that the concert was going to be successful. I wish that I had them selling tickets for me for every event I ever promoted or produced. I would never have had anything but sellouts.

The winds of change wrought by the Beatles were blowing across the world. Clothing and hairstyles had changed. Sexual mores and language had changed. The world that I grew up in was gone.

Nowhere was that more obvious than at Woodstock. Artie Kornfeld, John Roberts, Joel Rosenman and Michael Lang decided to stage a rock festival in an upstate New York town called Woodstock. When the town fathers of Woodstock cancelled the permits to stage the festival, the producers took it to Bethel, which was 50 miles away. The Rascals were invited to perform, but they had a previously booked engagement and I didn't want to disappoint the promoters of the event. And Gerry was once again pregnant and I couldn't leave her and the kids for four days.

I watched the news reports and saw the traffic jams and the vast crowds. I knew that the Beatles' appearances at Shea had given birth to the idea that enormous crowds could and would show up for the right kind of event. Later in the year, at Altamont in California, there was another huge event featuring the Rolling Stones. I hated that event because there was needless violence and loss of life and I knew that the security arrangements had been inadequate. The event was run very carelessly.

What was coming across loud and clear to me was that the gamble I had taken by putting the Beatles in Shea had set a precedent. Rock and roll was capable of drawing huge crowds in very large venues.

The new Madison Square Garden was being built on top of Penn Station, bordered by 33rd and 32nd Streets and Seventh and Eighth Avenues. It was to be a beautiful arena with almost 20,000 seats and state-of-the-art sound and lighting. Besides the basketball Knicks, the hockey Rangers, college basketball, and the Ringling Bros. and Barnum & Bailey circus that were already in place, music and concerts were contemplated as events for the new Garden. James Brown and the Rascals' earlier appearances at the old Garden had cemented that.

Several months before construction on the new Garden was completed, Alvin Cooperman, the head booker at the new Madison Square Garden, called me.

"Sid, you introduced Ned Irish to the revenue possibilities from music concerts at the old Madison Square Garden. How would you like to produce the first show in the new Madison Square Garden? We're going to have a lot of concerts in this place!"

"Sure, Alvin!" I jumped at the chance. It was a chance to be first again, and I appreciated being given the opportunity.

"Tell me, Alvin, what are you going to charge for the use of the new Garden?"

"Forty thousand a night."

"Okay, Alvin, I'll get back to you." Forty thousand was a lot of money, but, after all, the Garden was a brand-new facility.

I wanted the first concert to be a success. I wanted to do something a little different, and I also wanted to make sure that the audience would be well-behaved.

I called Manny Greenfield, the manager for Joan Baez. Manny lived in Boston and Joan lived in San Francisco. Joan was a hot artist at the time.

"Manny," I said. "They've built a magnificent new Madison Square Garden here in New York, and I have been awarded the inaugural concert. I'd love to present Joan."

"Hey, Sid, you know we're getting a lot of money for Joan these days."

"I'm sure you are. But I don't care about the money. I'll give you even more than you're getting! I really want Joan Baez to open the new Garden."

"Well, what's your offer, Sid?"

"How about $20,000, Manny."

"That's good. That's good! Let me take it up with Joan, and I'll call you back."

A few days later, he called back. "Sid, I have a problem."

"What's that, Manny?"

"Joan doesn't want $20,000."

"How much does she want?" I asked him guardedly.

"She only wants $5,000."

"What? Could you repeat that again?" I was sure that I had heard wrong.

"Yes, Sid. Five thousand dollars."

"Five thousand bucks, Manny? Could you explain that to me? I offered her $20,000."

"Sid, she only wants you to charge $2.00 per ticket for all seats on a first come, first served basis, and she and I both understand that at that price, you can't make any money. You might even lose money! No preferential treatment for anybody. Two dollars a ticket, first come, first served. She wants everybody who wants to see her to be able to afford a ticket."

I did a quick calculation. The sold out-house would only gross $40,000. Joan would get $5,000 and the Garden would cost $40,000. I would be losing $5,000. I wanted to be first in Madison Square Garden and Alvin Cooperman liked the idea of Joan Baez. I could afford to lose the $5,000.

"You got it, Manny. Five thousand dollars it is. All tickets, $2.00."

I called Alvin Cooperman at the Garden and told him the deal. He couldn't believe it. He also explained to me that because of Joan's political leanings, he was going to have to put on extra security just in case there was some kind of a demonstration.

"Okay, Alvin. Whatever you need..." I began.

"No, no, Sid! We'll take care of the security ourselves. You're going to lose enough money."

Of course, the concert sold out immediately. The combination of Joan, the ticket price and the new Madison Square Garden ensured that.

I decided to put Joan on in the round, which meant that she would be dead-center in the middle of the Garden floor. Then, I thought, to enable everyone to have a chance to see her, it would be nice if the stage rotated ever so slowly while she sang and accompanied herself on guitar. She and Manny loved the idea and approved it as soon as they heard it. Manny just wanted me to make sure that the stage turned slowly enough to ensure Joan's safety.

The concert was an unforgettable event. I ordered rose petals by the bushel to be strewn all over the stage and at its base. When Joan came on to the stage to thunderous ovation, she was ankle deep in a carpet of rose petals. Gerry and Adam sat with me, and this time I chose to sit in the front row, which was uncommon for me. Usually I like to sit several rows back. I wanted Gerry and Adam to experience and smell the rose petals.

Joan was wonderful and the audience loved her. At the end of her first encore, Adam, my five-year-old son, with no encouragement whatsoever from his parents, chose to walk up onto the stage and give Joan a rose petal. She leaned down and kissed him and the Garden erupted. People started to stream down from the higher seats towards the stage. The ushers wanted to stop them, but I told the head usher to allow them to come down and that I would take the responsibility. During her second encore, Joan was on stage with hundreds of people sitting on the rose-petal-strewn floor, singing along with her while the stage slowly turned. It was a magical moment.

Alvin Cooperman and the Garden hierarchy were so elated with the Joan Baez concert that they cut the price of the house by $5,000.

"You did such a great job! Thanks!" Alvin said. "We don't want you to lose money, Sid."

It was a very nice gesture, and I appreciated it.

At around this time, Sly Stone and his band, Sly and the Family Stone, burst onto the music scene. I had heard about him and read about his act, and once I heard his records on the radio, I understood why he was gaining momentum like a tidal wave.

David Kapralik, Sly's manager, called me. He had signed Sly and the Family Stone to Epic while still an A&R (Artists and Repertoire) man and had quit his A&R position at Epic to become the group's manager when he realized how big they were going to be. David and I knew each other from the business. I liked David a lot and I respected his guts for having quit a successful A&R job to manage Sly.

"Sid, I'd love it if you could present Sly at the Garden."

"I'd love to David. I've been watching what's going on. This kid could be the biggest!"

"I know. That's why I quit Epic. Listen, Sid, you don't have to put up your own money. I'll take care of that. I just want you to handle the Garden, put together the rest of the bill, and put your name on the promotion. And, I'll pay you for your time."

"I'd be glad to do it, David."

I called Alvin Cooperman, my buddy at the Garden, and secured the date February 13th and explained that I would need to use the entire room because I would have three other acts besides Sly and the Family Stone on the bill, and I needed all the seats.

"We can't do this in the round like Joan. It won't work, Alvin. We need to set up a proscenium stage (staging where the stage is in the front of the room), but we need to sell the entire room. I can't help it, some of the fans will only be seeing the performers' backs."

"Anything you want, Sid."

I booked the opening acts, Fleetwood Mac and Grand Funk Railroad. I also decided that I wanted to have a young comedian who I used to kid around with at the Bitter End perform, so I booked Richard Pryor.

The concert sold out immediately. I started to get calls from all over the United States and Canada for tickets. All the record executives and music people were calling. It wasn't the same level of excitement as with the Beatles, but it felt somewhat similar. In retrospect, it's easy to understand why: Fleetwood Mac, Grand Funk Railroad, Richard Pryor and Sly and the Family Stone on one bill. I could have sold out a 100,000-seat stadium. People were offering me scalper prices for my reserve tickets, but I refused to be tempted.

I was really looking forward to the show, particularly because I wanted to help Richard Pryor.

Fleetwood Mac opened the concert and did their half-hour. I thought that they were great and that they would be a big act in very short order.

I sat in the fourth or fifth row on the aisle so I would be available to deal with the constant stream of messages and questions that were being sent to me, without disturbing anyone who was sitting near me. At some point, I got a message that Sly had not yet arrived. I learned later that this was part of his modus operandi. I hurried to find someone in Sly's entourage and was told not to worry because he was at a nearby hotel and would be on stage on time. I went back to my seat.

Richard Pryor came on next. I had instructed him to do 18 minutes and he agreed. His opening line was, "Good evening, ladies and gentlemen!" Richard paused for effect, and slowly looked around the packed Garden. "I don't know what a kid like me is doing in a fuckin' rock'n'roll show like this!"

I was stunned. I didn't believe what I was hearing. Alvin Cooperman of the Garden was sitting in the front row with his two teenaged daughters. I took a quick look at him. I thought and hoped that maybe that was the worst of it and Richard wouldn't say anything inflammatory again.

Richard then said, "I want all you folks to relax and loosen your ties." I looked at Alvin again, and I could see his head swiveling around. I knew he was surveying the affect that Richard was having on the crowd.

Richard continued his opening monologue, "I'm so flabbergasted to be in the company of these great musicians and these great people..." he paused and surveyed the entire Garden. "And look at this fuckin' place, it's filled to the rafters!"

By now, I was trying to figure out how far I could slide under my seat. The head usher was with Alvin Cooperman, pointing in the general direction of my seat. It was three or four minutes into Richard's set and I was thinking, Oh my God! We're going to have another 14 minutes of this profanity! By now, all the ushers were looking for me and I was trying to slide further down into my seat. One of them rushed over to me and said, "Mr. Bernstein, Mr. Cooperman wants to see you."

"Tell him that I know what he wants and I'll handle it. I'll take care of it," I said.

Richard threw another one of his "fuckin'"lines out and, with that, Alvin Cooperman jumped up and rushed his two girls out of the room.

I hurried to the front of the stage and told Alan, my stage manager, to tell Richard immediately that he had to stop the profanity.

"Tell him, Alan, to stop immediately!" And I meant it.

Alan got Richard's attention and Richard came to the side of the stage to hear what Alan had to say. I could see Richard nodding his head in agreement. Alan hurried back to me and said, "It's okay, Sid, I told him what you said and he said he understands." By this time, the audience was probably wondering why Richard had left the mike and what was going on.

Richard sauntered back to the mike and, putting his hand over his eyes to shield them from the lights, began to look the audience over, as if to find one person. Me!!

"Folks," he said. "Please forgive me. The show must go on and I was starting to tell you a story that I'll finish in a minute, but I'm sure you want to know what just went on here and why I left the mike to talk to that man. (He pointed over to Alan.) Well, Sid Bernstein, the fuckin' promoter, asked me to watch my language!"

The audience was laughing so hard that they didn't hear him say, "What's wrong with that man?" You could almost see the waves of laughter. I hate profanity and always have. But, I must admit that Richard was hilarious that night. Richard, of course, went on to have a super-star career on stage, screen and television. But, I will never forget those 18 minutes. I wish him the best in his battle against multiple sclerosis.

Grand Funk Railroad went on after Richard. I had to get them to stretch their set and then stretch some more because Sly and his family showed up an hour and a half late, much to my anger and dismay. I will say, however, that once Sly started to sing and play, he was astonishing. His movements, his band, his persona, just took over and everybody forgot how late he was. But, the lateness was a tip-off to me. As far as I was concerned, his conduct would limit his career, and history unfortunately proved me to be right.

When the Beatles broke up officially in 1970, everyone in the music business was saddened. They had given so much to the music industry. Their great music and talent was no longer going to be packaged in the same way again. They would each go it alone. It was like a comet whose light and power had burned out. It is, unfortunately, a common occurrence in rock and roll that groups come together, make their contribution, then disband. Sometimes, they can be put back together. Most often, though, they cannot.

America was embroiled in the Vietnam war. Many changes were happening with drugs, clothing, hair and respect for authority. Society was in turmoil. I hated the war; I did not feel that America belonged in Southeast Asia. I had seen war firsthand as a soldier and the thought of American boys dying in the jungles of Vietnam was repugnant to me.

Peter Yarrow, of Peter, Paul & Mary, called me one day. I knew Peter from the Bitter End and had been a fan of Peter, Paul & Mary.

"Sid, I'd like to do a concert for peace, to protest the Vietnam war and I'd like to ask you to organize it."

Since I was against the war, I thought this was a chance to get involved and make a difference. I accepted Peter's offer immediately.

"I'm in, Peter. And I'll ask the Rascals."

"Great, Sid!"

In addition to the Rascals, we got Judy Collins and Harry Belafonte. We also got Jimi Hendrix, which was a coup (or so I thought).

Jimi Hendrix was a huge star. It was hard to find anybody bigger at that time.

We had proscenium seating for the concert. Some seats were behind the stage and we blocked them off, because it would have been impossible for anyone in those seats to see the stage because of all the equipment and set-up activities going on behind the scenes.

In this particular concert, we had built something akin to a wall to serve as a backdrop for the performers and also help magnify the sound. Hendrix was the second act to go on. He started to play and, after about a minute, he put his back up against the temporary backdrop and slid down the wall until he was eventually sitting on the stage. It was obvious to me that Jimi's weird behavior was drug-induced. I got to the stagehands and told them to take Jimi off the stage. No one, least of all the audience, was too happy about it, but I wasn't going to allow Jimi Hendrix to make a fool of himself. Jimi was an incorrigible druggie and this was only one of many occasions when he couldn't fulfill a professional commitment because of his drug use. How sad it was that a great talent lost his life at such a young age. The combination of fame, money and power is sometimes too much for these young performers and the pressure is unbearable for them. It's the other side of success.

The Peace Concert had a tremendous amount of support from the public and we were all proud to participate. For me, organizing the concert was a labor of love, and I believed very strongly in the cause.

It was a popular time to stage benefit concerts. Jerry Wexler of Atlantic asked me to organize a benefit for the Martin Luther King Foundation.

"Atlantic will provide all the acts, Sid. You just run the concert," he said.

I really enjoyed organizing concerts that supported worthy causes. When Jerry Wexler asked me to do the King benefit, it was a natural fit for me and I declined to have my name on the posters, handbills and radio ads. I did not want anyone to think that the concert was a commercial venture.

As promised, Atlantic involved most of their acts in the benefit. On the bill at the Garden, we had Sam & Dave, Sonny & Cher, Aretha Franklin, the Voices of East Harlem and the Rascals. The Garden was jammed and, at the end of the evening, I proudly announced from the stage that we had been able to raise $73,000 for the Martin Luther King Foundation.

Blood, Sweat & Tears was hot and I wanted to present them in concert, so I called Bennett Glazer, who managed them. I thought that they were a super group with a sensational lead singer, David Clayton Thomas. I told Bennett that I wanted to present Blood, Sweat & Tears at the Garden and he was very enthusiastic.

Bennett and I negotiated a $40,000 price for the band, and the Garden wanted their usual $40,000. I also allocated $15,000 for advertising and promotion. In addition, I decided that I wanted Miles Davis on the bill. Blood, Sweat & Tears was a horn band and I thought, who better to pair them with than Miles Davis, the king of the horn. Miles agreed to make the appearance for $5,000. I thought that this would be a dream show. Before anyone had bought a single ticket, I had put out $100,000. However, I was so sure that the concert was going to sell out that I even had the Garden tentatively reserve the following night so that I could accommodate the expected overflow audience.

During the spring months leading up to the concert, Blood, Sweat & Tears went out on a tour sponsored by the U.S. State Department. There was a backlash against the group because many of their fans felt that the group had sold out by associating with the Nixon White House. I don't know if they sold out politically, but I do know that they did not sell out for me at the Garden. Because of the negative publicity surrounding the State Department tour, I had to cancel the second day that I had reserved at the Garden and hoped that I wouldn't lose a bundle. There was a lot of money at stake and all of it was mine.

On top of all that, we began to get threatening phone calls and letters stating that people were going to throw bags of horse manure on the stage to protest Blood, Sweat & Tears having gone on the State Department tour. I immediately increased the number of ushers and security for the concert, which naturally increased the expenses.

We sold somewhere between 60 and 65 percent of the tickets. As I sat in the audience and listened to the great music of Miles Davis and Blood, Sweat & Tears, I knew that I was going to lose approximately $20,000.

Blood, Sweat & Tears finished their set, and I left my seat to congratulate them on their great performance as they came off the stage. As David Clayton Thomas exited, he stopped for a moment, shook my hand, and said, "Sid, don't worry. You're not going to lose any money."

I returned to my seat and Blood, Sweat & Tears came back for an encore. After the show ended, I went to the dressing room to say good-night and pay the band. All the members of the band were there and so was Bennett Glazer.

"Why the long face? You broke even."

"What do you mean?" I asked. My calculation was that I had lost $20,000.

"We're reducing our fee by $20,000. You broke even."

It was a wonderful gesture that I will never forget. These were young guys with great sensitivity and a manager with a lot of heart.

In April 1970, *Billboard* magazine invited me to speak at their annual convention. That year the conference was being held in Mallorca, off the coast of Spain. Gerry was quite pregnant with our fourth child, but she was given medical permission to travel, so we decided to go. We had a wonderful time. Mallorca is very beautiful place and Gerry enjoyed herself immensely.

I spoke on a program with Bill Graham, the legendary manager and West Coast impresario who was involved with Jefferson Airplane, Santana, the Grateful Dead and others. Also on the panel was Paul Marshall, a top show business attorney, and Lee Eastman, a leading labor lawyer whose daughter Linda, was a big Rascals fan and Paul McCartney's new wife. A huge number of people attended our panel. Bill Graham, who I had never had the chance to meet, was a dynamic speaker. I was the last speaker on the schedule and I chose to speak about music being an international language.

After I finished speaking, a man who was the head of a major German record and publishing conglomerate approached me and said, "Mr. Bernstein, if we had more gatherings like this and more speakers like you, we wouldn't have to worry about the brotherhood of man and peace in the world. I will not forget what you have said here."

Nor will I forget that moment!

On June 13, 1970, our third son, Beau Bernstein, was born. I was working constantly, but all I wanted to do was go home and be with my family. In fact, the Rascals often tell stories of my attending sessions at the recording studios and falling asleep shortly after my arrival. I remember thinking that if I fell asleep often enough, the Rascals would stop asking me to come to the studio. I really wanted to spend as much time as I could at home with my family.

On one of my visits, I was enjoying a nice snooze when I was awakened by a commotion coming from the studio. The four Rascals were in the studio with Arif Mardin and Tom Dowd and they were arguing about Eddie Brigati's procrastination in completing a lyric. Felix Cavaliere was angry and berating Eddie, as usual, for his tardiness in completing the lyric. Gene, Dino, Arif and Tom stood apart from the fray and watched. I watched the scene from the darkened control room as the debate between Felix and Eddie escalated. After a few minutes, I decided that I had to try to do something to diffuse the tension. I stood up and removed my loafers and trousers. I was wearing a pair of underwear that I refused to discard because my mother had darned them for me many times. There were patches in many colors on them. I let my ample belly hang over and proceeded to tiptoe into the small area between the control room and the studio as unobtrusively as I could. I then burst through the door and streaked across the studio floor in my socks and underwear. I was a sight to behold! Everyone started laughing so hard that the animosity and anger was quickly forgotten. Eddie completed the lyric and everyone returned to work.

However, all was not well in Rascal land.

Peter Yarrow wanted to do another peace concert, but now he wanted to do it in an outdoor stadium, to get as large a crowd as possible.

"Sid, we did so well last winter at the Garden! Let's do it again this summer."

The war was on everyone's mind. The protests in the streets were increasing and the college kids were becoming more and more agitated. I felt even more passionately that this war was not ours to fight and we should get out of Vietnam.

"Peter, this time we'll do it at Shea and have 55,000 people."

"Great, Sid! Great! Let's do it!"

We had to organize the concert quickly. In my entire career as a promoter, I never had to organize such a big concert in such a short amount of time. I had to pick a date when the Mets would be on the road. We got tickets and a program book printed quickly. My job was made a little easier because the Rascals recruited some of their peers to appear. We had Richie Havens, Miles Davis, the Staple Singers, Paul Simon, Janis Joplin, Steppenwolf, Creedence Clearwater Revival, the cast of *Hair*, Peter Yarrow and the Rascals on the bill. Murray the K was the MC. We started at noon and the concert ended at 9:30 in the evening. That place was rocking!

I remember that during the Rascals' rendition of *People Got to Be Free*, a worldwide number one record, Murray the K had to stop the boys in mid-song. Shea Stadium management requested that we stop the concert because the 55,000 people in the stadium were jumping up and down so hard that the stadium was actually shaking. The reason was that the lower stands at Shea are built on rails, underpinned by springs so that they can be moved for football games. What a sight it was to actually see the stadium palpatating, and I understood why management was concerned. Peter Yarrow got up and sang *Puff the Magic Dragon* and asked everyone to stop jumping on the seats. That did the trick.

Another thing I remember was Janis Joplin showing up as high as a kite. It was so sad to see. Janis was in the VIP holding area and I was trying to talk her out of going onstage. She kept insisting that she wanted to go on, but that she wanted to wait until it was dark because it would be more dramatic. Finally, I had to inform her that I would not let her perform because I was honestly afraid that she might fall off the stage and get hurt.

My final memory of the peace concert was our aborted attempt to stage a similar concert in Philadelphia. Stewart Mott, a scion of the family that built the General Motors Corporation, was a friend of Peter Yarrow's and came up with the idea to take the summer peace concert to Philadelphia. We had planned to hold the concert at the newly constructed Veterans Stadium and had booked the stadium even before the Shea concert happened.

However, Frank Rizzo, the Mayor of Philadelphia, refused to approve the concert because he was worried that there might be some demonstrations. The truth was that the Mayor was politically right-wing and supported the U.S. participation in Vietnam. The bottom line was the city of Philadelphia refused to grant us a permit, and we even went to court several times to try and get that permit. Throughout my many appearances in the courthouse in Philadelphia, I became friendly with some of the Mayor's young aides. I was very surprised to see some of those same assistants to Mayor Rizzo at the Shea peace concert, walking around with walkie-talkies, checking out the proceedings. I hoped that these aides would see how well-run the concert was and give the Mayor a favorable report. Unfortunately, we never got a permit to produce a peace concert in Philadelphia.

I had booked Grand Funk Railroad as one of the opening acts for Sly and the Family Stone at the Garden. Terry Knight very capably managed Grand Funk, and they had made a lot of progress since their earlier appearance at the Garden. They had become a huge act. I considered Terry Knight one of the brightest and best managers I had ever met. One day, he called me.

"Sid, I need your help. I want to put Grand Funk Railroad in Shea Stadium. You don't have to put up a dime; I'll pay for everything. All I want you to do is handle the arrangements with the people at Shea and let me use your name as the concert promoter. If you agree, I'll give you 25 grand."

Grand Funk Railroad was a happening group. I thought it was the easiest $25,000 I would ever make.

"Why not? You got a deal!"

"Oh, yeah, Sid. One more thing…I want to break the Beatles' revenue record for a single concert, which you set in 1965. Can you please scale the tickets so we could gross a little more than they did?"

"Sure, I'll do it. With my name going on the posters and the publicity, it'll look like I'm breaking my own record. I love it! Let's do it!"

I made three times as much from that promotion than I did from both of the Beatles concerts. And it was easy; I made all the arrangements in three days. We filled up Shea Stadium and the place was jumping. We took in around $330,000. Everyone thought that I was responsible, but it was really Terry Knight and Grand Funk Railroad.

William Morris is a great and powerful theatrical agency. It is one of the leading talent agencies in the world and has an impressive client list. The tradition at William Morris was to put all the newly hired and aspiring agents in the mailroom and see if they could work their way up. The thinking was that if someone had the drive, creativity and ambition to get out of the mailroom, they would probably turn into a successful agent.

One day, I got a phone call from David Geffen, an agent who had recently emerged from the mailroom. I had seen him at clubs and concerts and we became friendly.

"Sid, we just signed Laura Nyro, a new girl who's a fantastic singer/songwriter. She has an album that's going to be released on Columbia Records soon. She needs a manager and I would like to recommend you to her. I think you would work well together."

"Okay, where can I hear her?"

"She just moved to the city. She has no furniture in her apartment, but she does have a piano and some folding chairs. Why don't you meet me there later today and you can hear her."

He gave me the address and I went over after work. David introduced me to Laura, who was quite shy. I sat on one of the folding chairs. The young woman sat at the piano with her back to us. When she started to play, I could tell immediately that she was very good. I was very tired after a long day at the office and it didn't help that I couldn't see her face. Before long, I fell asleep. It's not easy running one of the hottest bands in the world and raising four young kids at the same time. I wasn't getting much sleep at all.

David jabbed me in the ribs and whispered to me, "Hey, Sid! You're snoring and she can hear you. She's getting angry. Come on! Stay awake!"

"I'm sorry," I whispered back. "She's really great. Should I apologize?"

"No, don't say a word."

When Laura finished singing, I told her how much I enjoyed listening to her. Then David and I left.

It turned out that Laura and Felix Cavaliere of the Rascals were friendly. She told Felix that I had fallen asleep while she was playing for me and that she never wanted to speak to me again. Felix tried to defend me, but to no avail.

The next time I spoke to David, he told me that he believed in Laura so much that he was planning to leave William Morris to become her manager.

My falling asleep while Laura Nyro was playing gave David Geffen, now of Dreamworks, the opportunity to become her manager and subsequently develop his own fabulous career. David Geffen is extremely talented and I have no doubt that he would have found another way to initiate his success, but I'd like to think that my untimely nap helped him get there just a little faster.

The Rascals' recording contract with Atlantic was up for renewal. I began to negotiate with Jerry Wexler and Ahmet and Nesuhi Ertegun. I explained that I wanted the Rascals to remain with Atlantic, that we had lived up to our end of the original agreement, even though we probably could have renegotiated our contract when the Rascals started to produce one hit after another. I expected that Atlantic would want to make an offer that rewarded our loyalty.

When Jerry Wexler got back to me, he was less than encouraging. He told me that the last Rascals album had done poorly because Felix had become a disciple of the Swami Satchadananda and the music had gone off on a tangent. The brass at Atlantic was not sure that the group could recapture its winning ways. Jerry's counter-offer was not really what I had in mind. I told him that I needed to think it over, but what I really wanted to do was test the waters elsewhere. I was annoyed at Atlantic. When they were desperate for a white act to help them become a more mainstream label, the

Rascals had helped put them on the map to such a degree that Atlantic now had many white acts and had become one of the major record companies in the world. I felt that Atlantic should show its appreciation for what we had done for them.

Word spread that the Rascals were looking for a contract with another record company. I got many calls. Rocco Laginestra, the head of RCA, called and asked me about signing the Rascals. I welcomed the opportunity to work with him. RCA wanted the Rascals and offered a million-dollar advance. It was really tempting. Clive Davis from Columbia called. Clive was a former lawyer who had the magic touch when it came to songs, artists and records. He offered me basically the same deal that Rocco and RCA had.

I recommended to my boys that we sign with Columbia because I felt that Clive and Columbia would be a perfect fit for a group like the Rascals who wanted to produce their own records with minimal supervision. I loved Rocco and respected his business acumen. But Clive Davis was a music guy, and the Rascals needed a music guy. The boys agreed with me, and were looking forward to working with Clive.

I called Atlantic and told Jerry Wexler that the Rascals were going to sign with Columbia. He wished us luck. I then called Clive and told him of our decision, and he was quite pleased.

"Sidney," Clive said, "listen, we should try to keep this between us. Next week we're having the Columbia Records International Convention in Freeport, the Bahamas. We bring in Columbia people from all over the world to talk business and have some fun. What I'd like to do is fly the Rascals in secretly and surprise everyone at the convention with the signing. We'll put them behind a curtain while I make my opening remarks. After I finish, I'll introduce the Rascals as our newest artists. It will be very dramatic!"

"Sounds great to me, Clive. And you can be sure we'll keep things quiet."

The Columbia lawyers worked feverishly to get the contract ready for the Rascals to sign. The contract was finally ready three days before we were to leave for Freeport. We had a meeting to review the contract. The attorneys, accountants, members of the Rascals and I sat around a conference table. Steve Weiss opened the meeting.

"Fellas, I'm going to give everyone around this table a copy of the Columbia Records contract. We are going to read through it paragraph by paragraph. You may ask questions at any time. I worked very hard on this with the attorneys from Columbia. Sid has negotiated a terrific deal for you and we need to have this finished before you take off for Freeport."

Steve began to read and we breezed through the contract rather quickly. Some questions were asked, but no one voiced any objections. Everyone seemed happy. The boys liked the idea of signing with Columbia and were enthused about working with Clive Davis. And the million-dollar advance didn't hurt, either.

Steve passed a pen to each of the guys and they were poised to sign.

With his pen poised in mid-air, Felix said, "Listen. I want to know just one thing. Are we going to give value for value received? This is a lot of money we're getting and I just want to know if all of us are going to give value for the money."

I, of course, knew that his remarks were directed at Eddie, and I immediately became nervous.

Felix looked at Gene and asked him if he was okay with the deal. Gene was already envisioning the new car he was going to buy; he looked at Felix and nodded his okay. Felix then asked Dino, and he nodded his agreement.

Eddie gave Felix a searing look. "Felix, what the hell are you talking about?" he said in an accusatory and derisive way. Eddie then stood up, dropped his pen and stormed out of the conference room. Everyone was in shock. I quickly raced out after Eddie. He was waiting for an elevator.

"Eddie, what are you doing? There's a million dollars on the table! Are you nuts? What in heaven's name are you doing? Come on back. We'll work it out."

Eddie was carrying an album with him and put it in front of his face, shielding my view of him. I think he was crying. He was still a kid, just 23 or so at the time. The elevator doors opened and he got in. As the doors closed, he said, "Forget it, Sid. Just forget it."

I did not see Eddie Brigati again for two years.

I went back to the conference room. The remaining Rascals were discussing what to do now. We wanted to sign the contract and show up in Freeport as we had promised Clive.

Gene had friends who had a group based in Rochester, New York called the Brass Buttons. They were a Rascals cover band that played all of the Rascals' songs. Their lead singer Jay Capozzi looked like Eddie. Gene suggested that we call and find the lead singer of the Brass Buttons to replace Eddie. I was pleased to see Gene so on top of things and thinking on his feet.

I felt that I had to call Clive and explain the situation. I told him that I thought we would have a replacement for Eddie and asked Clive if he was still interested in signing the group.

"Sid," Clive said, "get those contracts signed and over to me ASAP! We're prepared to make the announcement at the convention. I want the band there."

"Fine," I said. I was relieved, and I hoped that Eddie would miraculously have a change of heart.

We arrived in Freeport undetected the day before our scheduled appearance. The boys immediately set to rehearsing with Jay Capozzi who had come down from Rochester to replace Eddie. I found a remote studio where they could rehearse. Jay was a very good singer who was cooperative and anxious to please.

On the opening night of the convention, we sneaked into the hotel. The ballroom was packed. As Clive began making his opening remarks, the boys got into position behind the closed curtain.

"This had been a wonderful year for Columbia," Clive concluded his remarks. "We have reached new heights in sales and revenues. And, ladies and gentlemen, behind this curtain, we have our latest talent acquisition. And they will lead us to even greater heights. It is my pleasure to present them to you. Ladies and gentlemen—the Young Rascals!"

The curtain parted and the audience went wild. The Rascals went into their first song. I was sitting at a table right near the front.

Tony Orlando, who was running Columbia's publishing company at the time, slid over to me and whispered, "Hey, Sid. Is that Eddie Brigati up there?"

Putting my finger over my lips, I motioned to him to be quiet.

"Sid," he whispered again. "Is that Eddie?"

"Tony, would you please be quiet?"

Of course, Tony Orlando was so attuned to everything in the music world that he knew something was amiss.

Jay Capozzi did a great job. Only Tony Orlando said something to me, but others in the room must have known that Eddie was missing from the band.

I could see the handwriting on the wall. The Rascals were in a free-fall. Eddie Brigati was gone for good and Felix could never find another lyricist who could lock into his music. I was the captain of a sinking ship.

My fondest memory of the Rascals' time at Columbia actually has nothing to do with them. One day at the beginning of the contract, I went over to the Columbia recording studios on East 52nd Street to see how things were going. The building housed many recording studios and rehearsal rooms. Even though I had directions to the studio where the Rascals were, I got a little lost. I began opening doors, looking for them. The third or fourth door I opened was in semi-darkness. I saw two adults and two children on the floor, sitting on a blanket, having a picnic. Not wanting to disturb anyone, I quickly turned to leave. I heard a familiar voice say, "Hello, Sid." I turned back to see who was speaking to me. I saw Linda and Paul

McCartney having a picnic with their children, taking a break from recording. We said hello and talked about the Rascals on Columbia. They wished me luck with the Rascals' new deal.

When I left to continue my search for the Rascals' studio, I thought to myself that I had just witnessed a wonderful scene. Linda and Paul might have been the biggest stars in the universe. But to those young children, they were just Mom and Dad.

Clive was happy and true to his word. He took the Rascals into the studio and they began to record with their new lead singer. But the chemistry was gone without Eddie. Despite the rancor and animosity, he and Felix had been able to turn out hit songs. Without Eddie, there would be no more hit songs. The long, slow decline of the Rascals had begun. The requests for appearances diminished and with that, so did their price. Twenty months later, it was all over.

Although the Rascals did not achieve the longevity in show business that I had envisioned for them, for two-and-a-half years in the late 60s, the Rascals were the number one band in the U.S. and a favorite of other great bands the world over. And I was proud to have been their manager and grateful for all the success that they had enjoyed.

Felix Cavaliere is an extremely intelligent man. During the Rascal years, he was the musical soul of the group. Felix had a strong social conscience and always insisted that the opening acts at all their concerts be black acts. I was especially proud that Felix had such enlightened views. He has a natural aptitude for business and he made some shrewd real estate acquisitions using some of the money that he made with the Rascals. He now lives in Nashville, where he writes and is involved in the music business. Felix is a workaholic.

Eddie Brigati is a good-natured soul with a great sense of humor and an outgoing personality. He always treated his family in the most exemplary way. Eddie went out of his way to take care of and provide the good things for his family. I really identified with him as far as family and relationships were concerned. He has energy to spare and was a wonderful front man for the group when things were going well. He and Felix had great professional chemistry and together wrote many of the Rascals' hits, and some of their songs became rock classics. Eddie currently lives in New Jersey. We have not spoken in years.

Dino Danelli is a great drummer with a unique style and a sense of showmanship. With his erect posture on the drum stand and his ability to twirl the drumsticks, Dino's solid beat added great energy and excitement to the act. Dino was the quiet one who rarely had anything to say. He lives in New York and is now a record producer. Dino is also a fine artist and painter. We talk from time to time.

Gene Cornish came from Rochester and his ambition and drive resulted in his inclusion in the Rascals. Gene was attracted to the finer things in life and had a penchant for fancy cars. Gene thought quickly on his feet and was great in a crisis. Gene lives in New Jersey, is still involved in the music business, and we have stayed in touch over the years.

In 1999, the Rascals were inducted into the Rock and Roll Hall of Fame in Cleveland, Ohio. I was happy and proud to see them receive such a well-deserved honor. I always knew that the Rascals would stand the test of time.

By the time our fifth child and second daughter, Casey Bernstein, was born, on November 25, 1971, the Rascals had broken up. I was beginning to reevaluate many aspects of my business life. My overhead was high, the financial burdens great and the Rascals, a band that was soon to be extinct, had eroded my income and had exacted a tremendous monetary and emotional price that left me drained.

The Rascals' breakup put tremendous pressure on me financially and caused difficulty within my family. I had put all my financial eggs in that one basket and we certainly had had a great run. The Rascals had made many hit records and generated considerable amounts of money. We were all living the great life.

Gerry and I had acquired a large, expensive apartment in Manhattan to accommodate our growing family. We had household help. All the kids were enrolled in private schools. I had a car and driver.

During those great Rascals years, I had pulled back from concert promotion and had turned down all other acts that approached me about management. I was quite content with my life, both personally and professionally. The most important thing to me was spending time with Gerry and the kids. The Rascals success enabled me to be an ever-present father and husband and I was most grateful for that. I relished the time I spent with my family.

However, when the Rascals broke up, the steady cash flow dried up almost immediately and my income was severely impacted. It put a strain on our family; while my income was decreasing, our expenses were increasing.

Chapter 16: SINATRA AND ELVIS

ABE MARGOLIES WAS CLOSE WITH JERRY WEINTRAUB and his wife, Jane Morgan. Jerry was a manager and promoter and Jane was a chanteuse, an American singer who sang French songs. He managed John Denver as well as Jane. He also had the rights to promote Frank Sinatra, Elvis Presley and the Moody Blues. Jerry was a very powerful person in the music business. Abe had always thought that Jerry and I would make a good team.

Jerry and I knew each other from the business. He had quite a personality. He was handsome and extraordinarily persuasive—a super salesman.

When Jerry's partners at Management Three, Bernie Brillstein and Marty Kummer, left, Abe went to Jerry and told him that now would be the right time to approach me about joining him as a partner in Management Three.

Jerry and I had a meeting of the minds immediately and thought we would work well together. He offered me a very generous salary and benefits package.

Marvin Zolt, the head of business affairs at Management Three, said, "Listen, Sid. You're coming in as a partner, but it's my feeling that we should wait before we put the partnership agreement into a contact. Why don't you and Jerry have a trial period, sort of like a courtship? You'll get a heck of a salary, but let's wait to do the contract."

Marvin was a decent guy and so convincing that I agreed to wait up to a year before signing a contract. Also, I assumed that Abe would always be available to mediate any dispute I might have with Jerry. I went to work and was able to bring Billy Fields with me. There was lots of action. There was never a dull moment with acts like Sinatra, Elvis, John Denver and the Moody Blues constantly needing attention. Something was always happening.

I was working in my office one day at Management Three when my secretary Marilyn buzzed me and said, "Sid, there's a lady on the phone who says she's Shirley MacLaine."

"Great, who's this loony?"

" No, Sid, she sounds like a serious person."

Still doubtful, I told Marilyn to put the call through.

"Hello. Is this Sid Bernstein?"

"Yes," I replied.

"This is Shirley MacLaine and I was told to call you."

"Who are you?"

"Shirley MacLaine!" she laughed.

I was Sid the Music Man. Why would the movie actress Shirley MacLaine be calling me? I decided to play along.

"Okay, Shirley. How can I help you?"

"Sid, the people at the Garden said that you're the guy to call."

"For what?"

"Well, I'm planning a show at the Garden called Women for McGovern. It's all about and for women who support George McGovern for President. The people I spoke to at the Garden said that you could help me put the show together."

"What would you like me to do, Shirley?"

"I was hoping, Sid, that you would co-produce the concert with me."

"Well, what would we be producing?"

"I can get some really interesting women to appear, but I haven't the faintest idea how to deal with the Garden, the unions, tickets, staging…everything. I need help, Sid. Would you be interested?"

"Yes, I support the Senator. I'd be glad to help you."

"Good. Would you like to have dinner with me this evening at my apartment so we can discuss the details?"

"Of course, Shirley. I'd be happy to," I said. I wasn't about to turn down a dinner invitation at Shirley MacLaine's apartment.

That evening, I walked a few blocks from my office to Shirley's apartment. When I arrived, Pete Hamill, the columnist and author, was standing in the kitchen in an apron, cooking soup. Pete and I were acquaintances.

After a sumptuous meal that included some of Pete's soup, Shirley listed the performers that she had lined up for the concert, and it was a most impressive list of women: Dionne Warwick, Tina Turner, Mary Travers (of Peter, Paul & Mary), Judy Collins, Mama Cass Elliot (from the Mamas and the Papas), Marlo Thomas, actress Melina Mercouri, Broadway stars Gwen Verdon and Chita Rivera, the legendary Bette Davis and Mrs. Rose Kennedy, mother of the slain President. To spice the show up (as if it needed any more spice), Shirley had lined up celebrity ushers: her brother, Warren Beatty, Sen. Gene Tunney, Robert Redford, Eli Wallach, Jack Nicholson, Paul Newman, Alan King and James Earl Jones. Not a bad group to be associated with.

I took care of all the necessary arrangements. It was easy, especially since Shirley had already lined up all the talent.

Naturally, every seat was filled and it turned out to be an amazing night of entertainment. During the planning, Shirley and I only had one argument, over giving her top promotion credit on the posters and programs. She didn't want to be named first, but I insisted that she have the honor. I won.

"How could you do this to me?" wailed Jerry Weintraub. Jerry was a lifelong Republican. "It's embarrassing! My Republican friends are lambasting me!"

I just turned my palms heavenward.

I remember telling Shirley, "I think I might get fired. Jerry Weintraub is for Nixon and I'm embarrassing him!"

We were all laughing, except for Jerry. He was uptight about the whole thing.

I didn't have too much time to worry about Jerry's embarrassment over the McGovern concert because I was preparing to attend *Billboard* magazine's annual convention in Geneva, Switzerland. Gerry wanted to take the kids to the sunny beaches of Hawaii rather than the cold, snowy Alps, so I traveled to Switzerland by myself. I had a great time seeing many friends from the record business. My speech about concert promotion and the potential concerts have as vehicles for charitable fundraising was very well-received. Somehow everything at the convention seemed to be running behind schedule and my speech ended later than originally scheduled. I had to rush to the airport as soon as I finished my speech.

Bob Altshuler of Arista Records and I jumped into a cab and made a mad dash to catch the last plane to Paris. I wanted to make my connection for the flight back to the U.S. I was anxious to get on the plane and begin my journey to Hawaii to join Gerry and the kids on vacation. I hadn't given Gerry an exact date for my arrival in Hawaii, but since I had finished my business in Europe, I was ready for a vacation. The cab didn't move fast enough, and Bob and I missed our flight. Bob had some business to attend to in Paris and he persuaded me to take a train from Geneva to Paris.

"C'mon, Sid," Bob said. "I really need to get to Paris, so take the train with me and spend the night in Paris. You can catch an early flight back to the States."

I wasn't interested in spending the night in Geneva, so I agreed to take the train with Bob. The trip from Geneva to Paris takes four or five hours. Bob and I purchased our tickets, but because we had not made reservations, we had to share our compartment. The compartments had the sliding doors with two benches that face each other. The other two in our compartment were a lovely French couple returning to their home in Paris after enjoying a Swiss holiday. I took the opportunity to converse in French, which slowly began to come back to me. Bob, who didn't speak any French, followed the conversation as best he could. Whenever he seemed to be lost in the conversation, I explained to him about what we were talking about.

When we crossed the border between Switzerland and France, the train stopped for a passport check. As we proceeded into France, the conductor began calling out the names of the next stops the train would be making. After the first stop, the conductor called out the name of the next stop, "Dijon." When I heard "Dijon," the first thought that flashed in my mind was Claudy, our wartime relationship and the unanswered letters.

"Bob, did you hear the conductor call out Dijon?"

"Yes, Sid, I believe he said Dijon."

The French couple also nodded their heads. "Oui, monsieur, Dijon."

I told the French couple about my experiences in Dijon during the war. I related the story of Claudy.

"She was my first real sweetheart," I told them in French. "Ma premier cheri."

I was really curious about Claudy. I began a debate in my head: My family was on vacation in Hawaii, and stopping in Dijon and beginning a search for Claudy would only delay my return to the States for a day. I thought about whether I should get off the train in Dijon and try to find Claudy to see what became of her in the past 27 years. My traveling companions could probably see the debate raging within me.

Bob, who had hoped that I would spend the evening with him in Paris, said, "Go, Sid. Do it. Go."

The French couple said to me, "Allez vous. Allez vous. Go. Go."

The conductor came to our compartment and my companions explained my dilemma to him. He said, "Monsieur, allez vous. Allez vous. C'est romantique. Go, go. It's so romantic."

By that point, if I didn't get off, I had a feeling that Bob, the French couple and the conductor would have thrown me off. So, I decided to get off at Dijon.

It was pouring rain in Dijon. I got thoroughly soaked walking the two blocks from the train station to the Grand Hotel, where I had stayed 27 years before. Fortunately, the Grand Hotel had a vacancy. As I was filling out the check-in card, I asked the concierge if he would be kind enough to look up the name Vilfroy in the local telephone directory. I gave him the address that I had remembered from 1945.

"Yes, there is a Vilfroy listed," the concierge told me in French. "But not at the address you have given me, sir."

"Would you please dial the number for me?" I asked him in French.

The concierge dialed the number, but no one answered.

"Nobody is answering. Here is the number and address, sir. It is late, perhaps they will be returning soon."

I thanked the concierge for all his efforts and went up to my room. I peeled off my wet clothes and soaked in a hot bath. When I got out of the bath, I tried the number again, but there was still no answer. I proceeded to get dressed, and I wondered if I should go out and revisit the streets I had not seen since I was a soldier. I decided to go out, but before I went out, I tried the number once more, but still no one picked up the phone.

I left my room; thankfully it had stopped raining, and I started walking to the place where I had run the nightclub for soldiers. It was now called Café Central, but interestingly enough, it was still a nightclub. It was 10 PM and the cinemas were letting out. People began filtering towards Dijon's main street. I wandered among them, looking for a 19-year-old girl and her mother who I had last seen in 1945. I had no luck spotting Claudy or Madame Vilfroy among the moviegoers, so I began looking in the windows of the restaurants around the town square. Memories were flooding through me.

Since I could not find Claudy, I decided to go back to my hotel room and try the phone number once more. There was still no answer. Disheartened and disappointed, I went to sleep.

I did not sleep well, but I awoke to a warm and sunny day in Dijon. I ate breakfast and then decided to walk to the address that the concierge had given me the night before.

As I walked up the hill in the daylight, I could see how much Dijon had changed in the postwar years. The town had virtually doubled its size. Many new buildings had been built. I found the address and looked at the building directory listed on the front door. The name Madame Vilfroy was clearly printed next to a bell. I rang it several times, but got no response. It was a summer Saturday morning and I thought that perhaps Madame Vilfroy was on holiday somewhere. Even though it was getting hotter and sunnier with each passing minute, I was determined to speak to someone either coming into or going out of the building. I waited about 10 minutes and then a young man carrying trash walked down the stairs and opened the front door.

I stopped him and said in French, "My name is Sid Bernstein and I am an old friend of Madame Vilfroy. I was wondering if you might know her?"

"Certainly, monsieur. She is a friend of my mother's."

"I have been calling her on the telephone since last night and I rang her bell here this morning, but I am not getting an answer," I explained. "By chance, would you know where she might be."

"Wait one moment, sir. Wait here and I will be right back."

The young man ran up the stairs and returned a few moments later with a woman he introduced as his mother. She explained to me that Madame Vilfroy had recently fallen and was away convalescing.

"Would you possibly know Madame's daughter Claudy?" I asked the woman in French. "Does Claudy still live here in Dijon?"

"Oh, yes, monsieur," she replied. She instructed her son to go back to their apartment to get Claudy's address.

My heart was pounding.

"Her name is Bonheur and she is married to a doctor," the woman informed me while we were waiting.

The young man returned.

"They live on the Rue Liberte." The woman gave me Claudy's exact address.

I was deeply grateful to them for their assistance and thanked the young man and his mother profusely.

I began walking towards the Rue Liberte. The morning had grown considerably warmer and my shirt was soaked with perspiration. I was disheveled and sweating, but I was determined to complete my mission.

I found the building and rang the bell. My stomach was churning, my mouth was parched and my heart was hammering in my chest.

I could hear the door click, so I opened it and walked up the two flights to Apartment 2C. The door had frosted glass. I rang the bell and a redheaded woman in her forties opened it and greeted me.

"Bonjour," she said in French. "How may I help you?"

Answering her in French, I said, "Madame, I have not been in Dijon for a very long time and I am looking for some friends I had made when I was a soldier here at the end of World War II. I went to Madame Vilfroy's building and a neighbor kindly informed me that she was recuperating out of town from a fall. The neighbor told me that her daughter Claudy lives here. Would you be able to help me?"

The woman looked at me and said in English, "I am Claudy, Sidney." Please step inside. I want to call my husband."

I started to shake. Memories of my youthful self and thoughts of what might have been with a young, beautiful Claudy came over me.

I stepped inside Claudy's apartment and as she turned away to get her husband, I became overwhelmed with emotion and began to sob. I'm sure that I looked like a complete and utter mess. I was grateful that the vestibule was somewhat dark.

In a few moments, Claudy returned and a tall, handsome man who resembled the movie star James Stewart followed her. Fortunately, I had gotten a hold of myself before Claudy and Dr. Bonheur returned. They invited me into their home and explained that they were waiting for their two sons to return for lunch before they all left for their country home on holiday. The table was set for four places.

"Would you please join us for lunch, Sidney?" Claudy asked.

Claudy could not have been more gracious. I was thrilled that she harbored no ill feelings towards me for never answering her letters all those years ago. I accepted her invitation immediately. Claudy, Dr. Bonheur and I sat down at the table.

"I have heard so much about you," the doctor said. "And I even know what you looked like in 1945."

"How is that?"

Claudy produced a picture album and brought it to the table. She opened it, and on the front page was a picture of a 19-year-old Claudy with me at the fountain at the center of Dijon that her mother had taken. As I sat there looking at Claudy, I did not see a middle-aged wife and mother, but the beautiful young woman I knew and had left behind.

Claudy and I sat around the table and talked about our families and what had transpired during the past 27 years. The doctor sat there listening raptly.

Claudy's two teenage boys came home. They were handsome young men with blond hair. Claudy introduced them and explained that I was an old friend who had been in Dijon as a soldier during World War II. We made room for the boys at the table and continued talking. I told them about my three sons and two daughters and I extended an invitation to the two boys to come to New York and visit. I suggested that two of my sons could visit them in Dijon. A Bernstein-Bonheur exchange program. Claudy's sons' eyes lit up when I mentioned visiting New York. The boys asked me what I did for a living and I told them that I was in the entertainment business.

We finished eating and it was time to think about saying good-bye. Claudy explained that they had a long drive ahead of them. I realized that I needed to start thinking about getting to Paris and catching a flight home.

I walked Claudy and her family to their car. I asked Claudy to remember me to her mother and to express my disappointment in not seeing her. I also asked Claudy to convey to Madame Vilfroy my gratitude for her wonderful treatment those many years ago of a young soldier away from home. We exchanged addresses and phone numbers and promised to be in touch. We said good-bye and they drove off. I walked back to my hotel.

On my walk, I reflected on how ironic life is. I had not answered Claudy's letters those many years ago, because I had concluded that since Claudy was not Jewish, nothing would come of our relationship. It was a poor excuse, since I had ultimately married a woman who was not Jewish.

I thought about how I always looked back on my relationship with Claudy with bittersweet feelings. I had always cherished my memories of the lovely young woman I knew. The time I spent with Claudy helped make the time waiting to return home after the war more livable. I was pleased that my reunion with Claudy had been so warm and friendly. I was happy that she did not seem to harbor any ill feelings towards me for not having answered her letters. I was also happy for her that she had made a good life for herself and had a beautiful family.

I checked out of the hotel and caught the next train to Paris. When I arrived in Paris, I learned that I could not get a flight to New York until the next morning, so I checked into the Georges V, one of the finest hotels in Paris. After I checked in, I changed clothes and then decided to visit my favorite café on the Champs Elysses, which served the best pastries in Paris.

I walked into the café and saw Larry Uttal, president of Bell Records. Larry had attended the *Billboard* convention and had stopped in Paris on business before going back to New York.

"Sid!" Larry exclaimed. "Come sit with me."

I was happy to see a familiar face and joined Larry at his table. I ordered a hot chocolate and my favorite chocolate éclair.

As I savored the delectable pastry, I said to him, "Larry, I have to tell you what happened to me after I left the convention."

As I related my odyssey of the last day and a half, Larry began crying.

"I'm glad you went back to Dijon, Sid. If you ever want to make a movie about this and need backing, count me in."

Unfortunately, Claudy and I did not keep in touch. Her sons never came to visit in New York. My children never went to Dijon. I committed the same sin I had committed years before. I never called or wrote, I just let it go.

During my time at Management Three, I watched Jerry deal with Elvis' legendary manager, Colonel Tom Parker, as well as Sinatra's lawyer and advisor, Mickey Rudin. Jerry had a certain kind of finesse that I admired and I learned another way to deal with people.

One of the reasons Jerry asked me to join him at Management Three was because he was stretched thin, as both Colonel Parker and Mickey Rudin always expected to deal directly with him. Whenever one of them called demanding to speak to Jerry, I had to keep them occupied until Jerry became available. I began to have a working relationship with both the Presley and Sinatra organizations.

We were responsible for the Elvis tours whenever they arose. Colonel Tom Parker had a unique relationship with his star. The Colonel got 50 percent of what Elvis made and kept everyone, except a very few people known as the Memphis Mafia, away from him. Colonel Parker was born in Holland, but had affected a southern accent after living in the South for so many years. I got to know the Colonel from our phone conversations and during his visits to the office. I had also flown on the Colonel's private jet several times. I had concluded that he had an inordinately large ego. We spent some time together, but somehow I could not warm to him.

Colonel Parker was a consummate professional. He saw to every detail. On one occasion, we flew to Miami on the Colonel's private jet to check on hotel accomodations for Elvis. On another, we went to Richmond, Virginia, to check on a concert venue.

One day, the Colonel showed up at the office unexpectedly. Jerry was on the road with one of the other acts, so I had to entertain the Colonel.

"Sidney," he said to me in his fake southern accent. "Would you like to go to lunch with me?"

"Sure, Colonel. What did you have in mind?"

"Well, how about the Blue Grotto? I know you like Italian food and I love that place."

"Great, Colonel. Let's go! I know that restaurant from way back; it's a good one."

We traveled down to Little Italy in the Colonel's limo and were welcomed as kings upon our arrival. The Colonel was a frequent patron at the Blue Grotto; he loved Italian food almost as much as I did. We had quite a gastronomic experience with plenty of spaghetti, meatballs and garlic bread.

Smacking his lips, the Colonel expressed his delight. "This is the best garlic bread in all of New York," he said between mouthfuls.

Out of the blue, he leaned across the table and said, "Hey, Sid. You don't really like me, do you?"

I almost swallowed my spoon, but managed to reply, "Whadya say, Colonel?"

"Let me put it to you this way, Sid. You're not very fond of me. I've seen you with others and you seem to be more guarded and reserved in my presence. What is it?"

I thought for a minute, trying to formulate a tactful response. "You're right, Colonel. I don't really like you as much as I should."

"Well, Sid, c'mon. Be honest. You can tell me. What's the problem?"

At this point, I just wanted to finish lunch and escape. What had started out as a simple lunch had turned into a potential disaster for me and Management Three. The Colonel was Elvis Presley's manager and a client of Management Three. I didn't want to be responsible for souring what had been a successful business relationship.

"I respect you a great deal," I began hesitantly.

"C'mon, Sid. Tell me. Tell me."

"I don't know, Colonel. I'm usually very open with people, but with you, I find it difficult to be open. I usually become close to the people I work with, but I can't seem to do that with you. I don't know what it is. I really have to think about it."

"Okay, Sid. Would you think about it? I really like you and it would mean something to me to know why you hold back with me."

That night, I thought about what I had said to the Colonel at lunch. My first observation was that the Colonel really had been open and honest with me and I still could not be open and honest with him. I thought about a recent trip I had taken with him to check out a venue for an Elvis appearance. Colonel Parker looked at the manifest (the report on ticket sales, seats sold, scale of the house, etc.) and said to me, "Sidney, look at this. You and I just walked through the orchestra section of this arena and you saw me stop and make a notation. Do you remember me saying that I thought the space we stopped at could hold another 14 to 16 seats?"

"Yes, Colonel. I do."

"When I stopped there, Sid, did you wonder why the space was open?"

"No, I didn't."

"Well, when Elvis comes in here to do this concert, there will be seats here with people in them. Somebody is trying to steal seats from us, Sid."

Then I remembered once seeing the Colonel actually selling Elvis program books at a concert and I asked him why he was doing that.

"The reason I'm here, Sid? You probably think I'm an old, foolish man to be selling dollar programs. We sell so many of these programs at a concert that I want to make sure that they don't slip some of the non-licensed programs in with the official ones. I also want to get a look at the folks who buy these programs. I want to see their style and what they're like. I find that it helps me do my job better if I have a picture of the fans. I need contact with Elvis' fans."

I then remembered how many people resented the fact that the Colonel never let them get close to Elvis. As I was thinking about the Colonel, I remembered that even though he kept people away from Elvis, he had once granted me access to one of the greatest stars in the history of show business as a favor.

I had been pushing Jerry to use his relationship with the Colonel to persuade Elvis to hold a press conference before his next appearance in New York. I had gotten many phone calls from the press, requesting some access to the King.

"Sid, you know how the Colonel is about the press. He won't do it. You want him to allow local high school and college newspapers to interview Elvis.

You're crazy, man! *The New York Times* is one thing, but this is ridiculous!"

I wouldn't give up. "C'mon, Jerry. It'll be a wonderful opportunity for these kids to see Elvis. We'll rent a big room and you and the Colonel can control everything. It'll be terrific. You and the Colonel can handle the *Times* and the rest of the media. Let Elvis talk to the kids."

I bugged Jerry so much that he finally relented and spoke to the Colonel. A few days later, he came out of his office with a big smile on his face. "You win, Sid."

"What did I win, Jerry?" I asked, hoping that it was finally the promised partnership and money.

"The Colonel agreed to do the press conference. Set it up, Sid."

"Great! I have a list of the names of the kids who have been calling us. I'll start contacting them immediately."

"Remember, Sid. You wanted this. You asked for it, right?"

"What do you mean, Jerry?" I asked suspiciously.

"Well, Sid," Jerry laughed. "You are going to see *the* Elvis press conference."

We set up the press conference in a large room at a hotel on Long Island. Jerry Weintraub introduced Colonel Tom Parker, who emerged in an outrageously large cowboy hat with his phony southern accent.

"Hi, y'all," he waved as he sat down before the assembled audience of 200 to 300 high school and college newspaper men and women.

The Colonel talked endlessly. He was a captivating speaker and had the kids laughing. He took some questions, too. He was really entertaining, a master showman.

After about 40 minutes, he slapped his forehead and said, "Why, y'all, I've been goin' on and on, I completely forgot that Elvis is waiting back there. I do appreciate that y'all came, but I suppose you're waitin' on Elvis!" The Colonel motioned to one of the road crew. "Could y'all get Elvis out here? Tell him it's time for the press conference."

Elvis came out from behind the curtain with his sunglasses on, dressed in black from head to toe. He waved to the crowd, "How y'all doin'?" he drawled. "It's nice to see y'all here and I thank you for coming. I really appreciate it. I love New York City! It's such a fantastic place. I suspect that y'all be at the concert, so why should I take your time now? We'll have a real party." He turned to leave, gave them two raised hands with the peace sign, waved and said, "Been fun talkin' to y'all. Thankya vera vera much. God bless."

Poof! He was gone. He was there for two minutes and the kids loved every second.

The Colonel returned, did another ten-minute monologue, and then he was gone, too.

That night, thinking about the Colonel, I concluded that he was not the egomaniac I had previously thought. I realized that he was incredibly intuitive and clever and he had picked up on the reservations I had about him. I lamented the fact that I had not been warmer towards him. Colonel Tom Parker was brilliant and unique.

I regret that I never had the opportunity to tell the Colonel that I had misjudged him. We spoke several times after our lunch at the Blue Grotto, but I never got to tell him in person how much I respected and admired him.

One day, Jerry came into my office with a big smile on his face.

"Sid, listen to this. I just got a call from Warner Brothers Records. They're offering us $100,000 if we can do an album on how to play chess. They want us to go to Reykjavik, Iceland, to sign Bobby Fischer to make an instructional chess album. Fisher's in Reykjavik now, competing in a world championship against Boris Spasky, the Russian champion. What do you think? Should we go over and give it a shot?"

Bobby Fischer was one of the all-time great chess champions and was also known to be quite an eccentric. I knew that Jerry didn't want to go to Iceland alone; he enjoyed having me as a traveling companion.

"Sure, Jerry. Let's go. $100,000 is easy money if we can get Bobby Fischer on board. I know that Paul Marshall is his attorney. I'll give him a call and see if he can help us meet Bobby."

I called Paul Marshall, a well-known entertainment attorney, and explained why we wanted to meet with Bobby Fischer. Paul thought it was a great idea and offered to try to arrange a meeting with Bobby, Jerry and me.

"But, remember," Paul warned, "this kid is a little strange. You might make the trip and never get to meet him."

Jerry and I went to Reykjavik. What an incredible place! The sun was still blazing at eleven o'clock at night! There were kids playing in the streets. The people were magnificent to look at. The men looked like Vikings and the women were Nordic goddesses. Of course, I discovered all the great restaurants in Reykjavik. Jerry and I stayed in a four-star hotel where the hot water was supplied by underground thermal springs. The main thing I remember from my time in Iceland, however, was the light. Day and night, the sun was shining.

Visiting Iceland was one of the most fascinating experiences I have ever had. I absolutely recommend going if you ever have the chance to travel to that magical land. If you go in the summer, you will look at your watch and it will say 11:30 PM and the sun will be shining as brightly as it did at 11:30

AM. If you go to Iceland in the summer, don't forget to take your sunglasses.

Try as we might, Jerry and I never got near Bobby Fischer. He was so eccentric that it was impossible to make contact with him. I even tried to enlist Bobby's sister to help us get an audience with him, but even she couldn't facilitate a meeting. After about five days of trying, we packed our sunglasses and went home.

Although I was working at Management Three mainly as a talent manager, I still had a reputation in the industry for staging benefit concerts. I really enjoyed working on concerts, particularly if I felt that I was supporting a worthy cause. One day, Geraldo Rivera called and asked me to work on a benefit for Willowbrook, a home for mentally challenged people. At the time, Geraldo was married to Edie Vonnegut, author Kurt Vonnegut's daughter. Because of my work on the concert, we all got friendly—Geraldo and Edie and Gerry and I. I got to know Geraldo and see how talented he was, and I thought that he would achieve great success as a TV journalist.

I thought that Management Three should manage Geraldo. Jerry Weintraub thought it was a good idea, and when I suggested it to Geraldo, he enthusiastically agreed.

Geraldo was working for ABC television. He had a penchant for getting into mischief and I would have to visit ABC from time to time to bail him out. The first executive I met at ABC was Marty Pampadour. He and I worked out a good system of communication and we were able to keep Geraldo out of trouble. After Marty moved on, I had to develop a similar relationship with the new executive, Michael Eisner. The same Michael Eisner who today is the chairman of the board of the Walt Disney Company. Mike Eisner and I were able to keep Geraldo out of trouble and negotiate a deal that got Geraldo a nightly show, which was a great catalyst for his career.

I also got Don Imus to join the roster at Management Three. I thought that he was a unique talent with something interesting to say. I think that my early confidence in Imus and what he was doing was right on target. I am happy to see him achieve great success with his nationally syndicated radio show. I am particularly in admiration of the great work that Imus does on behalf of Tomorrow's Children. He is an example of how star power can contribute to a worthwhile cause.

Jerry had discovered John Denver while visiting the Bitter End. Jerry signed John to Management Three and had gotten him several appearances on Merv Griffin's TV show. Merv and John Denver really hit it off. The appearances John made on TV and in many important clubs around the country fueled his recording career, and soon he was selling records by the carload. I began to think about John Denver, his career, and the best way to take him to the superstar level.

I suggested to Jerry that it was time for John Denver to have a breakthrough engagement in New York. Jerry agreed and we arranged a concert for John in Carnegie Hall. We got tremendous support from RCA, John's record company. Management Three and RCA pulled out all the promotional stops: posters, ads, handbills—you name it. John Denver got the first-class treatment he deserved, and the concert was a huge success.

Jerry threw a post-concert party at his apartment for some of his friends. I remember that when I got to the party, the apartment was so jammed with people that they spilled into all the rooms, including the bedroom. The only spot where I could find a place to sit was on Jerry's bed. There were other people sitting on the bed as well, and I had a very nice conversation with a couple from Texas who knew Jerry quite well because they were neighbors each summer in Kennebunkport, Maine. That was my first encounter with Barbara and George Bush.

After John's big event in New York, I explained to Jerry that it would be a good idea to do something similar in California to help with record sales. He agreed, and we booked John into the Greek Theatre, an important theatre in LA.

I went to our office in Beverly Hills and did the Bernstein Special: posters, handbills, and carefully placed ads. We took Jerry's convertible, hired two young guys and started our hit-and-run poster campaign. Thank God, that Caddy convertible was a fast car because we came close to getting arrested there on more than one occasion. Los Angeles is certainly not New York. The authorities there were much tougher about having permits for hanging posters. John Denver was a big hit in Los Angeles. His career was really taking off.

Peter, Paul & Mary were doing eight specials for the BBC TV in London. They invited John to appear with them. Upon hearing John Denver, the BBC brass flipped and immediately offered him his own eight-show TV series. Jerry Weintraub didn't like the paltry sum that John was being offered and he procrastinated getting back to the BBC. The BBC, anxious to do a deal, called and invited us to come to London to see if we could come to a financial meeting of the minds for John Denver to do the eight-show series. Jerry dragged his feet. I convinced him that we needed to get to England and finalize a deal with the BBC quickly. I kept explaining to him that England was the gateway to continental Europe and John needed the exposure so that his records would be as successful there as they were in the States.

I was so persistent with Jerry that he finally agreed to do a deal with the BBC. To celebrate John's first appearance on the BBC, Jerry and I decided to go to England with our wives for what now became a vacation.

Jerry threw a party after John's first television broadcast and we invited clients, music business friends and industry executives. I had brought the Moody Blues to America for their first visit, and ten years later Jerry became their American manager, so we invited them to the party. Mike Pinder, a member of the Moody Blues, brought Ringo Starr. I was happy to see Ringo and we embraced. For the next hour and a half, Mike Pinder and Ringo Starr talked about the colors of the sky, the shape of clouds and the end of the rainbow. I didn't know what those guys were on, but I do know that they were seeing things that escaped me. But it was nice seeing Mike and Ringo anyway.

I was greatly saddened when John Denver lost his life in a plane crash. He was a great American singer and songwriter, and a very fine man. I am proud that I had just a little to do with his career and grateful to Jerry for allowing me to play a small role in John's journey to stardom.

It takes many qualities to be a really big star, and John Denver had them all. Talent, commitment, sincerity, heart, belief, love and warmth. John had the ability to connect with his audience and touch their souls. He had respect for people of all ages and colors, and equal affection for the poor and the privileged. John Denver was an exceptional person.

While I was at Management Three, I got a call from John Lennon and Yoko Ono's office requesting that I come to a film studio in New York so that I could have my knees filmed. John and Yoko were working on a project in which they would film prominent people in the music industry walking past a camera with their pants rolled up above their knees. Although I thought the project was a bit odd, I agreed and set up a time for them to film me.

On the day I was scheduled to be filmed, I showed up at the studio in the West 60s and was greeted by John and Yoko. They instructed me to roll up my pants to expose my knees and walk down a line on the floor. I never knew what the film was for and I never asked John or Yoko for an explanation. I never saw the film; I don't even know if it was ever completed or released. I did it because John and Yoko asked me to. I could never refuse John. He was very special to me. It's too bad I never had a chance to ask him what the film was for. I'd still like to know. I can just see it now—"And, the Academy Award for Best Knees goes to...Sid Bernstein!"

After working at Management Three for more than a year without any mention of the promised partnership with Jerry, I began to get antsy. To be sure, I was well-paid, the action was steady, fun and interesting. But, with the birth of our sixth child and fourth son, Etienne Bernstein, on January 25, 1973, there were now eight of us in the Bernstein family. Gerry in particular was worried about having financial security for herself and the kids, and that security would be assured if I got the partnership I had been promised.

I started dropping hints around the office. I wasn't insistent or anything like that, but Jerry realized what was on my mind.

One day, I sat down with him and said, "Listen, Jerry, I've been thinking about this partnership thing. I really need to get it resolved."

"Sid, why don't we see how we get along?"

We were getting along beautifully. Jerry had surprised me several times with generous increases in my salary. Two years was enough time to see how we got along. The truth was that Jerry was just stalling me. He really didn't want any partners at Management Three. I realized that Jerry had dangled the partnership in front of me so that I would join Management Three.

I went to Marvin Zolt and voiced my concerns. "Sid," he said, "you've come a long way here and you know how much Jerry respects you and how generous he is. Let it go for a while."

I explained to Marvin that I needed to take this step for my family's financial security. I needed to know where I stood with Jerry.

"Marvin, I'm asking you to find out from Jerry whether he's going to come through with a partnership or not."

"Okay, Sid. I'll try to talk to him."

A week or two passed with no reply, so I called Jerry myself. He was on a yacht somewhere with Frank Sinatra and Mickey Rudin. I didn't want to be put off anymore.

"Jerry, I have decided that I'm going to leave. I want to give you notice. I'm not in a rush, though, so how many weeks would you like me to stay to tie up loose ends?"

Jerry Weintraub is subject to quick decisions and pulls no punches. He gets hot quickly.

"Leave today. Right now," he blurted.

Jerry was furious and didn't speak to me for three years after that. Maybe my timing was off. In retrospect, I feel that we should have had that talk face-to-face. The bottom line is that I was promised something and I never got it. I felt that I held up my end of the bargain, but I felt that there had been no reciprocity. So I left. I was disappointed, hurt and frustrated, but I really didn't have time to dwell on it or feel sorry for myself. The days in the office with Jerry were never dull. He was brilliant, he knew the game and how to play it and, yes, he was quite generous. But I had made my decision and it was too late to turn back. It wasn't an easy decision to leave, but I had to secure my family's future.

Abe Margolies said that I made a big mistake!

BOOK FOUR

BASHERT

Chapter 17: **STARTING OVER**

I TOOK AN OFFICE AT 505 PARK AVENUE AND WENT TO WORK.
The Stylistics were hot. They had had several hit records. I booked them into Carnegie Hall, we sold out, and I made some quick money. The success I had with the Stylistics led me to put Harold Melvin and the Blue Notes into Carnegie Hall. The concert sold out using the old Bernstein formula. I was back in action.

I struck a deal to represent Bruce Morrow. Brucie wanted to get off WABC radio. He had worked there for years and was tired. He wanted to go to another station. I helped get him a job at WNBC radio with a big pay raise and some occasional appearances on NBC news shows reporting pop music.

Deodato was a famous Brazilian pianist and award-winning conductor and arranger. He had a number one record on MCA records titled *The Theme From 2001*. Deodato's son Cassius attended the same school as my eldest son Adam. Deodato and I became friendly after seeing each other at PTA meetings and school functions. Somehow, one thing led to another, and I began getting him bookings and managing his career.

I had left Management Three in a hurry because that's what Jerry Weintraub wanted. His immediate dismissal of me left me in a state of shock, but I had landed on my feet. Slowly but surely, I was reestablishing myself as an independent promoter and manager.

Bill Graham called me from San Francisco.
"Sid, I got the George Harrison/Dark Horse tour. Since you are the one who first brought the Beatles to the States, you should present George at Madison Square Garden."

Naturally I agreed, and of course, it was a sell out and an exciting musical evening.

I remember walking around the Garden during the performance and having an usher tell me, "Sid, there are some friends of yours 12 rows from the stage. The guy is wearing a big black hat. Go take a look, but be very nonchalant about it; we don't want a riot."

I casually walked up the aisle. I spotted the young woman sitting there with the man in the black hat. She gave me a big smile and a wave. The guy with the black hat winked and gave me the thumbs-up sign. I waved and smiled and kept walking. Paul and Linda McCartney were enjoying the music of their buddy George Harrison.

When I went backstage to see George after his concert, he was chanting, burning incense, and seemed to be praying. I didn't want to disturb him so

I waved, he waved, and I went home. That was George—the quiet one.

Felix Cavaliere had finally patched up the ill feelings that Laura Nyro had towards me after I had fallen asleep the evening that David Geffen took me to her apartment to hear her music. David Geffen had moved on, and she needed a manager. I was more than happy to add her to my growing client roster. She was extremely talented.

Because of that earlier negative experience, I wanted to do a super job for Laura. My untimely nap and the fallout that ensued had always disturbed me, as I prided myself on my professional conduct. After Laura had assembled one of the best bands I ever heard, I decided to present her at Carnegie Hall. Everything was thought-out and executed in a first-class manner. The lighting, staging, publicity and advertising all had my undivided attention. I was determined that this concert be a triumph for Laura.

I decided on an extra little touch. Upon presentation of her ticket, each female concert attendee would receive a beautiful long-stemmed daffodil. I got a well-known florist to supply the flowers for me, and I also hired additional staff to stand right behind the ticket takers and hand every woman that walked into Carnegie Hall a daffodil. The flowers were very expensive and the finest that money could buy. They were just beautiful. Laura was unaware of this little touch that I had planned for her concert.

Every seat in Carnegie hall was filled. I made sure that Laura stayed in her dressing room for an extra 15 minutes so that everyone would be seated and that a sea of daffodils would greet her.

When the band members came out, I could see the surprise on their faces when they saw the flowers.

Finally, Laura was introduced. Laura Nyro was a very quiet, unassuming person. She was extremely gentle and demure and had a very modest demeanor as well. I always considered Laura to be the quintessential "flower child."

Laura was greeted by thunderous applause. Being the modest person that she was, she walked out with her head somewhat bowed and her eyes on the stage. When she got to her mike, she looked up to acknowledge the ovation. As she caught sight of the waves of daffodils, her mouth fell open in surprise and a big smile crossed her face.

"Thank you! Thank you!" she said. The audience in the orchestra seats was waving the daffodils, the crowd in the upper balconies was standing and waving the flowers, and Laura was clearly overwhelmed. It was an event before she sang her first note.

Laura was a dear friend and loved my children. When she finally had one of her own, she said that her child gave her all the love and happiness she needed. Laura died several years ago after battling breast cancer. She was a very sensitive poet who wrote beautiful lyrics. It is a shame that she was taken from us at such a young age. What a lovely lady Laura was.

I loved being on my own again; I liked having my independence. The financial pressures were enormous, but I was getting by and having fun.

Abe Margolies introduced me to Joe Taub. Joe Taub is a born salesman with eyes like Paul Newman and a mane of white hair that is something to behold. Joe, his brother Henry, and Frank Lautenberg had started a huge business called ADP. Eventually, they sold ADP to the public and became wealthy. Frank Lautenberg became a U. S. Senator from New Jersey. I think that Henry stayed active in the business to some degree. Joe retired at a very young age.

Joe became very friendly with Enzo Stuarti, the great vocalist, who was his neighbor in New Jersey. When Joe wanted to help Enzo, he came to me for advice. Enzo had been on *Ed Sullivan* and other TV shows, but he had never been in concert. I recommended to Joe that we do my Carnegie Hall formula and invite reviewers and press. Joe agreed and helped sell most of the tickets; the concert sold out. Enzo began to get more concert dates and Joe Taub and I had a budding friendship.

Joe found out that I had left Jerry Weintraub and came to my new office one day and asked, "Sid, how can you leave Jerry Weintraub? You've got six kids! How can you just walk away? He has Sinatra, Elvis, and John Denver! How can you do it?"

I explained to Joe what had happened with Jerry and what I was planning next. In the hour that Joe and I were talking, several famous people called my office. Since Joe seemed amenable, I took the calls. Of course, Joe only heard my end of the conversations, but the names of the people I was talking to impressed him.

"Sid," he said to me, gesturing to the floor. "You have oil flowing right alongside your desk. It's in your territory, right under your chin, but you don't have a ladle to pick it up. You're not taking full advantage of the opportunities that I know you have coming your way. I'm sitting here, listening to you talk on the phone and important and well-known people are constantly calling you. *They're* calling *you*!"

"You're probably right, Joe. What do you suggest?"

"You need to take advantage of these opportunities. I want to come back here and spend some time with you."

For the next month, Joe came and sat with me in the office or came to lunch with me. He was clearly trying to get a handle of how the music and entertainment business was run, what the financial side was like and what he could bring to the endeavor. Joe gave me advice and I liked what he had to say; he and I decided to be partners. I was excited to have a partner who dressed like a king, looked like a movie star and had substantial financial resources. Before long, Joe Taub was pumping money into my new company.

Joe had weekly massages and he considered them to be his exercise routine. He believed that the massages helped keep both his body and mind in balance. Joe insisted that I have a massage before any important meeting or event.

One day, Joe and I were sitting in the office and a young lady walked in.

"Mr. Bernstein, you won't remember me," she began. "When I was a young girl in my early teens, I lived in Teaneck, New Jersey. My name was Phoebe Laub then and my friends and I would go to your shows at the Academy of Music. I saw the Rolling Stones, the Moody Blues and other groups there. My friends all had money and could buy tickets, but I couldn't, so I just went along for the ride. You had a little office at the Academy of Music and my friends and I would come and say hello to you. Often, after my friends would rush to get to their seats and I would turn to go home, you would produce a ticket from your pocket so I could attend the concert. You would tell me, 'This seat is not with your friends, but it will get you into the concert.' I would call my mom to tell her that you had given me a ticket and that I would be returning home with my friends. I have never forgotten that. And now, Mr. Bernstein, I am looking for a manager."

"Really? Have you been to see anyone else?"

"Yes, I saw Jerry Weintraub just yesterday."

"He's great. He's marvelous. He has Sinatra, Elvis, the Moody Blues and John Denver. Why are you here?"

"I don't want him. I want *you* because of the way you treated me when I was a kid."

"Okay, Phoebe. I understand. What can I do for you?"

"Mr. Bernstein, I have an album that was put out by an independent label and it has sold 700,000 copies. Now, I'm moving to Columbia Records. My name is Phoebe Snow."

As soon as she said "Phoebe Snow," I knew who she was. Her story had been featured in the trade papers because it wasn't often that an indie label sold 700,000 copies of anything. Of course I was interested in managing her. Joe, Phoebe and I began to discuss a formal business relationship.

After signing Phoebe, Clive Davis invited her to appear at Columbia's convention, which was held in Toronto that year. Phoebe asked me to accompany her to Toronto and Joe Taub urged me to go, even though we hadn't yet signed her to a contract.

I flew to Toronto with Phoebe. She was happy to have me act as her manager. When we arrived, Clive wanted to introduce Phoebe around and have her sing. Phoebe was reluctant because she had no one to accompany her on the piano. A young Columbia artist who was also at the conference volunteered to be her accompanist. I'll never forget the night that Phoebe Snow and Billy Joel dazzled everyone at the Columbia Records convention in Toronto.

Joe Taub took Phoebe Snow under his wing. He helped her, but she had so many problems that we couldn't get her career off the ground. We would book an engagement for her and she would cancel. She would have a date for a recording session and then not show up. It was an impossible and discouraging situation. I had seen this erratic and unprofessional behavior before with Judy Garland, Jimi Hendrix and Sly Stone. I knew that Phoebe probably wouldn't make it, but it wouldn't be for lack of talent. Joe Taub was like an uncle to her and he really tried to help her in every way possible. Phoebe had an amazing amount of talent, and she had two great friends—me and Joe—in the music business who were more than willing to help her. But she couldn't help her own best friend—Phoebe Snow!

A musician friend of mine called one day.

"Sid, I just got off the phone with Melba Moore. She heard that I knew you, and she was asking me about your qualifications as a manager. Of course, I gave you the best recommendation. If she calls you, listen to her story. Her marriage has just ended. She currently has some career problems—no record label, no agent, and no manager. But, Sid, you know she's enormously talented."

"Yes, I've seen her on TV and she can really sing. But, I've also heard some industry rumors about her that spell trouble."

"It's all untrue. Give her a chance, Sid. If she calls, talk to her."

The next day, Melba did call me and we made an appointment to meet. Only a half-hour elapsed before I concluded that she was a lovely, genuine human being. All the stories I had heard about how difficult she was were almost immediately forgotten.

"Melba, what would you like to do?"

"Well, Sid, I'd like to start fresh. I'd like to start right from the beginning, and I need the counsel and advice that a manager like you can provide. I know that I present a challenge, but I hear that you're a man that would take on such a challenge."

"I'd like to think about this. Let's meet again tomorrow and we'll continue exploring the idea."

The next day, she came to my office and I told her that I was willing to take on the challenge of resurrecting her career.

"I don't want to sign a contract yet, Melba. Let's see how we get along."

"Sid, you would be willing to work with me without a contract?" she asked quite unbelievingly.

"Yes, I'm prepared to do it that way."

I can't explain it. Maybe the stars were lined up right or something like that, but my efforts on behalf of Melba bore immediate fruit.

I called Art Kass at Buddah Records, and he made a record deal for Melba right on the phone. Then I called Nat Lefkowitz, chairman of William Morris, to talk to him about Melba. He insisted that we have lunch. At the lunch meeting, I could see that Nat was a little reluctant about Melba. He had heard the same stories I had heard. I knew that I had to sell him on the "new and improved" Melba.

"Nat, this is not the old Melba. This is a different lady. She is unattached and her major problems are behind her. She is a shy, modest and very gentle person. And, I think she is going to be a star again soon."

"Sidney, if you can guarantee that she will behave professionally, we'd be willing to sign her and give it a shot."

Melba must have thought that I walked on water. Within two weeks of her coming to my office feeling down and with seemingly few prospects, she now had a manager, a hot record label and a top booking agency.

We went to work and, in a slow, steady progression, her career began to be revitalized and re-energized. She made some television appearances and her price for live shows began to escalate almost immediately. We had won back her respectability. I even put her in a benefit show with Alan King, Carol Channing and Frank Sinatra. Melba Moore was coming back, big time.

However, Melba evidently needed to have a man in her life and shortly after we met, she fell in love with Charles Huggins, the entrepreneur/owner of Frank's Restaurant, a very famous eatery in Harlem. Charles was a handsome, bright guy, and Melba married him. After about a year into the marriage, she came to my office to speak with me.

"Look, Sid, Charles wants to be in the music business and he wants to manage me."

I can't say that I was shocked, but I had a feeling that this was not going to be the best thing for Melba. We were on a roll and she was threatening the chemistry.

"Melba, are you sure that you want to do this? Are you sure that you want to leave here?"

"He's my husband, Sid. He really wants to be in the management business. He wants a change from the restaurant. What do you think?"

"Melba, you have become very dear to me and I consider you my friend. If this is going to bring you happiness, and if you're sure it's the right thing to do, then you go and do it. You have my best wishes."

Having her husband also be her manager didn't help Melba's career, but it sure helped Charles Huggins. He used it as a stepping stone to sign and manage record producers, and he became very successful. Unfortunately, his marriage to Melba wasn't as successful. They eventually got divorced.

One day in Spring 1974, I ran into my friend Arthur Aaron on the street. Arthur had been a big fan of the Rascals and had gotten friendly with a couple of the guys. I would see him from time to time at their appearances. After exchanging family information, we got into a discussion about the Beatles.

"Sid, do you think the Beatles will ever perform as a group again?" Arthur asked me.

"I don't know, Arthur. But I sure would like to have an opportunity to try and put them back together again."

"Well, what do you think it would take?"

"Probably $10 million," I laughingly responded.

We chatted for a few more minutes and then went our separate ways.

The next morning, Arthur called me. "Sid, I spoke to Arlen Specter (the four-term senior senator from Pennsylvania in the U.S. Senate), and he thinks that the First Pennsylvania Bank might be interested in putting up the money for a Beatles reunion. Should I ask him to pursue it?"

"Sure, why not? We'll never get it done without the money. Ask him to proceed with the bank."

That afternoon, Arthur called again. "Sid, we have a lunch appointment with the chairman of the bank on Thursday, in Philadelphia."

On the following Thursday, I met Arthur and we took the Metroliner to Philadelphia. We picked up Arlen and walked over to the bank.

I remember that John Bunting, the chairman of First Philadelphia Bank, had the most interesting office. It was on three levels, with a desk and a sitting area on each level. After introductions, we were ushered into the chairman's private dining room, where we were met by an executive vice president of the bank. We spent the next 45 minutes enjoying lunch and chatting. The chairman and his vice president were interested in Beatles stories, so I told them a few. After dessert and coffee was served, the chairman, looking at me intently, asked, "Mr. Bernstein, how can we help you?"

"Well, Mr. Bunting, as you know, there is still great interest in the Beatles. Everywhere I go, people are always asking me about the Beatles and whether or not they're going to reunite. As you are also aware, it has been years since they played and sang together, so it's a long-shot at best. I think, however, that money might be a catalyst to getting them back together. I would like to offer them $10 million for a one-time closed-circuit concert to be broadcast all over the world," I concluded.

"And where would you present the performance?"

"I think that it should be in a time zone that would maximize the worldwide viewership."

The chairman asked me some more questions, which I answered, and then he stood up, extended his hand and said, "It's an interesting idea, Sid. Let us think about it, and we'll get back to you."

I thanked him for his time and the lunch. We shook hands all around and Arthur and I headed back to New York.

The very next morning, Arthur called me. "Sid, Arlen just called from Philadelphia. The bank says they'll put up $12 million—$10 million as an advance against whatever you negotiate with the Beatles, and $2 million for infrastructure. All we have to do is get the Beatles to agree."

"That's great news, Arthur! I'll get to work on it right away!"

"Yeah, and one more thing, Sid. The $10 million is open-ended. As long as Bunting and his team are running the bank, the money is there."

"Thanks, Arthur. Tell Arlen I appreciate his efforts, and we'll keep him posted."

I decided early on that I would not go directly to the Beatles. Industry etiquette dictated that I deal with their representatives to effect any business dealings. A flurry of letters and phone calls and more letters and phone calls between layers of lawyers, accountants and advisors that insulated them ensued. It was impossible to get any definitive word about anything.

Also, the Beatles evidently had issues amongst themselves, particularly John and Paul. We couldn't even get them together as a group to present our proposal. It was a sad thing for me because I knew how millions of Beatles fans were yearning for a reunion. I wanted to see it myself. I vowed to keep trying.

Naturally, I was very disappointed that once again I could not facilitate a Beatles reunion. I knew that the boys were leading their own lives and still had unresolved feelings among themselves that prevented them from getting back together. I'd always had some kind of plan to orchestrate a Beatles reunion in the back of my mind, but as the realization of the enormous difficulty of facilitating such a reunion sunk in, I put it on the back burner. I yearned for the days when I could make a call to Brian Epstein and get it done.

Then came ABBA.

Lou Levy, who had discovered the Andrews Sisters and had founded the highly successful Leeds Music Publishing Company, called me from London. "Sid, I just came back from the Eurovision Song Contest in France. You know, the annual international song writing and performing contest—"

"Yeah, I know Eurovision, Lou," I interrupted.

"Sid, there's an act that appeared there that won the contest unanimously. Two guys and two girls from Sweden. They call themselves ABBA. You have to get on a plane immediately and go see Stig Andersen. Stig is a friend of mine. I've already told him about you, but don't wait for his call. I'll give you his number in Stockholm. You call him! Call immediately! He's the group's manager, publisher and producer. He's the guy, Sid."

Lou knew his stuff. As soon as I hung up with him, I called Stig Andersen in Stockholm. He knew right away who I was.

"You fit in with my plans, Sid! When are you free to come to Sweden?" Stig asked.

"Well, Stig, Lou is so enthusiastic about what you and ABBA are doing that I would like to visit you as soon as possible. I can leave New York in two days."

"That's good, Sid. Make your reservations and let me know when you're arriving in Stockholm. I'll have you met at the airport."

Three days later, Stig met me at the airport in Stockholm. He was a young man in his 30s. I could tell almost immediately from our conversation that this was a guy with "smarts." I had been around long enough to know the real thing when I saw it. We went to his offices, which housed one of the biggest music publishing companies in Sweden.

"Sid, the group is not here in Stockholm. They're vacationing at their summer home. I am going to see them tomorrow; I bring them provisions weekly."

"Provisions, Stig?"

"Well they live on a little island in the Baltic Sea. It's out of the way and quite secluded. It's really the only way that they can escape the scene that goes on around them when they're here in Stockholm. They've become so popular here that it's hard for them to get any privacy."

What Stig said reminded me of what had happened to the Beatles in England at the height of their popularity.

The next morning, the sky was ominously cloudy, but Stig and I drove to the edge of the sea, car fully loaded with food and beverages.

We loaded the stuff onto a boat and took off. The weather got increasingly more threatening. We kept passing the many islands in the Baltic. After a while, the sky got black and the sea became extremely choppy. Stig must have seen the expression on my face because he asked me if I wanted to turn back.

I swallowed hard and said, "No, Stig. I've come this far. Let's go. If you've got an oar, I'll row so we can get there faster."

He laughed. "No oar, Sid. Just the engine."

We finally got to the island and as soon as the boat touched shore, the clouds parted, and the most beautiful sun appeared. As we alighted, the two male members of ABBA, Bjorn and Benny, came forward to greet us. They represented the B's in ABBA and both were very handsome young men. We proceeded to unload the boat and carry all the food to a cabin. We put the food down and one of the guys said, "Stig, we're glad you're here, because we have to move the baby grand up the hill to another cabin, which we rented to use as our music room."

I had come to sign a group and had, in a short period of time, become a sailor, food delivery guy and now a moving man. I pitched in, and we lugged that baby grand piano up the hill and into ABBA's new rehearsal room. My back was aching.

When we got to the new cabin, the other two members of ABBA met us, a gorgeous blonde and an equally beautiful redhead, Anna and Annifrid, the wives of Bjorn and Benny and the A's in ABBA. I thought to myself, if these young people can sing as good as they look, we really have something here.

One of the girls smiled and said, "So they enlisted you to help with the piano, ya?"

Holding my back, I responded with a laugh, "Did they ever!"

She said, "Does your back hurt? We'll rub it down." We were all laughing by now.

We sat up there in their music cabin, talking and listening to their music for two or three hours. It was super. We made a deal right on the spot for me to be their American manager.

When we were on our way back on the boat, Stig said, "Sid, you really made an impression on ABBA. They thought you were this very important man from the States. Your willingness to help with the piano made it for you with them!"

I forgot about my aching back. Just shows you what a little schlepping can do, I thought.

Stig asked me to stay in Stockholm for an extra few days because ABBA was going to perform, and the press was eager to meet the man who had brought the Beatles to America and would now be doing the same for ABBA.

The next day, I met with the press at Stig's office. Naturally, most of the questions were about the Beatles. On the day after the press conference, one of Stig's assistants came rushing to the hotel.

"Mr. Bernstein!" she said as she held out one of Stockholm's daily papers. "Look! You are on the front page of the paper!"

I took the paper and there was a picture of ABBA and me. She translated the caption, "Sid Bernstein—the American manager of the Beatles has arrived in Stockholm." Of course, it was a mistake. I was the Beatles promoter, not their manager. I understood that Stig had purposely made the mistake to the reporter because it added weight and importance to my signing of his group, ABBA.

I attended ABBA's concert the next night and thought they were fabulous. I went home with great expectations.

I always believed that ABBA could have been one of the all-time great acts. They were superb writers, terrific singers, and their physical appearance was positively stunning. But, I think what held them back was a decision that Stig Andersen made. He wanted to wait until ABBA would have two back-to-back number one records in the U.S. They had big records to be sure, but getting two back-to-back happens to few acts. It is rare indeed. Stig kept waiting and waiting, and he wouldn't let me at least break ABBA in New York, which I could easily have done. Stig's waiting dissipated the momentum in the U.S. and momentum is hard to come by. ABBA was successful in the few appearances they made in the U.S.; however, they never got to be the superstars that I had hoped they would be.

My great initial excitement eventually turned to disappointment for me.

The story turned out well for ABBA, though. Stig took them to Australia, and they broke every conceivable attendance record and became megastars there.

Shortly after my association with ABBA ended, John Lennon called me at my apartment.

"Sidney, listen. I'm taking some friends out to dinner. They say they want Italian food. You're the expert on Italian food. Where should I take them?"

"Paolucci's, John. Paolucci's is the best. It's on Mulberry and Grand Streets, in Little Italy."

"Oh, yeah, Sid, I remember that. You told me and my mates that the first time we ever met you at the Plaza Hotel."

"You're probably right, John. I had completely forgotten. Paolucci's is the place and there are two items on the menu that you have to order. Shrimp fra diavolo as an appetizer, start with that. Then you want to order the veal Parmesan."

"Wait a minute, Sid!" John interrupted. "I won't remember these names and for sure I can't spell them, so I'm going to put Harry on."

Harry Nilsson, John's buddy and a great songwriter and artist, got on the phone. "Sid, how the hell are you? How are all your kids?"

"Great, Harry! Everybody is fine. I hope you're behaving yourself!" We both laughed.

John and Harry had become notorious for their over exuberant-partying. The press kept printing stories of John's and Harry's wild escapades.

"Listen, Sid. The Englishman here can't spell his own name. What are those dishes again?"

I repeated the names of the dishes to Harry, and he could spell everything correctly.

"Sid," he said, before handing the phone back to John, "is Paolucci's as good as the restaurant you took me to in Hawaii?"

"You bet, Harry. And then some!"

John took the phone back, "Thanks, Sid. We're going."

Two days later I was sitting in my office when two messengers came in carrying two of the largest fruit baskets I had ever seen.

"Who are those for?" I asked.

"Sid Bernstein," came the reply.

"I never ordered anything."

"Sir, the card says Sid Bernstein. Are you Sid Bernstein?"

"I am."

"Well, then, these are for you."

I took the envelope with the card and ripped it open. The card said, Thank you ever so much. We had an incredible time. It was signed, Harry and John.

The next time I went to Paolucci's, Dominic Paolucci, the owner, told me that the group of rock and rollers I had sent to the restaurant were all famous people. "Sid," he said, "they were all so well-behaved and courteous! And, they left the biggest tip in the history of the restaurant!"

Lee Guber ran the Westbury Music Fair and the Valley Forge, Pennsylvania, summer theatre, and also produced Broadway shows. At the time, he was married to Barbara Walters, the TV journalist and daughter of my old boss at the Latin Quarter, Lou Walters. Lee approached me one day with a request that I help him stage a big rally at Madison Square Garden for Congressman Hugh Carey, who was running for Governor of New York. Lee also asked me if I could persuade Melba Moore, who I was managing at that time, to open the show for Frank Sinatra. Sinatra was a friend of Carey's and had agreed to appear. Lee explained that Carol Channing had agreed to appear and that Alan King was set to be the MC.

"Sid," Lee said, "we need you to deal with the Garden, the unions, the tickets, etc. You know the Garden better than anyone else."

"Flattery will get you everywhere, Lee. I'll do it."

I wasn't about to turn down promoting a bill with Alan King, Carol Channing and Frank Sinatra. I was also interested in getting Melba the exposure. I took care of all the necessary arrangements in two days.

On the night of the concert, I went to the Garden early to make sure that everything was running smoothly. Everything seemed to be in order except for the fact that Congressman Carey's plane was delayed in upstate New York where he was attending a fundraiser. I got messages saying that Carey would be about a half-hour late. Not great, I thought, but not entirely uncommon.

I asked Alan King to stretch his routine a little and to tell the other performers to do the same. I then went to sit in my seat in the orchestra section and enjoy the show, as was my custom. About 20 minutes after I sat down, Jilly Rizzo, Frank Sinatra's good friend, came to my seat and said, "Sid, the Boss would like to speak to you."

"Okay, Jilly, I'll be right there. I just want to watch the end of Melba's set."

"No, Sid. I think you ought to come right now. It's getting a little hot in his dressing room."

"All right, we'll go now." I rose to follow him.

We were sharing a joke as we walked towards the dressing room. I had my arm around Jilly. Halfway there, he slipped out of my grasp and said, "Sid, I forgot something. Why don't you go see Frank and I'll meet you there in a few minutes."

The warning signal went off in my head. Jilly was abandoning ship. When I got to the door of Sinatra's dressing room, Tiny, his bodyguard, said, "The Boss is a little hot."

I opened the door and walked in. I introduced myself to the great Frank Sinatra. "Mr. Sinatra, I'm Sid Bernstein, the producer of this event."

"Hi, Sid." He extended his hand. "I've heard a lot about you from Jerry Weintraub."

Sinatra turned to the mirror to straighten his bow tie. He was in shirtsleeves and I was amazed to see that he had a potbelly. I had always thought of him as a slim man. Looking at me through the mirror, he said, "Sid, what's holding up the show? It looks like we're 25 minutes behind already. What's up?"

"Mr. Sinatra, Congressman Carey was attending a fundraiser in Rochester and his plane was delayed. As soon as he gets to La Guardia Airport, we're going to get him here as quickly as we can. My information is that the Congressman's plane should land quite soon."

Turning from the mirror and looking directly at me, he said, "Sid, Jilly tells me that you are an expert on Italian food. Jilly says that you're the man. He says that you know your pasta and pizza. Tell me, Sid, where's the best pizza in New York?"

For years, I had gone to Patsy's up in Harlem for pizza. Often I would hear that I had just missed Frank Sinatra. I also remembered hearing that, from time to time, the Warner Brothers plane would transport pizza from Patsy's to Los Angeles for Frank Sinatra.

"Patsy's, Mr. Sinatra," I answered. "Patsy's has the best pizza."

"Man, that place is great. I still go up there sometimes when I'm in town."

He was flexing his suspenders. We were now buddies in food. I could see that Sinatra was no longer bothered by having to wait for Hugh Carey.

"But, Mr. Sinatra, the pizza I remember best of all was made at a little restaurant in the South Bronx that had a coal oven like Patsy's. It's the only pizza that could even dare to be compared to Patsy's."

"Knock off the 'Mr. Sinatra' business, Sid. You can call me Frank." He leaned forward conspiratorially. "So which restaurant is that?"

"Well, I remember that it was on Cortland Avenue, about 10 blocks from Yankee Stadium, but it's been gone now for some time. It was called Delli Venneris."

"What did you say?" he asked me, his eyes widening. "Did you say Delli Venneris?"

"Yes, Frank, Delli Venneris."

"Sid, you have just hit me square—and I mean square—in my *la banza*," and he smacked his stomach with his clenched fists. "I haven't heard that name in 20 years! That place was a masterpiece!"

I did not want to tell him that years ago, after a veterans' meeting, Milt Pollack and I drove to Delli Venneris late one winter night. It was about 11:30 PM, the streets were desolate and the wind was blowing up the canyon of apartment buildings. There was a solitary limousine parked in front of Delli Venneris. Milt and I parked behind the limo and went inside. Al Delli Venneris greeted us and motioned us to sit down.

"Sid, I'll be right with you. Right with you!" he said. "I have something in the oven." And he went into the kitchen.

"Okay, Al. Take your time."

I looked around the darkened restaurant and whispered to Milt, "Don't be too obvious, but if you look at the back of the restaurant, I think you'll recognize some people sitting there."

Milt turned slowly and whistled through his teeth. "Wow, Sid! That's Ava Gardner and Frank Sinatra!"

"That's right, Milt!"

As I stood in front of Frank Sinatra at the Garden, I wondered if he remembered going to Delli Venneris with Ava Gardner.

"Do you remember how they used to drop the corn meal on the paddle before they put the pizza into the oven?"

"I sure do, Sid. That place was great."

All of a sudden, he changed topics on me. "Sid, do you know the Prime Minister of Israel?

"No, Frank, I don't. You're probably not going to believe this, but I've never been to Israel."

"You've never been there?" he asked incredulously. "You gotta go there, Sid! That place is marvelous. The spirit is unbelievable and the generals that I know there are some of the toughest guys I've ever met. I've done some work there. They love American music in Israel. You gotta get over there sometime soon, Sid."

"I know, Frank. I plan to go when I get some free time."

There was a knock on the door and someone announced that Congressman Carey was in the building. I turned to leave as Frank put his jacket on.

"Sid, take care," he said. "Maybe we'll run into each other some day at Patsy's."

With Frank's passing, I am saddened to think that it is now impossible for us to run into each other at Patsy's, or anywhere else. Suffice it to say that Frank Sinatra left an indelible mark on the American cultural landscape. He was an original. And he knew his pizza!

I had seen Woody Allen in one of his early comedic performances at the Bitter End. I thought that he was so funny and clever, I vowed to myself that one day I would present him in one of my shows.

The opportunity arose when I presented Count Basie and Mel Torme at Carnegie Hall. For some reason, I felt that Woody would fit on the Jazz bill. I paid him the princely sum of $750. Woody put on a great show and never questioned his inclusion on the bill.

It takes great courage and confidence for an act to appear on a bill that is a little offbeat. There is never any assurance that the audience will respond favorably. The audience for this Basie/Torme show came to hear jazz. They got the bonus of also seeing and hearing one of the great comic geniuses of the 20th century. I knew that they would love Woody and accept him, but I'm sure that he wasn't convinced of that when he accepted the date.

Courage is a hallmark of live performers. No matter how good you think you are, regardless of how much confidence you possess, you still have to get up in front of a live audience who has paid money to be entertained and are now sitting there thinking, show me. That's why we call it show business and why the good ones make the kind of money that they do. Failure and humiliation in front of a crowd is just a missed step, a missed note, or a missed line away.

The one thing I know is that Woody Allen has courage.

Helen Reddy and Jeff Wald, her husband who was an agent at William Morris, called me to ask if I would organize a concert to benefit Ramsey Clark's U.S. Senate campaign, at Avery Fisher Hall in Lincoln Center. I agreed to do the concert. I was excited with the list of stars scheduled to appear: Paul Newman, Joanne Woodward, Harry Chapin, Neil Simon, Julie Harris, Harry Belafonte, playwright Adolph Green, Dustin Hoffman, Tom Paxton, basketball star Dave DeBusscherre, Phyllis Newman, Jack Gilford, Patrick O'Neal, Dick Shawn, Marlo Thomas and Kevin McCarthy. It was a star-studded cast and Avery Fisher Hall is a magnificent venue.

It had become easy for me to put on an event like this. I had produced so many shows that I could arrange the entire event with just a few days' work. I truly enjoyed the action and I could always take a memorable experience or anecdote away with me.

What I remember most from the Helen Reddy & Friends concert was the opportunity to work with Paul Newman. On the day of the event, Paul and I spent about four hours arranging the schedule for the show. We discussed who would open the event, the order of the performers, how long each act would be onstage, etc. We did the run-through on paper because not everyone was able to attend the rehearsal.

I had heard that Paul Newman was a prodigious beer drinker, but that it did not affect him at all. In the four hours that we spent together, he drank beer as though it were water. I was amazed that he could put away so much beer and not have it affect his mental capacities in any way. Paul Newman is a most magnificent-looking man, as most any woman would tell you. I was impressed with his manner and style; he has a glow about him that's difficult to describe.

My 12-year-old daughter Denise spent those four hours with me. After Paul and I completed our work, I went home to change clothes and prepare for the concert. On the drive home, I said to Denise, "Paul Newman is really the most handsome man."

"C'mon, Daddy, you're much better looking than him!"

Not exactly, but that's my Denise!

Despite the fact that my association with ABBA did not work out the way I thought it would, I was always interested in bringing European groups to the States. One day, David Stein, a friend of mine who was on the cutting edge of what was happening in music everywhere, called me. He told me about a Scottish group called the Bay City Rollers.

"Sid, this band is the hottest group in England now! They have some hits and they are causing Beatles-like hysteria. Their gimmick is that they wear tartan plaid and the kids are buying Rollers merchandise faster than it can be manufactured. And, Sid, I have the newspaper articles to prove it."

"Send me the articles, David. I'll take a look," I said. I read the press that David sent and started to pick up some English magazines on my own. What David had told me was true. It was like déjà vu. Kids waiting for hours to get a glimpse of the Bay City Rollers, sold-out concerts, the use of the word hysteria. It was enough for me. I decided to go see this latest phenomenon for myself.

The Rollers were on Bell Records in the U.S., which was headed by Clive Davis, who was also president of Arista Records. I decided to give my old buddy Clive a call.

"Clive, I'm thinking of going over to Scotland to meet with the Bay City Rollers. I want to bring them to America."

"Please, Sid, don't do it."

"Why not?"

"Because they don't play their own instruments. They use studio musicians. You're known throughout the business for your credibility and integrity, Sid. If you bring these kids to New York, you'll absolutely lose your credibility. Leave it alone."

I knew that Clive was a purist. For a group to feign playing their own instruments was not kosher with him. Today, groups like the Backstreet Boys and N'Sync are megastars without playing their own instruments. It's all in the timing.

"I appreciate what you're saying, Clive, and I'll think about it, but I can't promise you I won't go check it out. I really feel like I have to see them. But, I will give some serious consideration to what you've said."

Clive could hear that I was anxious to go and check out the Bay City Rollers, so he even had Barry Reiss, a mutual friend who worked at Arista, call to try to dissuade me.

Nothing could deter me, though. I decided that I would go. Just because I was going didn't necessarily mean that I would definitely bring the Rollers to the U.S. I had to see for myself. I had nothing to lose and maybe everything to gain.

When I settled into my seat on the plane over to Scotland, I saw Barry Reiss sitting near me, having been dispatched by Clive to go check out what was happening with the Bay City Rollers in Scotland. I thought it was hilarious. Barry and I were heading to Glasgow, which was the kick-off city for the Rollers' 38-city tour of the British Isles.

Barry and I were staying at the same hotel, so we drove from the airport to the hotel together. Looking out the car window, we saw that the streets were full of kids wearing tartan plaid.

"Look at this," I said to Barry. "Look at what's going on here."

"Yes, Sid, something is definitely happening."

When we got to the hotel, there were several hundred kids milling about. They all were wearing tartan plaid. The kids were there because they thought that the Rollers might be staying at the hotel, since it was the finest hotel in Glasgow. However, the Rollers weren't staying there at all; they actually came from their homes in nearby Edinburgh for this first concert.

All night long, I heard the kids in the street outside my window singing Rollers' songs and having a great time. I knew then that I was on to something.

The next morning at breakfast, I asked Barry if he had heard the kids' singing.

"Who could sleep? They kept me up all night," he said groggily.

Tom Paton, the manager of the Rollers, had been expecting me and left my ticket for entry to the first of two shows that day at the front desk of the hotel. As I walked to the nearby theatre, I could see hundreds of young kids accompanied by their parents heading in the same direction. Across from the theatre, there was a huge trailer truck with three windows cut into its side from which Bay City Rollers merchandise was being sold. Caps, vests, scarves, kilts, shirts—you name it. They were doing big business and everything was in tartan plaid.

Barry and I looked at each other and I could see that he was beginning to grasp just how popular the Rollers were. The show was just about what I had expected. No one was sitting in his or her seat. The kids were screaming and swaying to the rhythm of the music, with the tartan scarves held behind their heads. It wasn't the Beatles, but it sure did bring back memories.

The Bay City Rollers were five very good-looking young men who sang reasonably well. They were not playing their own instruments. Sitting in the audience, I found it intriguing that the parents seemed to be enjoying themselves almost as much as the kids.

After the show, I went backstage to see Tom Paton, the Rollers' manager. He was very interested in having the Bay City Rollers come to America as soon as possible. I invited him to come back to my hotel with me to discuss the possibilities, and since it was just a few blocks away, he readily accepted. Paton wanted to make a deal quickly, so we wrote out a contract and signed it right then and there in the hotel. The contract was for one year and it called for me to represent the Bay City Rollers in America.

I went back to the theatre with Tom for the second show. Whereas the first audience had been predominantly young kids in the 8 to 12 year range, the evening show had older kids, mostly teens and overwhelmingly female. They were jumping up and down on the seats and screaming, and it reminded me of the first and only time that the Rolling Stones played Carnegie Hall.

I was very excited and my mind was bursting with ideas for the Rollers' trip to the U.S. I hired a photographer to take pictures of the scene in Glasgow. It was in some ways reminiscent of what I had experienced with the Beatles. Unfortunately, those similarities did not extend to the music.

I went back to New York. On my return, the first person I called was Howard Cosell, the famous sportscaster and TV personality, who was preparing to launch a new TV show, *The Howard Cosell Show*, which would be almost a carbon copy of the *Sullivan* show. The show was slated to be broadcast on Saturday nights from the Ed Sullivan Theatre. The new show was debuting at the height of Howard Cosell's illustrious career.

Abe Margolies had introduced Howard and me to each other at Abe's Steak House, which was the restaurant Abe opened after Les Champs closed. We would often dine at the restaurant together.

"Howard, I just came back from Scotland where I signed a very exciting act that I think you should put on your first show. The Bay City Rollers could help put your new show on the map."

"Sid, I appreciate your calling me with this opportunity, but you really need to talk to the producers of the show, Alan King and Rupert Hitzig. They handle that part of the show," said Howard. "You know Alan. Call him and discuss it with him. I have no objection whatsoever. If they say it's okay, we'll put the Bay City Rollers on our first show."

I called Alan King and set up an appointment to see him at his office. Howard Cosell attended the meeting, along with Roone Arledge, who was Howard's boss at ABC and producer of the immensely successful *Monday Night Football* telecasts, which had catapulted Howard to TV stardom. I began the meeting by pulling out the pictures of the crowds in Scotland that the photographer I hired had taken. I passed the pictures around.

"This, gentlemen," I said, "is by no means the Beatles. But, not since the Beatles has there been a hysteria and reaction to a group like this by the young kids in Britain. I stayed in a hotel in Scotland and was kept up all night by kids wearing Bay City Rollers clothes and singing Bay City Rollers songs. Those kids were out there all night! It's my prediction that if you put the Rollers on your show, you'll have to have police barricades around the theatre and kids will be lined up for days waiting for tickets. It'll get you tremendous press coverage. I'm suggesting that you to do a remote from Great Britain featuring the Rollers for your first show. You'll televise, via satellite, a concert in London that I will arrange with the group's manager. You'll show your audience the hysteria, the kids wearing tartans and the whole scene around this good-looking young group. The following week, you'll telecast the Rollers live from The Ed Sullivan Theatre. I guarantee you'll need those barricades and police security. The Rollers will put *The Howard Cosell Show* on the map."

They bought it on the spot. Everyone in the production group was very excited. The deal was made just as I had outlined it. The remote first, then the Rollers live the following week.

On the night of the first *Cosell* show, the Bay City Rollers played a concert to a packed small theatre in London. Tom Paton had set up the show. Tom gave instructions that the kids in the audience be allowed to rush the stage. Security was purposely lax. The result was that the American viewers of *The Howard Cosell Show* saw pandemonium. The Rollers sang *Saturday Night*, which was their song in current release in the U.S., and the kids overran the stage and knocked down the lead singer.

The following week, as promised by Cosell, the Bay City Rollers came to the U.S. to be on his show. There were several busloads of kids and members of the press who were at the airport to greet them.

On the Saturday morning prior to the show, the Rollers went to rehearsal at the Ed Sullivan Theatre.

From rehearsal, I called Gary Smith, with whom I had worked on *Hullabaloo*. Gary was working in England, producing a TV show. I told him that I was at a rehearsal with the Rollers at the Ed Sullivan Theatre in New York.

"What's that screaming I hear, Sid?"

"That's the kids screaming for the Rollers who just got here. They're appearing on *The Howard Cosell Show* live this week. Last week they were on via satellite from England. Gary, they'll be back in Britain next week. Is there any chance you can use them for one of your shows?"

"Sid, you're not going to believe this, but I'm here preparing to do an Ann-Margret special. The Temptations, who were supposed to appear, just cancelled. They can't make our show. Can you get the Rollers here within the next four days?"

"I sure can, Gary."

"You got a deal, Sid."

We had the Rollers on TV so often in those few weeks that their record, *Saturday Night,* soared up the charts and went to Number 1.

I was booking them all over the U.S. and getting $25,000 a night. Clive Davis was a very happy man. He momentarily forgot that the Bay City Rollers didn't play their own instruments.

Tom Paton worked with me for the year, as contracted. After the year was up, he went with ICM, a large booking agency, because he thought he could save some money in commissions. What he gained in financial terms, he lost in drive, involvement and creative thinking. An agent is not a manager. I was the Bay City Rollers' manager in America. They got management skills, dedication and experience. When they made the change, they got agents who wrote orders. They lost the momentum and dedication that I had brought to their team. Their star dimmed and they were soon gone.

In 1976, the Boat People became a big issue. Many desperate and beleaguered people were braving unknown seas on rickety boats fleeing from tyranny and oppression in Cambodia and Vietnam. Men and women with young children, miserably adrift on the seas. The pictures on television were heart-wrenching. No one wanted to take these people in. It reminded me of the Jews fleeing Hitler's Europe 35 years earlier.

I wondered if I could do something to help alleviate the suffering of the Boat People. To be sure, I could donate some money, which, of course, I did. But, as only one concerned citizen, I knew that whatever I did could not even begin to address the tremendous issues and needs of these refugees.

Taking $60,000 of my own money, in addition to contributions I got from Felix Cavaliere of the Rascals, Laura Nyro, and my childhood friend Jerry Rosen, I wrote and placed a full-page ad in the Sunday edition of *The New York Times* and the Paris edition of the *International Herald Tribune* imploring the Beatles to reunite and perform at a concert to raise money on behalf of the Boat People. I knew that these ads would be seen by millions of people. I got many calls and letters thanking me for having taking the initiative.

On the Monday after the ad ran in *The New York Times,* Hans Janitchek, the assistant to the Secretary General of the United Nations, called and asked if I would come to his office. As we sat in his sun-drenched office overlooking the gleaming East River, he said, "First of all, understand that everything we say in here is being heard by someone out there. They are always listening." And he pointed out the window. I don't know who "they" were, but I could imagine. It was very cloak-and-dagger.

"Mr. Bernstein," Hans continued, "you have no idea what an impact your ad has made here in the UN. The halls are buzzing with excitement. For quite a while now, the Secretary General has been exploring the possibility of reuniting the Beatles for the benefit of UNICEF. He has met with no success at all. Because of your association with the Beatles, you probably stand as good a chance as anyone to effect a Beatles reunion. The Secretary would like you to know that he and the entire UN community will help you in any way we can."

Hans told me that members of the UN would probably be calling me and that I should be careful.

"They will try to use you," he warned me.

Our meeting was long and exciting. I really hoped that the influence of the UN might be instrumental in helping make the benefit concert for the Boat People a reality. Of course, no one could predict what would happen. Still, I could not have been more pleased that my ad made such an impression with the members of the United Nations.

In the days following my meeting with Hans Janitchek, I got many calls. The British and, interestingly, the Israeli ambassadors to the UN called. The British ambassador explained that the British government had made attempts to reach out to the Beatles and convince them to reunite for a worthwhile cause. They had not met with any success at all. The Israeli ambassador pledged to help in any way he could to get the Beatles to agree to perform at a benefit concert. He was very sincere in his offer, but nothing at that time could entice the Beatles to agree to play together.

The country that ultimately took in the most Boat People was Israel. That did not surprise me at all. Jews have a long memory. They remembered what it was like to look for asylum and not be able to find it.

The Beatles were still embroiled in their internal problems and none of them responded directly to my ads. Paul McCartney said in an interview he granted to the Paris bureau of the *International Herald Tribune* that I was heaping too much responsibility on him and his mates. He also said that no matter how hard they tried, they could not save the world. John Lennon, in an interview, was asked what he thought of the ads and he told the reporter from *Playboy* that the ads were just "Sid with his Yiddish schmaltz, on bended knee doing Al Jolson." John's comments really hurt.

I believe that the good Lord granted those four boys something special and that they never really understood the influence they had and how powerful their music was and how truly beloved they were.

One day soon after, my daughter Denise and I were walking on Lexington Avenue. We were just about to cross 80th Street when a huge limousine made an abrupt stop in front of us. The door flew open and a very well-dressed, thin man jumped out of the car.

"Sid! Hello!"

Denise, who was about 14 at the time, was startled and speechless.

"Hi, how are you? This is my daughter Denise."

"Hi, Denise," he said and took her hand. "It's nice to meet you."

"Sid, I wish those guys [the Beatles] had accepted your offer in the ad. The ad was beautiful."

"I wish they had, too. It would have been quite an event. I'm sure you would have been there."

"Oh, yes, Sid. We would have been there."

We talked for a few more minutes. Then he looked at his watch and said, "Got to run along, I'm late for an appointment with Ahmet. Goodbye, Denise." He shook Denise's hand and jumped back into the limo.

Denise was absolutely awestruck. "Oh my God! Mick Jagger!"

After the limo departed, I chastised myself for not having asked Mick to spearhead the charity concert for the Boat People. He was friendly with each of the Beatles. Perhaps he could have galvanized them to action.

John Lennon and Yoko Ono lived in The Dakota, a stately old apartment building on the corner of 72nd Street and Central Park West. Some of my favorite restaurants and bakeries were near The Dakota and I spent a lot of time around there. From time to time, I would meet John and Yoko on the street as they were going about their daily lives. We had a standing joke. Every time we met, John would introduce me to Yoko and she would always say, "John, how many times are you going to introduce me to Sid?" It was our little joke.

Several weeks after I had heard about John's interview in *Playboy*—when he said that my ad for the Boat People was "just Sid's Yiddish, *schmaltz*, on bended knee doing Al Jolson"—I saw John and Yoko on 72nd Street. John saw me and called out, "Sid! Sid!" We hugged each other and he introduced me (yet again) to Yoko. It was our usual routine and we all laughed. We spent just a few minutes talking. After I walked away from John and Yoko, I understood that what John had said in *Playboy* was simply his sense of humor and nothing more. John had exhibited no anger or hard feelings. As always, he was warm and friendly.

I realized that I had misinterpreted John's comment and I felt that my relationship with John was intact and would continue forever.

Chapter 18: **AND THEN CAME LAURA**

I HAD BEEN WORKING ON MY OWN AT MY PARK AVENUE OFFICE for several years. I enjoyed the freedom of working independently and also the range of projects I could get into. Even though I felt that I was successful working on my own, I was always interested in exploring all business opportunities.

In the early and mid-1970s, the New York Knicks basketball team was in its heyday. I would often take my sons to games. I had great seats that were given to me by Don Kirschner, the creator of The Monkees and a legend in the music business. The seats were right behind the Knicks' bench. In the row behind me sat another father, whose sons were a little older than my two oldest sons, Adam and Dylan. I only knew his first name, Al, and we would exchange small talk while our kids screamed and cheered for the Knicks. Al was such a big Knicks fan that a few times, after the Knicks had won a close one, he happily hugged and kissed me.

One day, my secretary buzzed me and said that Alton Marshall was on the phone.

"Alton Marshall?" I asked. "I don't know anyone by that name, but put him through."

"Hello, this is Alton Marshall."

"Hello, how can I help you?" I asked tentatively.

The caller sensed that I didn't know who he was. "Sid, this is Al from the Garden. Al, the guy who sits behind you and your basketball maniacs at the Garden!"

"Alton, I'm sorry. I just knew you as Al, so when my secretary said Alton Marshall, I was puzzled."

"No problem, Sid. I realize that you know me as Al, the basketball father, but I also happen to be the president of Rockefeller Center. Sid, I would like to talk to you about a business proposition and I was hoping you would come over to my office at your convenience."

We made an appointment for the following day.

Alton Marshall had a magnificent suite of offices at Rockefeller Center. I had to go through three different secretaries before I got into his inner sanctum. Al was as friendly and charming there as he was in the Garden.

"Sid," he began, "perhaps you've been reading in the papers that the Rockefeller family wants to close Radio City Music Hall. Don't believe it; nothing could be farther from the truth. We want to do everything we can to keep it open. Your reputation as a promoter is well-known and we would like you to consider coming in as the producer and promoter of our shows."

"Well, Al, that's very flattering, and of course I'm interested, but I think that what you have in mind will be very expensive."

"Yes, but it won't cost you a dime. We'll put up the funds to pay for the acts that you think are appropriate. We'll give you the money you'll need for advertising and promotion. We'll even provide you with office space right in the Music Hall. In essence, we'll be your partners, Sid."

He could see the excitement on my face.

"When would you like to start?"

I smiled. "How about today?"

We shook hands and I left. I rushed back to the Park Avenue office, anxious to tell Billy Fields, Marilyn Rubenfeld and Barbara Davies that we were moving to Radio City Music Hall.

I thought that booking acts to appear at Radio City Music Hall would be easy. Radio City is one of the most famous venues in the world. As the home of the Rockettes and the world-renowned Easter and Christmas spectaculars, the Music Hall had over the years become as popular a tourist attraction as the Empire State Building and the Statue of Liberty. It was supposed to be easy; I had the money to buy any act I wanted and to pay for advertising. It should have been easy, but I had the most awful time.

I started calling agents to book acts, but I got stonewalled. In the years since I had stopped promoting, Ron Delsener had moved in and become a promotion powerhouse. While I was busy managing my acts, Ron had become the top promoter in New York and had established allegiances everywhere. Every time I inquired about the availability of an act for the Music Hall, I was told, "Oh, Delsener has that act." I could not book any act of note.

I spoke to Lee Guber about my predicament and he told me that he thought he could help solve my dilemma.

"Sid, I'm always booking acts for my summer venues. I think that if I ask to book them into Radio City, no one will refuse me. I can get the acts for you. Let's be partners."

I really had no choice. I liked Lee and we were old friends, but I had hoped to do this on my own. However, the cards were stacked against me. Lee had the leverage. If the agents and managers wanted to keep their acts working for Lee at his Westbury, Long Island, and Valley Forge, Pennsylvania, venues during the key summer months, they would have to honor Lee's requests to appear at Radio City. I accepted Lee's offer to be partners.

The first act we put in Radio City was Jethro Tull. They were hot and sold out for the weekend. We had three shows scheduled and had to turn away many fans. In one fell swoop, Radio City became a pop music venue.

Lee Guber demonstrated his clout. In short order, we had Marvin Gaye, David Soul, Patti LaBelle, Sammy Davis, Jr., Linda Ronstadt, Frankie Valli,

Buddy Rich, Nancy Wilson, Sarah Vaughan, Stan Getz, Maynard Ferguson, Paul Anka, Arthur Fiedler and the Boston Pops and others. The relationship that we had with Radio City and Alton Marshall could not have been better. We received first-class treatment, but we couldn't make any money. We always had to pay the Music Hall's rental from the first proceeds. We also had to pay for the labor, and those were union costs, which were high because they were fixed by contract, and, of course, we had to pay the acts as well. The partnership was great for Radio City Music Hall because they got their rental fees, but we couldn't make any money. We put on many concerts, but we couldn't make enough money to make it worthwhile. After two years, we threw in the towel.

One of my fondest memories of working at Radio City Music Hall was when John Jackson, our production manager at Radio City, tried to help me once again execute a Beatles reunion. One day I told him about my most recent attempt to reunite the Beatles. I explained that the proper way to reach the Beatles was through their representatives and that I was reluctant to buttonhole the boys individually. It had to be done through their representatives or to them as a group. I also mentioned to John that I had a $12 million dollar financial commitment that Arlen Specter had helped arrange with a bank in Philadelphia, but that I had ultimately run into a brick wall. I was having great difficulty finding an opportunity to sit down with the Beatles to give them my proposal.

John suggested that I call Gary Stevens who was his best friend and somebody who could get in touch with practically anyone on the planet. Gary Stevens was, among other things, the press agent for Johnny Carson. Gary came to see me at my office, and we kicked some ideas around. Gary believed that we needed someone with unquestionable credentials and a worldwide reputation to penetrate the insular world of the Beatles.

"You need someone like Prince Phillip," he said.

"Prince Philip? You mean the husband of the Queen of England?"

"None other," said Gary.

I decided to put Gary on retainer so that he could explore the possibility of having Prince Philip intercede with the Beatles' representatives on my behalf. Gary contacted a friend at the United Nations, who gave him Prince Philip's number at Buckingham Palace. Gary dialed the number and spoke to an assistant to Prince Philip's aide. During the conversation, Gary explained that I was the promoter who had first brought the Beatles to the U.S., and it was my intention to stage a Beatles reunion, with all the proceeds going to various charities. The assistant's interest was piqued and assured Gary that the Prince would hear about our proposal. The assistant also explained that the Prince's favorite charity was the World Wildlife Conservation Fund.

About a week later, Prince Philip called Gary Stevens from Buckingham Palace. At first, Gary had a hard time believing that it was really Prince Philip on the phone.

"Old chap, what's this all about and should I get involved?" the Prince asked Gary.

Gary told the Prince how a successful Beatles reunion would mean millions to various charities, including the World Wildlife Conservation Fund.

"That makes a lot of sense to me. What exactly are you instructing me to do?"

"Prince Philip, if you could call all four of the individuals—Paul McCartney, John Lennon, Ringo Starr and George Harrison—to bring about this reunion for charity, it would be a beginning."

"Yes, old chap. But I don't know their addresses or phone numbers or who their agents are. Tell me about this chap Bernstein."

"Sid Bernstein is the man who brought the Beatles to America the first time they came over. He is also the man who subsequently presented them at Shea Stadium in the first-ever stadium concert in U.S. history." Gary could tell that the Prince was taking notes because he spelled Shea S-H-A-Y, until Gary corrected him.

"Tell me, Mr. Stevens, does Mr. Bernstein have a date in mind for this concert?"

"Not yet."

"Well, let me look into this. I'll call you back or you can call my assistant. Let me give it some thought."

Two or three weeks passed and Gary heard nothing from the Prince or Buckingham Palace. Finally, Gary called the Palace and a female assistant to the Prince spoke to Gary in a rather abrupt manner. "If we have any news for you, we will call," she curtly replied.

Two weeks later, Prince Philip called Gary personally, at about midnight London time.

"Mr. Stevens," said the Prince. "I have been working on this and frankly I am running into a stone wall. There are so many layers of people, lawyers, accountants and the like, shielding the principals."

"You understand, Prince Philip, how much money this could mean for charity?" Gary asked the Prince.

"I know, and I wish I could help you! You're a nice man, and I'm sure Mr. Bernstein is a nice man, too, but I cannot continue running into a stone wall. If you have any further ideas, please call me, Mr. Stevens."

Gary did a great job enlisting Prince Philip, but the timing was wrong.

The Beatles still had many issues amongst themselves that needed to be resolved and nothing would get them back together until those issues were resolved.

I never got a chance to thank Prince Philip for his efforts, but I really appreciated him taking the time to make the attempt.

One day after school, Gerry took some of the kids for ice cream cones at Baskin Robbins on 85th Street and Madison Avenue. As they were ordering, Paul McCartney came into the store with two of his kids. Naturally, Gerry recognized Paul. They had never had an occasion to meet, since every time I was promoting a Beatles concert, Gerry was pregnant and did not attend. She introduced herself and the kids to Paul. He was delighted to have finally had a chance to meet her. Gerry and Paul chatted for a while while the kids enjoyed their ice cream cones.

As Gerry was getting ready to leave, Paul asked her to send his best regards to me. Then he added, "Mrs. Bernstein, your husband is one of the most decent men in our industry."

What Paul said was something that meant a great deal to me and it's something that I will never forget.

It was during our stay at Radio City that I discovered Laura Branigan.

On the weekend that Linda Ronstadt played Radio City, I decided to go to the Music Hall very early and observe her rehearsal and sound check.

I wanted to get there early to consult with the stagehands and crew and to make sure that everything was perfect for Linda. I wanted everything to be just right for her sold-out shows. Linda was a friend of mine.

As I approached the Radio City Music Hall backstage entrance, a group of people were walking in the opposite direction. In the group was a tall, extremely beautiful young woman with long, flowing hair. She and I made eye contact and we both smiled. I kept walking. As I reached the stage door, I heard a voice.

"Mr. Bernstein! Oh, Mr. Bernstein!" As I turned to see who it was, I was thinking, "I hope it's that girl." Sure enough, it was.

"Do we know each other?" I asked hopefully.

"Well, you don't know me, but I know who you are. My name is Laura Branigan. I've been meaning to call you for six weeks. I'm a singer, and I need a manager."

"So why didn't you call me?"

"I wasn't sure you'd take my call, Mr. Bernstein."

"I understand, Laura, but you should have called. I speak to everyone. All you have to do is call the switchboard at Radio City and ask for me."

She said that she would be calling soon. We said good-bye and I went into Radio City to see to the arrangements for Linda Ronstadt. Miss Branigan went on her way.

When I got to my office, I told Marilyn, Barbara and Billy that I had met this absolutely gorgeous and stunning girl who said she was a singer in need of a manager. "I hope she calls," I said. "If she can sing half as good as she looks, look out!"

The very next morning, while we were busy fielding calls regarding Linda's concerts, Marilyn buzzed me. "Laura Branigan is on the phone, Sid. Let me put her off. What do you need this for right now? We're getting hundreds of calls for tickets to see Linda! We don't have the tickets, we're sold out and it's too hectic. Let me put her off."

"Wait a minute, Marilyn. I believe she's the girl I met yesterday. I want to talk to her."

I picked up the phone and chatted with Laura briefly and made an appointment to see her the next day. When she arrived, everyone in the office stopped working and took a look at her. She was stunning. Laura and I talked for a while in my office, and then she asked if she could sing for me. I took her into the rehearsal room that was next door to the office. As we went in, Marilyn whispered, "Sid, you don't have time for this! We're too busy!"

"It's okay, Marilyn. Just 20 minutes. That's all I need."

Once we were in the rehearsal room, Laura sat at the piano. "This is a song I wrote called *Memories*."

She began to play and then closed her eyes and started to sing. Her voice and the lyrics were magical. Laura performed with great feeling and emotion. I hadn't experienced such powerful feelings from a performer since Judy Garland. The tears were streaming down my face; I rushed to dry my eyes before she opened hers. She finished and opened her eyes. "Are your ready for the next song?" she asked.

"No, Laura. You don't have to do any more. I've heard enough."

"Don't you want to hear any more? I have two more songs that I think are pretty good." Clearly, she thought she had failed her audition.

"No, Laura, I've heard enough. What would you like me to do for you?"

"I'd like you to manage me."

"You got me, Laura. You got me. I'll manage you. Come next door and speak to Barbara Davies, my business manager. Tell her who your lawyer is and we can begin working out a deal."

After a few weeks, we signed a contract with Laura, and I felt that I had uncovered the next Judy Garland. I knew she had star quality.

Laura had never really performed before live audiences. I felt that she needed to sing in front of small groups at first so that she could get audience feedback and gain confidence. I began to invite friends and acquaintances of mine to come to the rehearsal room at lunchtime to hear Laura sing. I felt this would be a great learning experience for her. We usually had seven to twelve people come to these lunchtime mini-concerts. Laura would sing four or five songs, and most of the people who heard her told me that she looked and sounded great. Everyone seemed to love what she was doing, and I could tell that she was gaining confidence.

Eight or ten weeks into this regimen of the mini-concerts, I called Shirley MacLaine to invite her to a lunchtime concert and meet Laura.

"Sid," she said. "I'll come, but I don't have much time because my editor is in town. I really can't stay long."

"Just 15 minutes is all, Shirley. It'll only take 15 minutes."

When Shirley arrived, there were already about 14 or 15 people in the rehearsal room. Shirley, with her fur coat and matching hat, made quite the entrance and caused a bit of a stir. Shirley loved Laura. What was to be a brief 15-minute stay for Shirley turned into a half-hour, and then an hour. Everyone else left, but Shirley stayed to talk to Laura and was very warm and encouraging to her.

As I walked Shirley out of the building, she said, "Sid, this girl is going to be a star. You really have something here."

Finally I felt that Laura Branigan was ready to be heard by the record companies, and I began to invite the A&R men and other record executives to our musical lunch events.

Bob Summer, the president of RCA attended one session. He loved Laura but when he sent his A&R people, they reported to him that they did not hear a hit in any of the original songs that she had sung. RCA passed on her. After each record company representative came to hear Laura, I would hear the same response. The A&R people from the various companies loved Laura, but they didn't hear a hit. The truth is, they were supposed to find her a hit. That's what the R in A&R stands for: Artists and Repertoire. An A&R person's job is to find a hit song for the artist. The great A&R men like Clive Davis find a song for artists that they believe in. Sometimes I think that it's a lost art today. No one seems to have the patience to search and listen to the number of songs it takes to find a perfect match for a particular artist.

I was promoting Laura as a singer/songwriter. Maybe the representatives from the record companies thought that we were insisting that we record only her own songs, but that was not the case. If someone had presented a song written by someone else that both Laura and I thought was well-suited to her, we would have agreed to record it.

To my sheer amazement and disbelief, no record company showed any sincere interest in signing Laura Branigan. In hindsight, however, I really shouldn't have been that amazed. After all, hadn't almost every record company on the face of the earth rejected the Beatles?

I refused to give up. Someone asked me why I had not invited anyone from Atlantic Records to meet Laura. I thought about it and concluded that my reluctance stemmed from the fact that I thought the Atlantic Records people were still a little unhappy with me because I had moved the Rascals to Columbia.

However, I decided that I would call Ahmet Ertegun. He was charming and cordial. And he invited me to bring Laura up to Atlantic so that she could sing for him.

"Ahmet, I'm not going to bring her to the office. You're going to be conducting business, fielding phone calls from Mick Jagger and who knows who else, and she'll get lost in the shuffle. You won't be paying attention, and this girl deserves your complete attention. It won't work at your office."

"So how can I hear her, Sid? You don't have any tape on her. Where can I hear her?"

"At your home, Ahmet. I want to bring her to your townhouse."

"I don't have a piano in my home."

"Are you kidding me, Ahmet? One of the world's preeminent music mavens and you don't have a piano in your home? Wait till I tell everyone that!" We both laughed.

"Sid, it's true, but my brother Nesuhi has a piano at his apartment. We can go there. Let me ask him, hold on." I heard him on his other line speaking to Nesuhi in French. In a moment, Ahmet came back on the line.

"Sid, Nesuhi thinks I'm crazy, but because it's you, he's agreed. When can you bring her up?"

We made an appointment for the following Friday. The day arrived and it was rainy and wet. Laura and I made our way to Nesuhi's apartment on Fifth Avenue. A butler was offering drinks and Mica Ertegun, the famous interior decorator and Ahmet's wife, was there, along with Ahmet and Nesuhi. I introduced Laura and she began to sing. Almost immediately, everyone was tapping their toes and swaying to the music. When Laura sang *Memories*, everyone was moved and I thought I could see tears in Mica Ertegun's eyes. When Laura finished, Ahmet said that he wanted to talk but that he had to go home and change into his tuxedo as he and Mica had another engagement to attend that evening.

"Let me get a cab for you, Sid," he said. "You can drop me at home, and we can spend a few minutes talking." He told Mica that he would pick her up after changing, said good night to Laura, and he and I left.

Ahmet and I got into a cab. "Sid, what's the deal? What do you want to do?"

I felt bold. "Two albums the first year, if the first one doesn't hit. Four more albums after that, a $100,000 advance and big budgets for the recording sessions. I'm not sure about the percentage. We'll discuss that later."

"We'll let our attorneys work that out. You have a deal, Sid." We shook hands and that was it.

I called Laura and, when I told her the deal, she started screaming. We had gone from nowhere to almost everywhere in the course of one hour at Nesuhi Ertegun's apartment on Fifth Avenue.

Atlantic assigned Arif Mardin, their number one producer, to work with Laura. He loved her singing. Everyone worked very hard on the album. Three singles were released, but none of them made it, and the album was shelved. It was never released. The recording and release of the three singles took up almost two years, and we still had no hit.

One day when Laura and I were in the recording studio, Mick Jagger came strolling in wearing, jeans, a T-shirt and sneakers. I had never noticed before and was surprised to see how big Mick's feet were, and his white sneakers only accentuated their size.

"Sid, I heard you were recording and I wanted to pop in and say hello. I hear you have quite an artist recording here. People have been telling me that she's marvelous. I'd like to listen to her."

"By all means, Mick. Be my guest and have a seat."

He sat near me on a bench in front of the recording console and we chatted for a while. He was listening very intently to Laura record. Mick and I reminisced about the old days when I had presented the Rolling Stones five times in two years and how they had gotten me thrown out of Carnegie Hall. I reminded him about the time that the kids tried to jump over the orchestra pit at the Academy of Music. It was hard to believe that 10 years had passed since those wild times.

Mick told me that he loved the way Laura sang. And, knowing Mick, I'm sure he didn't mind looking at her, either.

After sitting and listening for awhile, Mick stood and said, "She's marvelous, Sid. I think you're going to have a big star and I wish you luck with her."

With that, he left. I thought about the fact that so many of these young men, who I had first met when they were barely out of their teens, had become megastars, and how gratifying it was to have played even a small part in their success.

During that recording time, I organized and funded a band for Laura and she did a few club dates. Reno Sweeny's, a New York Club, was the main venue where Laura performed and many people came to see her. Everyone felt that it was just a matter of time before Laura would be a star. She just needed that elusive hit record.

Atlantic brought in a new producer to work with Laura. He was a German who had had success in his homeland. To make him more appealing to American record buyers, he had changed his name to Jack White. Jack had a song that had been a hit in Italy and Germany and he owned the publishing rights. As soon as he played the song *Gloria* for us, I turned to Laura and said, "That's our hit!" I loved the song and knew that it would be a hit for Laura.

Atlantic sent Laura to California to record with Jack White. I made the mistake of not accompanying her, because while in California, Jack White's partner evidently planted seeds of doubt, discord and disharmony in Laura's head. I was about to get one of the great shocks of my life.

Larry Krutek, Laura's husband, called me one day before the projected release of *Gloria*, and said, "Sid, you have to raise $100,000 to promote *Gloria* for Laura."

"Larry, that's a lot of money to raise."

"I know, Sid. But you have to do it. Because if you don't, the record will go nowhere. We need to hire independent promo men and they're expensive."

"Larry, I believe in the record and I think that Atlantic, with their crack promo team, can break *Gloria*. I don't think that we need $100,000 worth of indie promo men. I'm confident that Atlantic will get the job done. But, if it'll make you feel better, I'll do my best to raise the $100,000."

I tried, but was unable to raise the money. Maybe my heart wasn't in it. Maybe the undue pressure that Larry was putting me under bothered me. Whatever it was, I didn't raise the money.

In retrospect, I now realize that the request to have me raise the $100,000 was part of a well-thought-out plan to displace me as Laura Branigan's manager.

Soon after this failed attempt to raise the $100,000, Jeff Grinstein called me at my office and said that he had heard that I was no longer Laura Branigan's manager. I knew Jeff from the days when he had been the president of the Bay City Rollers fan club. When Tom Paton, the Bay City Rollers' manager, pulled the group from me, Jeff, in protest, quit. When I began to manage Laura, Jeff became the president of her fan club. I respected Jeff, but when he related this rumor to me, I thought he was smoking funny cigarettes. I discounted what he said completely. "Forget it," I said. "It's ridiculous."

Just a half-hour or so earlier, I had gotten off the phone with Laura and everything seemed in order.

My office was the first one in the line of offices and everyone had to pass me first. Invariably, they would stop and say good morning to me. On the day that Jeff relayed the rumor about my not being Laura's manager anymore, Mitch, our promo man, came in and walked right by my office without saying a word. I thought that was odd. About a half-hour later, he called me on the phone from three offices down and asked me if I was sitting down.

"Yes, Mitch, I'm sitting down."

"Okay, I need to come in and tell you something, but I want to make sure you're sitting down."

"C'mon, Mitch. Come in and tell me your news. I'm sitting down."

He walked in, and I could see by the look on his face that something was terribly wrong.

"What is it, Mitch?" I asked him warily.

"Sid, I just came from Atlantic Records and everybody up there was asking me where you are and what was going on. When I questioned them, they said that there is a rumor being circulated that you are no longer managing Laura Branigan and that some woman named Susan has taken over.

"That's ridiculous, Mitch. I just spoke to Laura in our usual morning call, and she ended it as always, 'I love you, Sid.' It's ridiculous, Mitch. Just forget it."

It was now about 12:30 or 1:00 PM in New York. The first phone call I had that day from Jeff Grinstein had alerted me about this turn of events, and I had totally discounted it, but I had to take it seriously now. I was stunned. I didn't know what to do.

I didn't want to go home, because I couldn't imagine facing Gerry, who had warned me about Laura's husband many times before. "Sid, that guy is going to be your undoing," Gerry had said when she met Krutek before Laura and he got married. Nor did I want to have to tell the kids, who loved Laura as they would a big sister, what was happening. I was feeling so low, that if my office hadn't been on the ground floor, I might have jumped out of the window. I had worked with and nurtured Laura for five years. I had turned down the opportunity to manage other acts, some of whom had become big stars, so I could devote all of my energy to Laura's career. Laura was on the verge of stardom, and her complicity in this betrayal was so depressing that I was immobilized.

At around 2:00 PM, which was 11:00 AM in Los Angeles, I got a call from an agent from William Morris who I knew casually, asking me whether or not the rumors were true. "Sid, there's a story all over L.A. that you are no longer managing Laura Branigan."

"Discount it," I said. I just refused to believe what was happening. I wasn't ready to acknowledge it. It was just too shocking to me.

I decided to leave the office and go over to P.S. 6 and meet Adam, Denise and Dylan when their school day ended. I took them to Baskin Robbins for ice cream cones and we went to sit in Central Park. My two oldest children, Adam and Denise, noticed that something was bothering me and asked me what was wrong. I didn't let on; I just told them that I was tired. It was one of the worst days of my life. After dinner that night, I told Gerry what had happened. She wasn't a bit surprised because she had felt that Laura's husband was trouble from the beginning.

I had been in the business for over 30 years. I had achieved some success and suffered some failures. I had always tried to deal in good faith and fairness. Doing the right thing had always been paramount with me. The Rascals had self-destructed and now Laura had been disloyal. I felt heartsick. I needed distance from the entire business. I was ready for a change.

"Sid," my friends had said, "you are always willing to sit and talk to just about anybody. You dispense advice based on 40 years' worth of experience, and you never ask for anything in return. Stop giving it away for free! Hang up a shingle as a consultant and start getting paid for the advice!"

I decided to take their advice and see what it would be like to get paid for the advice I had so gladly dispensed for free for so many years.

After he heard about how my relationship with Laura Branigan ended, Abe Margolies wanted me to return to promoting immediately. He was ready to fund anything I wanted to do, but my heart wasn't in it anymore. I told Abe that I wanted to try being a consultant. Since other promoters like Ron Delsener and Bill Graham had basically taken my place, I felt that I didn't want to return to promoting full-time. I had lost contact with the venues, the agents, agencies, and acts.

I did, however, agree to promote Shecky Greene at Carnegie Hall. Shecky was a terrific comedian and a frequent customer at Abe's Steak House. I had met Shecky several times at Abe's Steak House and thought he was a very funny guy. As a favor to Abe, I promoted Shecky at Carnegie Hall, and it was a successful engagement. I also got the opportunity to present Mickey Gilley, the great country artist, at the Copacabana. The deal was right, so I took it and Mickey Gilley had a successful run at the Copa. For a minute, I considered going back into the promotion business full-time, but after giving it some thought, I dismissed the idea.

Eventually, Abe accepted my decision not to resume my career as a promoter. However, he insisted that I take legal action against Laura Branigan.

"I know you, Sid, you don't like confrontation, but I will not allow you to walk away from this," he said. "You will get the toughest, street-fighting lawyer you can find, and you will sue this girl. This is a gutter fight and you need a lawyer who will get down in the trenches with you."

I retained Barry Slotnick who was well-known but later became even more famous after defending Bernhard Goetz, a man who had protected himself with a gun when four young men tried to hold him up in the New York subway system. Barry is a great attorney, but he wasn't a music-business lawyer and, combined with his ever-increasing caseload, he found it difficult to move my case along. Abe thought that Barry was moving too slowly and suggested that we find another lawyer. We switched to Roy Cohn, whose national reputation as a tough, no-holds-barred street fighter had been made in the 1950s during the McCarthy hearings. Once again, it was delay after delay.

Finally, I told Abe that I thought a music-business attorney could get the case settled quickly. He agreed, and Marty Silfen, the young litigator we hired, got the case settled in a few days. I was awarded a settlement that was satisfactory, but no amount of money could make up for the heartache and hurt that Laura Branigan had caused me. Laura had a hit with *Gloria*, but her second hit, *Solitaire*, was not nearly as big. She's had a spotty career and has never came close to achieving the stardom that I had envisioned for her.

Chapter 19: **THE DEATH OF JOHN LENNON**

ON DECEMBER 8, 1980, I WAS AT FINE & SCHAPIRO'S RESTAURANT on 72nd Street right off Broadway. I was having a leisurely dinner with David and Sandy Brokaw, the sons of Norman Brokaw, the head of the William Morris Agency, who were the publicists for Mickey Gilley. David and Sandy were based on the West Coast. We were celebrating Mickey's highly successful run at the Copa. Celia Matthau, the former daughter-in-law of Walter Matthau, came into the restaurant to pick up a take-out order. She was a singer from California, so I asked her to join my dinner companions and me. As usual, the conversation turned to the Beatles and everyone wanted to hear Beatles stories. The time passed so swiftly that before long, the busboys were putting the chairs up on the tables and preparing the restaurant for closing. I told my guests that we had to leave, I paid the bill and we exited the restaurant. Once out the door, we turned left to make our way to Broadway. I hailed a cab for the two PR men from Los Angeles and instructed them to go up 72nd Street and then through the park to their hotel on the East Side.

"When you get to the last corner before the park, look to your left and you will see The Dakota; that's where John Lennon and Yoko Ono live." I bid them good-bye and hailed another cab to take me downtown to another appointment I had. I offered to drop Celia off and she accepted.

After I dropped Celia off, I proceeded to SPQR, a famous Italian restaurant located on Mulberry Street in the Little Italy section of New York. I had promised the owners that I would come to look at the nightclub they were opening above their highly successful restaurant. Lou took me upstairs to show me the new club he had built, and we talked about when the best time would be for the grand opening and which artist I thought should be the first to appear there. All of a sudden, I heard Luba, Lou's wife, say, "Oh no, oh no! It can't be true! I can't believe it! Oh my God! Sid! Sid! Come here, come here!" she cried. "You won't believe this! My girlfriend just called and said that John Lennon has been shot and that he's been taken to a hospital."

Who would want to shoot John Lennon? I thought.

"It can't be right," I said. "It must be a mistake."

Lou and I finished our conversation and he offered to drop me off on his way home. Since they lived in New Jersey, I asked Lou and Luba to drop me off on West 72nd Street and told them that I would take a cab through the park to my apartment on the East Side.

After they dropped me off, I hailed a cab and asked the driver to take me through Central Park to the East Side. The radio in the cab was on and the talk was about John Lennon.

"Señor," I said to the cab driver, "is this true what they're saying about John Lennon?"

"Yes, and this has been going on all night, every station. He's gone."

"What?!?" I blurted in utter disbelief. "John Lennon is dead?"

"Yes, they could not save him. He's gone."

By now we were approaching The Dakota at 72nd and Central Park West and I could see all the police lights and the tumult. I was in shock and rather disoriented. It was 1:30 in the morning. It was surrealistic. There were police vans and cars everywhere. The media with their cameras, satellite trucks and those bright lights were all over the place. There were what seemed to be thousands of kids with candles who were standing vigil. I took it all in sorrowfully, mourning the loss of my friend. The cab crawled through the traffic and finally made it across the intersection and into the park, and I was home in short order.

It was hard to believe that I had been a block or so away at Fine & Schapiro's restaurant and talking about John Lennon when he was gunned down.

Gerry, a sorry and forlorn look on her face, was waiting for me when I got home.

"Sid, you heard?"

"Yes, Gerry."

"The phone has been ringing ever since it happened. They're calling from everywhere. You have more than 25 messages. Sid, it's so late and you have a lecture at Hunter College first thing tomorrow morning. Get some rest."

I had completely forgotten that weeks earlier I had committed myself to speaking to the students in the music department at Hunter College. I looked at all the messages. The BBC, Paris radio, *The New York Times*, the *Daily News*, the *New York Post*, NBC, CBS, ABC, *Time*, *Newsweek*—the list just went on and on, and all of them wanted a statement about the terrible tragedy that had befallen John Lennon.

"I can't answer these tonight, Gerry. I'm bushed and heartsick. The only one I'm going to respond to is *Good Morning America*."

I chose to respond to that call because Alan Cohen, a producer at the show, had been a friend of mine for many years. I called him.

"Alan, this is Sid."

"Oh, Sid, thank you for calling me back. I'm sure that you are getting bombarded. I know the news must be devastating, but I've got to have you on *Good Morning America* tomorrow. Could you please do it as a favor to me?"

"Alan, I'm beat. I've had a terrible day and I'm basically in shock. Besides that, I'm committed to doing a lecture at Hunter College early tomorrow morning." I looked at my watch and realized that it was already tomorrow.

"We'll put you on first, Sid. No more than 10 minutes, I promise. I'll send a limo for you and I'll even give you a wake-up call at 6:15 AM. I'll have the limo drive you home as soon as you finish the interview."

I agreed; he was a good friend.

Promptly at 6:15 AM, the phone rang. I rushed to get ready, but I was exhausted and not looking forward to the day. The limo was at the front door when I emerged from the building. The ride to the ABC studios on the West Side took but a few minutes. My time on air with David Hartman went by in a blur. I don't remember what he asked or how I responded.

When I finished, the limo took me back home. The driver went by way of 72nd Street. When we got to The Dakota, there were throngs of kids with candles singing John Lennon songs. Radio, television and newspaper people were everywhere. It was the exact same scene I had seen at 1:30 in the morning. It looked like no one had moved all night.

Pat Collins, a New York TV news celebrity, saw me through the limo window and I cracked it open to say hello.

"Sid," she said. "You've got to say a few words, please."

"Pat, I'm exhausted and overwrought and I don't want to get out of this car."

She could see how shattered I was, so she let me go. "Okay, I understand, Sid," she said graciously.

When I got home, I tried to sleep. Gerry turned the phones off and I think I dozed for about an hour. The insistent apartment buzzer woke me with a start. The doorman said that there was a camera crew in front of the building, asking for me.

A voice came over the intercom, "Can we have a statement from you in front of the building, Mr. Bernstein? It'll just take a few minutes."

"I don't want my building or my home photographed. There are lunatics out there shooting people. I'm scheduled to give a talk at Hunter College in about an hour and you're welcome to come. I'll answer any questions you have at the college."

"All right, Sid. We appreciate it. Could you use a ride to Hunter?"

"Sure, we can drive over together and I'll do the interview there. Thanks."

They drove me to Hunter College. When we got there, the professor who had asked me to speak was waiting.

"Mr. Bernstein, thank you so much for coming. I wasn't sure if you would show up. I know how traumatic these last 24 hours must have been for you. Would you mind if we moved your talk to a different room than previously scheduled? It'll only take a few minutes to make the change. There are so many people who want to hear you speak this morning and we need a much larger room to accommodate them all."

I agreed to his request. I introduced him to the TV crew who had accompanied me to the college and got permission for them to film me at the lecture. While they were redoing the lecture room, I was taken to an office in the music department and given a seat with a footrest. I promptly fell asleep. In what seemed to be only a few minutes, I heard a knock at the door.

"We're ready for you now, Mr. Bernstein. Please follow me."

They had moved the talk to a large lecture hall, which was now completely full of people. People were everywhere, standing along the walls and sitting in the aisles. I was in a daze and surprised by the large contingent of newspaper people. I attributed the large crowd and numerous members of the press to the reaction that only the Beatles could generate in such a quick time and in such numbers. It was the incredible Beatles grapevine at work. They had found out about my talk at Hunter and passed the word along.

The professor introduced me. They had set up a mike at a lectern, but I was so tired that I asked to sit behind a desk. They moved the mike for me. The media all placed their mikes on the desk, too.

I began tentatively. "I was all prepared to talk to you as students on the subject of the music business. But, in view of the events of last night, that has to change. I don't know if I can speak about music right now, because the tragedy that happened not far from here has changed everything. A wife has lost her husband; children have lost their father; I have lost a friend; the world has lost a champion for love and peace. The voice of John Lennon will sorely be missed in the days ahead."

My voice was breaking and I was having a hard time controlling my emotions. From the corner of my eye, I could see one of the older newspapermen remove a handkerchief from his breast pocket and dab his eyes. That just made me feel worse.

"The world will sorely miss John Lennon."

I really couldn't say much more. I was at the end of my rope. The shock and lack of sleep did me in. I went home to escape into the oblivion of sleep.

The next day, a rumor surfaced that John Lennon's body was at the Frank Campbell Funeral Home. My sons Adam and Etienne wanted to go there, but the rumor was not true, so we went to The Dakota instead. There was a huge crowd stretched completely around the block, waiting to leave cards, flowers and gifts at the entrance to the great old apartment building. My boys got on the line and placed their offering on the iron gate that surrounded the building.

The following Saturday, New York's Mayor Ed Koch declared a day of commemoration for the slain John Lennon. The crowds gathered in Central Park. Ernie Anastos, a well-known and respected New York TV news anchorperson, called to ask me if I would agree to let him interview me in the park. I agreed to meet Ernie at the ABC TV truck. When I got to the park, I spotted the ABC truck surrounded by a large crowd.

Cousin Brucie helped me climb onto the TV truck platform. From there, I could observe the crowd of almost 100,000 people. Bruce Morrow and I stood on the platform of the news truck in the cold. Ernie Anastos interviewed us both. Moments before I spoke, a very light snow began to fall. Bruce leaned over to me and said, "Look at the snow, Sid. It's like angels falling from the sky."

It was a beautiful and poetic image befitting the occasion. And John Lennon.

Yoko Ono had arranged for John's ashes to be spread in the park where she, John and Sean used to walk.

Ernie Anastos asked me to make a statement.

From my vantage point, I saw my daughter Denise and two of her friends in the crowd. Through the loudspeaker, I could hear the song *Imagine*. Denise and her friends were crying.

I looked at all the sad and crying people and said, "Our tears are falling on this hallowed ground that now holds John Lennon's ashes."

Someone told me later that my remarks were seen throughout the world. After I left the park, I reflected on what had just happened and remembered the glorious past.

There would be no more chance meetings on the street. No more requests to see my knees. No more frantic calls for recommendations to restaurants or tickets to events. How do you replace that part of your heart? My friend John Lennon was gone forever.

Chapter 20: ENGLAND, HAWAII AND IN BETWEEN

IN 1981, CLIVE EPSTEIN, BRIAN EPSTEIN'S BROTHER, came to New York. I had never met Clive, but he called me to extend best regards from his mother Queenie, who was the first person I spoke to on that momentous day in 1963 when I had arranged with Brian Epstein to bring the Beatles to America. I invited Clive to have dinner with me at Paolucci's. He and I hit it off immediately. Clive had a wife and three children, so we talked about our families. Of course, we spoke about Brian. I told Clive the story of how Stigwood, Bernstein and Epstein almost became partners. "That would have been great for Brian, Sid. Too bad it didn't happen," he said.

Clive invited me to come to Liverpool. "I can't believe that you of all people have never been to Liverpool. You would enjoy the city and its wonderful people. I'd love for you to meet my family and, of course, my mother would love to meet you. Come visit Liverpool, Sid."

Clive and I developed a friendship. We exchanged letters and numerous phone calls. Finally, after some months, I decided to accept Clive's invitation. Gerry and I agreed that I would take Adam out of school for a week, and he accompanied me to Great Britain. Clive insisted that we stay at his home; he wouldn't hear of us staying at a hotel. He had a beautiful family and they were all cordial and great hosts.

We went to visit Queenie Epstein and we spent hours talking about Brian. She told me how much she missed him and how she could still hear his footsteps around the house.

I asked Queenie if I could visit Brian's grave, which was in the synagogue's cemetery. I met the rabbi of the community and he took me to the gravesite. I thanked Brian for his having given me the opportunity to participate in the making of music history. As I stood there in the front of the tombstone, which bears Brian's Hebrew name, I said a silent prayer: Thank you, Brian, for what you did for me. I will always treasure your memory. May your soul rest in peace.

While we were in Liverpool, Clive got Adam and me tickets to the repertory theatre that was featuring a play called *Lennon* about the life of John Lennon. The play was wonderful; it had great acting, humor and, of course, it had super music. It ended with the sound of three shots; there wasn't a dry eye in the room.

"Sid," Clive said, when he came to the theatre to pick up Adam and me, "the cast knows that you're here and they would like to meet you."

"Clive, look at me. I've been crying. I don't think that I'm in the mood to meet the cast."

"It's okay, Sid; they'll understand. Don't disappoint them."

Adam really wanted to meet the cast, so I went with him to the lavatory and splashed some cold water on my face. We then went to the dressing rooms to meet the repertory group, and spent some time with them. After a while, the cast departed and Adam and I were alone with Bob Eaton, the play's director.

"Bob, as you know, I'm a promoter back in New York and I'd love to bring the play there."

"Mr. Bernstein, it would be a realization of a lifelong dream for me to be able to direct a play in New York. Of course, I am very interested."

"Who do I have to talk to?"

"Call Jill, our business manager, tomorrow morning," he responded. "I'll alert her to your call."

The next morning, I called Jill. She informed me that an attorney would be calling me the following day. It was a quick and simple negotiation. We made a deal to bring *Lennon* to the United States.

Adam and I returned home, and I had a new and compelling project to attend to. After my initial conversation with the attorney in England, I thought it would be quite easy to bring the play across the Atlantic. I was wrong; it took two years before *Lennon* finally opened in New York.

Abe Margolies and Joe Taub put up most of the money for the play. I obtained the rest from other sources. The union rules in New York made it difficult to bring the original cast and director to stage the play. I had to choose between the director and the cast; it was either-or. I could not bring them both, so I chose the director. Without the British cast, it would be very tough to replicate the show I saw in Liverpool because they have an instinctive feel for both the language and location. However, I felt that Bob Eaton was talented enough to compensate and help the American actors to approximate the performance of the British cast. I would have to make the best of it.

The cast we assembled did a terrific job. One of the cast members was a young British actor named Greg Martin. He had been living in the States for a while and we were fortunate to have a Brit in the cast. He played more than one role in the play and was superb. Several years later I would meet the young actor's father, George Martin, and discover what a strong, mutual connection we shared.

Throughout my association with the Beatles in the 1960s, I had never had the opportunity to meet their legendary producer, George Martin. Several years after I had staged *Lennon*, at a luncheon held in the Grosvenor Hotel for the British version of the Grammy Awards, I finally had the opportunity to meet him.

I was in London to introduce Perry Mucheheide, an American friend of mine, to Cynthia Lennon, John Lennon's first wife. Perry wanted to put on a tribute to John Lennon in Milwaukee and I was doing some consulting for him. He wanted to meet Cynthia to get her feedback and support.

While we were at the Grosvernor, Perry heard about the awards luncheon and wanted to go. It was too late to call anyone for tickets.

"Perry, we aren't going to get in. Besides, I'm supposed to meet Clive Epstein's wife and daughter for lunch."

"Please call them and change it. Let's go to the awards luncheon instead."

Perry was insistent. So I called Barbara Epstein and asked her if we could meet for dinner instead of lunch; she agreed to the change in plans. She laughingly said that she and her daughter would use the time to go shopping.

I wasn't sure we could get in, but Perry and I went to the ballroom at the Grosvenor. I cautioned Perry that I thought our chances of getting in were slim. The ballroom was packed and it didn't look like there was room for even one extra person.

"Look how crowded it is," I said when we arrived. "Don't even try."

"Just sit down here for a minute, Sid."

I sat down in a seat just outside the entrance to the ballroom. I saw Perry talking with the two ladies who were collecting the admission tickets and he was pointing at me. Evidently, he explained to them who I was and that we had just arrived in England and were surprised to find out about the awards luncheon upon our arrival. He motioned to me to come over and he introduced me. The women were very nice and solicitous and told us to take any two seats we could find. Perry and I found a table near the back of the ballroom that had two empty seats. The table was right next to a set of stairs that led to the mezzanine. As we sat there eating, Perry grabbed my arm.

"Sid! Look! There's Linda McCartney!"

Linda McCartney was making her way up the stairs with one of her daughters. Perry implored me to introduce him to Linda. I told him that I would introduce him after the luncheon. In his enthusiasm to meet Linda, Perry was creating quite a scene at the table. I decided to stand at the foot of the stairs in anticipation of Linda's return. As soon as she saw me, she let out a scream.

"Sid Bernstein! What are you doing here?" She introduced me to her daughter Stella. "Stella, this is Daddy's friend Sid Bernstein from New York."

I introduced Perry, who was one of the Beatles' greatest fans. He was ecstatic.

"Where are you sitting, Sid?" Linda asked. I pointed to our table in the back.

"Oh, no. Come with me. You must say hello to Paul."

Linda took me by the hand and led me through the labyrinth of tightly packed tables. We finally reached the front of the ballroom and I could see Paul sitting at a table with his young son Jamie. When Paul spotted me, he stood up and gave me a hug.

"Sid, what are you doing here?"

"I came to London to work on a special project."

I could see that everyone was looking at me, trying to figure out who I was. At the next table, I recognized Elton John, Cliff Richard and the producer of the event who was from Capitol Records. He came over and said hello. We spoke for a moment and he took me to meet George Martin.

Upon meeting me, George greeted me warmly. "Sid, I just want you to know that my son Greg raves about you. I can't tell you how much I appreciate your treatment and support of him when he worked for you in *Lennon*. I feel like I know you so well!"

"That was your son, George?" I said in amazement. "He never told me that you were his father. What a wonderful young man he is. It is certainly a small world."

"Indeed it is, Sid."

Indeed it is.

George Martin is a gentleman and one of the most talented people I have ever met. He is a brilliant record producer. If Brian Epstein was the fifth Beatle, then George Martin is the sixth Beatle. His contribution to their music speaks for itself. George was an integral member of the team that carried the Beatles to their huge success.

Gerry had just about had it with show business. The Rascals had self-destructed, my venture at Radio City, which had seemed so promising at the outset, eventually turned out not to be profitable, and, finally, Laura Branigan had defected and was no longer my client. While I thoroughly enjoyed my consulting jobs, the work was not very steady. The cumulative effect of these events impacted so negatively on Gerry that she was ready for a major change in her life. The financial pressure on our family life was tremendous and Gerry desperately wanted out of New York and the entertainment business.

Gerry became involved with a program known as est that had been popularized by Werner Ehrhard. The program was a self-actualization course and it heavily espoused feminism. I began seeing changes in Gerry's thinking. I felt that I needed to find out how much est contributed to Gerry's new attitude, so I spent two weekends taking the course. Frankly, I thought the experience was a lot of bunk. I didn't get "it," and getting "it" was what est was all about. They should have called the course "It." More importantly, I felt that est was disrupting my family life. All of a sudden, I was confronted with a woman who was completely different from the one I married.

I guess that the precipitous drop in our income and, more importantly, how that would impact her life frightened Gerry. She wanted to make a major change in our lives; Gerry had never been crazy about the entertainment business. She suggested that we move to Hawaii and leave all the insanity of New York behind. We had taken many trips as a family to Hawaii and everybody loved it there. Hawaii is truly a paradise: perfect weather, magnificent vistas, warm and friendly people. Hawaii has it all. To make Gerry's idea even more compelling, I had always been treated like royalty whenever we went to Hawaii because the Rascals had been big stars there. Over the years we had developed many good friends there.

One of our friends was Fred Williams, who was a vice president of a real estate company. Throughout the years, we had stayed in close contact with Fred and were delighted when he ended up marrying one of our kids' favorite baby-sitters in Hawaii. I called Fred and informed him that I might be ready for a big change in my life.

Fred was put in charge of building a brand-new mall behind the Royal Hawaiian Hotel, the preeminent hotel in Hawaii.

One day, he called me. "Sid, you know so much about chocolate, maybe you'd like to open a chocolate shop here in Hawaii. I would see to it that you get the absolute number-one location in the new mall we're building. You could have the space that's right off the escalator at the entrance to the mall. Everybody who comes into the mall will have to pass your chocolate shop. It's a can't-miss location."

I told Gerry about Fred's proposition and she was very enthusiastic. I was reluctant to pick up the entire family and move to Hawaii. So Gerry and I devised a plan where she would go to Hawaii to open the chocolate shop and I would stay in New York. We decided that the kids would stay with me in New York. If the chocolate shop became as successful as we hoped, then the entire family would relocate to Hawaii.

Gerry went to Hawaii to open the chocolate shop. We didn't count on how utterly laid back the Hawaiian lifestyle was. Everything took forever; the pace of life was so slow. No one seemed troubled about any kind of delay in the construction of the mall. Gerry had gone to Hawaii with a budget and a carefully measured-timeline. The slow Hawaiian pace ate the budget up and soon Gerry started to run out of money.

While Gerry was in Hawaii, I took care of the kids. Etienne, at eight, was the youngest and Adam, at 17, was the oldest. My friend Lou Levy from England came to the apartment to visit me. He was hysterical listening to me supervise all six kids with the household chores. Lou had a writer friend and told me that when he mentioned my situation with the kids to her, she immediately thought that it would be a great story for *The New York Times*. Lou arranged for the writer to come visit and interview me.

Several weeks later, a story appeared in the *Times* about the father in Manhattan raising six kids by himself. Some weeks after the story appeared, I got a call from the president of Warner Television explaining that someone at Warner had read about the kids and me. They were wondering if I would consider giving Warner an option to buy my story because they thought it would make a great TV series. "Why not?" I said.

Warner actually paid me for an option to my story, but never went forward because they claimed that the market had dried up for family-oriented shows. They told me they were now looking for shows with more action.

After eight months in Hawaii, Gerry finally ran out of money. She called and said, "Sid, I'm coming home. Fred says it might be another year before the mall is completed and I just don't have the staying power."

"OK, Ger. Come home. We all miss you."

We agreed that she would come back to New York on the day we were planning a joint birthday celebration for my daughters Denise and Casey at Benihana, a Japanese restaurant that the kids loved. I didn't tell the kids about Gerry's return; I wanted to surprise them that their mom was coming home.

On the day of birthday celebration, the seven of us went to Benihana. While we were there, I kept glancing at my watch. I sat facing the door so I could spot Gerry when she arrived. The kids were having a great time and didn't notice that I was somewhat preoccupied. I saw Gerry come through the entrance and work her way to our table. I started to cry. At that point, the kids saw her and they all jumped up in excitement and rushed over to hug and kiss her. I was extremely lonely when Gerry was in Hawaii; I was thrilled that she was home.

Gerry was disappointed that her quest to open the shop had not been successful. I guess it was not meant to be. However, the seven of us were overjoyed to have her home again.

One morning, soon after Gerry's return from Hawaii, I was coming out of the bank after extracting some cash in anticipation of an impending trip. As I started to walk away after concluding my transaction, I heard a voice behind me.

"Hey, mate!" I just kept walking.

"Hey mate!" came the voice again.

Then I heard a woman's voice call my name.

I turned around and saw Paul and Linda McCartney with two of their children walking towards me. When they reached me, we embraced. Pointing to me, Paul said to his son Jamie, "You know, Jamie, this man knows about pizza! Nobody knows about pizza like Mr. Bernstein. Isn't that right, Sid?"

"Well, I guess so, Paul," I answered, somewhat sheepishly.

"Do you really like good pizza?" I asked young Jamie.

"Yeah, yeah!" he answered while rubbing his stomach in a circular motion.

"Me too, Jamie. I really love it and I have the size to prove it!"

All the grown-ups laughed.

"Listen, Sid," Paul said. "We're playing the Boston Garden tonight. We'll be back late, but tomorrow I'll give you a call. Maybe we can take all the kids, yours and mine, for pizza."

"That would be great, Paul! I'm going out of town for a few days myself. That's why I was at the bank. But we'll do it another time. See you guys soon!" And I hurried off.

We have yet to make that pizza date happen.

Abe Margolies and I spent a lot of time together in what turned out to be the last years of his life. Early one Sunday morning, he and I went to Barney Greengrass restaurant on Amsterdam Avenue. Barney's was famous for its variety of lox, eggs and onions and it reminded Abe and me of the food we grew up with. Whenever we went there, we would encounter well-known and influential people from all walks of life.

Abe had a habit of chewing on a toothpick after a meal. As we were walking home through Central Park after having enjoyed a leisurely breakfast, Abe started to choke.

"Abe, what's wrong?" I said, as he fell to his knees.

"Sid, I swallowed the toothpick," he gagged.

I tried not to panic. We were in the middle of the rather large Central Park and there was almost no one around at that early hour. I helped Abe up and somehow we made it out of the park. Abe's apartment building was just across from the park at 72nd Street and Fifth Avenue. When the doorman rang up to Abe's apartment, there was no answer. Rather than go upstairs, I rushed to a corner phone booth (these were the days before practically everyone carried a cellular phone) and phoned Dr. Ezra

Greenspan, Abe's doctor. Dr. Greenspan was a good friend of Abe's and was a pioneer in the field of chemotherapy. He also acted as Abe's personal physician. Over the years, Abe had been instrumental in raising large sums of money to help fund Dr. Greenspan's research. Luckily, Dr. Greenspan was at home.

"Sid," he said. "I live nearby. Jump in a cab and bring Abe right over to me."

When we got to Dr. Greenspan's home, he was waiting for us in the lobby of his apartment building. He took one look at Abe, and told us to go to Mount Sinai Hospital immediately.

"Sid, take him over. I'll go up and phone ahead. They'll be expecting you."

We cabbed over to Mount Sinai and were rushed into the emergency room where the waiting doctors met us. Dr. Greenspan was evidently an influential person at Mount Sinai.

As Abe lay there being examined, a myriad of thoughts rushed through my mind. I realized how dear and important Abe was to my family and me. I recalled how instrumental he had been in my life and how he had always been there for me. I thought how devastating it would be to lose him. I was afraid for Abe.

Fortunately, the doctors were able to dislodge the toothpick without any difficulty. When they finished working on Abe, he jumped up and, in his inimitable style, thanked everyone and whistled his way out of the hospital. He was Abe again. But, still, it had been a terrifying moment for me. It hammered home just how tenuous all of life is.

A professor from the New School for Social Research who was teaching a course on theatrical law contacted me. Since his course was not strictly on the law, he thought that his students should hear some of my experiences, and he invited me to lecture. I accepted the invitation. The assistant dean of the New School happened to be monitoring the class on the evening that I spoke there. After the class, he was waiting for me. He introduced himself and said, "Mr. Bernstein, I thoroughly enjoyed listening to you, and I'm glad I decided to sit in on the class this evening. I was wondering…would you consider teaching a course here at the New School?"

"Well, that's very flattering and I thank you for your kind words. I owe the New School a lot."

"How's that, Mr. Bernstein?"

"Well, many years ago, I took some courses here and one of my professors, Dr. Max Lerner, insisted that we read books about Great Britain. He was teaching a course about democracy and he felt that we needed to know about the British system. He gave us a reading list of books, which I couldn't get to because I was too busy. Instead, I began reading English newspapers, and that's how I learned about the Beatles and other British acts."

"How interesting. So you owe us?" laughed the dean.

"Yes, I do! But I have to tell you, I'm really not into reading lists, tests, papers, and the like, so what kind of a professor would I make?"

"It's not like that at all. We would just want you to come and tell your stories like you did tonight. Just show up and talk for an hour or so. That's it. We'll pay you for the number of lectures that you do each term, and you can do as many as 12 or as few as 8."

"Paid? You would actually pay me?"

"Certainly we would pay you. And you don't have to prepare, assign homework, grade papers or give tests. You just have to tell the students about your experiences and answer questions. Just give it a try," he said hopefully.

"Okay, you've convinced me. I'll give it a try."

Shortly after my conversation with the dean, I began my teaching career at the New School. Just as the dean had promised, I did not have to prepare a reading list or written assignments. I simply had to plan a topic for a lecture and speak. Sometimes, I would ask friends and colleagues with different areas of expertise in the entertainment industry to guest lecture.

Bert Padell, who is one of the most widely known business managers in the entertainment field, was someone I asked to guest lecture on a regular basis. Bert is a very dynamic speaker and the kids enjoy listening to him. Bert has a great time delivering his lectures, and he and I have shared the teaching load for some years now.

One day after class, Bert and I were sitting around shooting the breeze and he said to me, "Sid, you know what I'd love to do is speak to the music department at Harvard. I'd like to be able to say that I lectured at Harvard."

I had a client that I was doing some consulting work for who was a Wall Street broker and an alumnus of Harvard University, and I asked him if he could set it up so that Bert and I could lecture at Harvard. I explained that Bert was a very dynamic speaker and that I thought he and I would put on a good show for the academics at Harvard.

Two months later, Bert and I got an invitation to speak at Harvard. On the appointed day, we flew up to Boston and appeared before a large assembly of both students and faculty. Both Bert and I had a great time and I think that everyone who heard us that day did as well. Now on my resume, I can honestly say that I have lectured at Harvard!

I have been "teaching" at the New School for 15 years. I enjoy it immensely. I like being around the young adults of the student body. And, most of all, I hope that one day I will say something that will be as inspiring for one of my young students as the request Prof. Max Lerner made of me more than 35 years ago. I truly hope so.

In the spring of 1988, Abe Margolies decided to host a fundraiser for then Senator Al Gore of Tennessee. Senator Gore was campaigning to be the Democratic Presidential nominee. Abe invited about 60 or 70 of his closest friends to Abe's Steak House for a $1,000-per-plate luncheon. When I walked into the restaurant, I noticed that on the right side of the room was a rather large banquet table on a raised platform. I assumed that Senator Gore would be addressing the group from his seat at the banquet table.

The first part of the luncheon was a cocktail hour where I mingled with old friends. After a while, we were asked to take our seats. As I sat down, a young man approached me.

"You're Sid Bernstein, aren't you?" he asked.

"Yes, I'm Sid Bernstein. How can I help you?"

"Mr. Bernstein," the young man continued. "I'm an aide to Senator Gore and I don't know if you're aware that the Senator is a huge music fan and a big Beatles fan. Would it be OK if I brought him over?"

"Yes, I'd be happy to meet him. Why don't you take me over to his table?"

The young aide, whose name I've unfortunately forgotten, brought me over to Senator Gore and introduced us. "Senator Gore," the aide began. "This is Sid Bernstein, the man who brought the Beatles to America."

Senator Gore jumped up and shook my hand vigorously and proceeded to pepper me with questions about how I had come to discover the Beatles; what made me want to present them at Carnegie Hall; and how I conceived of the Shea Stadium concert. We spent the better part of 15 minutes talking and we were both enjoying the conversation. As we continued to speak, a large crowd gathered around us. I think that if I hadn't reminded the Senator about the real purpose for his appearance at Abe's, we might still be there. His parting words to me were, "I hope we meet again, Sid."

"I'll look forward to that, Senator," I replied, as I walked back to my table.

Personally, I'd prefer that our next meeting take place in the White House where I can once again talk music history with *President* Al Gore.

In 1988, all four of my sons were working at Camp Chipinaw in Bethel, in the Catskill Mountains of New York. Bethel is the town where Max Yasgur's farm is located. The Woodstock Music Festival had taken place there in August 1969, having been organized by four New Yorkers—Michael Lang, Joel Rosenman, John Roberts and Artie Kornfeld. They had expected 30,000 to 40,000 people. Instead, more than 400,000 people showed up that August weekend. The festival had initially been planned for Woodstock, New York, but the town fathers voted it down. Keeping the name Woodstock, the principals moved it to the 37 acres of Max Yasgur's farm in Bethel.

Gerry and I went up to see our boys on visiting day. The camp electrician, Evan Bloom, found out that I was at the camp. He introduced himself to me.

"You're Sid Bernstein, the music man. Would you mind if I asked you a question?"

"Not at all, Evan. What would you like to know?"

"Were you at Woodstock in 1969, Mr. Bernstein?"

"No, Evan. My wife was pregnant at the time and my band, the Rascals, had another booking, so I couldn't be there."

"Have you ever seen the site? It's only two miles from here."

"No, I haven't."

"Well, would you like me to show it to you?"

"I'm visiting the camp and my boys, Evan. I don't think I want to leave them so suddenly."

"That's okay. We'll take them along with us. I'll get permission from the camp."

Evan made the arrangements and we proceeded to drive the short distance to Yasgur's Farm. Evan escorted us to the monument that stands on the site in commemoration of the historic event. It's a big rock engraved with all the names of the performers and acts that appeared at the Woodstock festival in 1969. I stood in front of the monument, reading the names: John Sebastian, Canned Heat, the Butterfield Blues Band, Santana, Joe Cocker, Richie Havens, Country Joe McDonald, Joan Baez, Crosby, Stills, Nash & Young, ShaNaNa, Arlo Guthrie, Ten Years After, Sly & the Family Stone, Jimi Hendrix, Jefferson Airplane and The Who.

I could feel the vast crowd that was there nearly 20 summers before. It's hard to explain, but as I looked down at that large, open field, I could visualize the more than 400,000 people sitting there for three days and nights in the rain and mud, enjoying the music, each other and the experience. I could hear it, see it and feel it. It was an eerie spiritual feeling that gave me the chills.

"Evan, I saw the movie but it's hard to imagine 400,000 people fitting into this space.

"Yes, sir, Mr. Bernstein. I was 14 at the time and I saw it with my own eyes. I was here. There were 400,000 people here."

Just then a car started to come up the road.

"Mr. Bernstein, I'll bet you that car coming up the road has an out-of-state license plate," Evan said. "Every day, without fail, people from around the country come here to see this place and the monument."

Sure enough, the approaching car had a license plate from Montana. The passengers were a man, his wife and two kids. Evan asked the man from Montana why he was there.

"I was here in '69," he answered, "and I wanted my wife and kids to see this place."

"Mr. Bernstein," Evan said., "next year is the 20th anniversary of Woodstock. People have proposed an anniversary concert and the original group of producers has tried to put it together, but the town is adamantly opposed. They will not issue a permit."

"Of course they're opposed. You were here and saw what happened in 1969 yourself. The roads were paralyzed; there wasn't enough food or water, and it's a miracle that there wasn't a catastrophe here. Of course the town is against it."

"That's all true, but it was an incredible experience! I think you might just be the person who could get a permit."

We delivered my boys back to the camp and Gerry and I went home. That night, I couldn't sleep. I kept mulling over what Evan had said, and thinking about what I had felt standing in front of the monument. The next morning, excited and exhausted at the same time, I called Evan.

"Evan, who do I have to speak to?"

"Are you interested?" Evan seemed to practically jump through the telephone.

"Yes, I am Evan."

"Oh, my God!" he exclaimed. "Tell me, who do you want to reach? I know everybody!"

"Just let's start with whoever you think is the key person. Let's start at the beginning."

"The first person we need to talk to is the Sullivan County Supervisor."

"Okay, set it up."

Evan set up the meeting with the County Supervisor, who explained to me that everyone was frightened of the project. "We've turned down several people, including the original producers, Sid. Everyone is afraid of a recurrence of what happened in 1969. It took us months to recover from Woodstock. Just take a look at our roads. We can't handle it!"

"I'm aware of that, but I'm thinking of something much smaller in scale than the original festival. I'd make absolutely certain that there would be lots of security and people to handle the traffic. I don't want to create havoc."

"You're not going to bring the Beatles here are you, Sid?"

"I wish!" I laughed. "No, of course not."

"Okay, what you need to do now is talk to some of the town managers. They will have to sign off on this before it can happen. There are town and county ordinances that we've passed as a result of Woodstock. You cannot have a mass assembly of over 10,00 people. It's the law."

"Can that possibly be changed? We'll need to sell at least 20,000 tickets to amortize the general costs and the cost of the extra security."

"You'll need to take that up with the town managers."

The first thing I did was talk to June Gelish, the owner of Yasgur's Farm. She agreed that for $250,000 we could use the property for an anniversary festival.

"But, Sid, I don't think you can get the necessary permits," she cautioned.

I had a feeling that I could somehow get the venue, so I began to contact and meet with the town managers. We contacted Alan Scott, the Town Manager of Bethel. At first, he told us that we needed to get all the other town managers on board because we needed to undo the ordinances that forbade a gathering of more than 10,000 people. Neither he nor any of the other officials were too encouraging. We then embarked on what turned out to be a five-year campaign to try to stage the festival. We decided to state our case to local residents. I spoke at many town meetings, boards, schools, Mason and Kiwanis meetings, synagogues and anywhere people would listen. I turned it into a referendum where the will of the people would carry the day.

Alan Scott did everything he could to thwart our efforts. He sabotaged, fought and went so far as to propose his own choice, Robert Gersh, as the promoter of the festival. Scott did that after it became evident to him that we were making headway with the people of Bethel. He saw that the local residents wanted it to happen and they wanted me to do it. We had developed a workable plan, and the people of Bethel knew that we were sincere in our efforts and would keep our word to them.

Finally, at a heated and acrimonious public meeting attended by an overflow crowd of Bethel residents, by a show of hands, we prevailed over Scott's candidate, Robert Gersh. All the campaigning and negotiations took so long that we were now talking about having a 25th anniversary Woodstock Festival instead of the 20th. We were awarded the right to proceed with the festival on Yasgur's original site, subject to approvals from the appropriate state and local authorities.

I had beaten Scott in the town council, but he kept fighting me. He gave an interview to *The New York Times*, where he said that I didn't have the money to produce the festival. He enlisted the sheriff, Joe Wasser, and the D.A. to try to talk me off the project. He refused to give up or give in to the will of the people.

When the original group that had put on Woodstock in 1969 heard that I had prevailed at Bethel and was moving ahead in my plans to stage Bethel '94 (The name I gave to the anniversary festival), they decided that they needed to respond. They went to the town of Saugerties, New York, and got a permit to stage the 25th anniversary of Woodstock on Winston Farm. They owned the name Woodstock. They got a commitment from Polygram Records and John Scher, a concert promoter whose company had been bought by Polygram, to put up $19 million dollars for their anniversary festival. Scher and the original group were upset that I had obtained the right to use the Yasgur property. We tried to partner with them, but after several meetings, at which I offered to give up my top billing, we gave up the idea of a joint promotion. They didn't understand that there was no way the people in Bethel were going to give them permission to do Woodstock on Yasgur's Farm. Having averted disaster back in '69, the wary townsfolk were not about to tempt the fates once again.

[Scher was so angry that he tried to buy every act that we had. He put deposits down on all of the acts that we wanted but hadn't signed yet. They put their festival on in Saugerties. They ended up spending close to $20 million dollars. There was looting, arson and violence on the last day of their festival. It was a mess. People came from Saugerties to our site, and told us that the real spirit of Woodstock was in Bethel. How could it not be? What did Saugerties have to do with what had happened in Bethel in 1969?]

I raised $1 million dollars from investors in Philadelphia and was promised the balance by a local insurance company that would put up an additional $5 million dollars. Notwithstanding the admonitions of the sheriff, who threatened me with arrest, and the D.A., we kept forging ahead.

We paid Mrs. Gelish the $250,000 for the use of Yasgur's Farm, and we began planning the festival in earnest. We worked hard to get our festival on. We made a deal with the adjoining farm for use of its road for entry and egress purposes. We retained Howard Rubenstein, New York's preeminent PR man, to handle our public relations, and we moved our command center to the Concord Hotel, whose management, the Parker Family, graciously assisted us in any way they could. We contracted with Ticketron to sell our tickets. We fought the fight to get the final approvals and the money that had been promised. As far as I was concerned, our festival was on.

Suddenly, the insurance company reneged on their commitment. They did, however, supply the toilets. We were millions of dollars short. The festival was just a few days away. We knew that there had been tickets sold in New York and that people were on their way. We also knew that the acts were en route. We had no stage, no lights, no sound system and almost no money.

I got a call from the largest local radio station in the area that had a big signal, which could be heard hundreds of miles away.

"Sid, we hear that you're short the money to stage the festival," the interviewer, Bob Wolf, said.

"Yes, that's true, but we're still going forward," I told the radio audience.

"Do you have the acts?" Wolf asked me.

"Yes, we booked them a while back and gave them deposits, so we expect they'll be here."

"And what about the sale of the tickets?"

"Well, we know that tickets have been sold, so we believe that the ticket holders will be here and expect to see a show."

"So what do you need, Sid?"

"I need a generator. I need lights. I need sound and a stage. I need carpenters and electricians."

"What are you going to do? You don't have the money and you need all this stuff before you can have the festival. What are you going to do?"

"I'm going to move forward," I said. "I'm going to the Farm, and I'll find a way to put on this festival."

"And how about your threatened arrest because you don't have all the necessary permits?"

"I guess they'll just have to arrest me. I'm carrying on. People are coming, and I'm going to try to put this festival on for them. I refuse to disappoint all the people who are involved in this effort and the music fans who want to be here."

"Well, there you have it, ladies and gentlemen," Wolf said. "That was Sid Bernstein, the promoter of the Bethel '94 Festival, speaking to you from the Concord Hotel, saying he's going ahead."

As soon as I hung up from doing the radio interview, the phones in my room at the Concord started to ring. The first call was from a man who owned several flatbed trucks.

"Sid, you got your stage," he said. "I have flatbed trucks. We'll put them together in a row, and it'll make a perfect stage. I heard you on the radio, Sid! I'm dispatching the trucks immediately. You'll have your stage in 90 minutes. I know where to send them."

Carpenters and electricians began calling. "Count us in, Sid. When do you want us at the Farm?"

The support that we got was overwhelming. Someone supplied us with a generator. We were provided with the sound. My youngest son, Etienne, rode 600 miles on a motorcycle to help with the festival. Everything we needed materialized, and we held our festival. The estimate was that over the weekend of August 13-14-15, 1994, 100,000 people filtered in and out of Max Yasgur's historic farm.

The festival had been scheduled to run for three days, but lasted for five. We never had even one untoward incident. No violence, no theft, nothing but fun and music. Richie Havens, who brought along a film crew to film the festival, Country Joe & the Fish, ShaNaNa, Melanie, the New Rascals, Sarah McLachlan, Joe Walsh from the Eagles, Leslie West, Arlo Guthrie and David Pirner from Soul Asylum showed up at Bethel '94 and gave the people a festival to remember.

We didn't make money. In fact, we lost close to $1 million dollars. But we all got an education. You're never too young or too old to learn, and this was an education about corruption, greed and the disregard for citizenry by elected officials.

The people were having none of it. They wanted Bethel '94 to happen, so they voted for it, and then they backed up their vote with lights, generators, stages, carpentry, electrical work, food, hotel rooms and accommodations of all sorts. It was a lesson in what The People can do. I said as much from the stage when several of the acts pulled me onstage to praise me for having the perseverance to put on the festival despite all the problems. I gave all the credit to the people of Bethel and the surrounding towns. "Without these terrific folks," I said, almost in tears, "these five days of peace, love and cooperation could not have happened. God bless you all."

Paul McCartney wrote an oratorio, Liverpool Oratorio, which was being performed at Carnegie Hall in November 1991. Benji Greenberg, a great Beatles fan and collector of Beatles memorabilia who I came to know over the years, bought tickets and insisted that I be his guest. We sat with his brother Billy in the Diamond Horseshoe of Carnegie Hall. About ten boxes away from us sat Paul and Linda McCartney. The irrepressible Benji kept holding up his BEATLES9 license plate, and finally Paul saw it and gave Benji the thumbs-up sign. Benji's BEATLES9 license plate is valid in New York State and can be used on any car that Benji chooses to register it to. Benji will always be a little boy when it comes to the Beatles, and there's just no way to dampen his enthusiasm.

After the Oratorio had been performed, we went to the reception that Carnegie Hall was feting for Paul. The management of Carnegie Hall had heard that I was "in the house" and, at intermission, two Carnegie Hall officials came into our box.

"Mr. Bernstein!" one of them said. "It's so nice to see you! We did not know that you would be in attendance, and we would like to invite you to a reception that we are having for Mr. McCartney after the performance. Would you like to come with your friends?"

I accepted the gracious invitation. After the concert, we went to the reception room at Carnegie Hall. The room was packed with guests and many members of the press. It was quite a crowd. We arrived before the guest of honor and sampled some of the marvelous hors d'ouvers, which I believe were catered by the Russian Tea Room located next door to Carnegie Hall.

When Paul and Linda arrived, there was a blinding burst of flashbulbs and the press immediately besieged them.

Benji started pulling me towards Paul. "Sid, please! I have to meet him!"

"Benji," I said., "take it easy! You'll meet him. Just give the press and this crowd a little while to cool off. You'll meet him."

Benji was not going to leave Carnegie Hall until he met his all-time hero, Paul McCartney. I didn't feel like pushing myself to the front of the crowd that was around Paul and Linda. I told Benji that as soon as the crowd thinned out, I would take him over to meet Paul. Finally, the crowd began to disperse and Linda saw me. "Paul," I heard her say to her husband. "Look, Sid's here!" Paul smiled and finished a conversation he was having with a member of the press.

Benji and Linda were discussing Westchester County, the New York City suburbs where Linda had been raised. While Benji and Linda were talking about her hometown of Armonk, I told Paul that I had particularly enjoyed the music and the wonderful children's chorus that had performed in the Oratorio. I asked him if Benji's brother Billy could snap a picture. As always, Paul graciously agreed. Benji pulled out his BEATLES9 license plate for the picture and Paul said, "Hey, I saw you in the Hall! You were holding up the license plate!" Benji was in seventh heaven. I winked at Paul. We took the pictures, I kissed Linda and thanked Paul for his graciousness. I was thrilled that I could make a dream come true for one of the world's great Beatles fans, the irrepressible Benji Greenberg!

I will say this for Benji: he is living proof of the adage "nothing succeeds like persistence."

After the toothpick scare with Abe, I would make sure that we scheduled time to spend together. We never planned anything particularly exciting; we would grab a bite to eat or just sit in the park. We just wanted to spend time together. One day, as we were sitting in Central Park, he said to me, "You know, Sid, I haven't been able to eat lately. I seem to have completely lost my appetite"

"What's wrong, Abe? Gert (Abe's wife) has told me the same thing. She says you're not eating as you usually do."

"Sid, don't you know that I'm a respiratory invalid?"

I didn't know what that meant, but by the look on his face, I could tell that whatever it was, it wasn't good. "Abe, you have to start eating. You have to push yourself."

There was an umbrella-hot dog cart across from where we were sitting. We had been raised on hot dogs and we both loved them.

"I'm going to get a hot dog from the vendor over there. Can I get you one?"

"Sure," he said glumly.

I got the two hot dogs. I took a bite out of mine and savored it. Abe bit into his and immediately threw it over his shoulder into the bushes.

"Let's walk, Sid. I want to watch the kids playing softball." Abe loved to watch the kids play softball in the park. As we walked, I noticed that Abe was shuffling and not really picking up his feet. I knew then that Abe was very sick.

Not long after that meeting, Abe became bedridden. He was diagnosed with lung cancer. It was ironic that a great benefactor of chemotherapy research could not be helped when he needed it. Abe deteriorated quickly. I went to see him every day, whether he was at home or in the hospital. It is a terrible thing to watch your best friend waste away. I was losing Abe right before my eyes. In the end, Abe came home from the hospital to die.

At his funeral, hundreds of people from every conceivable walk of life attended. Abe had known them all—the sinners, the saints and everyone in between. He was a larger-than-life character who touched the lives of countless people. Abe was a special gift to all who knew him.

Reader's Digest used to have a monthly feature entitled "The Most Unforgettable Character I Ever Met." Readers would write in, telling about someone who had touched their lives and left an impression on them. I never wrote to *Reader's Digest*, and to be sure, I have through my life met many unforgettable characters, but the most unforgettable, without question, was Abe Margolies.

In all the years that Abe Margolies financed me and we did many shows, concerts and productions together, never, ever, did he take one penny from me. Never. I think about him every day. Abe was as unique and giving a man as I ever met, and I loved him dearly. All he ever wanted to do was help his family and friends. I miss Abe Margolies terribly.

My son Dylan wanted to go see Paul McCartney on the night he appeared on *Saturday Night Live* in 1993. We got some tickets and went to the

Saturday Night studios at NBC in Rockefeller Center.

After the show, there was a long line of people waiting to say hello to Paul. One of Dylan's former schoolmates was an usher and saw Dylan and me standing on the line and took us by the hand and moved us to the front of the line. As we were standing in front of Paul's dressing room, the door opened and he and I made eye contact. "Sid!" he exclaimed, and excused himself from a group of people that he was talking to in the dressing room. He came out and greeted Dylan and me.

"Which Bernstein is this?" he asked as he shook Dylan's hand. I told him it was Dylan, my second-born son, and Paul exclaimed, "The last time I saw you, you were a little boy!" Dylan had grown into a young man.

We chatted for a moment or so, and then left. I didn't want to monopolize any more of his time since there was a long line of people waiting to see him.

Whenever and wherever I have close proximity to any act that I have ever had anything to do with, I always make it a point to try to say hello. It's the courteous thing to do, and I would never want it to be known that I had attended a performance and not tried to extend my congratulations and best wishes.

Paul McCartney is and has always been a very gracious and real person. He has seen the top of the mountain more than once. His talent and artistry speaks for itself and, if anything, he has improved with age. I feel privileged to consider him a friend and I am proud of what he has accomplished and how he has conducted his life. Long live Sir Paul!

In 1993, Cynthia Lennon invited me to come see her son Julian perform at the Beacon Theatre in New York. Julian had developed a musical career and was an Atlantic Records recording act. I brought two of my sons, Beau and Etienne, along with me to the Beacon. I sat with Cynthia; my two boys were a few rows behind us. The theatre was packed. Julian came onstage with his band, and was greeted by the very enthusiastic crowd with great applause.

I had met Julian at the China Club in New York City and had found him to be a very friendly and engaging young man. He sounded and looked a lot like his father; it was uncanny. My great affinity and affection for his father made it an almost given that I would like Julian as well. I often wondered how John Lennon's prolonged absences from his first son's life had affected Julian's childhood. I admired Julian's great musical talent and ability, but the thing that I most admired about him was the close, loving relationship he had with his mother. Julian and Cynthia's relationship resonated with me.

Every so often, I glanced over at Cynthia watching her son perform and I sensed the great pride and love she felt for Julian. Cynthia's eyes were positively glowing. The Yiddish word for such swelling pride is *nachas*. There is no precise translation of *nachas* into English; it's a combination of love, pride and hope. It is an incredible feeling.

Whenever I am in an audience, whether as a promoter, manager, agent or just a ticket holder, I have a habit of periodically observing the rest of the audience to see and feel what they are experiencing. As I was scanning the audience that night in the Beacon, out of the corner of my eye I saw Yoko Ono and her son Sean Lennon come quietly into the theatre and take two seats. The seats were in the section to the immediate left of where Cynthia and I were sitting. I knew that Cynthia and Yoko had not seen each other for many years. Midway through his performance, Julian paused and thanked the audience for coming and then he said, "I would just like to say that my younger brother is here in the audience."

Most people in the theatre had not seen Yoko and Sean come in. When Julian informed the audience that Sean was there, there was an unmistakable charge of excitement in the air. I turned to look at my two boys, and they nodded as if to say, "We saw Sean and Yoko come in!"

And then Julian said, "Sean, would you please come up to the stage?"

Sean left his seat and walked up the aisle to thunderous applause. The two Lennon boys put their arms around each other and began to sing *Stand By Me*. It was an unforgettable moment. Julian and Sean share a great resemblance to John. The moment was so touching and tender that there was not a dry eye in the theatre. Julian and Sean finished their song and, of course, there was a standing ovation. It was one of the most moving and dramatic scenes I have ever witnessed.

After the show, Cynthia, unaware that I had previously met her son, invited my two boys and me to meet Julian. I told her that I had already met him, but I wanted to go backstage to congratulate him on his performance and to introduce him to my two sons.

We went upstairs, and I introduced Beau and Etienne to Julian. We talked for a few minutes and Julian invited us to a post-concert party that Atlantic was throwing for him at the Hard Rock Café. Naturally, my boys were itching to go, so I accepted the invitation. We went to the Hard Rock and sat at a table with Cynthia and Julian. We were there for about 20 minutes when Yoko and Sean walked in. I asked Beau and Etienne to move so that Sean and Julian could sit together. As my boys got up to move, Yoko and Sean came over to the table. Yoko and Cynthia greeted each other and a photographer snapped a picture of them saying hello that was seen in newspapers all over the world just a day or two later. I'm not sure, but I think that this was the first time in many years that Yoko Ono and Cynthia Lennon had been in each other's presence. Yoko was very gracious and friendly to everyone, and told me how handsome and polite my sons were.

We were all just parents enjoying our kids.

Nineteen ninety-five was the 30th anniversary of the Beatles' first appearance at Shea Stadium. Many people say that is the single most important concert in the history of rock & roll because it proved beyond any shadow of a doubt that rock & roll acts could fill such a large venue.

Kevin McCarthy from the New York Mets organization called me.

"Mr. Bernstein, my name is Kevin McCarthy and I am part of the management team that runs Shea Stadium and the Mets. My father was the head grounds keeper at Shea on August 15, 1965. I was two years old at the time. I've been hearing about you and that incredible night for most of my life. My father will never forget it. I also happen to be a huge Beatles fan and it's a great pleasure to be talking to you. Mr. Bernstein, this coming August 15th, we are planning a program commemorating the 30th anniversary of the Beatles concert here at Shea. The Mets will be playing a day game and we would like to give you the honor of throwing out the first ball. Would you consider doing it?"

"How nice. Can I bring my family?"

"Certainly. Bring your family and friends."

I agreed to do it.

On the morning of August 15th, I went to Central Park to throw some stones so that I wouldn't embarrass myself when it came time for me to throw the ball from my seat in the stands to the catcher. It had been a very long time since I had thrown a ball.

We went to Shea Stadium as a group on August 15th. My family, friends and I had lunch in the Diamond Club and we all had a great time. Kevin McCarthy and the Mets were great hosts. After lunch, I went to a studio in the stadium to pre-record on videotape some remarks about August 15, 1965, that would later be shown on the Jumbotron, the large screen in centerfield. I spoke of that amazing night 30 years ago when the four boys from Liverpool took New York by storm and made music history.

When it came time to throw the ball, I found that my throwing practice paid off, as I threw the ball without too much difficulty. It was a fun experience for my family, friends and me. I'm grateful to Kevin McCarthy for coming up with the idea.

More than 50 years after I first met Red Buttons, the boxing fan enthusiastically rooting for the underdog, I called Red and asked him if he would be the master of ceremonies at a benefit that I was producing for the 25th anniversary of Daytop Village. I was doing consulting work for Daytop, which is a well-known drug and alcohol rehab center in New York City. He was very gracious in accepting my offer and gave a magnificent performance at the benefit. I thought of Red and his performance when I was planning Daytop's 30th anniversary gala five years later. Once again he accepted and, once again, he was magnificent. The Bronx has surely turned out some wonderful people and Red Buttons is one of them.

In early 1998, Mayor Barbara Cooke and the City Council of Liverpool invited me to come and speak at a memorial for Brian Epstein. They felt that Brian hadn't been recognized enough for his accomplishments and contributions to Liverpool. In honor of Brian, the city was planning to rename the Neptune Theatre the Brian Epstein Theatre. The theatre seated about 300 people and catered to productions that were somewhat offbeat and outside the mainstream.

There were to be several speakers at the memorial, and I was asked to speak for about seven or eight minutes. I felt that I had to accept. This was, after all, for Brian Epstein.

"I'll be there," I said. "When do you need me?"

I did not ask for airfare or expenses for participating in the memorial and I was later told that this made a great impression on the organizers of the event.

I flew to Manchester, which is 20 or 30 minutes from Liverpool, one day before the ceremony. Robby Quinn, who has become a dear friend of mine, and Joe Flannery picked me up at the airport. We drove to Liverpool, stopping to look at the houses where Paul, George, Ringo and John had spent their childhood. It really put me in the proper mood. They dropped me at the Moat House, a lovely and quaint hotel. After resting for a while, Robby Quinn picked me up again and we had a late lunch and spent the time talking about Brian and Liverpool. When I went back to the hotel, several members of the City Council came by to say hello. They were all very solicitous and made me feel very welcome. My relationship to Brian and the Beatles seemed very important to the Liverpudlians.

The next day, a Friday, at noon, I went to City Hall for the ceremony. I met the Mayor and she asked if I would extend my speech to 20-25 minutes. Several of the other speakers had unexpected emergencies and cancelled at the last minute.

"Madame Mayor (I did not know until later that the proper way to address her was Your Lordship), for Brian Epstein, I would stand on my head and speak for 24 hours if you asked me."

"Oh how, lovely," she replied. "You'll not be needing to stand on your head, Mr. Bernstein, and 20 or 25 minutes would be perfect."

The program began with some Beatles music performed by local talent and then some remarks by the president of the City Council and another City Council member. Someone read letters from George, Ringo, and Paul, who all said that they could not attend in person but that their thoughts and warmest feelings were extended. What the boys said in their letters was quite beautiful and moving. I wish I had the text of each of the letters because I would reprint them for you verbatim. After the reading of the letters, the Mayor gave me a terrific introduction. As usual, I went to the podium without any notes.

I told the assembled audience, which included Brain Epstein's nephew Henry (Clive's son), about how I had first come to speak to Brian and how we had started doing business together over 35 years ago. I explained to them that Brian and I never had a written contract throughout the duration of our business relationship. I told them some of the stories that you have read in these pages, and I told them how I felt about Brian Epstein. I spoke from my heart, and when I finished the speech, I received a standing ovation. Many people came to me afterwards to tell me how much they had enjoyed my remarks and how much it meant to them and Liverpool that I had taken the time to participate in the ceremony honoring Brian Epstein.

There was a buffet following the ceremony. I was sitting at a table enjoying the food and conversing with some people when the Mayor, the president of City Council and two members of the Council approached.

"Mr. Bernstein, could you please excuse yourself for a few minutes? We would like to speak with you in private."

I stood up and walked over to the group, with what I'm sure was a quizzical expression on my face.

"Mr. Bernstein," the Mayor said. "We have just had an informal meeting of the City Council members here today and we have unanimously selected you as the first-ever Ambassador from the City of Liverpool to the United States."

After having addressed the Mayor as Madam, Mayor, and Mrs. Mayor and been corrected several times, I said, "Your Lordship, I'm deeply honored. Absolutely honored! Thank you and the City Council." I didn't know what else to say.

So, if you ever happen to meet me one of these days, please remember to refer to me as Mr. Ambassador!

After accepting the Ambassadorship, I was introduced to Bernie Michelson, who was the owner of a music and record shop called Hessy's. In their formative years, the Beatles had bought much of their equipment and hung out with their peers from the Liverpool music scene at Hessy's.

"Mr. Bernstein, I would be honored if you would be our guest this evening at our home for the Sabbath meal."

Someone distracted him for a moment and Robby Quinn was able to whisper to me, "I think you should go there, Sid. Bernie knew the boys when they were in Liverpool and his home is only two doors away from where the Epsteins lived."

I accepted Bernie's invitation, which was one of a number of dinner invitations that I had received throughout the day.

Bernie and Sarah Michelson have a beautiful home and a lovely family. During the meal, Bernie brought out an old ledger of accounts and showed me some of the entries. I read from the ledger. I saw George Harrison's name and next to it the make of the guitar he had purchased and a record of the monthly payments. I found another entry for Ringo Starr and his purchase of drumsticks. There was one for John Lennon for the purchase of assorted equipment, what he had paid and what the balance was. I got a big kick out of that ledger.

Bernie told me that he had been extremely fond of "those four boys." They were real Liverpudlians, very ambitious and complete gentlemen. He had known Brian well, as they had practically been next-door neighbors. It was a lovely evening and I am glad that Bernie's was the invitation that I had accepted.

About four or five weeks after returning home, I got a call from Robbie Quinn in Liverpool, telling me that there had been a plaque in my name delivered to the City Council, naming me as the Ambassador. Robby needed my address so that the plaque might be mailed to me.

"Robby, don't mail it. I want to pick it up in person."

I had an idea that I wanted to explore. I went to Liverpool to collect my plaque. When I arrived at City Hall, there were about 12 or 14 people in the Mayor's office and some members of the press and a representative from the BBC. My friend Stan Satlin had accompanied me. The Mayor conducted a brief ceremony and presented me with a plaque officially naming me Liverpool's Ambassador to the United States.

In my response, I explained how deeply honored I was and that Liverpool and its people meant a great deal to me and had played an important role in my life. I also expressed the sentiment that I wished I could do something to repay the honor that was being bestowed upon me. The citizens of Liverpool, of course, felt that I had done something for them 35 years ago and they were repaying me.

I spoke to the press and after the ceremony, several members of the Council, Stan and I went back to the Moat House to enjoy some refreshments and speak about the idea that was taking shape in my head. We had been sitting there for a short while when a desk clerk summoned me to the phone.

I couldn't imagine who would be calling me and for a moment I feared that something had happened at home with my family. I took the phone.

I heard Joe Flannery's voice. "Sid, I am sorry to have to convey such sad news, but I just heard on the telly that Linda McCartney has succumbed to cancer."

I was shocked. I had seen Linda not long ago and she had looked wonderful, radiant and full of life. I knew that she had been fighting breast cancer, but I thought she was winning.

"I just saw her a few months ago at Carnegie Hall, Joe. How sad! I had been telling people how good she looked. What a terrible tragedy!"

"I'm sorry, Sid."

I hung up the phone and felt a wave of sadness. I took a moment to myself and thought about Linda. I had known her since she was a young girl in New York. She had been one of the Rascals' earliest and biggest fans. Linda was a talented photographer and she had shot many pictures of the Rascals. She was lovely and vivacious, and her marriage to Paul had been both loving and successful. They had a wonderful family. I had considered their enduring marriage to be a tribute to them, considering that marital musical chairs is so prevalent among members of the entertainment industry. My heart went out to Paul and their children.

I returned to the small gathering. I didn't want to ruin the party so I didn't mention the phone call. However, several people must have seen the sadness etched on my face and asked me if anything was wrong. I replied by saying that I had received some unsettling personal news, and no one brought it up again.

I found it ironic that the subject of the meeting we were having at the Moat House was cancer and cancer research. I was raising the issue because I had an idea about bringing a worldwide music festival to Liverpool in the millennium year, with all proceeds going to cancer research. It was my way of trying to repay Liverpool for the honor they had bestowed upon me. I also wanted to do something in Abe's memory. Immediately prior to the phone call about Linda's passing, the Liverpudlians had been telling me about the Roy Castle Foundation. Roy Castle had been a Liverpool boy who became famous as a musician and entertainer in England. He had developed cancer at the height of his career and spent his last months talking about cancer and raising money for research and care. Upon his death, Liverpool had honored Roy with the formation of the Roy Castle Foundation, a research center in Liverpool dedicated to finding cures for cancer. I started to think about ways to support and increase these efforts, and that's how I got the idea for the music festival in the millennium.

After I received the Ambassadorship from Liverpool, Stan and I conceived a plan to hold a music festival in Liverpool. When Stan traveled to Liverpool with me when I received the plaque naming me Ambassador from Liverpool to the U.S., he could see that the Liverpudlians and I had formed a mutual admiration society.

"Sid," he said, "you are liked and honored by these folks. I think that if you were ever to collaborate with them, it could be tremendous."

I had an idea in the back of my mind that if we were to do any collaboration at all, that it would be for cancer research. It would be my tribute to Abe Margolies' memory.

At that time, the Labor Party was in power in Liverpool and Stan and I had become friendly with some of the Laborites on the City Council. We explored the possibility of staging a music festival. Mark O'Conner, an attorney in Liverpool, and Steve Stewart, an accountant at Ernst & Young, provided me with office space and lots of good advice whenever I was in Liverpool. They were encouraging and helpful.

Naturally, having the Beatles perform was on everyone's mind. Often during my many festival-planning trips, people would ask me whether I thought the surviving Beatles would reunite for the festival. My response was always the same: "No! This is not about the Beatles; it's about Liverpool and its people."

I didn't think that we should try to impose our wishes on Paul, George or Ringo. I had learned during the time of the Boat People benefit that any initiatives to perform would have to come directly from them. Against my better wishes, I was convinced by practically everyone involved to try to talk the surviving Beatles into playing together. After all, "hope springs eternal in the human breast." So, I contacted Paul McCartney and he graciously, but unequivocally, declined. There was no point in calling George or Ringo then; there would be no Beatles reunion.

When the Labor Party lost the election of 1998 to the Liberal Democrats, it put a damper on our evolving plans. The Liberal Democrats listened, but did not have the same enthusiasm for the project as the Laborites did. For the time being, the thought of a music festival in Liverpool is dead.

I still harbor the hope that maybe one day we can make the music festival a reality. Where better to hold a world music festival than in the city that gave birth to the greatest music revolution in history? Imagine having crowds like those at Woodstock, with a worldwide television audience looking on, and having all the proceeds, every penny, to benefit the fight against cancer. "You may say I'm a dreamer, but I'm not the only one." The people of Liverpool dream the same dreams.

Chapter 21: **OH, WHAT MIGHT HAVE BEEN!**

Through the years, I have been presented with several opportunities that I could have taken and, in hindsight, probably should have taken. Each time, I had a compelling personal or professional reason for not pursuing the idea further. And while I'm not sorry that I didn't take advantage of these opportunities, I often wonder what might have happened if I had.

Early in my career as a promoter, I had a fantastic ten-day run of shows at the Paramount and was in the lobby meeting and greeting the fans when this extraordinarily handsome giant of a man walked in alone.

"Hey, mister," he said. "Where's Mr. Sid Bernstein? I want to talk to him."

"I'm Sid Bernstein. How can I help you sir?"

"Look," he said to me. "You got James Brown appearing here; you got Sam Cooke; you got Jackie Wilson; you got the biggest acts in the world. I'm a big act. I want to get up there on that stage of yours. I don't sing; I don't play an instrument; but I will do business for you. I want to be in this show for a couple of days. How long you gonna be here?"

"Well, we have about a week to go."

"I won't cost you much. I just want to be on that stage, and I want to talk and perform for the people, but I don't sing and I don't play, Mr. Bernstein."

"We just don't have time in the shows to add another act. We'd love to have you, but there's just no room."

"Well," he said. "You're missing a good thing, Mr. Bernstein. I'd do a job for you."

"I know," I responded. "Let's do it the next time. I give you my word, the next time we do this, you're in."

He went in to see the show, and in retrospect I wondered if I should have just let him walk onstage and say hello to the crowd. Even though changing the headliners in those 10 days of Christmas shows was effective, accepting his offer to appear onstage would have been a great public relations coup.

Muhammad Ali sure was a handsome and commanding presence, a great fighter and a born showman. I'm sorry that I didn't take him up on his offer and give him an opportunity to appear onstage. I have no doubt that he would have electrified the audience.

Working on the Newport Jazz Festival in the summer of 1961 was a very hectic time. I had to do a great deal of planning and organizing from my office in New York. I had no time or interest for any other project, especially one that would mean lots of additional energy and focus.

In the days and weeks leading up to the Festival, Billy Fields, Gerry's roommate Nada Rowand and I were working 18 hours a day in an office above Howard Johnson's on 46th and Broadway in New York. The phones were ringing off the hook. John Drew was calling every five minutes from Newport. We were besieged for tickets. We were also dealing with the logistical nightmare of arranging transportation for all the acts in and out of Newport. The three of us were doing the work of ten people. Right in the middle of all of this frenetic activity, a young girl came into the office.

"I'm looking for Sid Bernstein," the young girl said in her unmistakable New York accent.

"I'm Sid Bernstein," I said as the phone rang. "Excuse me, young lady. I've got to take this call. We are trying to put on the Newport Jazz Festival and it's a little crazy around here. Please bear with me if you will."

When I hung up, she tried to tell me her story again, but we kept getting interrupted by the ringing phone. Slowly, and in fragments between the phones and the interruptions from Billy and Nada, I learned what she wanted.

"I'm a singer and I'm looking for a manager and Eddie Blum (who was an assistant to Richard Rodgers, the composer) asked me to come to see you." Mentioning Eddie Blum's name gave her immediate credibility with me. Eddie was a friend of mine, and I respected him. I looked at her more closely. She was rail thin, and was wearing ill-fitting clothes topped off with a strange hat.

I said to her, "Please forgive me. I can't give you the attention you obviously deserve. I don't want to be discourteous to you and I would never short shrift a friend of Eddie's. Would you please call me when all of this is over?"

"When would that be, Mr. Bernstein?"

"In about six weeks. We are committed to doing a promotion in Hartford with Brook Benton and Connie Francis right after Newport, so early August would be a good time. I will be happy to sit and talk with you then and listen to you sing."

She was disappointed, but agreed to call me in six weeks.

In the ensuing days and weeks, I concentrated all of my energies on the events in Newport and Hartford and forgot about the brief encounter I had with the young singer.

After Newport and a few days after we got back from Hartford, Gerry saw an ad in a local paper that piqued her interest.

"Sid, remember that girl that Eddie Blum sent up to see you? You know the one who you were too busy to talk to? Well, it says here in this ad that she's appearing at the Bon Soir in the Village. Would you like to go listen to her sing?"

"Sure, Ger. Let's go."

That night, we went to the Bon Soir. What I saw there was nothing short of mesmerizing. The waif who appeared in my office looked more polished and sophisticated onstage (especially without that silly hat). While her singing was fabulous, what I noticed most were her magnificent hands. She had the long, elegant fingers of a concert pianist. Her graceful manner and poise made her presence electrifying.

When she ended her set, Gerry and I went backstage to say hello. As we walked in, I saw my old friend Marty Erlichman, who was the manager of Tommy Makem and the Clancy Brothers, a very popular and successful Irish folk group.

I asked Marty, "What are you doing here?"

"I'm signing this girl. I met her when she was on the same bill with Tommy and the Brothers at the Blue Angel, and I liked her so much that I'm going to manage her."

I backed off completely; I would never dream of poaching on someone else's act. Because I had been too busy making arrangements for Newport and Hartford to talk to this girl, Marty Erlichman had seized the opportunity. And I lost the chance to manage Barbra Streisand.

During the height of the Rascals' popularity, I established a new office at 75 East 55th Street, in the same building as Bert Block, a well-known agent. Also in that building was my friend Albert Grossman and Mort Lewis, who managed the Brothers Four, a very hot folk act.

One day, I was working in the office and got a call from Frankie Valli. Frankie and the Four Seasons had had many hits. I had presented the Four Seasons when I produced the Paramount holiday shows and we had stayed loosely in touch over the years.

"Sid, we broke up with our manager," Frankie said, "and I'd like to talk to you about the possibility of you taking us on. I know how busy you are, and I don't want to come to your office because of the tumult I'm sure is going on there. Would you consider coming to my home in New Jersey? I heard you like Italian food, so I promise you the best home-made Italian meatballs you ever ate!" Frankie had evidently done some research.

"Frankie, you're on!" I said. Who could pass up the promise of the best meatballs ever?

A few days later, I drove to Frankie's house. We spent a fun few hours together. The meatballs were fabulous. I listened to Frankie's tales of woe about the group's former manager. But, I had also done some research of my own. There were stories of how the Four Seasons used to fight amongst themselves. There was even a story of them getting embroiled in a verbal battle, as they were walking to catch a plane, which became so heated that they missed the flight!

I begged off. "Frankie, I'm gonna miss these meatballs, but I'm just too busy. It wouldn't be fair to you and the guys. I don't think I can do the job you need done. I'm sorry. You deserve a full-time manager."

I didn't take on Frankie and the Four Seasons because I didn't want to get in the middle of another squabbling group. I was in the middle of one battling group and that was enough for me. But I sure did enjoy those meatballs!

Very often, friends and associates in the business would give my name to aspiring singer-songwriters and bands who were looking to establish themselves in the music scene. I made a point of meeting with the young musicians who came to my office, no matter how busy I was. I enjoyed hearing new talent and tried to be as encouraging and helpful as I could.

One day a handsome young man walked into my office and introduced himself. I recognized his name and knew that he had written a number one song for The Monkees.

"How can I help you?" I asked.

"I need a manager."

"Well, I don't think that, as a songwriter, you need a manager."

"That's true, but I want to start singing and performing. I also play the guitar. I think I could use a manager now for guidance and to help me become a performer."

"I understand," I said. "The first thing you ought to do is go down to the Bitter End and ask for Billy Fields and Freddie Weintraub. They run talent showcases and they can help you with your presentation. Billy, in fact, was a vocalist and left a performing career to manage the club. He can really be helpful to you. Then, I think you should come back here at your convenience, bring your guitar and you can audition for me."

He stood up abruptly, looked at me and said, "I'll call you."

Years later, I found out that my use of the word "audition" had so offended him that Neil Diamond didn't want to have anything to do with me.

Maybe I should have said, Come back and play me some of your songs. Or, Let me hear your music. Anything but, You can audition for me. Not in my wildest dreams had I ever imagined offending anyone, especially such a great talent as Neil Diamond. He was a very sensitive kid.

On another occasion, a short young man came into my office while my secretary Sherry was at lunch. I motioned to him to sit down as I was finishing a call. When I hung up, I looked up and gave him my full attention.

"Mr. Bernstein," he said, "would you have a few minutes for me?"

"Certainly. How can I help you?"

"Look, Mr. Bernstein, I would like to talk to you about management."

I looked at this very nondescript young man and wondered what this kid needed a manager for, so I asked him.

"Well, a friend and I have a record coming out on Columbia. It should be out in the next week or two, and I'd like to get a manager and an agent, as we have neither. Up until now, I've been doing the bookings myself."

"Do you have the album or anything I could listen to?"

"No, but the record will be out in a week or two. I should have brought a tape but I forgot. I saw your name in a directory in one of the industry magazines, so I decided to come to your office. There were a few other names who are listed as having offices in this building, too."

"What do you do?"

"Well, I write and play the guitar, and my friend and I sing," he answered.

"Tell me…who else do you have on your list?"

He looked down at a paper and he said, "Albert Grossman and Mort Lewis."

"That's a good start you have there," I said. "Both men are friends of mine, and both are terrific managers. In fairness to yourself, you should stop in at both their offices and try to see both Albert and Mort. Also, try to meet Bert Block on this floor because he's a great agent and you said you need an agent. You can use my name to help you get in the door. After you've seen everybody, come back and see me and let me know how you made out."

"Thank you, Mr. Bernstein. You've been very helpful. Can I drop my album off to you when it's released?"

"By all means. I look forward to hearing it!"

He left and went on his quest for a manager and an agent. The next day, Mort Lewis called me.

"Sid, I want to thank you for sending that kid up to me yesterday. He's really an interesting and very bright kid. I spent quite a bit of time with him, and I'm going to take him and his buddy on."

"You're welcome, Mort. I remember the kid, but I forgot his name."

"His name is Paul Simon."

While I was still working with Jerry Weintraub at Management Three,

I began to hear talk among industry friends about a musical revue called *Grease* being performed by a theatrical company in Chicago. The word of mouth about *Grease* was great, so I decided that I had to go and see it for myself. I tracked down the name of the theatre in Chicago where *Grease* was playing and called the manager. He confirmed that the show was becoming very successful and that there was a lot of buzz in Chicago about it. I explained to the company manager about my background, and he invited me to come to Chicago to see the production.

"People are talking about the show and sales are building very nicely," the manager informed me.

In my opinion, nothing makes a show successful like word of mouth. Not advertising, not hype, not promotions. Not even critical acclaim can match the effectiveness of word of mouth to generate ticket sales.

As it turned out, my friend Dick Clark, the enormously successful TV host, producer and entrepreneur, had also heard about *Grease*. Dick was based on the West Coast and he heard that I had been calling the theatre in Chicago, making inquiries about the show.

Dick called me. "Sid, we're old friends and we go back a long way. I understand that you're interested in that show, *Grease*, in Chicago. Why compete? Why don't we work on this together? It's been a long time coming; we really should do something together, don't you think?"

"I agree. I would love to be partners with you, Dick."

Dick and I discussed a plan and we agreed that if we were to be successful in acquiring the rights to the show, we would become partners. During our conversation, I got the idea that Dick was planning on flying to Chicago from L.A. to begin negotiations to acquire the show for a Bernstein-Clark production. Dick had the impression that I was going to fly from New York to Chicago to handle the negotiations.

Several weeks passed and I had not heard from Dick. I called him and asked if he had made any progress with *Grease*. Dick told me that he was waiting to hear from me about my meetings in Chicago. We both said "uh-oh!" together. Neither Dick nor I went to Chicago because we each thought that the other was going to go. It was a classic case of miscommunication.

A young couple from New York traveled to Chicago and made a deal with whoever owned the rights to *Grease*, to buy it and bring it to New York. The rest is history. *Grease* made millions of dollars on Broadway. It eventually became a blockbuster Hollywood film starring John Travolta and Olivia Newton-John.

Dick and I can only laugh through our tears.

No matter how involved I was managing Laura Branigan's career, I would still keep an eye out for any interesting and talented young musicians who would perform in clubs throughout New York City. I would frequent several clubs and became friendly with some of the owners and managers, who would let me know when certain performers would be appearing.

Rick Newman was one of the club owners with whom I was friendly. He owned Catch A Rising Star, a popular nightclub not too far from my home that featured up-and-coming comics. I would often stop by to say hello to Rick and see who the next great comedy stars might be. Even though it was a comedy club, from time to time Rick allowed singers on the stage at Catch A Rising Star.

On one of my visits, I heard a young singer who had a voice that wouldn't quit. She looked like she weighed less than 100 pounds, but she could she could really power up when it came to her singing. What a killer voice! She was a favorite of mine and I went out of my way to hear her whenever she performed. Rick always made sure that I knew when she would be singing. Whenever Rick called, I would drop what I was doing and make my way to the club. Rick was also taken with her and he eventually became her manager.

One day, Rick called me. "Sid, the other night after you left, the A&R guy from Chrysalis Records came in with Barbara Skydell from Premier Talent and they flipped over your favorite singer. They are both going to sign her. She's all set. I'm managing her; she's going to record for Chrysalis, and Premier is going to handle her bookings. But here's my problem: you know I'm a café owner. What the hell do I know about management? I'd love for you to be my partner in this deal. Sid, we'll be co-managers."

"Listen, Rick, I'm so involved with Laura Branigan that I couldn't even think of taking on another responsibility. I really can't do this to Laura. I'm sorry, but I just can't do it."

"Okay, I understand."

When Rick's singer's record came out on Chrysalis, it was an immediate hit.

Bert Padell, Rick Newman's business manager and a friend of mine, called me up.

"Sid, are you crazy? You told Rick that you don't want to be his partner in the management of his female artist? Are you nuts? Her record is a runaway hit! Chrysalis is shipping records as fast as they can press them! I'd really like to meet with you so we can discuss this further. Please come to my office, as soon as you can."

When I got to Bert's office later that week, Rick Newman was there, too. Rick spoke first.

"Sid, I'm sorry, but I had to tell Bert about our conversation because I need help. I know you like Laura Branigan and are committed to her career, but why should that interfere with what I proposed? I'll do my share, but I'd really rather have you as my partner. As I told you, this management stuff is really not my thing."

Bert piped in. "Sid, you're crazy to turn this offer down. You and Rick are good friends; you get along. It'll be great for both of you. C'mon, Sid!"

"I'm sorry. I can't to it to Laura."

"You see, Rick? I told you," said Bert. "The guy is nuts!"

As I walked out of Bert's office, I was somewhat disappointed. I felt a real friendship with Rick and I would have liked to help him with Pat Benatar.

Not long after turning down Rick Newman's offer to manage Pat Benatar, I got a call from a female singer who I had known and whose work I admired. She invited me to lunch at a well-known restaurant, and I could never turn down the opportunity to have a delicious meal with lovely company.

While we sat at the table waiting for our order, she said, "Sid, I need a manager. My husband has been managing me, but we're getting divorced and I don't want him to manage me anymore. My career's doing well, so I feel that I need someone with whom I can feel comfortable and who will take care of me. Would you consider being my manager?"

"I don't have to think about it. I've been working on Laura Branigan's career for quite a while now, and I don't really think it would be fair to take on another female artist. Your career has taken off and you are going to need lots of attention. You deserve to have someone who can devote the time and energy necessary to maintain your career. I'm sorry, but I'm not taking on any new female singers right now."

"I appreciate your loyalty, Sid. It's refreshing to see. I can promise you that it wouldn't make a difference to me. You could manage us both."

"I know, I'm sorry, but I just can't do it to Laura," I said to Melissa Manchester.

I often wonder what would have happened if I had said yes to all those great artists who wanted me to become involved in their careers. I have no doubt that it would have been rewarding, but I have no regrets. For whatever reason, it just wasn't meant to be. That's life.

Chapter 22: **THE ATTACK ON GEORGE HARRISON**

ON FRIDAY, DECEMBER 31, 1999, I WAS SHOCKED to learn that a crazed individual who had an irrational obsession with the Beatles had broken into George Harrison's estate outside of London and attacked George and his wife Olivia.

My first reaction was "Oh, no, not again!" I wondered whether we were going to be confronted with another tragedy like the one we experienced nearly 20 Decembers ago when John Lennon was shot.

My second thought was that it was quite ironic that George, who had always been the Beatle most private and reclusive and concerned with security, had not been immune from an attack that threatened his life.

The television reports began to filter through the various news media and report that George and his wife were expected to make complete recoveries. I breathed a sigh of relief.

And once again the phone calls started coming from all over the world. I started to field telephone calls from media outlets asking for a statement. I told them all basically the same thing—I was thankful that George would be okay and yet terribly sorry that he had to suffer physical pain and considerable mental anguish before he would be able to put this terrifying incident behind him. I explained that my relationship with George, while always cordial, had not been as close and continuous as my relationship with John and Paul. I attributed this to the fact that John had become a New Yorker and we had the opportunity to meet and interact from time to time. Paul married Linda who was a huge fan of the Rascals and also was from a New York suburb. Paul and Linda spent a lot of time in and around New York with their family, so we had the opportunity to see each other on various occasions.

Ringo lived everywhere but New York and consequently we never had many chances to reconnect.

George was another story altogether. He shunned the limelight and stayed pretty much to himself. His homes were always protected and, as I said before, he had always been very concerned with security. I liked George from the moment that I met him in the Plaza Hotel room so many years ago. I found him to be introspective and reserved, yet highly spiritual. He is a gentle man and a gentleman.

George is a man of great sensitivity, which he demonstrated on one of the Rascals' trips to Great Britain. The Rascals were in London for some performances, and George invited them to come to a studio where he was recording. After being in the studio for but a few minutes, George received a call regarding an emergency at his home and left the studio immediately. Later that day, he called to apologize profusely and made plans to send his limo the next day to pick the Rascals up and bring them to his home for a visit. The next day, as planned, George's limo came to our hotel and picked the Rascals up and drove them to his home, where they spent several hours hanging out and listening to music. Even though it was a tough time for George, he was determined to extend his hospitality and spend the time with the Rascals.

More than 30 years after the Beatles broke up, it is still impossible for them to find the peace and privacy that I am sure they must crave. But the truth is that they will never be free from the unrelenting interest, curiosity and adoration of their fans. And furthermore, all of us who had anything to do with the Beatles will always be expected to provide insights into that unbelievable chapter of entertainment and cultural history. The music and the hysteria have ensured that.

Chapter 23: **BASHERT**

I HAVE BEEN INCREDIBLY FORTUNATE AND BLESSED IN MY LIFE. My parents could not have been more loving or nurturing. My friends have been true, loyal and unbelievably supportive. My wife has been my devoted partner and confidant. Together, we have raised six of the nicest people you will ever meet.

I have never measured success by accolades, honor or money. I believe my life has been successful because of how loving, caring and supportive my family is.

Some people may say that I have been very lucky.

I have saved this story for last because I think that it exemplifies what I believe has been a recurring theme in my life: the presence of providence and the role that destiny plays in all our lives.

As I mentioned earlier, Benji Greenberg is one of the world's great Beatles fans. He has a Beatles memorabilia collection that is both extensive and valuable. He is crazy about the Beatles.

One day Benji called to tell me that Paul McCartney was going to be videotaping for MTV at the Ed Sullivan Theatre for the introduction of a new album.

"Sid, could you please get some tickets so that we can go?"

"Benji, I don't think I'm going to go. I'll listen to the album when it comes out, but I really don't want to go watch a TV shoot. I've seen enough of them in my life. I will, however, try to get you a ticket."

I started by calling Joe Dera, a longtime friend of mine and Paul McCartney's publicist.

"Joe, I need a ticket for Paul's MTV shoot. Can you help me? My friend Benji Greenberg is desperate to go."

"Sid, I don't have any tickets. I've given all mine to the press. But, if I come across an extra one, it's yours."

Next, I called John Eastman, Linda McCartney's brother.

"Sidley (his nickname for me), not only don't I have any tickets, but Joe Dera's office is calling me to see whether or not I can give back the few extra tickets that they gave me! I had to disappoint them because I've already given them all away. I'm really sorry, I just don't have any tickets."

Benji kept calling me. "Sid, please! I have to be there!"

I kept telling him that there were no tickets, but I was working on it. Benji can be very insistent, and when it comes to the Beatles, the word no does not exist.

Finally, on the day of the taping, Joe Dera called. "Sid, we don't have a ticket, but if your friend Benji will come to the door, my right-hand lady Rachel will walk him in."

"Thanks, Joe. I really appreciate it. Benji will be there."

I called Benji, who vowed to get to the Ed Sullivan Theatre. Because of a nor'easter, the weather had been terrible all day and the trains from Westchester had been cancelled. The roads were flooded out, and I wondered if Benji could make it into Manhattan.

Benji said, "I'll get there, Sid, even if I have to run all the way."

On the evening of the taping, Jackie Mason, the great comedian, called me.

"Sid, could you meet me at the Edison Hotel this evening? Herman Badillo (a local New York politician) is thinking about running for Mayor and he wants my support. You're good at this stuff, and I value your opinion. Would you please come?"

"Jackie, first of all, I'm about to have dinner with my family. Secondly, have you looked outside lately? There's a nor'easter under way! It's been raining torrentially all day! I'll never get a cab. I don't think so, Jackie."

Jackie implored, "Sid, the meeting with Herman isn't until 8:30. By then you'll be finished with dinner, and maybe the weather will let up. Please try to come."

I decided that I didn't want to disappoint Jackie. I thought I'd try and make it downtown to the Edison. After dinner, I took my raincoat and told Gerry and the kids that I was going to make an attempt to get a cab and go meet Jackie, "…but don't be too surprised if I'm back up here in 15 minutes." The rain was still coming down in buckets, and I didn't have much hope of making it to the Edison.

When I got downstairs, I could see that, although there was hardly any traffic, the rain was so heavy that the vehicles that were on the road were moving very slowly. Visibility was extremely poor and everyone driving was being extra careful. Cabs were repeatedly passing me up; some were empty but they probably couldn't see me behind the curtain of rain that was falling. I was very cold and wet. I thought of going back upstairs where it was warm and comfortable, but a cabby spotted me from the opposite side of the street and began working his way laterally across the avenue. He came to a stop in front of me and I jumped in.

"The Edison Hotel, please." The foreign-born cabby seemed to me to be a new driver in New York and was unfamiliar with the location of the Edison Hotel. I had to reassure him that I could direct him there. As we slowly proceeded downtown, I opened my coat and got comfortable. I put my hands down on the seat and felt some sort of chain. I pulled the chain out from where it had become lodged in the crack of the seat and saw that it had a plastic rectangular card attached to it. I asked the cabby to turn on the passenger light: to read the laminated card. It read:

I slapped my cheeks and pinched myself. Was I dreaming? When I determined that this was no dream, I looked around for the angels. I read and re-read the card to make sure I wasn't mistaken. I was stunned and in total wonderment.

I immediately told the cabby that our destination had changed. I told him to make a right on Second Avenue and 53rd Street and to head west on 53rd Street until I told him to stop. When we got to the Ed Sullivan Theatre, I jumped out of the cab and ran to the stage door. Flashing my newly discovered staff pass, I asked the two security men, "Will this get me in?"

"This will get you anywhere you want to go," one of them responded.

"Come right in," the other one said, as he opened the door.

I walked into the theatre. The seating area was dark and Linda and Paul were onstage playing with the band. I spotted an empty aisle seat and slid into it. Joel Siegel, a well-known New York theatre, movie and TV critic, was in the next seat. He and I were old friends, and I whispered a hello to him and couldn't help adding, "You wouldn't *believe* how I got here."

"Sid, who more than you should be here?"

I smiled and let it pass. I removed my wet raincoat and settled in to watch the taping.

The music was pure McCartney and the time flew. When the performance ended, I told Joel that I was going to try to say hello to Paul and Linda and asked if he and his fiancée, who was with him, cared to join me. Joel replied that they hadn't eaten dinner yet and they were starving. He invited me to join them at the Stage Deli after I had seen Paul and Linda. I told Joel that I would see them later.

I made my way to the door that led to the dressing room wing of the theatre. The memories of that wild night when the Beatles did their first

Sullivan show flooded my mind. I asked the two security men guarding the dressing room access if I could proceed. When they saw the staff pass around my neck, they opened the door for me. I walked towards the elevator that would take me to the dressing rooms. John Eastman was there, waiting with his family.

"Sidley!" he exclaimed. "How did you get in?"

"John, it's just too long of a story, and you wouldn't believe it anyway. I just want to say a quick hello to Paul and your sister. Would that be okay?"

"Sure, go right ahead. Take the elevator. They're upstairs." I showed the elevator man my pass and he took me up. When I got off the elevator, Richard Ogden, Paul's manager, was in the small waiting area outside the dressing rooms.

"Hey, Sid! What are you doing here?!" he said as he greeted me.

"Oh, Richard, it's a long and unbelievable story."

"Where's Paul?" I added.

"Over there in the first dressing room."

I walked towards the open door of the dressing room where a security man was standing, but Paul saw me through the open door and came out. "Sid!" he exclaimed as he walked out. We hugged and Paul asked, "Are you alone, Sid?"

"I couldn't bring my family, Paul. It was tough enough for me to get in, let alone the whole family. And, besides that, the story of how I managed to get here is amazing!"

"How did you get here, Sid? Tell me what happened," he said, with a look of great interest on his face.

I quickly related the entire story to Paul. "I felt like an angel had put the staff pass there, Paul, I really did."

"It was the hand of God," Paul said as he tapped my forearm. "The hand of God."

"In Yiddish, Paul, you would say that it was *bashert.*"

"*Bashert?*" Paul liked the word. "*Bashert?* What does it mean?" he questioned.

"Destiny or the hand of God."

"And how do you spell it?"

"B-A-S-H-E-R-T. Bashert," I spelled it for him again, and he repeated it a few times.

"Paul, where's Linda? I want to say a quick hello."

"She's in the next dressing room," and he pointed to a closed door. "She'll be surprised to see you."

I went to Linda's dressing room and knocked on the door. Linda answered. When she saw me, she was indeed surprised. She greeted me warmly, hugged me, and kissed me on both cheeks. She introduced me to several elderly people who were in the dressing room visiting with her.

"This is Sid Bernstein, everyone! The man who introduced Paul to America!" I said hello to her visitors.

"Linda, I just wanted to see you and say hello," I said as I kissed her cheek, and made my exit.

As I was walking to the elevator, I saw Paul talking to John Eastman and pointing toward my staff pass. As I got closer, I could hear him say to his brother-in-law, "...the will of God, or the hand of God."

"Paul, are you telling John the story?"

"Will I ever forget it, Sid?"

"And what is that Yiddish word you taught me? I want to tell John."

"*Bashert*, Paul. *Bashert*."

Author's Epilogue

I have spent the better part of the past year working on this book and renewing my friendship with Sid Bernstein.

As Sid's proceeded to tell his story, his innocence, lack of guile, genuine concern for people and gentleness struck me. I wondered whether readers would believe his story. Did I really expect people living in the year 2000 to believe that this man would turn down opportunity after opportunity because he felt that his obligations to his parents and family took precedence? Where was the anger and rage when situations demanded it? Where was the greed so commonplace in the music business? How could he be an integral part of so many legendary events and not have a gargantuan ego? Where was the self-promotion so characteristic in men of great accomplishment? Where was the preoccupation with sex, drugs and gossip that is so prevalent in rock and roll? How can anybody be so naïve?

The truth is that Sid Bernstein is a man from another time. A time when you tried to find what was best about someone. A time of civility. A time when you didn't pry into other people's personal lives. A time when parental respect and family loyalty were paramount. A time when you weren't measured by your monetary success. A time when being a mensch mattered most of all.

Sid is human, to be sure. So human that he can, even now at this stage of his life, still dream the dreams that legends are made of. So human that he envisions events and projects that would be daunting for a man half his age. Childlike in his goodness and gentility. A child who still believes that all things are possible.

You will have to search very far and very wide to find someone like Sid Bernstein.

—Arthur Aaron

Music Industry Glossary

Manager: One who advises and guides an artist with his/her career. The manager is paid a percentage of the gross earnings of the performer.

Business Manager: One who controls an artist's finances. The business manager pays the bills and often advises the artist on how to spend and invest their money. The business manager generally is paid a percentage of the performer's gross earnings.

Agent: One who procures live-performance engagements for an artist. The agent negotiates the contract, helps set the fee and tries to ensure a comfortable working environment for the artist. The agent generally is paid 10% of the gross salary that the artist earns for the performance.

Publicist: One who interacts with members of the press and the various media on behalf of an artist. The publicist helps the artist choose where, when and with whom to grant interviews. The publicist also helps to create a positive public persona for the artist and their music.

Promoter/Impresario/Presenter: One who presents an artist in live performance. The promoter/impresario/presenter secures the venue (the place where the artist will perform), prints the tickets and programs, arranges for publicity and press coverage and is responsible for the sale of tickets. The promoter/impresario/presenter hires the artist and is paid either a flat fee, a percentage of the gross or a share of the profits after deducting expenses.

Artists & Repertoire (A&R): At a record company, the staff person charged with finding and signing a new recording artist, and then helping the artist find the right producer to supervise the recording sessions. The A&R person often searches for material for the artist to record.

Producer: In the recording business the producer is the one who brings together all the elements required for the record-making process. The producer procures the recording studio, works with the recording engineer, the songwriter(s), the arranger, the musicians, the vocalist(s) and others to provide the atmosphere and the organization necessary to make recordings. The producer can be a member of the record company's staff or an independent brought in from the outside. The producer generally is paid a percentage of the recordings sold by the artist(s).

Index

Aaron, Arthur 233-234
ABBA (Anna, Benny, Bjorn, and Annifrid) 234-237, 243
ABC-TV 220, 264
Abe's Steak House (Manhattan) 245, 261
Academy Awards 9, 222
Academy of Music (Manhattan) 141, 151-152, 172, 230, 258
Adderley, Cannonball 66
ADP (see "Sen. Frank Lautenberg")
Aida (at Carnegie Hall) 109, 111, 121, 130
Alan (stage manager for Richard Pryor show) 195
Ali, Muhammad 295
Allen, Fred 8
Allen, Woody 176, 241-242
Altshuler, Bob 210-211
American Broadcasting Co. (see "WABC" and "ABC-TV")
American Guild of Variety Artists 63
American Legion 39
American Veterans Committee (AVC) 40, 42; Harry Hopkins chapter 39
Anastos, Ernie 267
Andersen, Stig 235-237
Andrews Sisters, The 235
Animals, The 140-141
Anka, Paul 252
Ann-Margret 246
Anti-Semitism 5, 18-22, 64-65, 67, 92
Apollo Theatre (Harlem) 5, 55-59, 61, 76
Arista Records 210, 243
Arledge, Roone 245
Arlen, Harold 49
Armstrong, Louis 58, 66
Aronowitz, Al 131, 134
Artists and Repertoire (A&R) 193, 256, 301
Arts & Leisure (see The New York Times)
Aspinall, Neil 156
Associated Booking Co. 177
Astaire, Fred 70
Atlantic City Jazz Festival, The (N.J.) 60

Atlantic Records 153, 163, 165-167, 169, 175, 181, 182, 197, 202-203, 257-260, 286-287
Aurelio, Dick 155
Auster's Egg Cream Stand 76
Avery Fisher Hall (Lincoln Center) 184, 242

Bacharach, Burt 164-165
Backstreet Boys, The 243
Badillo, Herman
Baez, Joan 191-193, 278
Bailey, Pearl 183-184
Band, The 176
Banks, Murray 41
Barclay, Eddie (Barclay's Records) 182
Band, The 176
Barge, The (The Hamptons) 153-154, 163-165
Barney Greengrass (Manhattan) 274
Barron, Hank 110, 115, 119, 121
Bart, Ben 63, 185-186
Bart, Jan (see "Sol Strausser")
Barsalona, Frank 177
Basie, Count 60, 66, 120, 136-137, 241
Baskin-Robbins 254, 261
Bassey, Shirley 120, 130, 136
Battle of the Bulge 30
Bay City Rollers 243-247, 259
Beatles iii, 63, 139, 140, 141, 142-146, 177, 179-182, 184,187-188, 189-191, 194, 189-191, 194, 201, 227, 236-237, 245, 247-249, 257, 263, 266, 268, 269, 277, 289, 291, 293, 303-304, 305, 307
  Preparations for first trip to the U.S. 100-130
  The Ed Sullivan Show 126-127
  Carnegie Hall 131-136
  Professionalism 135
  First Shea Stadium concert 150-162
  Second Shea Stadium concert 166-175
  Break-up 195-196
  Refuse to be reunited 233-234, 247-248, 252-254
Beacon Theatre (Upper West Side) 286
Beatlemania 100-101, 111, 114, 116, 121, 122-123, 125, 127, 130, 133, 135, 156-157, 159-162, 171, 243
Beatty, Warren 209
Bee Gees 179-180
Belafonte, Harry 38, 196, 242
Bell Records 215, 243
Bellson, Louis 184
Benatar, Pat 302
Benihana (Manhattan) 273
Bennett, Dagal 86
Bennett, Danny 86
Bennett, Sandy 86
Bennett, Tony 76-88, 102, 103, 105, 109, 111-112, 120, 136-137, 166, 172
Benton, Brook 59, 67, 296
Berle, Milton 15, 44, 46, 47
Bernstein, Adam iv, (birth) 137-138, 141, 146-147, 187,192-193, 210, 227, 250, 261, 266, 268-269, 273, 277-278, 279, 305-306
Bernstein, Beau iv, (birth) 199, 210, 277-279, 286-288, 305-306
Bernstein, Casey iv, 207, (birth) 210, 273, 305-306
Bernstein, Denise iv, (birth) 141, 187, 210, 242-243, 249, 305-306 261, 267, 273, 305-306
Bernstein, Dylan iv, (birth) 187, 210, 250, 261, 277-279 286, 305-306
Bernstein, Etienne iv, (birth) 223, 266, 273, 277-279, 283, 286-288, 305-306
Bernstein, Gerry (Geraldine Gale) iv, v, 52-54, 56, 60, 70, 83, 85, 87-88, (marriage to Sid) 89-95, 112, 116, 119, 127, 129, 130, 136-138, 141, 153, 156,174, 180, 187, 190, 192, 198, 207, 210, 214, 220, 223, 254, 260-261, 264-265, 268, (tries moving to Hawaii) 271-273, 278-279, 296-297, 305-306
Bernstein, Ida 3, 15, 36, 38, 47, 73, 86-87, 90-91, 93-95, 116-117, 119, 126, 153 (death) 189-190, 199, 305
Bernstein, Israel 3, 15, 36-38, 47, 86-87, 90-91, (death) 93-94, 305
Bernstein, Leonard 52
Bernstein, Rachel 3, 15, 36-39

313

Bernstein, Sid (S.B.)
  Nicknames
    "Bernie" 29, 32
    "Buddy Burnside" 22-23
    "Mr. Sidney" 60
    "Sidney Bernstein" (adoption) 15
    "Sidley" 308
    "Simcha" 3, 36, 37, 91
    "Your boy, Sidney'" 33, 59
Berry, Chuck 189
Bethel '94 Festival 277-283
Biegelman, David 65, 68
Billboard 175; (annual convention) 198, 210, 215
Bitter End, The 176, 194, 196, 220, 241, 298
"Black is Black" (Los Bravos) 182
Blair, Sallie 49-51
Blakey, Art 66
Blazers (London) 181
Block, Bert 297
Blood, Sweat & Tears 178, 197-198
Bloom, Evan 278, 279
Bloom, Julius 82, 107
Blue Angel, The (Manhattan) 297
Blue Grotto, The (Little Italy) 216, 219
Blue Notes, The 227
Blues Project, The 176-178, 179-180
Blum, Eddie 296
Blumenfeld, Roy 176
Bonheur, Claudy Vilfroy 34-37, 211-215
Bonheur, Dr. 213-214
Bon Soir (Greenwich Village) 297
Bond, James 136
Borge, Victor 87
Boston Garden, The 274
Boston Herald I67
Boston Pops, The 252
Bowes, Major 10, 12, 13,
Brando, Marlon 9
Branigan, Laura 254-262, 271, 300-302
Brass Buttons, The 204
Brass Rail, The 14
Brasserie, The 90
Breen, Bobby 8
Brian Epstein Theatre, The (Liverpool) 289
Briarwood Singers 131, 135
Brigati, Eddie 153, 199, 204-206
Bright, Jackie 63

Brillstein, Bernie 208
British Broadcasting Company (BBC-TV) 221, 264, 291
Brokaw, David 263
Brokaw, Norman 263
Brokaw, Sandy 263
Bronx Coliseum, The 6, 8
Bronx Hospital, The 21
Brothers Four 297
Brown, Charlie 46, 49
Brown, Cynthia 46
Brown, Eva 53
Brown Derby, The (Catskills) 46-47
Brown's Hotel (The Catskills) 4, 46-47, 49
Brown, James 63, 184-186, 191, 295
Brown's Playhouse (The Catskills) 47
Brown, Ruth 49, 57-59
Brubeck, Dave 66
Buckingham Palace 252-253
Buddah Records 232
Bunting, John 233-234
Burden, Eric 141
Burnside, Buddy (see "Sid Bernstein")
"Burnside Chat, The" (AVC Bulletin) 39
Burton, Laurie 166
Bush, Barbara 221
Bush, George 221
Bush, Mrs. (see "Morningside Hotel")
Butterfield Blues Band 278
Buttons, Red 9, 289

Café Au Go Go (Greenwich Village) 176
Café Central (Dijon) 212; (as GI nightclub) 34-35
Camp Chipinaw (The Catskills) 277
Camp Upton (Long Island), WWII 27
Campo, Pupi 46
Canned Heat 278
Cannibal and the Headhunters 156
Cantor, Eddie 8, 9, 46, 47
Cantor Show, The (see "The Eddie Cantor Show")
Capitol Hotel (Broadway) 44
Capitol Records 114, 117, 124, 126, 271

Capitol Theatre, The (Broadway) 10, 13
Capozzi, Jay 204-205
Carey, Gov. Hugh 232, 238-241
Carlin, George 77, 120
Carnegie Hall iii, v, 52, 70, 78-86, 102, 105-111, 113, 115, 117, 119-120, 121, 122,130-140, 152, 157, 175, 177, 182, 184, 189-190, 221, 227-229, 241-242, 245, 258, 261, 277, 283-284, 292
Carnegie Hall (film) 105
Carroll, Diahann 183
Carroll, Jean 73
Carson, Johnny 252
Carter, June 189
Caruso, Enrico 4, 10
Cash, Johnny 189
Cashbox 175
Cassius (son of Deodato) 227
Castle, Roy 292-293
Catch A Rising Star 301
Cavaliere, Felix 153, 169, 182-183, 199-200, 204, 206, 228, 247
CBS studio 126, 135
CBS-TV 264
Central Hotel (Dijon) 33
Central Park 3, 95, 183, 261, 263, 267, 274, 284, 288
Channing, Carol 232, 239
Chapin, Harry 243
Charles, Ray 49, 62, 66, 163, 183
Chevalier, Maurice 87
China Club, The (Manhattan) 286
Chitlin' Circuit 59
Christie's iii,
Chrysalis Records 301
Citibank 151
Clancy Brothers, The 297
Clapton, Eric 179
Clark, Dick 300
Clark, Ramsey 242
Clark, Rudy 169
Cliff, Jimmy iv, v,
Cliffwalk Manor Hotel (Newport) 67
Cocker, Joe 278
Cohen, Alan 264
Cohen, Emil 47
Cohn, Roy 262
Coleman, Dr. Lester 71-72
Coles, Honi 58
Collins, Judy 196, 209

314

Collins, Pat 265
Coltrane, John 66
Columbia Broadcasting System (see "CBS-TV")
Columbia Records 78; 82-83; 86; 103; 163; (international convention) 203-206, 230-231; 257
Communist Party, The 23
Comeback Diary 32-33, 35
Concord Hotel, The (The Catskills) 4, 281-282
Conrad, Johnny 62
Cooke, Barbara 289
Cooke, Sam 63, 295
Cooper, Alice 176
Cooperman, Alvin 191-193, 194-195
Copacabana, The (Manhattan) 78-79, 261, 263
Coquelin, Le 89
Cornish, Gene 153, 181, 199, 204, 207
Cosell, Howard 245
Cosell Show, The (see The Howard Cosell Show)
Cotton Club Revue (Los Angeles) 49
Coughlin, Father 18
Country Joe and the Fish 282
"Cousin Brucie" (see "Bruce Morrow")
Cream 179
Creedence Clearwater Revival 200
Cronkite, Walter 116
Crosby, Chris 63
Crosby, Stills, Nash & Young 278
Cross-promotion (or "cross marketing") 173
Cugat, Xavier 41
Curbelos, The 43, 46
Curtiss, King 63, 156, 163
Cushman's Bakery 5
Cyrcle, The 174, 179

D-Day 28
D-5 28
Daily Express, The (London) 99-100
Daily Mirror, The 21, 30
Daily News, The (see "The New York Daily News")
Dakota, The (Central Park West) 249, 263-266
Dakota Station 60

Daley, Don 20
Damari, Shoshana 190
Danelli, Dino 153, 182-183, 199, 204, 206-207
Darin, Bobby 76
Dark Horse Tour (George Harrison) 227
Dave Clark Five, The 140-141
Davies, Barbara 251, 255
Davis, Bette 153, 209
Davis, Clive 204-206, 230-231, 243-244, 256
Davis, Miles 49, 56-60, 197-198, 200
Davis, Sammy, Jr., 251
Daytop Village (Manhattan) 289
Dean & Jean 63
DeBusscherre, Dave 242
Decca Records 163
Delli Venneris (South Bronx) 240-241
Delsener, Ron 251, 261
Denver, John 208, 220-222, 229-230
Deodato 227
Depression, The 6, 17
Dera, Joe 305-306
Diamond, Neil 298
Diamond Club, The (W. 47th St., N.Y.C.) 58-59
Diano, Frank 29-30
Diccio, Al 172-173
Dickinson, Angie 164-165
Dion and the Belmonts 76
Doc (stagehand at Carnegie Hall) 122
Domino, Fats 49, 59-60
Dorsey Band, The (see "The Tommy Dorsey Band")
Dowd, Tom 165-166, 199
Dreamworks 158, 200
Drew, Eleanor 62, 64-65
Drew, John 62, 64-68, 296
Dubrow's (Brooklyn) 28
Durante, Jimmy 65
Durbin, Deanna 8
Dylan, Bob 164, 176

Eagles, The (see "Joe Walsh")
Eastman, John 305, 309
Eastman, Lee 198
Eastman, Linda 198 (see also "Linda McCartney")
Eaton, Bob 269

Ed Sullivan Show, The 18, 112, 125-128, 135, 229, 245
Ed Sullivan Theater (Manhattan) 245-246. 305-307
Eddie (see "Old Chelsea Post Office")
Eddie Cantor Show, The 18, 9, 14
Ehrhard, Werner (see also "est")
Eisner, Michael 220
Ellington, Duke 60, 66
Elliot, Mama Cass 209
Emergency First Aid Station (Shea Stadium) 162
EMI Records 114
Empire Room, The (Waldorf-Astoria) 87
Empire State Building, The 251
Epic Records 193
Epstein, Barbara 187, 270
Epstein, Brian 101-107, 116-118, 122-126, 128-130, 132-135, 143-145, 147, 151,155, 160, 164, 169-175, 177, 179-184, (death) 186-188, 234, 268, 271, 290-291
Epstein, Clive 268, 270, 290
Epstein, Henry 290
Epstein, Queenie 103-104, 143-144, 150-151, 187, 268
Erlichman, Marty 297
Ernst & Young 293
Ertegun, Ahmet 153, 163, 165, 169, 202, 249, 257-258
Ertegun, Mica 257
Ertegun, Nesuhi 163, 202, 257-258
est (Ehrhard Seminar Training) 271-272
Eurovision Song Contest 235
Evans, Mal 156
Eveready Label Corporation, The 21, 23

Federal Bureau of Investigation, The (FBI) 22-23
Federal Communications Commission, The (FCC) 61
Ferguson, Maynard 60, 66, 252
Fiedler, Arthur 252
Fields, Billy 47, 67, 70, 72, 89, 115-116, 152, 157-159, 176, 189, 208, 250-251, 255, 296, 298
Fields, Freddy 65, 68-69

Fine & Schapiro (Upper West Side) 263-264
First Pennsylvania Bank, The 233-234
Fischer, Bobby 219-220
Fisher, Eddie 47
Flannery, Joe 289, 292
Fleetwood Mac 194
Flowers at concerts
  daffodils (Laura Nyro) 228
  rose petals (Joan Baez) 192-193
"Flight of the Bumblebee, The" (Esy Morales) 43
Font, Ralph 46
Food
  army 27
  chocolate 272
  eclairs in Paris 89, 215
  egg creams (recipe) 76
  hot dogs (with Abe Margolies) 285
  jelly doughnuts 5
  jellybeans 161
  lox, eggs, and onions 274
  meatballs 94, 297-298
  meat prices (see "sticker capaigns")
  napoleons 5, 70
  pizza 38, (Frank Sinatra and S.B., best in N.Y.C.) 240-241
  salami and chocolate 30-31
  shrimp fra diavolo 237-238
  spaghetti, meatballs, and garlic bread 216
  soup 6, (Pete Hamill's) 209
  veal Parmesan 38, 238
Ford, Henry 22
Forest Hills Tennis Stadium (Queens) 79, 111-112
Fort Dix 35
Fort Totten 28
Forum, The (Montreal) 70-72
Four Seasons, The (singing group) 63, 297-298
Fox, Manheim 189
Francis, Connie 44, 67, 296
Frank E. Campbell Funeral Home (Upper East Side) 266
Franklin, Aretha 163, 197
Franklin, Cass 45
Frank's Restaurant (Harlem) 232
Freed, Alan 61-62

G&R Cafe (The Bronx) 6

Gale, Kathleen 92-93, 149-150
Gallagher, Bill 82, 85
Gardner, Ava 241
Garfield, John 15
Garfield's Cafeteria (Brooklyn) 28
Garland, Judy 65-72, 73, 76, 80, 105, 120, 136, 231, 255
Gavin, Bill 167
Gavin Report, The 167-168
Gaye, Marvin 251
Geffen, David 158, 200-201, 228
Gelish, June 280-281
General Artists Corp. (GAC) 73-81, 83, 86-88, 90, 93-95, 99-102, 108, 110-112, 115, 116, 118-120, 126, 171, 173, 177
General Motors Corp. 200
Gentleman's Quarterly 164
George Washington Bridge 86
German-American Bund 22
Gerry and the Pacemakers 140-141
Gersh, Robert 280
Gertsman, Felix 78-79, 81
Getz, Stan 49, 60, 66, 252
Gilford, Jack 242
Gilley, Mickey 261, 263
Glaser, Joe 58, 177
Glazer, Bennett 197-198
"Gloria" (Laura Branigan) 259, 262
Goetz, Bernhard 262
Goldfinger 136
Goldberg, Maxie 4
Goldner, John 127-129
"Good Lovin'" (The Rascals) 169, 175, 181-182
Good Morning America (ABC-TV) 264-265
Goodman, Benny 133-134
Gore, Sen. Al Gore 277
Gore, Leslie 63
Gotterer, Barry 154
Graham, Bill 198, 227, 261
Grammy Awards (British version) 269
Grand Funk Railroad 194-195, 201
Grand Hotel (Dijon) 33, 211
Grateful Dead, The 198
Grease 300
Greek Theatre (Los Angeles) 221
Green, Adolph 242
Green, Charley 46
Green, Jackie, 177, 181
Green, Lenny 46

Greenberg, Benji 283-284, 305-306
Greenberg, Billy 283-284
Greenbriar Boys, The 189
Greene, Shecky 261
Greenfield, Manny 191-192
Greenspan, Ezra, M.D. 274-275
Griffin, Merv 220
Grinstein, Jeff 259-260
Grossinger's Hotel (The Catskills) 47
Grossman, Albert 176-177, 189, 297, 299
Grosvenor Hotel, The (London) 269-270
Grummond, Bill 79, 81, 111-112
Guber, Lee 238-239, 251-252
Gurock (Scotland) WWII 28
Guthrie, Arlo 278, 282

Hadassah 190
Hair 200
Halliwell, Bud 102-103
Hamill, Pete 209
Hampton, Lionel 66
Hanley, Bill 171
Hard Rock Café, The (Manhattan) 287
Harlow's 164-165
Harmonica Rascals, The 166
Harold Melvin and the Blue Notes 227
Harris, Julie 242
Harrison, George 124, 125, 130, 131, 160, 227-228, 253, 289-291, 293, 303-304
Harrison, Olivia 303
Hartman, David 265
Harvard University 276
Hauser, George 179
Havens, Richie 176, 200, 278, 282
Heathrow Airport 112, 113
Hendrix, Jimi 196, 231, 278
Herman's Hermits 140-141
Hessy's (Liverpool) 291
Hitler, Adolf 18, 19, 21, 22, 247
Hitzig, Rupert 245
Hoffman, Dustin 242
Holiday Paramount Show (see "Alan Freed")
Holloway, Brenda 156
Howard Johnson's 296
Hope, Bob 65-67, 105
Horne, Lena 87

316

Hotel Georges V (Paris) 215
Hotelings (Manhattan) 99-100
House of Flowers 183
"House of the Rising Sun, The" (The Animals)
Howard Cosell Show, The 245-246
Howard Theatre (Washington, D.C.) 59-60
Howe, Buddy 73-76, 81, 83, 86-88, 99, 101-102, 116, 118-120
Howe, Jean 119
Huggins, Charles 232-233
Hullabaloo 246
Hunter College 264-266
Hunt's Point Palace 17
Hurok, Sol 78
Hurt, Mississippi John 189
Hyman, Walter 49-51, 95, 110, 115, 118-121, 146, 153-154, 163, 167-169, 171,177

"I Ain't Gonna Eat My Heart Out Anymore" (The Rascals) 166-168
"I Left My Heart in San Francisco" (Tony Bennett) 82-83, 86, 136
"I Feel Pretty" (Gerry Bernstein) 53
"I Wanna Hold Your Hand" (Beatles) 117
Ice Palace, The (Haddonfield, N.J.) 68-70
ICM 247
Idlewild International Airport (Queens) 122
"If I Had a Hammer" (Trini Lopez)118
"Imagine" (John Lennon) 267
"Impossible Years, The" 168-169
Imus, Don 220
International Herald Tribune, The 247-248
Irish, Ned 184-186, 191
Iron Cross, The 22
Irving, Val 65
Isow's 105, 106, 115
Israel Bonds 14
Israeli All-Star Show 190
"It's Just a Matter of Time" (Brook Benton) 59

Jackson, John 252
Jagger, Mick 149, 152, 249, 257, 258

James, Carroll 114
James Monroe High School 9, 11, 14-16
Janitchek, Hans 247-248
Javits, Sen. Jacob K. 153
Jefferson Airplane 198, 278
Jensen Building 61
Jethro Tull 251
Jewish War Veterans 21
Jill (Bob Eaton's business manager) 269
Jilly's Restaurant (Manhattan) 190
Jimmie Lunceford Band, The 5
Joel, Billy 231
John, Elton 271
Jolson, Al 248, 249
Jones, Brian 138-139
Jones, James Earl 209
Jones, Quincy 66
Jones, Tom 165
Joplin, Janis 176, 200

Kalb, Danny 176-178
Kapralik, Dave 193-194
Kass, Art 232
Katz, Steve 176, 178
Katzenberg, Jeffrey 158, 174
Katz's Deli (Lower East Side) 30
Kaye, Sammy 42
Kelly (with cast on leg, at Carnegie Hall) 131-132
Kennedy, John F.: Sen. 38; Pres. (assassinated) 116-117,122, 209
Kennedy, Rose 209
King, Alan 169, 209, 232, 239, 245
King, Larry
Kingsbridge Armory 42
Kinks, The 140-141
Kinn, Maurice 100
Kirschner, Don 250
Kitchman, Leo 66, 128, 129, 156
Klein, Alan 63
Knight, Terry 200
Knock rummy, 7
Koch, Ed 267
Kooper, Al 176, 178
Kornfeld, Artie 190, 278
Krutek, Larry 259-261
Kuhn, Fritz 22
Kulberg, Andy 176
Kummer, Marty 208

La Guardia Airport 72, 240
La Playa Sextet 43
LaBelle, Patti 251
Laginestra, Rocco 203
Lang, Michael 190, 278
Lasher, Eve 39, 41, 44
Lasher, Jack 39, 41, 44
Latin Quarter (Manhattan) 45
Latin Quarter Management Company 45-46
Lautenberg, Sen. Frank 229
Lee, Brenda 76
Leeds Music Publishing Co. 235
Lefkowitz, Nat 232
Lefty's Pool Hall (The Bronx) 7, 16, 20, 23, 36, 42, 54, 58
Lennon 268-269
Lennon, Cynthia 270, 286-288
Lennon, John iv, v, 124-126, 130, 131, 158, 162, 175, 179, 181, 187, 222, 234, 237-238, 248-249, 253, (death) 263-267, 286, 289, 291, 303
Lennon, Julian 286-288
Lennon, Sean 267, 287-288
Lerner, Max 33, 99, 275, 277
Les Champs (Manhattan) 75, 245
Les Misérables 152
Levenson, Sam 41
Levy, Lou 235, 273
Lewis, Jerry 46
Lewis, Mort 189, 297, 299
Lewis, Patti 46
Lewis, Ramsey 66
Lewis, Vic 101-102, 118-119
Life I23, 116
Liff, Biff 53
Lindberg, Charles 22
Lindsay, Mayor John 154-155, 158
Lindsey, Mort 65, 68-69, 72, 80
Lindy's 14
Lipkin, Mrs. (see "Morningside Hotel")
"Liverpool Oratorio" (Paul McCartney) 283
Living Room, The (East Side nightclub) 76
Lloyd's of London 146, 171
London Times, The 99-100
Lopez, Trini 118
Los Bravos 182
"Love Me Do" (Beatles) 114, 117
Lunt-Fontanne Theatre (Broadway)

94
Lynne, Gloria 66

M&F Restaurant (The Bronx) 6
Machito 46
Mack (see "Old Chelsea Post Office")
Mack, Bessy 11, 12, 13,
Mack, Ted 11
MacLaine, Shirley 208-210, 255
Macombo (Los Angeles) 120
Madeline (WWII) 29-30
Madison Square Garden (52nd Street) 16, 17, 66, 127, 184
Madison Square Garden (Penn Station) 128, 129, 185-186, 190, 191-192, 194-195, 197-198, 200, 208, 227, 238-241, 250
Major Bowes Amateur Hour, The 10, 13
Major Bowes Traveling Amateur Show, The 10, 13
Makem, Tommy 297
Maltz, Bob 42, 58, 82-83
Mamas and the Papas, The (see "Mama Cass Elliot")
Mambo, the 48
Management Three 208-224 passim, 227, 299
Manchester, Melissa 302
Manchester Guardian, The 99, 101
Manero's (Greenwich, Conn.) 91
Mann, Manfred 140
Manze, George 20
Mardin, Arif 169, 199, 258
Margolies, Abe 16, 20, 22, (opens jewelry company) 36, 54-60, 62, 64, 66-68, 73-75,
  (opens Les Champs restaurant) 75, 91-92, 108-110, 116, 121-122, 133-134, 146, 171, 208, 224, 229
  (opens Abe's Steak House) 245, 261-262, 269, 274-275, 277,
  (death) 284-285, 292-293
Margolies, Gert 285
Marilyn (at Management Three) 208, 255
Mark Hellinger Theater, The (Manhattan)
Marshall, Alton 250-252
Marshall, Paul 198, 219

Martin, George 143, 269-271
Martin, Greg 269, 271
Martin Luther King Foundation 197
Mason, Jackie 306
Matthau, Celia 263
Matthau, Walter 263
MCA Records 227
McCarthy, Capt. 30
McCarthy, Joseph (McCarthy Hearings) 262
McCarthy, Kevin 242, 288
McCartney, Jamie 205, 271, 274
McCartney, "John" 130
McCartney, Linda (Eastman) 198, 205-206, 227, 270-271, 274, 283-284, 303, 305, 307-308
McCartney, Paul 123, 124, 125, 130, 131, 149, 158, 162, 179, 181, 187, 198, 205-206, 227, 234, 248, 253, 254, 274, 283-284, 286, 289-290, 292-293, 303, 305, 307-309
McCartney, Stella 205, 270-271
McDonald, Country Joe 278
McGovern, Sen. George 209
  (see also "Women for McGovern Concert")
McLachlan, Sarah 282
McWilliams, Joe 19-22
MCA Records 227
Mein Kampf 18
Melanie 282
Melody Maker, The 100
Melvin, Harold (see "Harold Melvin and the Blue Notes")
"Memories" (Laura Branigan) 255, 257
"Memphis Mafia" (Elvis Presley entourage) 215
Mercouri, Melina 209
Mercury Artists 46-49
Metroliner 233
Mets (see "The New York Mets")
Meyers, Larry 46, 49, 57, 59
MGM (Metro-Goldwyn-Mayer) 89, 168
Michelson, Bernie 291
Michelson, Sara 291
Mike (chauffeur for Walter Hyman) 153-154
Miller, Glenn 42, 134
Miss America Pageant 60
Mitch (promotion, Management Three) 260

Moat House (Liverpool) 289, 292
Moffatt, Tom 176, 178
Monday Night Football (ABC) 245
Monkees, The 250, 298
Montgomery, Gen. Bernard 28
Montreal Canadiens, The 70
Moody Blues, The 140-141, 208, 222, 230
Moon, Keith 181-182
Moore, Melba 231-233, 238-239
Moor's Motel (Provincetown) 94-95
Morales, Blanche 43, 45
Morales, Esy 43-45, 46
Morales, Humberto 43
Morales, Noro 41, 43, 46
Morgan, Jane 208
Morningside Hotel (The Catskills) 44, 46
Morrison, Charlie 120
Morrow, Bruce ("Cousin Brucie") 166-167, 173-174, 227, 267
Mott, Stewart 200
Mount Sinai Hospital 3, 275
Movie-Tone newsreels 6, 17
MTV 305
Mucheheide, Perry 270-271
Mulligan, Gerry 66
Munk, Chip 145-145, 156, 158, 170
Murray the K 122, 129, 156-157, 160, 174, 187, 200

Nathan's Famous (Coney Island) 28
National Broadcasting Co. (see "WNBC" and "NBC-TV")
NBC-TV 227, 264
NEMS (British holding company) 170-171
Neptune Theatre, The (Liverpool) (see "The Brian Epstein Theatre")
Nero, Peter 190
Nestlé 30
New Masses, The 23
New Musical Express, The 100
New Rascals, The 28
New School for Social Research, The 99, 275-277
New York Daily News, The 83, 264
New York Hospital 93-94
New York Knicks, The 184, 191, 250
New York Mets, The 142, 170, 288, 299
New York Philharmonic, The 184

318

New York Post, The 39, 83, 99, 131, 264
New York Rangers, The 184, 191,
New York State Boxing Commission 42
New York Times, The 83, 99, 217-218, 247, 264, 273, 281
New York Times Book Review, The 103-104, 143, 150
New York University 138
Newman, Paul 209, 229, 242-243
Newman, Phyllis 242
Newman, Rick 301
Newport Jazz Festival, The (R.I.) 60, 64-68, 70, 74, 76, 80, 102, 156, 161, 295-296
Newsweek 116, 264
Newton-John, Olivia 300
Nicholson, Jack 209
Nilsson, Harry 238
Nixon, Pres. Richard M. 197, 210
Nottingham (England), WWII 28
N'Sync 243
Nyro, Laura 200-201, 228, 247

Observer, The (Great Britain) 101
Ochs, Phil 189
O'Conner, Mark 293
Ogden, Richard 308
"Old Black Magic" (Sallie Blair) 49
Old Chelsea Post Office 147-149
Oldham, Andrew Loog 114-115, 138, 151-152, 172
Olympia Theatre, The (Paris) 118, 182, 187
Olympics, The 169
Omaha Beach 28
O'Neal, Patrick 242
Ono, Yoko 222, 249, 263, 267, 287
Orlando, Tony 205
Osborne Building, The 52
"Over the Rainbow" (Judy Garland) 69

Padell, Bert 276, 301-302
Page, Patti 76
Pagliacci 10
Paine, Tom 21-22
Palace Theatre, The (Broadway) 9, 14, 62, 76, 100
Palladium, The (London) 62
Pampadour, Marty 220

Paolucci, Dominic 238
Paolucci's (Little Italy) 125, 237-238, 268
Paramount Theatre (Brooklyn) 61-62
Paramount Theatre (Manhattan) 61, 63, 75-76, 100-101, 140-141, 185, 295, 297
Paris Radio 264
Park Sheraton Hotel, The (Manhattan) 139-139
Parker, Colonel Tom 127, 215-219
Parker family 281
Paton, Tom 244-247, 259
Patsy's (Harlem) 240-241
Payola scandals 61
Paxton, Tom 242
Peace Concert (New York, first) 196-197
Peace Concert (New York, second) 199-200
Peace Concert (Philadelphia) 200
Pearl Harbor 27
Pearson, Drew 27
People, The (Great Britain) 101
"People Got to be Free" (The Rascals) 200
Peter, Paul and Mary 176, 196, 209, 221
Peterson, Oscar 66
Phantom of the Opera, The 152
Phone Booth, The (Greenwich Village) 164-165, 167
Pinder, Mike 222
Pirner, David (of "Soul Asylum") 282
Playboy, 248, 249
Plaza Hotel (Fallsburg, N.Y.) 39, 44
Plaza Hotel, The (Manhattan) 117, 122, 123-126, 128, 129, 135, 157, 237, 303
Pleshette, Gene 61-62, 140-141
Pleshette, Suzanne 61, 140
I.P.M. I23, 30, 99
Pollack, Milt 240-241
Polygram Records 281
Popkin, Rae 15
Popular Mechanics I9
Posnick, Nat 83-84, 109, 121, 122, 130, 136
Precht, Bob 126
Premier Talent 177, 301
Presley, Elvis iii, 100, 127, 208, 215-217
(press conference) 218, 229-230
Prince Philip, H.R.H. 252-254
Press, members of the 134, 136, 217-218, 236-237, 265-266
Prospect Park (Brooklyn, WWII) 27, ("Blanket Hill") 28
Protocols of the Learned Elders of Zion 22
Pryor, Richard 176, 194-195
P.S. 6 261
P.S.10 4, 5
P.S.47 6
P.S.165 6
Puente, Tito 43, 46, 48
"Puff the Magic Dragon" (Peter Yarrow) 200
Purple Heart, The Order of The 32

Queen Elizabeth, H.M.252
Queen Elizabeth Hotel (Montreal) 70
Quinn, Robby 289

Radio City Music Hall 250-252, 254-255, 271
Radio Corp. of America (R.C.A.) 163, 203, 221, 255
Rascals, The (also "The Young Rascals") iii, 153-154, 159, 163-170, 172, 174-184, 186, 188, 190-191, 196-205
(break-up) 206, 233, 247, 257, 261, 271, 278, 292, 297, 303, 304
Ratner's Restaurant (Lower East Side) 35, 54
Raymond, Art 41
Reader's Digest 285
Record World 175
Red Rock Amphitheater, The (Denver) 86-87
"Red Rubber Ball" (The Cyrcle) 174
Redding, Otis 163
Reddy, Helen 242
Redford, Robert 209
Reid, Napoleon 4
Reiss, Barry 243-244
Reykjavik (Iceland), beauty of 219
Renay, Diane 63
Reno Sweeney's (Manhattan) 259
Resnick, Artie 169
Reuben's Restaurant 52

Reynolds, Joey 167-168
Reynolds News (Great Britain) 101
Rich, Buddy 252
Richard, Cliff 271
Ringling Bros. and Barnum & Bailey 191
Rivera, Chita 209
Rivera, Edie Vonnegut 220
Rivera, Geraldo 220
Riverhead (Long Island) 28
Rizzo, Frank 200
Rizzo, Jilly 239-240
Roberts, John 190, 278
Rock and Roll Hall of Fame (Cleveland) 207
Rockefeller, Gov. Nelson A. 131-132
Rockefeller Center 73, 250
Rockefeller family 131-132, 250
Rockettes, The 251
Rodgers, Richard 296
Rodriguez, Tito 43
Rolling Stones, The 114-116, (Carnegie Hall concert) 138-140, 151-152, 159, 166, 172, 177, 181, 189, 230, 258
Rolling Stones, The (audiences) 138-140, 245
Ronstadt, Linda 251, 254-255
Roosevelt, Pres. Franklin D. 16, 17, 18, 23, 27, 39
Roosevelt, Franklin D., Jr. 39
Rosen, Jerry 146, 171, 247
Rosenblatt, Yosele 4
Rosenman, Joel 190, 278
Ross, Rosalind 74
Rounds, Tom
Rowand, Nada 296
Roy Castle Foundation (Liverpool) 292-293
Ryan, Red 20
Rubenfeld, Marilyn 251
Rubenstein, Howard 281
Ruby and the Romantics 63
Rudin, Mickey 215, 223
Ruppiner Bar 6
Russian Tea Room, The 284
Rydell, Bobby 63

Saffain, Sol, 177, 182
Satchadananda, Swami 202
St. Catherine's Street (Montreal) 70
St. Vincents Hospital (Manhattan)
149
Ste. Marie, Buffy 189
Santana 198
Satescu, Iona 107, 139-140, 189
Sam & Dave 163, 197
Santana 278
Sapphires, The 63
Satescu, Iona 107-109, 116, 120
Satin, Lonnie
Satlin, Stan 291-293
"Saturday Night" (Bay City Rollers) 246, 247
Saturday Night Live (NBC) 286

Sawyer, Pam 166
Sayonara 9
Schary, Dore 168-169
Scheck, Barry 44
Scheck, George 44
Scheff, Phil 82
Scher, John 281
Schiffman, Bobby 55, 60
Schiffman, Frank 55, 60
Schrafft's 77-78
Scotland, Stan 73-74
Scott, Alan 280-281
Sebastian, John 278
Security procedures 123-124, 134, 141, 142-143, 154-161, 154-162, 172, 192, 198, 246, 280
Sha Na Na 278, 282
Sharon, Ralph 78, 80, 82
Shaw, Billy 49, 55, 56
Shaw, Lee 49, 56
Shaw Artists 48-60, 156
Shawn, Dick 242
"She Loves You" (Beatles) 117
Shea Stadium iii, v, 142-146, 150-11, 153-162, 164, 167, 171-174, 179, 190-191, 200, 253, 277, (Jumbotron) 288
Shearing, George 41, 66
Shore, Dinah 8
Siegel, Herb 83, 88
Siegel, Joel 307
Silfen, Marty 262
Simon, Neil 242
Simon, Paul 200, 299
Simone, Nina 88, 102
Simpson, O.J. 44
Sims, Jay 39
Sinatra, Frank iii, 45, 134, 190, 208, 215, 223, 229-230, 232, 238-241
Singer Bowl (World's Fair Grounds, Queens) 186
Singer Sewing Machine Co. 172
Sklar, Rick 166-167, 173-174
Skorous Organization 141
Skydel, Barbara 301
Slotnick, Barry 262
Sly & the Family Stone 193, 195, 278
Smith, Billy 159
Smith, Gary 246-247
Snow, Phoebe (Phoebe Snow Laub) 230-231
Social Justice 18
"Solitaire" (Laura Branigan) 262
(Judy Garland) 69
Sonny & Cher 197
Sotheby's iii,
Soul, David 251
Soul Asylum (see "David Pirner")
Sound of Music, The 60, 83, 92-94
Sounds, Inc. 156
Spassky, Boris 219
Specter, Sen. Arlen 233-234, 252
Spector, Jack 114
Spector, Phil 163-164
Spielberg, Steven 158
SPQR (Little Italy) 263
Stafford, Terry 63
Stage Deli, The (Broadway) 307
"Stand By Me" (Julian and Sean Lennon) 287
Staple Singers, The 189, 200
Stars & Stripes 33
Star Spangled Banner, The 9, 20
Starr, Ringo 124, 125, 130, 131, 158, 161-162, 174, 179, 222, 253, 289-291, 293, 304
Startime (TV) 44
Startime Revue, The 144
State Theatre, The (Hartford, Conn.) 67
Statue of Liberty, The 251
Stein, David 243
Steppenwolf 200
Stern's Department Store 18
Stevens, Gary 252-253
Stevens, John 189
Stewart, James 213
Stewart, Steve 293
Sticker campaigns 21-22, 23, 37
Stigwood, Robert 179-181, 187, 268
Stone, Sly (see also "Sly and the

Family Stone") 193, 231
Storch, Larry 62
Stouffer's 102
Straight, Michael 39
Strausser, Sol 9, 11-15
Streisand, Barbra 295-297
Stuarti, Enzo 229
Stylistics, The 227
Sullivan, Ed 86, 112-113, 127, 128, 157, 160-161
Sullivan, Sylvia 112-113
Sullivan Show, The (see The Ed Sullivan Show)
Summer, Bob 255
Sutton Cleaners and Tailoring Shop (Manhattan) 93

Tales of Robin Hood 28
Tamarack Lodge (The Catskills) 44
Taub, Henry 229
Taub, Joe 229-231, 269
Ted Mack Amateur Hour, The 11
Temptations, The 246
Ten Years After 278
Theme from 2001 "Also Sprach Zarathustra" (Deodato) 227
Theatre Three Productions 110, 115, 119
Thomas, David Clayton 197-198
Thomas, Marlo 209, 242
Thomas, Norman 18
Thomas, Rufus 63
Thompson, Jim 142-143, 145, 157, 170-171
Ticketmaster 173
Ticketron 58, 173, 281
Time 116, 264
Time Warner Cable 155
Tiny (bodyguard for Frank Sinatra) 239
Tiny (lead security man for Rolling Stones concert) 152
Tommy Dorsey Band, The 42
Tomorrow's Children (see "Don Imus")
Tooley, Bill 159
Torme, Mel 66, 241
Tracy, Kid 8
Travers, Mary 209 (see also "Peter, Paul and Mary")
Travolta, John 300
Tremont Terrace, The (The Bronx)

(see "The Trocadero")
Tremont trolley (The Bronx) 37
Trocadero, The (The Bronx) 41-42, 44-46
Tropic Holiday 144
Tunney, Sen. Gene 209
Turner, Tina 209
"Twist and Shout" (Beatles) 161

United Nations 247-248, 252
UNICEF (United Nations International Children's Emergency Fund) 248
U.S. State Department 197-198
University of Dijon 34
Uttal, Larry 215

V-1 rockets 30
V-E Day 30
Vale, Jerry 88, 102
Valli, Frankie 251, 297-298
Van Ronk, Dave 189
Variety 75, 77
Vaughan, Sarah 62, 66, 252
Verdon, Gwen 209
Verona (N. J., WWII) 27
Verve Records 178
"Vesti La Giubba" (Sol Strausser) 10, 11, 13
Veterans of Foreign Wars (V.F.W.) 39
Veterans Stadium (Philadelphia) 200
Vietnam War (see also "Peace Concert") 196, 199, 200, (refugees) 247-249
Vilfroy, Claudy (see "Claudy Vilfroy Bonheur")
Vilfroy, Georges 35
Vilfroy, Madame 34-35, 212-214
Voices of East Harlem 197
Vonnegut, Edie (see "Edie Vonnegut Rivera")
Vonnegut, Kurt 220

WABC (radio) 166-167, 173-174, 227
Wald, Jeff 242
Waldorf-Astoria Hotel, The 87, 145, 149, 187
Waldorf Towers, The 179
Wallach, Eli 209
Walsh, Joe (from "The Eagles") 282

Walt Disney Co., The 220
Walters, Barbara 45, 238
Walters, Lou 45, 183, 238
Warner Brothers Records 219, 240
Warner Television 273
Warren Theatre, The (Atlantic City) 60
Warwick, Dionne 209
Warwick Hotel (Manhattan) 155, 157, 173
Washington Square Park (Greenwich Village) 138, 141, 146
Wasser, Joe 281
Waters, Muddy 49
Watts, Charlie 138
Wein, George 60-61, 64, 67
Weintraub, Freddie 176, 298
Weintraub, Jerry 208, 210, 215-224, 227, 229-230, 239, 299
Weiss, Nat 179, 181, 187
Weiss, Norman 118, 171
Weiss, Steve 154, 163, 203-204
Weissberg, Gilda 107-108
Wells Fargo 155, 160-161
West, Leslie 282
West Side Story (see "'I Feel Pretty'")
Westbury Music Fair (Valley Forge) 238
WEVD 41
Wexler, Jerry 163, 165, 169, 197, 202-203
Whiskey A Go Go, The (Los Angeles) 120
White, Jack 257
Whittemore, Jack 49
Who, The 181, 278
Wilkie, Wendell 23
William Morris Agency, The 53, 74, 177, 200-201, 232, 242, 263
Williams, Alan 101
Williams, Fred 272
Williams, G. Mennen 39
Willowbrook benefit, 220
Wilson, Jackie 63
Wilson, John 23
Wilson, Nancy 252
Winchell, Walter 21, 33
WINS (radio) 61
WMCA (radio) 63
WMCA "Good Guys" 63, 114, 122
WNBC (radio) 227
WNEW (radio) 49
Wolf, Bob 282

321

Women for McGovern Concert 209-210
Wood, Biddy 49-51
Woodstock Music Festival (1969) 190, 278, 279, 280-281, 294
Woodward, Joanne 242
Woolworth's 5
World Wildlife Conservation Fund, The 253
World's Fair Grounds (Queens) (see also "Singer Bowl") 142, 155, 159-160
WOV (N.Y.C.) 41; "Pedro" 41
Wrigley Gum 22
Wyman, Bill 164

Yankee Stadium 6, 58, 143
Yarrow, Peter (see also "Peter, Paul and Mary") 196, 199-200
Yasgur's Farm (Max Yasgur) 278-281
Yiddishisms
  'bashert' (destined) 103
  'Bubba' (grandmother) 3
  'machers' (big shots) 169
  'mensch' (a real person) 174
  'nachas' (pride) 287
  'no chochmas' (no fooling around) 141
  'simcha' (happiness, party) 3
  'spielkes' (agitated, impatient) 102
"You Better Run" (The Rascals) 186
Young, Jesse Colin 189
Young Communist League (Y.C.L.) 18
Young Men's Hebrew Association (Y.M.H.A.) 21
Young People's Socialist League (Y.P.S.L.) 18
Young Rascals, The (see "The Rascals") 166
Youngman, Henny 81-82, 85
Young's Gap Hotel 14

Ziegfeld Follies, The 8
Zisselman's Farm 4, 5, 160
Zolt, Marvin 223